WOMEN AND ENLIGHTE
EIGHTEENTH-CENTURY ᴅ⅃ᴵᴛᴀᴵᴺ

During the long eighteenth century, ideas of society and of social progress were first fully investigated. These investigations took place in the contexts of economic, theological, historical and literary writings which paid unprecedented attention to the place of women. Combining intellectual history with literary criticism, Karen O'Brien examines the central importance to the British Enlightenment both of women writers and of women as a subject of enquiry. She examines the work of a range of authors, including John Locke, Mary Astell, David Hume, Adam Smith, Edward Gibbon, T. R. Malthus, the Bluestockings, Catharine Macaulay, Mary Wollstonecraft and the first female historians of the early nineteenth century. She explores the way in which Enlightenment ideas created a language and a framework for understanding the moral agency and changing social roles of women, without which the development of nineteenth-century feminism would not have been possible.

KAREN O'BRIEN is Professor of English at the University of Warwick. She is the author of *Narratives of Enlightenment: Cosmopolitan History from Voltaire to Gibbon* (Cambridge, 1997), which won the British Academy's Rose Mary Crawshay Prize.

WOMEN AND ENLIGHTENMENT IN EIGHTEENTH-CENTURY BRITAIN

KAREN O'BRIEN

University of Warwick

CAMBRIDGE
UNIVERSITY PRESS

CAMBRIDGE
UNIVERSITY PRESS

University Printing House, Cambridge CB2 8BS, United Kingdom

Published in the United States of America by Cambridge University Press, New York

Cambridge University Press is part of the University of Cambridge.

It furthers the University's mission by disseminating knowledge in the pursuit of
education, learning and research at the highest international levels of excellence.

www.cambridge.org
Information on this title: www.cambridge.org/9780521774277

First published 2009
Reprinted 2010

A catalogue record for this publication is available from the British Library

Library of Congress Cataloguing in Publication data
O'Brien, Karen, Dr.
Women and enlightenment in eighteenth-century Britain / Karen O'Brien.
p. cm.
Includes bibliographical references and index.
ISBN 978-0-521-77349-2 (hardback) – ISBN 978-0-521-77427-7 (pbk.)
1. English literature–18th century–History and criticism.
2. English literature–Women authors–History and criticism. 3. Women in literature.
4. Sex role in literature. 5. Women–Great Britain–History–18th century.
6. Sex role–Great Britain–History–18th century.
7. Feminism–Great Britain–History–18th century. 8. Enlightenment–Great Britain.
9. Great Britain–Intellectual life–18th century. I. Title.
PR448.W65O37 2009
820.909287–dc22
2008044207

ISBN 978-0-521-77349-2 Hardback
ISBN 978-0-521-77427-7 Paperback

For Peter

Contents

Acknowledgements

I am grateful to Warwick University and to the Arts and Humanities Research Council for a period of research leave that enabled me to complete this book. Most of the research was carried out at the British Library, the Bodleian Library and the National Library of Scotland, and I would like to thank the librarians there for their assistance. My warmest thanks to Isabel Rivers, Clarissa Campbell Orr, John Hines, Barbara Taylor and John Christie for excellent advice and careful reading of parts or all of the book. This book owes a great deal to the pioneering work of Jane Rendall, and to conversations with her during our time at the Institute for Advanced Studies in the Humanities at Edinburgh University. It benefited enormously from Barbara Taylor's Leverhulme-funded project 'Feminism and Enlightenment 1650–1850: A Comparative History' in which I was very fortunate to participate in 1998–2001, and which opened out a whole new world of scholarship and ideas to me. An earlier version of chapter 4 appeared in the book that came out of this project, *Women, Gender and Enlightenment, 1650–1850*, ed. Barbara Taylor and Sarah Knott (Basingstoke, 2005). Particular thanks to Linda Bree at Cambridge University Press for her patience and support. I have been lucky to have an editor who cares and knows so much about the eighteenth century. My thanks to Rochelle Sibley for expert note checking. The book started out as an MA course, and I learned a great deal from my postgraduate students at both Cardiff and Warwick Universities. Warwick University has been an intellectually rewarding, as well as a sociable and enlightened place to work. On a personal note, I would like to thank Helen Calcraft, Josie Dixon and Jackie Labbe for their support and friendship, and, above all, Cassy and Patrick O'Brien, devoted parents and superlative grandparents. My greatest debt is to Peter McDonald, a great cook, a great father to our children Louisa and Samuel, and a wonderful husband.

Introduction: the progress of society

Let me observe to you, that the position of women in society, is somewhat different from what it was a hundred years ago, or as it was sixty, or I will say thirty years since. Women are now so highly cultivated, and political subjects are at present of so much importance, of such high interest, to all human beings who live together in society, you can hardly expect, Helen, that you, as a rational being, can go through the world as it now is, without forming any opinions on points of public importance. You cannot, I conceive, satisfy yourself with the common namby-pamby, little missy phrase, 'ladies have nothing to do with politics'. . . . Female influence must, will, and ought to exist on political subjects as on all others; but this influence should always be domestic, not public – the customs of society have so ruled it.

(Maria Edgeworth, *Helen*, 1834)[1]

This is a study of the implications of the Enlightenment for women in eighteenth-century Britain. It explores the impact of the great discovery of the British Enlightenment – that there is such a thing as society, that humans are principally intelligible as social beings, and that society itself is subject to change – on both male and female writers of this period. It considers the degree to which investigations of society by Enlightenment writers were inflected, even, at times, motivated by their growing interest in women as distinct and influential social members. And it examines women as both subjects and authors of works of social enquiry in the light of the Enlightenment idea that society can progress by its own endeavour, not only economically but also in its moral relations, education and culture. The discovery of the progress of society entailed a re-evaluation of history, not simply as a series of political events and military conflicts, but as a civilising process. This re-evaluation brought with it, for the first time, the idea that women, as well as men, have a history, and that, far from being intelligible in terms of unchanging biological, scriptural or domestic roles, they too can change with changing times. Indeed, eighteenth-century writers

I

increasingly came to believe that the status and educational level of women in a given society were important indicators of its degree of historical progress, and a number argued that the low educational level of women in their own times was itself an impediment to further social improvement. This is not to say that the historical investigation of human sociability and the historicising of women were in themselves hospitable to what we would now call feminism: by which I mean the demand, first made at the very end of the century, for equal civil and political rights for women. But it is to say that Enlightenment philosophical and historical enquiries created a framework and a language for understanding the gendered structures of society without which nineteenth-century feminism would not have been possible. This study takes a long-range view, from the late seventeenth to the early nineteenth centuries, in order to convey the scale of this transformation. The transformation was apparent to commentators of this period themselves, as it is, for example, in the opening quotation above, to Lady Davenant, who speaks to the protagonist of Maria Edgeworth's 1834 novel *Helen* about the extraordinary increase in political and collective self-awareness that had taken place among educated women over the last hundred years, even though that increase stops somewhere short of claiming a fully political role in the life of the country.

In seeking to trace this transformation in the prominence accorded to women, and the depth of the Enlightenment engagement with them as social beings, as well as the growing confidence with which women writers themselves wrote of their own position in society, this study draws upon a variety of primary sources, some literary, some philosophical and theological, and some works of history, political economy and educational theory. In doing so, each chapter attempts to trace an evolving process of intellectual elaboration, debate and disagreement in which women are sometimes the main topic, but more often a subsidiary topic within a broader discussion of ethics, metaphysics, economics or, most frequently, 'manners' (by which the eighteenth century generally meant moral and social norms and culture). This book is less concerned with the social circulation of gendered representations in this period than with the explicit articulation of the moral, sociological and economic vocabularies through which women emerged as a distinct discursive category, and which women writers themselves deployed and refashioned in their own writings. It is, in other words, a work of intellectual rather than of cultural history, although it draws extensively upon cultural-historical and literary studies that have shed great light upon the deep, gendered symbolic patterns that infiltrated, at every level, political life and artistic creation in eighteenth-century Britain. The book ends in the early nineteenth century when women writers themselves sought to profit from the Enlightenment interest in their historical role and influence by writing works of historical biography and art history. It begins in an era when, as the Anglican educational writer and philosopher Mary Astell wrote, women were rarely the subject of history and history was of little interest to most of them: 'Since Men being the Historians, they seldom condescend to record the great and good Actions of Women; and when they take notice of them, 'tis with this wise Remark, That such Women acted above their Sex.'[2] Rather, it was in the arenas of theology and moral philosophy that the question of women's distinctive participation in the collective life of society, including but also beyond the realm of the household, was most thoroughly rehearsed. This earlier period was one in which ethical and religious writers sought to locate the foundation of morals in the constitution of human nature, and, in so doing, to determine whether morality springs from reason, sentiment, the affections or the moral sense.[3] A number of women writers responded enthusiastically to the emerging notion of the private affections as the source of moral norms in society, and of 'benevolence' (the selfless, well-meaning disposition we have towards fellow members of society) as the essence of moral behaviour. With this commitment to a sense of the wider social significance of their moral actions, women writers contributed, as we will see, to vigorous debate as to whether morality is primarily a matter of rational choice or sentiment, and whether it is benevolence or self-interest that holds society together. That debate about the kinds of moral and social enquiry that can be derived from the study of human nature occurred with particular intensity in England in the wake of works by Thomas Hobbes and Bernard Mandeville. The questions posed by their depiction of society as something held together by a combination of greedy self-interest and political coercion travelled north and lay at the root of Scottish Enlightenment philosophy and political economy. And in very many of these debates, the conduct of women – their selfless virtue, their consumer greed, their sexual manipulation of men – not only functioned as a case in point, but opened out a new analytical field which accorded them, for the first time, a complex and changing social identity.

By identifying the place of women in British Enlightenment debates, this book must inevitably take a view about the nature of the Enlightenment itself. In doing so, I have been particularly mindful of recent research that has breathed new life into the previously flagging field of Enlightenment studies, including books by J. G. A. Pocock, John

Robertson, Roy Porter and Jonathan Israel.[4] Robertson has made a compelling case for a return to a study of the Enlightenment 'which restores the primacy of its intellectual contribution', even as he situates his own study of the Enlightenment in Scotland and Naples within a thickly described social and political setting, as well as for an Enlightenment that was, above all, concerned with 'understanding, and hence advancing, the causes and conditions of human betterment in this world', through the study of human nature in society, and of the economic means to social improvement.[5] Within these terms of definition, Robertson is committed to a view of the Enlightenment as a unitary phenomenon, with local manifestations in Scotland, Naples and elsewhere, but with a very poor showing in eighteenth-century England.[6] By contrast, J. G. A. Pocock's four-volume study of Edward Gibbon starts from the premise, first articulated by him many years before, of a distinctive, conservative and Anglican English Enlightenment. This Enlightenment, strongly connected by religious ties and shared history to a continental Protestant tradition, was not, like its French counterpart, an affair of alienated, anti-clerical *philosophes*, but of an intellectual movement of academics, churchmen and politically involved intellectuals such as Gibbon and Edmund Burke (and he is emphatic about Burke's inclusion in this company).[7] This was a broadly Whiggish Enlightenment, concerned to preserve the constitutional arrangements, the (restricted) civil rights and religious toleration enshrined in the settlement of 1688–9, as well as to limit the power of churches or religious groups to 'disturb the peace of civil society'.[8] From this preoccupation with the need to preserve a civil social space from religious fanaticism and political tyranny, came both 'a history of mind and society together', and a programme for gradual social improvement.[9] Pocock's Enlightenment has some similarities with the self-confident and unradical English Enlightenment celebrated by Roy Porter in his *Enlightenment: Britain and the Creation of the Modern World*; although, for Porter, as not for Pocock, this Enlightenment was an indigenously British, precociously modern, somewhat secular affair, having its roots in the scientific and political revolutions of the late seventeenth century.

More congruent with Pocock's English Enlightenment, and of immense value to the present study, is the portrait of the enlightening process at work in English intellectual life in B. W. Young's *Religion and Enlightenment in Eighteenth-Century England*.[10] Young's specific focus is upon the liberal, anti-dogmatic and scientifically informed world of Anglican divines who variously adapted Newtonian physics and Lockean philosophy to the theological and institutional needs of the national church. In the process, they extended and updated the tradition of 'Latitudinarianism' that had grown up in the late seventeenth-century Anglican church, and had promoted freedom of conscience, reason and experience, rather than liturgy, doctrine and ecclesiastical organisation, as guides to religious truth. Many of the women writers discussed in this study, including Damaris Masham, Catharine Cockburn and Elizabeth Carter, can be situated within the broad framework of this 'late Latitudinarian' Anglican preoccupation with the uses and limits of reason, the happiness that comes from a moral life, the possibility of human progress, and the salvation that comes, not only from faith, but from active, good works.[11] And over and above these intellectual circles, such issues were at the heart of the lively debates between Anglicans and Dissenters, especially rational dissenters, who, as Young points out, shared a sense of belonging to an 'Enlightened age', a common debt to John Locke's philosophy, and a hostility to obfuscating superstitions and rituals.[12]

Rational Dissent, or Unitarianism, was, as a number of studies have shown, uniquely important for the development of the feminism of the late eighteenth and nineteenth centuries, and many major figures were either rational Dissenters, such as Mary Wollstonecraft, or Anglicans with great sympathy for dissenting views, such as Catharine Macaulay.[13] There were, of course, considerable political differences between broad-church Anglican supporters of the established government and its dissenting opponents, but historians have often emphasised these at the expense of their shared, self-consciously Enlightened perspectives on matters of theology, of the freedom of the will, and of the use of reason to improve our life on this earth and our chance of heaven in the next. John Robertson has recently speculated about the possibility for formulating the case for an English Enlightenment made up of these Latitudinarian Anglican and rational dissenting elements, starting with the Anglican 'emphasis on human free will rather than an all-determining divine will' on which 'the Rational Dissenters built a fresh conviction of the human capacity for virtue, and their feminist associates a new vision of a sexually egalitarian republicanism'.[14] He adds that, on this basis, 'it may not, after all, be incongruous to think of an English Enlightenment facing in both conservative and radical directions over the course of the century'.[15] Certainly, this idea of an English Enlightenment, encompassing a fruitful, if sometimes unstable, mixture of Anglicanism and Dissent, Whiggism and radicalism, helps to make sense of the evolving debate about the nature and role of women. It is also helpful for what it excludes, specifically the

High Church and evangelical elements of eighteenth-century intellectual life (always allowing for the complicating presence of Mary Astell). It is these elements, with their 'mystical critique of rational religion' and emphasis on innate human sinfulness, that Young positions as something akin to a 'counter-Enlightenment' in Britain.[16] Young's story stops short of the Evangelical revival of the 1780s and after, with its decisive rejection of what it saw as flabby Latitudinarianism and heretical rational dissent. But, for the purposes of this study, it is helpful to describe this, also, as part of a counter-Enlightenment, not least because it allows us to see how women Evangelicals themselves redirected the energies of the Enlightenment towards the moral tutelage of the young, the poor and the enslaved, conceding, in the process, that this must be their specialised female role. The closing section of this book considers the extent to which evangelical women, many of whom, from Hannah More onwards, played such a prominent part in nineteenth-century public life, can be said to have taken forward or defeated the legacy of Enlightenment ideas about women. It also, amid a story of partial failure, traces the legacy of the Enlightenment idea of the progress of society, and the place of women within that society, into early nineteenth-century political economy, including the works of Malthus and of the women political economists of this period.

That legacy was preserved, as a thread in nineteenth-century British Whiggism, by a generation of men who had learned about economics, the progress of society and the need for a rational education for men and women at the great Scottish universities, or, at least, by reading the classic works of the Scottish Enlightenment. The Scottish Enlightenment (which was partly clerical in impetus, like its English counterpart), and its extraordinary engagement with the place of women within its historical investigations of human society, lies at the heart of this study. The book traces the contours of this engagement, and explores the impact of earlier English theological and philosophical ideas in Scotland. It also seeks to account for the different ways in which these arguments about the role of women in the progress of civilisation were taken up in England; including, for example, Gibbon's approach to the history of women through a historically comparative legal framework, and the moralised, relatively conservative idea of the progress of society that Elizabeth Montagu and her Bluestocking circle derived from their friendships with Scottish writers such as Lord Kames and James Beattie. The rich traffic of ideas between Scotland and England is a constant theme of this book, as well as the powerful influence of French thinkers – Montesquieu in particular – on both sides of the border. One important set of ideas promoted by that traffic had to do with Scotland and England's Gothic and medieval past, its connection to their shared European heritage, and the long-term effects of the high status accorded to women by their ancestors. A growing interest in Gothic and medieval history fed into an Enlightenment narrative of Europe's transition from feudalism to commercial modernity, and assigned to women a privileged place in the history of European 'manners', in particular the manners associated with the culture of chivalry. This debate about women and chivalry played out in many different ways in Britain, but converged upon the question that would come to haunt the nineteenth century: to what extent is a culture of gender separation and of male deference towards women consistent with a modern, Enlightened civilisation? The answer from Catharine Macaulay, Mary Wollstonecraft and John Stuart Mill, delivered in historical terms supplied by the Enlightenment, was an emphatic 'not at all'; for them civilisation would remain, at best, only a work in progress so long as women were still living in the Dark Ages. Others, however, were less exercised by the failure of the progress of society to deliver rights for women than by the possibilities of a rich historical identity offered by this variant of Enlightenment history. The discovery that women have a history, indeed, that by their very social position they have a special insight into Europe's peculiar past, emboldened unprecedented numbers of women to write history: not only the history of women's lives (although by the early nineteenth century there was an avalanche of these), but of Europe's manners, literature and art.

The Enlightenment that lies behind the title of this book, then, is one primarily concerned with questions of human nature (male and female) and its selfish or benevolent tendencies; with morality as it operates for the good of society, but also as it relates to the moral law of God; with the institutional structures, manners and progressive development of society; with the cultural preconditions and cultural outcomes of commercial modernity (a chicken-and-egg question); with history as the record of progress and also as an aid to collective social self-understanding; and with the need to understand the economy and population growth in order to prevent injustice and disaster, and to promote further progress. This is not a secular or secularising Enlightenment, despite the central involvement of unbelievers such as Hume, but rather one that moves from theological debate about the pleasurableness and efficacy of worldly benevolence to questions of human agency in society, including the agency of women. These questions are, in turn, deeply entangled with one of the central arguments within the European Enlightenment: the extent to which men's social co-operation derives from their natural capacity for altruism (the Christian and neo-Stoic view) or from their self-interested passions and mutual needs (the Epicurean and Hobbesean view). Women writers, unsurprisingly, almost always aligned themselves with arguments for natural sociability (often tacitly derived from the philosopher Lord Shaftesbury), but, as we will see, this presented them with enormous difficulties when they came to reckon with the Epicurean foundations of contemporary political economy. The Enlightenment presented here is very much a Protestant one, with connections to continental Protestant writers such as Pierre Bayle (directly, and via Mandeville) and Poulain de la Barre (a French Catholic convert to the Protestant faith), but one that nevertheless treats the English and Scottish cases as separate, if mutually illuminating, intellectual constellations. It is also, with different resonances on each side of the border, largely a Whig Enlightenment in which prominent Whig Anglican divines, such as Gilbert Burnet, Joseph Butler and Thomas Secker, played an important role in encouraging female learning.

This model of the Enlightenment runs somewhat counter to the tendency of recent histories of feminism to focus upon Tory and Jacobite female opponents of the Revolution of 1688–9. This in itself, as I shall argue below, springs from an undue historical focus, in feminist history, upon Locke's political writings as marking a decisive conceptual separation between the public sphere of civil society and the private sphere. Much of this derives from Carole Pateman's influential thesis that the second of Locke's *Two Treatises of Government* (1689) inaugurated a new phase of political theory which specifically excluded women from civil society on the grounds of their natural subordination to men, and that civil society 'is not structured by kinship and the power of the fathers; in the modern world, women are subordinated to men as men, or to men as a fraternity'.[17] This has proved powerful as an analysis of the workings of modern liberal politics, but, in relation to historical accounts of women and the British Enlightenment, it has too firmly set the terms of discussion to questions of women's public and private identities. It has also, until very recently, led to an emphasis upon those women writers who dissented from the Whig culture of empirical enquiry, religious latitude and pragmatic politics, a culture that Locke in fact helped to shape. This, in turn, has downplayed some of the very real continuities that existed between the re-evaluation of women's spiritual, moral and rational capacities, need for education, and social influence that took place in the wake of Locke's work, and the works of the Bluestockings and more radical women writers at the end of this period.

   This study aims to explain some of those continuities without, it is
hoped, framing a Whiggish narrative of its own, either about the contribution of particular kinds of proto-liberal politics to the bettering
of women's lives, or about the rise of feminist thought. This period,
certainly, witnessed the creation of the conceptual categories that were,
ultimately, necessary to women's articulation of their demand for equal
civil and political rights. Yet it was also one in which the redescription, by
eighteenth-century writers, of women as influential members of the
intermediate terrain between the political and the private spheres that
they called 'society' was accompanied by the rise of increasingly polarised
notions of gender difference. That difference, discussed by many of the
writers in this study in terms of its social effects, was also increasingly
mapped on to ever more rigid and stable notions of the biological
differences between the sexes. That sense of underlying biological difference came from new medical theories about the workings of the body, its
nervous and muscular systems, and the connection between the body's
physical and psychic aspects.[18] It was also the product of broader cultural
anxieties in which femininity functioned as a portmanteau term of negative or positive value as Britain came to discursive terms with growth
of the commercial sector of the economy.[19] Such attributions, as Dror
Wahrman has argued, acquired intensified resonance in Britain during
the crisis of the American Revolutionary War, and they reflected back on
to gender ideology in ways that both hardened and moralised sexual
distinctions.[20] They were also, to some degree, symptomatic of public
disquiet about the involvement of women in party politics, something
female aristocrats had enjoyed almost as a matter of dynastic entitlement
for many centuries, but which, after the 1780s, became less and less
acceptable to the public.[21] The loss, to women as a group, of the dubious
leadership of such figures as Georgiana, Duchess of Devonshire, was not a
great one, and the explicit restriction of the franchise, for the first time, to
'male persons' in the 1832 Reform Act simply confirmed their de facto
political exclusion. In terms of political and civil rights, the period from
the late eighteenth century to the early nineteenth century was one of no
progress; indeed, there is evidence that the property rights of widows and
married women actually declined during this period.[22] There were a few
anonymous publications (notably *The Hardships of the English Laws in
Relation to Wives*, 1735 and *The Laws Respecting Women*, 1777) protesting
against this legal state of affairs, and, particularly in the 1790s, there were a
number of male reformers who, alongside Wollstonecraft, made the case
for political rights for women.[23]

HISTORICAL LOSSES AND GAINS

The static, or even deteriorating, legal and political situation of women, and the dichotomised, gendered language of much political and economic public debate did not, however, correspond to a diminishing sphere of social operation for women in this period. Indeed, the period gave rise to a growing number of opportunities for middle- and upper-class women to exercise their talents outside the family in both informal and institutionalised settings. Some of these opportunities were in relation to leisure activities (debating societies, commercial pleasure gardens, assembly rooms, theatres), others involved social intervention such as philanthropy, petitioning or campaigning (against the slave trade, notably).[24] Women not born to, or lucky enough to escape from, a life of agricultural labour, domestic service, manufacturing or other poorly paid work, did find remuneration as nurses, teachers or writers – the latter two enormously on the increase in this period to the point where, by the late eighteenth century, unprecedented numbers of women were teaching in or even running schools, and publishing novels and poems.[25] Recent historians have investigated extensively this enlargement of opportunities for women and the sense of collective female self-confidence that came with it. All of this has greatly complicated the case, forcefully made by Leonore Davidoff and Catherine Hall, for a dialectical process of middle-class identity formation and the emergence of an ideology of separate male and female spheres during the Industrial Revolution.[26] Davidoff and Hall's study provoked heated and productive debate, and historians now generally concur that the separate sphere idea was either a defensive reaction by men to the growing prominence of women in British life, or that women themselves encouraged and elaborated this ideology as a means of securing themselves a platform from which to act and speak as proper ladies.[27] Among those arguing the latter case, Eve Tavor Bannet has written that the achievement of Enlightenment feminism was a repositioning of the family, and of women within it, at the heart of the nation, and an assertion of 'continuity between the ordering of private families and the peace, prosperity and well-being of the state'.[28] A sophisticated version of this case has been made by Harriet Guest in her study *Small Change: Women, Learning, Patriotism,* when she argues that, even when women celebrate the domestic realm of the family, it often comes across as contradictory, 'strangely without content and lacking in definition'.[29] One reason for this apparent vacuum at the heart of middle-class separate spheres ideology is, she suggests, that 'domesticity gains in value as a result of its continuity with the social or the public, and not only as a result of its asocial exclusion'.[30] Guest traces a series of discursive shifts, from the mid eighteenth to the early nineteenth centuries, that eventually enabled women to 'define their gendered identities through the nature and degree of their approximation to the public identities of political citizens'.[31]

Guest tells a story of continuity and incremental progress. It differs from the argument advanced at the end of this study which places more emphasis upon the reconfiguration, even, to an extent, defeat (except among philosophical Whigs and radical Dissenters) of Enlightenment ideas about women that occurred in the wake of the Napoleonic wars and the public dissemination of Evangelical theology and morality. As we will see, most Enlightenment writing about women argued against the undue confinement of women to private or domestic spaces, and characterised that confinement as, at worst, perverted (citing the model of eastern sultans and their harems), or, at best, likely to deprive society as a whole of women's energising and conciliatory presence. It was for the second of these reasons that many writers also tended to regard both domestic drudgery and paid work by middle-class women as inherently oppressive and exploitative, and as something that took them out of social circulation (after all, there was a growing army of female servants to do most of the work for leisured women). Eighteenth-century writers' sense of the boundary between the domestic and social realms was generally fluid and informal. The ideological demarcation of the domestic, when it did occur with greater frequency in the early nineteenth century, was couched either in a personal language of self-conscious retreat from one's normal social existence, or in a more generalised language of nostalgia for a time when the country was little more than an alliance of virtuous homesteads.[32] This nostalgia was itself the product of the historicising of domestic and social life that took place in the eighteenth century, anchoring it to a narrative of the progress of civilisation. That narrative, adumbrated in many genres of writing, usually included the story of women's emergence from domestic seclusion, violence and enslavement by selfish men into a bigger arena in which they exercised both a stimulating and stabilising influence on the developing economy. The arena was often ill defined in spatial terms (though explicitly not the aristocratic world of the court) or remained largely a virtual one (of publication, or epistolary exchange). For some, notably Catharine Macaulay and Mary Wollstonecraft, it was a rehearsal space for female citizenship, and for others, like Catharine Cockburn and Elizabeth Carter, it was the familial and social domain affected by women's rational moral choices. As more restrictive and moralised versions of the domestic sphere emerged from the neo-conservative cultural reaction to the American Revolution and, still more, to the French Revolution, women writers fashioned accounts of their influence and moral activity that depended, not so much upon the continuity, as upon the *analogy*, of the domestic and the civil realms.[33] Some early nineteenth-century women historians, as we will see in chapter 6, found a profitable and appreciative market for historical accounts of women who, without ever setting foot outside their households, could not help but influence the world by virtue of their status as princesses, queens, royal consorts or wives of men of destiny.

POLITICAL ANALOGIES AND NATURAL LAW

The resurfacing, in the early nineteenth century, of analogies between the domestic realm and the state, is, in many ways, less surprising than the relative scarcity of analogies like these in most of the previous decades. Such analogies had formed part of a richly suggestive language of gender conflict in the late seventeenth century, when the place of women was discussed in a vocabulary derived from political theory (using terms such as duty, sovereignty, contract, 'passive obedience', the right of rebellion). During the first half of the eighteenth century, this language steadily disappeared, partly as a result of the waning of the bitter political controversy that followed the ousting of the Stuart royal family (often debated in terms of rape and family betrayal), partly because, after Mary II and Anne, there were no queens on the throne, and partly because Enlightenment writers from Hume to Burke and Jeremy Bentham discredited contract theories of politics. In the process, women writers lost a rich resource for thinking about gender relations as a microcosm of the political. Late seventeenth- to early eighteenth-century writers such as Astell, Delarivier Manley, Mary, Lady Chudleigh, Sarah Fyge Egerton and Lady Mary Wortley Montagu used the language of political allegiance and rebellion to spectacular effect in their writings about women. Astell in *Some Reflections upon Marriage* (1700), especially in the preface to the third edition of 1706, brilliantly probes the homology of domestic and political power, and exposes the hypocrisy of those who claim that authority is derived from the consent of the governed:

if the Matrimonial Yoke be grievous, neither Law nor Custom afford her [the wife] that redress which a Man obtains. He who has Sovereign Power does not value the Provocations of a Rebellious Subject, but knows how to subdue him with ease, and will make himself obey'd; but Patience and Submission are the Only Comforts that are left to a poor People, who groan under Tyranny, unless they are Strong enough to break the Yoke, to Depose and Abdicate, which I doubt wou'd not be allow'd of here.[34]

Astell deploys the Whig critique of arbitrary power (the framers held that James II had broken the 'original contract' between king and people, and had 'abdicated the government') in order to expose the reality of male power and tyranny to which women voluntarily subject themselves when they enter into the marriage contract. Juridical contracts or covenants in both the marital and political arenas are really just forms of customary subordination: 'For Covenants betwixt Husband and Wife, like Laws in an Arbitrary Government, are of little Force, the Will of the Sovereign is all in all.'[35] And custom, as Patricia Springborg has argued in her study of Astell, yields no right, and it may interfere with women's God-given entitlement to freedom from domination and moral autonomy.[36]

Astell's acquaintance and correspondent, Mary, Lady Chudleigh, distilled some of Astell's ideas in her poem *The Ladies Defence* (1701) in which the female protagonist, Melissa, complains about the hypocrisy of men who are Whigs in the coffee house, but Tories in the bedroom: 'Passive Obedience you've to us [women] transferr'd,/And we must drudge in Paths where you have err'd:/That antiquated Doctrine you disown;/'Tis now your Scorn, and fit for us alone.'[37] Montagu's letters, written during her residence in Turkey in 1716–18 and published in 1763, also make intricate and witty use of the intersecting languages of political and domestic politics as she repeatedly contemplates the paradoxical personal liberty of Turkish women within a despotic political system. She playfully evokes the despotism of the Ottoman Empire as a warning to the 'passive-obedient men' of the English Tory and Jacobite persuasion, while referring repeatedly to the 'privileges' and 'prerogative' of the Austrian and Turkish ladies ('the only free people in the Empire'), and to the 'principle of *passive-obedience*' that allegedly guides her conduct as the wife of a Whig ambassador.[38] Montagu's wryly subversive accounts of the sexual and social freedoms of Turkish women have a libertine flavour ('the Turkish ladies don't commit one sin the less for not being Christians'), but, also, strongly party-political overtones.[39] This is because many of the letters are addressed to Montagu's sister, the Countess of Mar, who had very recently followed her husband into exile in France, following his support of the Pretender during the Jacobite rebellion of 1715. Although Montagu disapproved of her brother-in-law's politics, she indirectly pays a compliment to her sister's loyalty to him in a letter to her, about the widow of the deposed and reputedly poisoned Sultan Mustafa II who stays true to her husband's memory and refuses to be reconciled to the new Sultan.[40] This letter implicitly acknowledges and explores the conflicting personal and political allegiances that structured the lives of aristocratic women of her era.

Montagu's Whiggish letters to her Jacobite sister are a case in point of the cross-party salience, in the early eighteenth century, of the politicised language of female liberty, passive obedience, marital contract, prerogative and duty. Undoubtedly, that language was deployed with peculiar force by those women writers, notably Manley, Astell and Aphra Behn, who were opposed to Whiggery in all its forms. However, as Rachel Weil has shown in her incisive study of the gender applications of political argument in this period, this language was manipulated by Whig, Tory and Jacobite writers to a variety of feminist ends.[41] Works by Tory women writers such as Manley's *Secret History, of Queen Zarah* (1705) and her *Court Intrigues . . . from . . . New Atalantis* (1711) gave biting satirical accounts of political and sexual betrayal, personal and political disloyalty and ingratitude in the behaviour of certain Whig grandees. A number of Whig women, such as Elizabeth Singer Rowe and Mary Davys, positioned themselves in self-conscious opposition to the Cavalier libertinism of figures like Manley and Behn, and variously drew attention to their virtuous femininity, Horatian retirement, provincial way of life and amateurism as means of understanding their writing.[42] Others writers, such as the author of *An Essay in Defence of the Female Sex* (1696, almost certainly by the Anglican physician and writer Judith Drake), combined a commitment to Locke's epistemology and modern learning with a Tory political outlook. Drake argued that women should be encouraged to develop the social and intellectual skills that would allow them to have a civilising effect upon men. Drake's argument anticipates the cases made for the mixed social spaces of mid eighteenth-century England when she says that men need to attain a 'mixture of Freedom, Observance, and a desire of pleasing': an 'Accomplishment' which 'is best, if not only to be accomplish'd by conversing with us'.[43] However modest they appear, it was arguments like these, more than the political language of gender protest, that were most effective in creating a sense of a civil identity for women in the eighteenth century. Certainly, the discursive politicising of male/female relationships went into sharp decline in the eighteenth century, after a brief period of revival during periods of intense party-political controversy such as the Exclusion Crisis and the decades immediately following the Glorious Revolution.[44] Constance Jordan, in her study of *Renaissance Feminism*, suggests that, in England in particular, the depoliticising of marriage (an institution described, in the sixteenth century, very much in terms of male household governance) had been underway since the mid seventeenth century.[45] This decline may well have reflected broader social shifts (as Lawrence Stone famously described them) in the composition and conception of the family as a small, domestic unit based on affective ties, although, in practice, it appears that these shifts occurred only to a limited degree in this period.[46]

A more stable line of discursive continuity from the seventeenth to the late eighteenth century came from the Renaissance feminist critique of natural law. Traditional, neo-Aristotelian natural law posited a hierarchical order of creation in which woman occupied a lower place, being physically weaker and naturally subordinate to man, and it prescribed different 'offices' (or duties) to each sex.[47] Natural law is accessible to reason and consistent with the divine law, and, for this reason, man-made, positive laws can only be just and valid if they do not violate its general principles. Renaissance sceptics, critical of this tradition, pointed to the enormous variations in laws and conventions, including those that governed women's lives, over time and across continents, and they analysed the power structures that motivated those arrangements. Such critiques could take the form of analyses of abuses of power and pleas for those in power not to exceed their rights, erudite enumerations of variations in social practice or demolitions of vulgar masculine prejudice.[48] Pro-women writers continued to criticise male abuses of power in these terms well into the eighteenth century: male power, wrote the Parisian salonnière the Marquise de Lambert, exists 'par la force plutôt que par le droit naturelle'.[49] These arguments were enhanced by the spread, from the mid seventeenth century, of Cartesian ideas about the partial autonomy of the mind from the body, and about the faculty of reason (naturally equal in all human beings) that enables people to distinguish between truth and received wisdom. Highly educated women in both France and England gained inspiration and method from Descartes' work for a variety of learned and scientific pursuits, as well as a philosophical basis for their claim, against the traditional tenets of natural law, to equal rational capacity.[50] Most impressively, the French philosopher Poulain de la Barre combined, in his series of feminist works in the 1670s, a rationalist, Cartesian critique of the common prejudices of mankind with a historically and geographically informed assault on the spurious universalism of natural law. In the most famous of his works, *De l'égalité des deux sexes* (1673), Poulain dissected the cumulative layers of custom and tradition that lead society to believe in women's 'natural' inferiority, and made the case for their physical cognitive and intellectual equality with men: 'En effet nous avons, tous hommes et femmes, le mesme droit sur la verité, puisque l'esprit est en tous également capable de la connoistre'.[51] Alongside this Cartesian argument for epistemological (and hence also spiritual) equality, Poulain makes the case for natural equality against those jurists who wrongly extrapolate the laws of nature from the unjust social conventions: 'les Jurisconsultes qui avoient aussi leur préjugé, ont attribué à la nature une distinction qui ne vient que de la coustume'.[52] Poulain asserts that there is no reason why women should not do most of the same jobs as men, and enjoy an equal share of power.[53] His writings have been the subject of a pioneering study by Siep Stuurman, which emphasises, above all, Poulain's originality in transforming Cartesianism into 'an Enlightenment *social* philosophy'.[54] Poulain's social philosophy consists in his construction of a conjectural history ('conjecture historique') of the subjection of women; this, Stuurman shows, begins with the division of labour within the family, and then the progressive exclusion of women from intellectual pursuits and proper education, reinforced by their socialisation into a life of frivolity.[55] Poulain often deviates into remarks about the natural superiority of women in certain areas such as conversation.[56] However, his work is remarkable, and for our purposes exceptionally prescient, in the way that it forges a feminist argument through an evolutionary account of society. Where earlier feminist critics of natural law had exposed the male will to power that lay behind seemingly incoherent variations in custom and opinion, Poulain sees a historical process of female subjection at work that can be read alongside the formation of laws and the state, and that might, in time, be changed.

Poulain anticipates the conjectural histories of Rousseau and of the Scottish Enlightenment, and his work was certainly known to the Marquise de Lambert and Judith Drake. Beyond this, the extent of the influence of this and his other works is itself a matter of historical conjecture. *De l'égalité* was translated into English in 1677, and also appeared, in a different, elegant and unacknowledged translation in 1758 under the title *Female Rights Vindicated*, supposedly 'By a Lady'. The work may have been known, in England, to Astell, William Walsh (author of *A Dialogue Concerning Women*, 1691) and John Toland.[57] Toland, a radical philosopher and freethinker, was well connected to continental intellectual circles (he knew Bayle, for example), and shared Poulain's desire to expose 'prejudice', especially in religious matters, but also, on occasion, in matters relating to the female intellect. In the preface to his *Letters to Serena* (1704, addressed to the learned Queen Sophie

Charlotte of Prussia), he writes that 'whether the Exclusion of Women from Learning be the Effect of inveterate Custom, or proceeds from Designs in the Men, shall be no Inquiry of mine', and yet goes on to discuss a number of distinguished female scholars, and the prejudice of men against them.[58]

A Cartesian critique of male 'prejudice', whether directly or indirectly inspired by Poulain, continued to surface, at intervals, in pro-female writing throughout the eighteenth century. The best-known reprise of this critique occurs in a work entitled *Woman Not Inferior to Man* (1739) by a writer who styles herself as 'Sophia'. Literary historians have assumed that this work is a partial and unacknowledged translation of Poulain, though it is, in fact, a free adaptation of his work written in a highly personal, disarmingly frank, female-identified voice (for example, her remark that men are 'stubborn brats').[59] Sophia is less interested in the historical and sociological aspects of Poulain's argument than in his analysis of the workings of male power, and she spends most of her work embellishing the parts of *De l'égalité des deux sexes* concerned with women's intellectual fitness for scientific enquiry and public appointments. Starting with the pseudo-Cartesian point that 'reason' is a 'prerogative that nature has bestowed' upon women (adapted and elaborated in England, as we will see in chapter 1, by Anglican women writers), Sophia contends that physical differences between men and women are minimal, and that the common view that they can't have jobs in the church, the government and the army is simply the product of male bias, stupidity and exclusion: 'Why is *learning* useless to us? Because we have no share in public offices. And why have we no share in public offices? Because we have no *learning*?'[60] Sophia intersperses her adaptation of the French author with English quotations from Rowe and Pope, and with references to Boadicea, Queen Elizabeth and to 'Eliza' (clearly, Elizabeth Carter), cited as a modern example of 'towering superiority of . . . genius and judgment'.[61]

Sophia's identity has long been a mystery, and it is not even certain that she was female, although she does write with a very pronounced sense of solidarity with her female readers. There are similarities of theme and tone with the sixth number of Lady Mary Wortley Montagu's *The Nonsense of Common-Sense*, in which she argues that 'vulgar Prejudices' against women's rational capabilities should be dispelled, not least because this leads men to the mistake 'of treating the weaker Sex with a Contempt that has a very bad Influence on their Conduct'.[62] This lends some support to the theory that Sophia was Sophia Fermor, daughter of the brilliant Henrietta-Louisa, Countess of Pomfret, the friend and correspondent of

Montagu.[63] Sophia herself gave a much clearer sense of her personality, background and circumstances in the second of her publications, a reply to an attack on her by an anonymous gentleman, *Man Superior to Woman* (1740). Sophia's answer, although it incorporates some more extracts from Poulain, is a forceful, often angrily sarcastic, attack on the way that men argue and coerce women into submission: 'does he take all the *Women* for such easy idiots that they are to be coax'd out of their natural right by every fawning sycophant, sneer'd out of it by every word-retailing witling, or braved out of it by every wife-beating bully?'[64] Sophia gives a series of portraits of male 'characters', given to libertinism, lust and brutality: Hectorius who beats his virtuous wife ('plates, cups, knives or whatever things come first to hand, are the vehicles by which he conveys his ideas to her'), Anarchus ('when a-bed frequently puking' on his wife), and men like Molybditis whose daughters quickly learn what they can expect from their spoiled brothers ('before little master is well breech'd, he is taught to lord it over his sisters').[65] Aside from the portraits, Sophia adapts and paraphrases snatches of Poulain to substantiate her argument, from the laws of nature, for women's original equality, and their right to autonomy (she points out that jurists 'themselves acknowledge dependence and servitude to be contrary to the design of nature').[66] Custom and history, she insists, are nothing but the usurpation of the 'rights and liberties of Women'.[67] For her, those 'liberties' are largely economic and intellectual. Sophia uses arguments from natural law to denounce the violence and sexual double standards of men, but stops well short of advocating greater social tolerance for women's sexual freedoms. Sophia also treats custom and history as monolithic and unchanging edifices, from which examples can be cited and counter-cited.

In many respects, Sophia's case for greater equality and esteem for women remains in a seventeenth-century mode, in that she does not take on board the accounts of the social formation of female identity that can be found, not only in Poulain himself, but in a number of writers, from the later seventeenth century, such as Drake and Locke. Locke's enormously influential treatise *Some Thoughts concerning Education* (1693), for example, describes how little girls are socialised into their customary roles as ornaments and man-pleasers: 'And when the little Girl is tricked up in her new Gown and Commode, how can her Mother do less than teach her to Admire her self by calling her her little Queen and her Princess? Thus the little ones are taught to be Proud of their Cloathes, before they can put them on.'[68]

So continues, Locke writes, a wasted childhood as girls' natural energy is spent on trivial pursuits instead of on improving the mind and exercising the body:

I have seen little Girls exercise whole Hours together, and take abundance of pains to be expert at Dibstones, as they call it: Whilst I have been looking on, I have thought, it wanted only some good Contrivance, to make them employ all that Industry about something that might be more useful to them; and methinks 'tis only the fault and negligence of elder People, that it is not so.[69]

Locke's own 'contrivance' was for a limited equality of education between girls and boys, but his analysis of the upbringing of girls here may have proved more influential than his prescriptions. Many eighteenth-century writers extended and elaborated this kind of analysis of female socialisation as part of more historicised accounts of the evolution of modern 'manners'. Some writers, from Locke's friend Damaris Masham to Wollstonecraft, also speculated about the educational and social preconditions for women to participate on an equal footing in male intellectual culture, in the ways that Cartesian feminists had hoped. But, given the growing sense of the pervasive force of manners in shaping the way people think, others could not help but confirm what a distant dream that equal participation really was.

LIBERTINISM AS SOCIAL ANALYSIS

Most of the writers discussed in this book advocated or practised a reasoned analysis of the customary treatment and education of women in order to understand, and, in some cases, to change the culture in which they lived. A few engaged in a more fundamental rethinking of the moral and social vocabularies through which women were understood, sometimes through philosophical or literary imaginative inversions of the social order. Foremost among these was Mandeville, remarkable for the prominence he accorded in his works to such matters as female modesty, chastity, intellectual capability and sexual exploitation. Few subsequent writers, male or female, owned up to liking or approving of Mandeville's works. Yet those works are worth pausing over here, not only because of their well-known impact upon the Scottish Enlightenment, but also because they conveyed to the eighteenth-century reading public the remnant of a rich tradition of continental scholarly exploration of the relativity of moral values, or *libertinage érudit*. This tradition had some bearing on the view of women, since the values of female chastity and modesty had always been, and were becoming ever more, from the late seventeenth century, points from which British society took its moral bearings.[70] The tradition of *libertinage érudit* had its origins in the revival of Epicurean ideas in the early seventeenth century, and was, in its rational probing of traditional knowledges, boosted by the subsequent spread of Cartesianism.[71] It was this intellectual current, more than any other of the seventeenth century, that moved European philosophers towards a consideration of the nature of man and the psychological, ethical and religious basis of his operations as a social being, and, along with this, towards an interest in women as social beings. Marie de Gournay's *Egalité des hommes et des femmes* (1622), to cite a prominent instance, was partly the result of her intellectual involvement with a circle of prominent *libertins érudits*.[72]

Pierre Bayle himself may be placed in this tradition, and was an author who, as David Wootton has shown, took an exceptionally open-minded and intense interest in sexual morality, and the degree to which the strict sexual morality enjoined by religion is in conflict with the promptings of nature.[73] Bayle, as Wootton argues, took an earthy, liberal attitude towards such matters as female sexual freedom and prostitution, and, in the article 'Patin' in his *Dictionnaire historique et critique* (1697, second edition 1702), he showed how sanctimonious social insistence upon female chastity can lead to women attempting abortions or killing their babies, because their fear of public shame overcomes the natural dictates of their consciences. Bayle's *Dictionnaire* was translated into English in 1710, and again in 1734–41, and was widely discussed in early eighteenth-century Britain.[74] Bayle's 'feminism' (as Wootton terms it) may well have rubbed off on acquaintances such as Gilbert Burnet (discussed in chapter 1). Much of the flavour and some of the substance of Bayle's covertly expressed religious scepticism and Epicurean vision of society (including its female members) reached British audiences through the works of Mandeville, who had very probably studied under Bayle when at school in Rotterdam. Mandeville moved to London in the 1690s to practise as a physician, and, in transit, became a Whig, supporting the Glorious Revolution, the Protestant succession and limited monarchy.[75] In the 1723 version of Mandeville's *The Fable of the Bees*, there is a discussion of infanticide, remarkably similar to Bayle's 'Patin', in which a fashionable young lady, seduced, impregnated and abandoned by a 'Powerful Deceiver', is driven to destroy her child.[76] Women like this, Mandeville observes, are so overwhelmed by censorious social attitudes towards them and so obsessed with the need to preserve their reputations, that they are likely to risk committing abortion or infanticide:

All Mothers naturally love their Children: but as this is a Passion, and all Passions center in Self-Love, so it may be subdued by any Superiour Passion, to sooth that same Self-Love, which if nothing had interven'd, would have bid her fondle her Offspring. Common Whores, whom all the World knows to be such, hardly ever destroy their Children . . . not because they are less Cruel or more Virtuous, but because they have lost their Modesty to a greater degree, and the fear of Shame makes hardly any impression upon them.[77]

This is, by eighteenth-century standards, a daring foray into a taboo subject, all the more so because of the degree of sympathy expressed for the mother who acts out of the socially invented passion of shame. It is also reminiscent of a passage in Defoe's *Moll Flanders* (1722) in which Moll, inured to shame by a career of bigamous marriage and concubinage, tells the reader that she would never think of terminating a pregnancy or committing passive infanticide by 'farming' unwanted offspring.[78]

Mandeville's discussion here is only incidentally pro-woman, and is primarily directed towards explaining how one kind of self-love (the natural one of women for their children) can be trumped by another, more powerful and socially inculcated kind of self-love (the fear of shame). His larger purpose, in *The Fable of the Bees*, is to develop the argument of Bayle – that men are naturally amoral and pleasure-seeking, and that they become socialised, not by religious prescriptions, but by laws that manage their natural appetites to the mutual advantage of all – into a thorough-going account of the way people really live in a modern city like London.[79]

Mandeville's work, in other words, played a pioneering role in taking forward the exploration of the cultural relativity of moral values, and the *libertinage érudit* of the seventeenth century on to a new, Enlightenment terrain: the analysis of economic behaviour, of the social genesis of moral rules, and the workings of sociability in civilised settings. His was, from the outset, a gendered account of those workings. The *Fable* started life as a short poem, *The Grumbling Hive: or, Knaves Turn'd Honest* (1705) in which Mandeville ironically imagines the economic disaster that would take place if women turned honest and gave up shopping: 'Weavers that join'd rich Silk with Plate/And all the Trades subordinate/Are gone.'[80] Mandeville's sympathies with women were, however, more extensive than this endorsement of their economic usefulness as consumers, and on one occasion he recollected fondly the active participation, less common in England, of women in his native Netherlands in family businesses.[81] Four years later, Mandeville published a work in a female voice, *The Virgin Unmask'd*, which, despite its promisingly erotic title, contained a serious discussion of the War of the Spanish Succession cast in the form of a dialogue between an elderly spinster and her young niece. Mandeville peppered the dialogue with remarks about the disadvantaged position of women; the aunt Lucinda explains to her niece how men 'have Enslaved our Sex: In Paradice, Man and Woman were upon an even Foot', and complains of the lack of female education.[82] The first edition of *The Fable of the Bees* (1714) contained an introduction (in which Mandeville stated his intention to tell men not 'what they should be' but 'what they really are'), an 'Enquiry into the Origin of Moral Virtue', and an apparatus of annotations ('Remarks' numbered alphabetically) to the original *Grumbling Hive* poem.[83] The main target of Mandeville's satire is contemporary moral cant – whether pious, sentimental or stoical – and the way people use it to delude themselves about the selfish passions and drives that really make society work. Looking beyond virtue and vice, he defends the social necessity of many practices which moralists designate as 'vicious', such as prostitution; prosecuting 'Courtezans and Strumpets . . . with as much Rigour as some silly People would have it' only leads to an increased number of seductions or rapes of other women.[84] Deep down, Mandeville insinuates, most people are far more motivated or restrained by considerations of social esteem than by the sanctions of religion or morality.

The Fable begins with the 'Enquiry into the Origin of Moral Virtue' which explains how savage man, a creature of unruly passions and appetites, becomes sufficiently self-restrained to live in society. Mandeville regards self-restraint, which Christians and moralists call 'virtue', as an important ingredient of social co-operation, but recognises that it entails an estrangement of man from his own nature, a 'Violence', as he puts it, which men are induced to 'commit upon themselves' by a group of politicians who 'have undertaken to civilise mankind' by manipulating the one potentially sociable passion innate to all human beings, pride.[85] From all this, it is clear that, for Mandeville, the civilising process involves a bending of human nature through a combination of external, legal restraint and subtle, coercive socialisation. The same, Mandeville argues, goes for women who are socialised into gender-specific roles in order to meet the practical requirements of their particular society. He discusses the different upbringings of boys and girls in the context of a general argument about the way in which moralists flatter people into thinking that they must be 'good' in order to be admired. On one occasion he gives a wonderfully vivid description of two little girls learning to be good and co-operative:

When an awkard Girl before she can either Speak or Go, begins after many entreaties to make the first rude Essays of Curt'sying: The Nurse falls in an extasy of Praise: *There's a delicate Curt'sy! O fine Miss! There's a pretty Lady! Mama! Miss can make a better Curt'sy than her Sister* Molly! The same is eccho'd over by the Maids, whilst Mama almost hugs the Child to pieces; only Miss *Molly*, who being four Years older, knows how to make a very handsome Curt'sy, wonders at the Perverseness of their Judgment, and swelling with Indignation, is ready to cry at the Injustice that is done her, till be whisper'd in the Ear that it is only to please the Baby, and that she is a Woman; she grows Proud at being let into the Secret . . . These extravagant Praises would by any one, above the Capacity of an Infant, be call'd fulsome Flatteries, and, if you will, abominable Lies; yet Experience teaches us, that by the help of such gross Encomiums, young Misses will be brought to make pretty Curt'sies, and behave themselves womanly much sooner, and with less trouble, than they would without them.[86]

When the girls grow up, Mandeville shows in Remarks L and M, they will become valuable consumers, benefiting, rather than endangering, society as encouragers of 'luxury' so long as politicians keep an eye on the balance of trade.

Thus, the first version of *The Fable of the Bees* presents femininity as one among a number of socially useful learned behaviours in complex, commercial societies, and treats contemporary public sanctimoniousness about female immorality and 'luxury' with implicit disdain.[87] At some stage after publishing the first edition of *The Fable of the Bees* and before publishing the 1723 version with its closing essay, 'A Search into the Nature of Society', Mandeville read Shaftesbury's *Characteristicks* (1711, revised 1714). In response to Shaftesbury's idea of man's natural sociability, Mandeville became less preoccupied with exposing the hypocrisy of those who give the name of 'vice' to socially beneficial practices, than with strengthening his idea of society as an artificial contrivance against Shaftesbury's vision of society as the spontaneous outgrowth of man's natural feelings. One major consequence of this new, anti-Shaftesburian strain of argument, in the 1723 *Fable*, is the far greater prominence given to the subject of women. More than half the revisions are concerned with this subject, which becomes the illustrative focus for Mandeville's contentions about nature and virtue. The first of these occurs in the greatly expanded Remark C on the artificially inculcated passions of honour and shame that motivate soldiers to action and women to modesty. Mandeville states that the modesty of women is the female form of shame, and merely 'the Result of Custom and Education'. It is purely social in orientation, and is designed to teach women to control their sexuality in public. Women are not naturally ashamed of their sexuality, and the blush on the cheek of the young lady disappears when she

contemplates sexual matters in private. They do, however, internalise the
social laws of censure, and blush in private if they overhear themselves
discussed disrespectfully.[88] Shaftesbury's philosophy gives no place to
female desire, whereas Mandeville believes that it is as strong as male
desire, but that the laws of 'the Polite and knowing World' demand that it
should be more closely concealed.[89] Chastity is a lesson which young
girls learn, 'like those of *Grammar*', as they do modesty, and neither is
inherently virtuous: 'Because Impudence is a Vice, it does not follow that
Modesty is a Virtue; it is built upon Shame, a Passion in our Nature, and
may be either Good or Bad according to the Actions perform'd from that
Motive.'[90]

A self-aware society, less in thrall to religious notions of 'virtue' and
Shaftesburian notions of 'politeness', Mandeville appears to argue, would
not impose such unnatural sexual self-denial upon women. Not only
would a heftier dose of Dutch sexual frankness lessen the incentive to
commit abortion or infanticide, but it would also deter wealthier people
(whom he scornfully refers to as 'the fashionable Part of Mankind') from
inflicting arranged marriages on their daughters. As he observes in the
newly added Remark N:

it is the Interest of the Society to preserve Decency and Politeness; that Women
should linger, waste, and die, rather than relieve themselves in an unlawful
Manner; and among the fashionable Part of Mankind, the People of Birth and
Fortune, it is expected, that Matrimony should never be enter'd upon without a
curious Regard to Family, Estate, and Reputation, and in the making of Matches
the Call of Nature be the very last Consideration.[91]

Mandeville's libertine critique of the effects of contemporary sexual
morality upon the lives of women and his sensitivity to the cruelties they
endure, had its intellectual roots in the work of Bayle, but also affinities
with the contemporary literary libertinage to be found in Manley, Eliza
Haywood and other writers of amatory fiction. Their works, similarly,
explore the female suffering caused by the tension between women's
natural propensity to pleasure and the moral rules (neither transcendent
nor natural, but hypocritically and self-servingly imposed by moralising
men).[92] In Manley's *Secret History, or Queen Zarah* (1705) one of the male
characters refers to sexuality as a 'natural Right', adding (in a way that
invites the reader to think of women) that 'they are wretched who enjoy
not that Liberty'; and, in her fictionalised autobiography, *The Adventures
of Rivella* (1714), she also explores the social workings of the discourse of
female 'shame' through the device of a sympathetic but uncomprehending

male narrator.[93] The simple message of Mandeville's writings that there are two sets of rules – the official, religious and moral ones and the real, unacknowledged laws of social behaviour – found echoes in the fictional stories of enterprising harlots from Moll Flanders to Fanny Hill.

From the time of Richardson's *Pamela* (1740), respectable novel writers progressively distanced themselves from libertine views of this kind, but libertinism continued to evolve throughout the century, and to nurture a degree of ethical scepticism and experimentation, especially with regard to orthodox ideas about female sexuality.[94] Gibbon and Hume owed something to this current of philosophical libertinism, as we will see, but, before the very end of the century, only Mandeville made his unconventional, liberal sexual views a platform for practical reform in Britain.[95] A year after the second edition of *The Fable*, he published anonymously a pamphlet entitled *A Modest Defence of Publick Stews* (brothels) in which he developed the case, set out in Remark H of the original *Fable*, for legalised and publicly regulated prostitution as a means of protecting respectable women from seduction and rape. This included a plan for properly supervised brothels in which the women would be protected from violence, and provided with medical facilities to control the pox and to reduce the mortality of their offspring.[96] He also stated that female chastity is unnatural from a physiological point of view, reprising his ideas about female honour as a form of learned behaviour, and elaborating a new notion of 'artificial Chastity':

To counterballance this violent natural Desire, all young women have strong Notions of Honour carefully inculcated into them from their Infancy. Young Girls are taught to hate a *Whore*, before they know what the Word means; and when they grow up, they find their worldly Interest entirely depending upon the Reputation of their Chastity. This Sense of Honour and Interest, is what we may call artificial Chastity; and it is upon this Compound of natural and artificial Chastity, that every Women's real actual Chastity depends.[97]

Mandeville sees how the whore as a figure of 'vice' is necessary to the discursive construction, in his time, of 'real' chastity as the materialisation of a physical state as a social mode of being. Most commentators and conduct book writers of Mandeville's time would have found his alternative notion of 'artificial chastity' pernicious and irreligious, since chastity was generally regarded as one of the 'offices' of women prescribed by natural law. However, there are some striking similarities with Hume's discussion of female chastity in his *A Treatise of Human Nature* (1739–40), which he designates as one of the 'artificial' virtues, the product, not of nature, but of social convention, education, and the requirements of husbands and father'.[98]

Hume is unlikely to have read *A Modest Defence of Publick Stews*, but Mandeville did have a very significant impact upon his thinking, as he did upon Francis Hutcheson, Adam Smith and other Scottish Enlightenment philosophers.[99] Hume criticised Mandeville's argument about the artificial nature of moral and legal rules by suggesting that, far from being imposed by skilful politicians, they came about through the historical evolution of sociability. This development of Mandeville's thinking would have far-reaching consequences. By and large, Mandeville had more to say about the workings of society than about its historical progress, although in his later works, however, his thinking did develop some historical perspectives. For instance, *The Fable of the Bees. Part II* (1729), a dialogue work written in defence of the original *Fable*, outlines, as a historical argument, the idea that rules of morality and codes of behaviour are reinvented at each stage of the civilising process. Mandeville never called this process 'improvement', as his Scottish Enlightenment successors were to do, but this work contains the seeds of an evolutionary account of female virtue in which sexual continence can be read as an index of social development. And in a subsequent dialogue work entitled *An Enquiry into the Origin of Honour* (1732), Mandeville wrote about honour and shame as historically contingent passions, different in meaning and social effect in different societies, such as ancient Rome, barbarian Germany or medieval Europe. One of the interlocutors in this dialogue characterises honour (whose male form is courage and whose female form is chastity) as a fundamentally medieval idea which has survived into the present: 'I make no Doubt, but this Signification of the Word Honour is entirely Gothick, and sprung up in some of the most ignorant Ages of Christianity.'[100] Mandeville was discussed seriously by those, like Hutcheson and Hume, who attempted to account for morality in naturalistic terms, and they followed him in including the ethical categories that pertained to women, such as chastity, compassion and modesty, in their discussions. His work also excited serious, uniformly hostile discussion among the devout, especially those moral rationalists committed to the notion that reason allows us to discover God's immutable moral law. Among these, the celebrated High Church Anglican devotional writer William Law mounted one of the most cogent attacks on Mandeville's work in a pamphlet entitled *Remarks upon a Late Book, Entitled, The Fable of the Bees* (1724), in which he argued that reason does play a vital part in enabling people to act well. Mandeville had suggested that compassion, far from being a moral behaviour, is merely an impulse of nature to which weak-minded women are particularly prone. Law counters that 'To say that Women have the *weakest Minds,* is saying more than you are able to prove. If they are more inclin'd to Compassion, through a Tenderness of Nature, it is so far from being a *Weakness of their Minds,* that it is a right judgement.'[101] Most of Law's criticisms are levelled at the wrong-headedness of Mandeville's view of history as one in which wise politicians suddenly impose civility on the savages.

PRELIMINARIES

Whether on historical ground or in relation to his excessive or insufficient ethical naturalism, or to his denial of the reality of benevolence, the terms of the controversy over Mandeville's works were also those of the Enlightenment debate about women. At the heart of the debate was the question as to whether sociability or self-interest was the real basis for society, and, in either case, what was the point of women's entry into the present functioning, past history and progressive future of society itself. The first chapter of this book starts, on the other side of the argument from Mandeville, with those writers who made the case for the benign impact of women upon a social order that depends for its survival, upon individual human virtue and piety. It is concerned with the creation of a Whig Anglican Enlightenment in early to mid eighteenth-century England that was favourable to female learning and female social influence and activity. It begins with the work of Locke, and with the response from his pupil Lord Shaftesbury, from Cambridge Platonist religious writers, and from theologians from Samuel Clarke and Gilbert Burnet to Joseph Butler. It explores the engagement of women writers with the theological and philosophical debates, prompted by their work, about the extent to which we can know God by examining the realm of nature, about the nature of reason, the capacity of reason to access God's moral law, and the sources of our obligation to be virtuous. It also looks at the questions pertaining to the operations of virtue in a social context. In particular, it considers women's response to arguments, between Locke and Shaftesbury, about the sources of moral norms in society, and the degree to which morality has a natural foundation in the human mind. The chapter examines the search, in the work of Mary Astell, Damaris Masham, Elizabeth Burnet and Catharine Cockburn, for an ethics and epistemology hospitable to the rational and moral capacities of women that would enable them to act as philosophers and agents within and beyond the domestic sphere. It investigates, following both Shaftesbury and Mandeville, the extent to which they considered self-love or benevolence, or a combination of the two as the basis for social co-operation, and the extent to which benevolence, rather than private devotion, ought to be the main business of a purposeful life. The chapter then moves forward in time to the philosophical and devotional writings of the Bluestocking circle of women writers, particularly those of Elizabeth Carter and Catharine Talbot. It seeks to place these within the Latitudinarian Enlightenment, and to show the deep impact upon their work of their friend Butler, one of the most influential moral philosophers of the century, in formulating their ideas of active female virtue, free will and the ability to arrive at a degree of understanding and certainty about this world and the next through the exercise of reason.

Chapter 2 moves to Scotland, where attempts by Enlightenment thinkers to create a science of human culture yielded the most extensive engagement with the role of women ever undertaken in European intellectual history. It begins with moral philosophy, and with the critique of Locke's social contract and of Mandeville by Francis Hutcheson, Hume and Smith. Within a natural law framework, Hutcheson elaborated an inclusive theory of natural benevolence, and of society as the benevolent outgrowth of familial ties, as well as an unusually egalitarian idea of marriage and family life. Hume and Smith rejected the idea of the objective moral realm asserted by Hutcheson, Clarke, Butler and others, and developed naturalistic accounts of virtue as something that arises from our passions. For Hume this included the insight that justice is an 'artificial', rather than a natural virtue (and justice includes, he writes, the injunction to female chastity). With this idea of artificial virtues came the idea of human sociability as a historical development (rather than as the product of a social contract), and, in the writings that followed, of the place of women within that evolving history of moral and legal rules. Most of the chapter is concerned with the development of Scottish 'conjectural history' with its exploration of the relationships between morality, the law and social customs (including, prominently, those that affect the status of women) that naturally occur at different economic stages of society. Natural jurisprudence remains a framework for these discussions, but the chapter identifies two somewhat different lines of enquiry: that of Lord Kames, James Beattie and Dugald Stewart (concerned with the historical emergence of the inner moral sense, including a sense of justice towards women, and also with the blunting of that sense by modern luxury), and that of Smith, his pupil John Millar and William Robertson

(concerned to give an empirical account of the natural progress of society –
including the gradual diminution of cruelty to women). South of the
border, partly through their close connections to the Bluestocking circle,
Beattie, Kames and Stewart had the greater impact. On all these Scottish
writers the extensive discussions of women in the work of Montesquieu
played an important part, and there was even, in England, a female
Montesquieuan, Jemima Kindersley. And there was a shared tendency
to see history as a great gender divergence, with male and female roles
becoming ever more polarised as societies become more complex, and
with an intensification of (not instantly gratified) sexual energies being
associated with greater economic productivity . The contrast, in the work
of Scottish writers, between complex societies and hunter-gatherer or
pastoral tribes, was sharpened by their reading of the new anthropology
from France, but often in ways that implicitly excluded the 'primitive'
peoples described there, with their allegedly brutal treatment of their
women, from the European trajectory of progress.

   In some of the anthropological writings of the Scottish Enlightenment,
as well as later works such as James Dunbar's *Essays on the History of
Mankind* (1780), the study of 'manners' became detached from the
framework of natural jurisprudence, and linked more closely to the
investigation of ethnic and cultural specificity. A similar detachment of
economics from moral philosophy and jurisprudence would take place
early in the nineteenth century. Chapter 3 explores some of the ways in
which this more diffuse notion of manners informed the historical culture
of the second half of the eighteenth century, particularly in relation to
Britain's changing sense of its Roman, Ancient British, Celtic, Gothic and
medieval pasts, and how women increasingly came to be identified as the
carriers of that cultural and ethnic heritage. It tells the paradoxical story of
the analytical dilution and historical enrichment of the conjectural history
of manners, and of the emergence of more specialised (and in many ways
more limited) ideas of women's roles as guardians and carriers of those
manners. It looks at the part played by numerous literary histories,
historical works, plays and other literary sources in the development of
a gendered ethnic consciousness, and of a sense of temporality that
included, but was more complex than, 'progress' as women came to be
seen as bearing and preserving the traces of the remote past. The genea-
logical contours of that past, especially, were a matter of vigorous controversy between Scottish, Welsh and English writers – a controversy that
invariably included the status and virtue of women in ancient societies,
things that were now understood to be key indicators of ethnic personality

and of levels of civilisation. The chapter shows how the 'Ossian' debates intersected with wider arguments about Celtic versus Germanic women, and how the emergence from the 1760s of an ideal of Gothic femininity and of female 'affective patriotism' served both to confirm and complicate conjectural historical models of European progress. The Roman republican ideal of the austere woman who sacrifices her feelings for the good of the state, although it continued to provide inspiration to writers such as Catharine Macaulay, declined in popularity, succumbing, in part, to a prevailing philosophical climate in which private affections and self-regard were not perceived to be at odds with public benevolence. Gibbon played an important part in this respectful but sceptical re-evaluation of the relevance of Roman history to modern Britain, as well as providing his own highly original analysis of the appalling legal predicament of women in ancient Rome. The final part of the chapter is concerned with the rediscovery of medieval chivalry, in the wake of Scottish Enlightenment history, and also of literary and antiquarian scholarship by Sainte-Palaye (and his translator Susannah Dobson), George, Baron Lyttelton (assisted by his friend Elizabeth Montagu), Thomas Percy, Thomas Warton, Beattie, Clara Reeve and others, as the legacy of Gothic manners. Chivalry was for them as later for Burke, the defining and enduring characteristic of Europe's gender order, the forerunner of civilised manners, and the model for social relations more generally. The revival of chivalry as an ideal reached its height in the 1820s, and its enduring legacy was the creation of the idea of the lady as a kind of inherited, historically venerable rank to which all women can aspire. Although some women writers and readers readily took the chance for cultural and moral guardianship that the cult of chivalry afforded, others, notably Wollstonecraft and Macaulay, deplored it as a means of writing women out of the history of social progress.

Macaulay, the most effective critic of Burke's chivalry and the major female historian of the eighteenth century, is the subject of a dedicated chapter 4. A committed radical republican who believed that there had been no real improvements in English politics or society since the end of the Commonwealth, Macaulay fits awkwardly into a British Enlightenment concerned with the progress of society. Before her final *Letters on Education* (1790), she expressed little overt interest in the progress of women. Modern commentators have either puzzled over her seemingly gender-blind assumption of masculine republicanism, or have explored the strategies through which she laid claim to female political spokesmanship. This chapter seeks to establish, through a detailed reading of her historical works, that

Macaulay set out to modernise the classical idea of liberty in the light of Enlightenment ideas (particularly those of Hume) about the social and economic forces that shape historical development; that she formulated her own 'science of politics' by reviving, in opposition to Hume and others, Locke's idea of the right of resistance to authority permissible within the social contract; that she sought to combine Locke's ideas of individuals asserting their rights with classical notions of active, vigilant citizenship in ways that accorded a role for all men and women in the improvement of the nation's political culture; and that, above all, she promoted the idea of rational self-cultivation as a qualification for citizenship, including, she strongly hints, citizenship for women. These political ideas are underscored by Macaulay's theological writings which, in the tradition of Clarke and Cockburn, locate the moral obligation to act for the public good in the objective, eternal distinctions between right and wrong by which God himself is constrained. Like her Latitudinarian predecessors, she argues that these distinctions are discoverable by our reason, and that morality is a matter of rationality not, as for Scottish moral philosophers, of sentiment. She parts company with her predecessors, however, when she declares that morality is also a matter of 'necessity', and that we do not have free will to choose the bad once reason has allowed us to understand the good.

Education, for Macaulay, plays a vital role in allowing us to determine our true 'rational interest' and so inevitably to follow the right moral and political path. This was the subject of her last work, the *Letters on Education* (1790), which had a considerable impact on Wollstonecraft in its analysis of the processes of moral cognition, of the distorted, excessively gender-specific personal identities produced by the current state of education and manners, and of the potential for female education to hasten the progress of civilisation. Chapter 5 shows how, following Macaulay, Wollstonecraft adapted the British Enlightenment languages of manners and conjectural history to a powerful critique of the denigration of women in modern society. Wollstonecraft set out to reverse the Enlightenment tendency – taken to extremes by modern writers on chivalry, and absorbed into Rousseau's account of women's supporting role in the creation of male citizens – to judge manners by their social effects, rather than by their moral content, and to treat femininity as a kind of rank, or ascribed social identity. She linked this, in her *Vindication of the Rights of Woman*, and also in her later *Historical View* of the French Revolution and in her account of Sweden, to a historical analysis of modern Europe as at once hyper-civilised and feudally retarded, and having failed to realise the benefits of the commercial stage. Wollstonecraft's solutions, it is argued, were more gradualist than revolutionary, in that she thought that an individual female and male reclaiming of moral autonomy, followed by reformation and realignment of morality and manners, needed to precede political change, and to bring about the implementation of civil and political rights, as had happened in America. In her beliefs about morality – as a matter of rational choice and reflection, not sentiment, and as issuing from an objective moral realm – Wollstonecraft was very much a thinker in the late Latitudinarian tradition, particularly as it was mediated by her minister Richard Price. In seeking to reintegrate, for feminist purposes, this theology of individual rational autonomy with the language of manners and the progress of society, Wollstonecraft's work exposes, with particular clarity, the tensions between the Scottish and English strains of Enlightenment, and between the idea of society as a product of self-interest or as an aggregate of private affections and public benevolence. She acknowledges the commercial stage to be the one most likely to deliver a better life for women, yet insists that women's stake in that kind of society cannot simply be as pleasers, socialisers and consumers. Their private affections and moral conduct must be connected to public benefits to enable them to become fully themselves, and to enable the state to reach a higher state of civilisation. Most of Wollstonecraft's female predecessors advocated this civic integration in terms of philanthropic benevolence, but she was the first, in Britain, to say that, for women's 'private virtue' to become a 'public benefit, they must have a civil existence in the state, married or single' (see pp. 184–5).

The final chapter looks forward to the nineteenth century, and to the ways in which the idea of the progress of society (for men as well as women) fragmented and regrouped in the years following the Napoleonic wars. It is in two separate parts, one concerned with women historians, the other with women and political economy in the wake of T. R. Malthus's *Essay on the Principle of Population*. A common context for both parts is the rising influence of Scottish Common Sense philosophy, of the kind promoted by Montagu and her circle, and in particular of the Edinburgh philosopher Dugald Stewart and his circle (including Maria Edgeworth, Anna Laetitia Barbauld and Elizabeth Hamilton); also the decline of the Latitudinarian Anglican consensus in religious thinking (despite the considerable success of the work of William Paley), the ongoing rise of Evangelicalism, and the temporary defeat, in the first two decades of the century, of Enlightenment philosophical Whiggism by a new 'throne-and-altar' ideology. The first part explores the ways in which a generation of women historians made money out of the Enlightenment association between women and history, and the promotion, by Bluestocking writers such as Hester Chapone and Sarah Scott, of history as an essential part of women's education. The chapter records the considerable contribution of women historians and authors of semi-fictional history, such as Hamilton, Ellis Cornelia Knight and Susannah Dobson, to the further expansion of the affective, imaginatively engaging possibilities of the history of 'manners'. It shows how later historians, such as Mary Berry, continued their work of rewriting the history of female 'influence' in the domain of manners, not in terms of unintended sexual agency, but in relation to a progressive narrative of their spiritual, rational and benevolent social agency. It explores the elevation, in this period, of certain female exemplars (notably the seventeenth-century Roundhead supporter, Lucy Hutchinson) as nationally serviceable points of sympathetic entry into history. And it gives an overview of works, by Mary Hays, Lucy Aikin, Elizabeth Benger, in two emerging genres of women's popular history – royal biography and art history – paving the way for women's dominance in this field from the mid nineteenth century onwards. In the case of biographies of queens and princesses, these works can be characterised as extending the Enlightenment history of manners into new, emotional territory. Far from simply creating a niche area for women historians, these histories gave emblematic significance to the stories of elite women, who found themselves in positions of immense influence through no endeavour of their own, having to make hard choices but, at least, assured of historical recognition for those choices. Over and above the possibilities they offered to women readers, these histories, in dramatising the encounter between a responsible individual and the intractable, opaque world of power, gave a privileged role to the female character in history in mediating the national past, and a sense of what it feels like to be a pawn in the progress of society.

The second part of this chapter begins with Jane Austen's ambivalent attitude towards history, and her scepticism, despite her intense engagement with the social workings of manners, about whether society actually progresses. In some respects, her work approximates to a late, Malthusian version of the Enlightenment in its endorsement of the possibility of improvement within the limits imposed by the economy, warfare and numbers of people. Malthus is discussed as a figure of the Enlightenment, broadly hospitable to Latitudinarian natural theology (although ever sceptical about the possibility of human benevolence), and deeply, if sometimes critically, engaged with what his Scottish forebears had to say about women as beneficiaries or victims of social progress. Malthus's work inevitably placed female reproduction at the heart of political economy. When, in the revised version of his *Essay*, he emphasised 'moral restraint' as an alternative to over-population, he discussed the changes in social attitudes towards women that would need to come about to make this an effective strategy. Other population theorists, such as Stewart, saw female education as an important intervention in social progress. The entanglement, in the debates about population, of female education, political economy and social progress encouraged some women writers – among them Priscilla Wakefield, Jane Marcet, Hannah More and, later, Harriet Martineau – to regard political economy as *in itself* a form of female education. Yet, in the figure of More, in particular, we reach the limits of Enlightenment: committed, as second-generation Bluestocking, to the ideals of rational autonomy and female education, she nevertheless contributed to the transformation of the Enlightenment project for the progress of society into one in which the lower orders of society were 'progressed' by their spiritually enlightened 'betters'.

Anglican Whig feminism in England, 1690–1760: self-love, reason and social benevolence

In this chapter, I will look back to the late seventeenth century, and forward to the mid eighteenth in order recover the broader philosophical and theological contexts within which debates about women's place in the social order were conducted. Locke's idea of the social contract had its foundations in a materialist epistemology, given its fullest treatment in his *Essay Concerning Human Understanding* (1690), and in his views on ethics – a subject never addressed fully or separately by him, but in part retrievable from his writings. It was in these broader fields of epistemology and ethics that women writers, including Mary Astell, made their most significant interventions. They ensured, by their example as female commentators on philosophical and religious matters, and, still more, by arguments directly relevant to women, that they had some voice in the profound philosophical reshaping of epistemology and ethics which took place in the wake of Locke's work. Women writers engaged intensely, often critically, with the theological implications of Locke's philosophy, and with the critical response to his work that came from theologians of the Cambridge Platonist school and from Shaftesbury. As we will see in this chapter, a number of women writers – including Damaris Masham, Catharine Cockburn, Elizabeth Burnet, Elizabeth Carter and Catharine Talbot, sought to synthesise, from the raw materials of these philosophical debates, ideas of ethics and epistemology hospitable to the rational and moral agency of women. These debates came primarily out of a religious and moral philosophical, rather than explicitly political, context, and took place largely within the 'Latitudinarian' ideological wing of the Anglican Church. Latitudinarian Anglicanism endorsed the values of religious toleration (very limited, in the case of Roman Catholics), free rational religious enquiry, undogmatic, generally non-mystical faith based on reason and scripture, and salvation open to all (as opposed to Calvinist ideas of divine election), taking good works as a sign of saving faith. This chapter will address the role of women writers in the advancement of the (mainly Whig) Latitudinarian English Enlightenment of the early to mid eighteenth century, and the ways in which they asserted, within this influential movement, the deep interconnection between private ethical conduct and the well-being of church and state.[1]

Much has been written about the role of women in the Evangelical Revival from the early eighteenth century, and about their participation in the intellectual movements inspired by Rational and other forms of Dissent later in the century.[2] This chapter looks instead at the role of women and of questions of femininity in what might be seen, at least until the latter part of the century, as the tolerant religious mainstream. Latitudinarian Anglicanism formed the bridge between the established church and Dissent, creating a middle ground capacious enough for later radicals such as Catharine Macaulay, yet closed to deism, freethinking and other forms of unbelief. Although it occupied the middle ground, Latitudinarianism was never uncontentious. Its qualified endorsement of religious toleration was often the subject of fierce public debate, especially early in the eighteenth century when concerted attempts to curtail the civil rights of Dissenters issued in the Occasional Conformity Act of 1711 (repealed 1719), excluding them from public office. Mary Astell's support of this Act (she wrote three pamphlets on the subject), and her opposition to the Toleration Act of 1689, mark her opposition to the politics (if not the theology) of Latitudinarianism. Her biographer, Ruth Perry, describes her as 'the inevitable female projection of the English Enlightenment'.[3] Yet, according to the different genealogy offered here, Astell may be seen to have stood outside the tide which ran from earlier debates about the rights of Dissenters and their membership of the political community to late eighteenth-century assertions about the civil rights of women. As in the introductory chapter, the case made here is that Whiggism, in its political and established religious forms, was not, as Carole Pateman argued, inherently antipathetic to arguments promoting the status and rights of women, and that it was in fact, in the longer run, the medium in which such arguments most flourished. This is, nevertheless, a case which cannot be made without due recognition of the complex and enduring influence of Astell's extraordinary work, from Clarissa Harlowe's decidedly Astell-ian piety and holy death to Sarah Scott's utopian female community in *A Description of Millenium Hall* (1762).[4] As a philosopher, Astell was both a Cartesian and indebted to Cambridge Platonism, and she pushed into new feminist territory its emphasis upon reason as the inner candle of the Lord and the path to truth.[5]

The clash between Cambridge Platonist and Lockean ideas formed one of the main axes of theological debate in the early eighteenth century.

There were sharp differences between the epistemological idealism of the Platonists (who argued that our reason enables us to discern the true, perfect forms of the things that we otherwise perceive only imperfectly with our senses) and Locke's empiricism, as well as between the Platonists' Cartesian idea of the mind as an immaterial entity separate from the body, and Locke's hypothesis that material entities could think. There were also important areas of agreement on morality as the great end of religion, on the importance of reason as the instrument for knowing God and on the need for education to cultivate that reason. The tensions and commonalities between these two ways of looking at cognition, ethics and faith were particularly productive for those concerned with the mental capacities, education and moral conduct of women. No woman writer, not even Locke's friend Damaris Masham, accepted uncritically his epistemology, according to which we derive all knowledge – including our knowledge of God and of morality – through our experience and reflection upon the material world. Nor were women writers willing to endorse Locke's view, persuasively caricatured and criticised by Shaftesbury, that morality was primarily a matter of law and enforcement, public opinion, praise and shame, since this seemed to them to open the way back to the demeaning libertinism of the Restoration. For many, including Catharine Cockburn and the Bluestocking writers, Locke's work did not provide an adequate foundation for an idea of moral obligation arising from our certain knowledge of eternal truth, and they drew deeply upon latter-day Platonists, such as Samuel Clarke, in order to create their own accounts of how rational men and women arrive at moral certainty. Bringing together elements from Locke, Clarke, Shaftesbury and (later) Joseph Butler, women writers created synthetic accounts of epistemology and ethics that emphasised, above all, the exercise of reason within a domain of knowable and immutable truth. They were committed to the notion that, through education and personal endeavour, women could attain the status of rational beings, capable of arriving at a reasonably secure level of religious certainty and of acting as both philosophers and effective moral agents within and beyond the domestic sphere. From this commitment followed their consideration of the nature and purpose of reflective inwardness, something both Locke and the Cambridge Platonists regarded, in their different ways, as basic to the mind's acquisition of knowledge. They also engaged in some further debate about the social and institutional structures within which higher levels of female reflection might take place.

Astell made the most celebrated and influential contribution to this debate, in the first part of her *A Serious Proposal to the Ladies* (1694), when she advocated an Anglican intellectual retreat for women to develop their mental powers. Others preferred to emphasise more worldly settings and more practical purposes for the cultivated female mind. Astell wrote extensively about the process by which the unfettered female mind arrives at moral truth, as well as the obligations which such discoveries place women under to love and obey God. Yet, as we will see, she had relatively little to say about the kinds of moral obligations women are under to their fellow creatures in everyday life. Other female moralists found her approach other-worldly and overly rationalist (in the sense of endorsing an intuitive, rather than collaborative idea of reason). They attempted to develop an ethics and a theology rooted in the notion of men and women's innate sociability, and favourable to female social action (as Carter remarked, 'Society is the true Sphere of human Virtue').[6] For them, Locke's account of civil society, in the second of his *Two Treatises of Government*, as something designed to satisfy the need for self-preservation, sounded too competitive and too individualistic. In the wake of Shaftesbury's moral philosophy, they found themselves in a philosophical climate in which the non-competitive, gregarious instincts of nurturing and kindness were valued ever more highly, and became the basis of a familial and communitarian, rather than contractual account, of social origins. Alexander Pope, in the third book of his *An Essay on Man* (1733–4) – a work enormously popular with women readers – gave an account of the history of civilisation in which society grows naturally out of family ties.[7]

Astell explicitly rejected the Whig and Lockean idea of natural equality and of civil society as the product of a social contract. Many other women writers also rejected these ideas, but silently and without anti-Whig animus or resort to patriarchal models of the state. For them, the idea of an individualistic humanity prior to society was a myth easily discredited simply by looking at the natural and selfless bond between mothers and children.[8] Many, from Catharine Cockburn to Elizabeth Montagu, believed men and women to be naturally benevolent. Their belief that, in Cockburn's words, benevolent virtue is 'the law of their nature' gave them their inner sense of 'moral obligation'.[9] Women writers responded enthusiastically to the positive evaluation, in the works of philosophers from Shaftesbury to Hutcheson and Hume, of the private affections as the source of moral normativity in society, but they rarely allowed themselves to slide into sentimental irrationalism. Therefore, most remained committed to the notion that true virtue, though often prompted by affection, can only really be the quality of a self-reflective, rational being. A major and persistent concern, especially for writers such as Talbot, was the degree of conflict between self-interest (or 'self-love') and love for others ('benevolence'). Here again Pope, with his insistence upon the congruence of enlightened self-regard and altruism ('Self-love thus push'd to social, to divine/Gives thee to make thy neighbour's blessing thine'), was a major source of philosophical inspiration.[10] Most of the women writers discussed here came to understand benevolence neither as a delusion of egotism nor as a potential distraction from the duty to love God, but as the main business of a virtuous, socially purposeful life. With these philosophical underpinnings, the word benevolence – key in the philosophical writings of Clarke, Butler, Hutcheson, and, in Pope's *Essay* – came to endow the moral agency of women with public significance.

A FEMALE CHRISTIAN EPISTEMOLOGY

In this first section, I will attempt to map the philosophical journey made by women writers in the wake of Locke's work, from questions of knowledge to the practical ethics of benevolence, and to connect this to a broader idea of Whig Anglican Enlightenment favourable to female learning and to female social activity. I will treat questions of epistemology and ethics separately, but will try to show how they were intimately related. The journey began when Locke's *Essay Concerning Human Understanding* gave new urgency to the perennial questions, how do we know, and, in the process of acquiring knowledge of the world, how do we derive our ethical rules for conduct, and, above all, how do we know God? These questions exercised Astell from an early age, and were given clarity and new meaning after her reading of the *Discourses upon the Beatitudes* (1690) by the eminent theologian John Norris. Norris's epistemology (he thought that we see all things in God, and that our reason enables us to access the eternally valid truths and ideas which can only subsist in the mind of God) derived both from the Cambridge Platonists and from the French rationalist thought of Descartes and Malebranche, and it was one with which Astell found herself in substantial agreement. Norris was also the earliest critic of Locke's empirical epistemology, and, in his *Cursory Reflections* on Locke's *Essay*, voiced his profound unease at the idea that all knowledge can be traced to experience: 'what a strange *Adventure* is it in Philosophy to make the Idea of God to come in by our Senses, and to be derived from Sensible Objects! . . . what is there in the Material World that can resemble God?'[11] Astell also agreed with Norris that, since from a Platonist perspective, love is the highest form of knowledge, God is the only really worthy cause of our love, but she wrote to him to discuss the relationship of that love to the lesser affective mode of human benevolence. The exchange of letters between them, eventually published as *Letters Concerning the Love of God, Between the Author of the Proposal to the Ladies and Mr. John Norris* (1695), has been discussed in detail by Patricia Springborg, along with the anonymous *A Discourse Concerning the Love of God* (1696), which Astell claimed was an attack on her by Locke but in fact came from Locke's close companion, Damaris Masham.[12] Masham was the daughter of the leading Cambridge Platonist theologian Ralph Cudworth and a former friend of Norris, but this work marks her departure from idealism and from rationalist ideas about human love for pure abstract forms. She defends the importance of sensory experience, and objects to the way Astell and Norris's theory of knowledge orientates humans away from society, making it, she says, 'impossible to live in the daily Commerce and Conversation of the World, and love God as we ought to do'.[13] The obligation to live a productive, socially useful life is for Masham binding, in different ways, on both men and women. She contests Astell's and Norris's distinction between, on the one hand, the true love of the divine and, on the other, the benevolent love of others, by way of a careful refutation of Norris's account of causality and human motivation. What she offers is an empirical philosophical regrounding of the biblical injunction that we must love our neighbours as ourselves, one which connects our sensual experience of the world, our early sensations of pleasure and the love of other creatures that they bring, to the way mature human beings come to know and understand the 'Author of those things which afford us pleasing Sensations, who therefore is supreamly to be loved'.[14]

Astell was certainly stung by this work, not least because it advanced views diametrically opposed to her own about knowledge, piety and moral obligation from a very similar standpoint of commitment to female intellectual equality. While she pondered these questions, she brought out her next book, *A Serious Proposal to the Ladies, Part II* (1697), in which she gave a detailed consideration of how best to cultivate the mind. This work offers guidance to women wishing to engage in an active mental search for knowledge and virtue, written on the model of Antoine Arnauld's *L'Art de penser* (1662). It is designed to help them 'Disengage our selves from all our former Prejudices' (and there are some, perhaps not accidental, similarities to Poulain de la Barre's Cartesian project here), especially those which set limits to the female intellect, and to enable them to conceptualise and articulate such truths as human beings can grasp 'with the greatest Clearness and Life'.[15] Astell also explains, in more detail than before, the relationship between cognitive activity, the cultivation of the cognitive powers and moral obligation:

The Sum of our Duty and of all Morality, is to have a Temper of Mind so absolutely Conform'd to the Divine Will, or which is the same in other words, such an Habitual and Intire Love to God, as will on all occasions excite us to the Exercise of such Acts, as are the necessary consequents of such a Habit.[16]

Astell's belated reply to *A Discourse Concerning the Love of God* came in 1705, in the form of her major work, *The Christian Religion, As Profess'd by a Daughter of the Church of England* (1705). Here, she downplays questions of how we know and love God in favour of a thorough, point-by-point consideration of the lived life of Christianity, and the duties which our God-given freedom and rationality impose upon us as solitary and social beings. This is Astell's defiant answer to the apparent accusation by the author (Masham) of *A Discourse* that she had assigned an unduly subordinate role to human benevolence. Yet, as we will see, it steered this most uncompromising of female philosophers in the direction of prudential moralising. It is also her fullest and most angry attack on Locke (who had died the previous year), whom she now knew to be the author of *The Reasonableness of Christianity* (1695), and suspected to have been a Socinian, a materialist and far too accommodating of radical Dissenters.[17] Astell insists again that knowledge of God comes from within: 'I find indeed a light in my Mind, directing me to the Author of my Being; making it necessary to Adore, to Love, to Devote my self to Him.'[18] Our purpose is to find out and conform ourselves to God's will; refusing to do so, she states repeatedly, is the act of a 'libertine'.[19] For women, 'our Duty to our Selves consists in making the best use of our Talents, and hereby aspiring to the highest degree of Happiness and Perfection of which we are capable', and this is for her a form of self-love.[20] This may entail a life of courageous 'singularity', devotion and retirement ('Women who ought to be Retir'd, are . . . design'd by Providence for Speculation'), since this is the path to what she calls, in a refinement of arguments earlier advanced in *Some Reflections upon Marriage*, 'true Liberty'.[21] Here the connection between Astell's feminist rationalism and Toryism again becomes apparent:

true Liberty . . . consists in making a right use of our Reason, in preserving our Judgments free, and our Integrity unspotted, (which sets us out of the reach of the most Absolute Tyrant) not in a bare power to do what we Will; much less in a petulant Censuring and Judging our Governors, which is not Liberty but Licentiousness.[22]

The price of this inward liberty, Astell concedes, is conformity to male expectations about a woman's reputation. Astell spends a long time considering the social requirements on women to be modest, humble and chaste, and explaining, even though she says that it is God's opinion that really counts, how to obtain and keep the outward appearance of all these things. A woman of honour, she writes, will avoid giving even the appearance of scandal: 'she owes so much to her self and the World as to give it all the satisfaction in her power'.[23] In making the case that women should render unto the male Caesar his due, she can sound almost as though she is endorsing an instrumental view of morality ('Humility and Modesty do also help to gain Reputation, for they are decent and amiable Vertues').[24] In reality, she is concerned only to advise women on how to put at bay the conversational and fashionable world in which female reputations are made and destroyed, the better to cultivate their inner lives. Astell's treatment of what she calls, in the title of book III of *The Christian Religion*, 'Our Duty to our Neighbour', is nevertheless evasive. She presents this duty largely in passive terms (women should not corrupt men by flirting with them, for example), and she is most concerned with the ways in which our love of others can often slip into a kind of idolatry, detrimental to our love of God.

To a hostile commentator like Damaris Masham, Astell's most substantial work seemed to point up the previously covert relationship between an idealist epistemology, Tory political quietism, unapproachable feminism, prudential morality and a lack of social responsibility. Masham responded the same year with her most remarkable work, *Occasional Thoughts in Reference to a Vertuous or Christian Life*, in which she gave her own, alternative account of women's obligations to civil society, and in which she embarked upon a pioneering consideration of the socially constructed nature of female and male 'virtue'. Masham opens the work with an investigation of the means by which men and women can arrive at true faith and the capability of genuinely virtuous action, by cultivating their rational understanding of scripture and morality. Moral agents, including women, need first 'a rational assurance of the Divine Authority of the Scriptures, and a liberty of fairly examining them' since these 'are absolutely necessary to the satisfaction of any rational Person'.[25] Thus far, despite a different underlying notion of reason, Masham is in agreement with Astell, especially in her estimation of women's intellectual capacities: 'I see no Reason why it should not be thought that all Science lyes as open to a Lady as to a Man.'[26] What is new in Masham's argument is her account of women's virtue in relation to the legitimate and illegitimate demands made by fellow members of society. This discussion is aimed squarely at Astell, as well as engaging, as we will see later, with the section of Locke's *Essay* in which he discusses the 'Law of Fashion, or private Censure'. Most people, Masham argues, lack a proper understanding of Christianity and allow their notions of morality to be governed by social expectations. The problem is particularly acute in the case of women who care only for what men think of them, and who can therefore only ever achieve a partial, male-defined kind of virtue:

> The other thing which I imagine faulty, does more peculiarly concern the Sex, but is yet chiefly practis'd in regard of Those of it who are of Quality, and that is, the insinuating into them such a Notion of Honour as if the praise of Men ought to be the Supreme Object of their Desires, and the great Motive with them to Vertue: *A Term* which when apply'd to Women, is rarely design'd, by some People, to signifie any thing but the single Vertue of Chastity.[27]

There follows a historical and sociological consideration of the rules of morality in different ages and places. The term virtue, Masham argues in a passage that closely echoes Locke's *Essay*, needs to be clearly understood as a social and historical construct: 'For by a Vertuous Man, in all Countries of the World, or less Societies of Men, is commonly meant, by those who so call any one, such a Man as steadily adheres to that Rule of his Actions which is establish'd for a Rule in his Country, Tribe, or Society.'[28]

Masham then argues that the difference between a virtuous person and a truly religious one resides not in the quality nor even in the motives for his or her actions, but in the source from which they derive their sense of obligation to be good. Good people who believe in 'a Superior Invisible Power' do not just see rules as rules, but as divinely sanctioned duties, and these can only be known through the study of both scripture and the law of nature.[29] Women who possess a fully rational understanding of their ethical obligations are answerable to God alone for their conduct. All deference to social expectations – *pace* Astell – deprives them of moral authenticity and spiritual depth. Astell had argued, in *The Christian Religion*, that the difference between 'a Christian endeavour to obtain a Good Reputation is distinguish'd from Vain-glory, by the *motive*, which in the former is Obedience to God'.[30] Masham is more uncompromising on this point: women should aim purely at virtue, not simply at a good reputation, whatever their motives, and this virtue should be at least in part a matter of good public works. Masham's *Occasional Thoughts* sets out in some detail a Latitudinarian project for women's social action, as philosophers, wives, and, above all, as educators of children. Women of higher social standing are under particular obligations in this respect: 'it should be consider'd by these, that no one is Born into the World to live idly; enjoying the Fruit and Benefit of other Peoples Labours, without contributing reciprocally some way or other, to the good of the Community'.[31] There are certainly many areas of agreement between Astell and Masham that transcend their ideological positions at opposite ends of the political, ecclesiological and Lockean spectrums. Both sought to promote the idea of female intellectual improvement and education on grounds of free will, of salvation open to all and of a rationally intelligible Christianity, legible in nature and enforced by scripture. And both enlarged their initial investigation of the ways in which we come to know God into one about ethics and the civic role of women. Yet their late works also reveal the profoundly divergent kinds of feminism that can arise from different Christian epistemologies. For Astell, female autonomy must be grounded in a heightened sense of knowing, and therefore loving and caring for others, through God. Masham was concerned that this kind of Platonist epistemology could lead to prudential morality, especially in the case of women, because it does not provide an adequate set of terms for our love and obligations to our fellow creatures. The points of view of both writers had an enduring impact upon eighteenth-century conceptions of women. But it was, perhaps, the sociological side of Masham's work that looked most to the future, particularly her exploration of the tension between socially ascribed and divinely prescribed ideas of female virtue.

ETHICS AND THE OBLIGATION TO BE A GOOD WOMAN

Masham's interest in the mechanisms for enforcing moral behaviour stems from her reading of Locke's *Essay*, as well as her familiarity with the highly critical reception of his *Essay* on this point.[32] Locke's idea of morality was fundamentally juridical in the sense that it depended upon the idea of some kind of law together with some kind of enforcement. On the theological plane, this laid him open to repeated charges of what modern philosophers call 'theological voluntarism' – the idea that we must obey God, not because he is good but because he tells us what to do, and because he can reward us if we do and punish us if we do not. As a moralist (insofar as he wrote about ethics), Locke was accused of equating virtue with the common prejudices of mankind. The accusation was not entirely fair, but Locke certainly did handle the idea of human moral systems with a measure of scepticism and sociological objectivity likely to antagonise some sections of his readership. A hint of *libertinage* in Locke's moral thinking can be glimpsed in his early, unpublished Oxford lectures on natural law (*c*.1663–4) in which he used the testimony of cultural difference – across different countries and epochs – to challenge the idea that human beings have internal principles of right and wrong. Locke's 'scepticism about the cultural universality of moral assumptions', as it has been described, is in evidence when he considers the supposedly universal requirement on women to be modest and chaste: 'What is one to say of modesty and chastity', he asks in one of the lectures, 'if among the Assyrians women were accustomed and encouraged to take part in banquets stark naked . . . while among other nations it is unlawful for women to go out in public, even though veiled, or to show their faces, or be seen by strangers?'[33] In *An Essay Concerning Human Understanding*, he adduces a range of quasi-anthropological evidence to prove that morality has no innate aspect, and that the principles of morality are not imprinted on the human mind from its beginning but known through the application of man's rational faculties.[34] Men, Locke observes in a chapter entitled 'Of other Relations', generally construct their moral ideas and judge moral actions according to three sets of rules: the 'Law of God', the 'Law of politick Societies' and the 'Law of Fashion, or private Censure'.[35] The first two, which he takes to be reasonably self-explanatory, generate an understanding of actions as, respectively, sinful or dutiful or as criminal or innocent. The third law 'of private Censure' gives an idea of 'vertues and vices', and these, Locke explains with unobtrusive scepticism, are merely social ascriptions of value which have much more to do with the collective policing of social norms than with actual good or evil:

Thus the measure of what is every where called and esteemed *Vertue* and *Vice* is this approbation or dislike, praise or blame, which by a secret and tacit consent establishes it self in the several Societies, Tribes, and Clubs of Men in the World: whereby several actions come to find Credit or Disgrace amongst them, according to the Judgment, Maxims, or Fashions of that place.[36]

Since it is internalised by each member of society, this law of private censure is more powerful and effective than any other mechanism of social regulation. There is, Locke asserts, not one man 'of ten thousand, who is stiff and insensible enough, to bear up under the constant Dislike, and Condemnation of his own Club'.[37]

Contemporary critics charged Locke with equating virtue with the common measure, and of implying that virtue is really only a name for the things that society chooses to endorse and encourage. Locke, who was puzzled and angry at being misread in this way, defended himself against this charge in the preface to the fourth edition of the *Essay*: 'The taking notice that Men bestow the names of Vertue and Vice, according to this Rule of Reputation is all I have done, or can be laid to my charge to have done, towards the making Vice Vertue, and Vertue Vice.'[38] Masham in her *Occasional Thoughts* clearly addresses this debate from a somewhat critical female point of view, and airs her concern that the 'Law of Fashion, establish'd by Repute and Disrepute' leads all too often to a shallow Christian education for women.[39] Far more anxious than Locke about the power of social persuasion, she sees the 'Law of Fashion' as a form of false consciousness for women which clouds or obstructs their relationship both to themselves and to God. She comments ruefully that 'the Law of Fashion or Custom, is still to be obey'd, let Reason contradict it ever so much', and then goes on to lament the fact that so many men make female frivolity and idleness fashionable.[40]

Masham's reservations about Locke's moral philosophy were shared and amplified by his former pupil, Anthony Ashley Cooper, the third Earl of Shaftesbury, author of a number of philosophical works compiled as the enormously popular *Characteristicks of Men, Manners, Opinions, Times* (1711, revised 1714). From his earliest works, Shaftesbury insisted that virtue does have a natural foundation in our minds, and that legal and moral sanctions are much less important than our moral intuitions. Moral and legal rules are not in themselves capable of making us virtuous, but they may be embodied in a virtuous people or magistrates, in which case 'it is the *Example* which chiefly influences Mankind, and forms the Character and Disposition of a People'.[41] This is because, Shaftesbury argues, the example set by virtuous leaders finds an echo in the natural promptings to virtue inside all of us: 'as to Punishments and Rewards, their Efficacy is not so much from the Fear or Expectation which they raise, as from a natural Esteem of *Virtue*, and Detestation of *Villainy*'.[42] Shaftesbury was the originator of an alternative ethical theory of 'moral sense' according to which human beings possess an intuitive capacity to judge right and wrong, along with an innate emotional orientation towards their fellow creatures: 'there may be implanted in the Heart,' Shaftesbury speculated in his 'Inquiry concerning Virtue, or Merit' (originally 1699, but much revised), 'a real Sense of Right and Wrong, a real good Affection towards the Species or Society'.[43] This moral sense is partly an empirical faculty which enables us to judge others. When rational human beings see a display of 'natural affections' (that is, those affections that tend to promote the good of others) they approve of them as harmonious and beautiful. But the moral sense is also active, practical and creative, and enables people to cultivate themselves as higher moral beings. The higher moral beings he had in mind were certainly men, especially men able to take part in the public discourse of a free society. Shaftesbury had virtually nothing to say about women other than that they might be a distraction from male social interaction: "Tis no Compliment to them, to affect their [women's] Manners, and be *effeminate*. Our Sense, our Language, and Stile, as well as our Voice, and Person, shou'd have something of that Male-Feature, and natural Roughness, by which our Sex is distinguish'd.'[44] Moreover, Shaftesbury's explicit theism rendered him, as we will see in the letters between Elizabeth Carter and Catharine Talbot, a deeply suspect figure, not the sort of influence a pious-seeming female writer could openly embrace. Nevertheless, Shaftesbury's response to the moral-philosophical aspects of Locke's work, and his wider philosophy of the moral sense, are important for our purposes here because of the enormous impact he had upon the debate about the ethical make-up of women, as well as upon eighteenth-century moral philosophy generally.[45] For one thing, his philosophy drew deeply upon Cambridge Platonist ideas about natural human virtue and sociability, and the need for rational reflection as the basis for truly virtuous action. These he placed in the context of everyday social interaction in civil society. For another, he gave generous place to the role of family life and parental love in the development of those natural affections. His politics were of the classical kind, tending to draw sharp distinctions between the public and the private realms. Yet the difference between the kinds of moral agency possible in the public and private spheres was less important, in terms of the well-being of society as a whole, than the difference between social and anti-social kinds of moral dispositions. For this reason, Shaftesbury played an enormous, if not always fully acknowledged role, in the eighteenth-century re-evaluation of the social significance of domestic life, and, by implication at least, the social efficacy of actions and choices made by women within the family.

In his philosophical works Shaftesbury identifies two principal types of affection: the natural affections 'which lead to the Good of The Publick', and the self-affections 'which lead only to the Good of The Private'; although opposite in their ends, there is, ultimately, no tension between the two types of affection since 'the Wisdom of what rules' has ensured that it is 'according to the *private Interest* and *Good* of every-one, to work towards the *general Good*', and that the reward of natural affections (which includes 'Love to the Offspring') is pleasure (including what he calls the pleasure of '*merited Esteem*').[46] He calls '*unnatural Affections*' those which do not tend 'either to any Good of The Publick or Private; but contrary-wise'.[47] Misanthropy, or the desire to live without human company, is high on Shaftesbury's list of unnatural affections leading to morally perilous '*Estrangement* from human Commerce'.[48] To become a virtuous, moderate person, it is necessary to balance one's natural and self-affections. Everyone has their own individual emotional timbre (in a striking phrase, he calls this the 'Oeconomy of the Passions'), but, in order to remain good and sane, they must stay in tune in their own key.[49] If everyone achieves this, the result will be a society of autonomous but complementary beings all exhibiting, in a variety of forms, that virtue which 'upholds Communitys, maintains Union, Friendship, and Correspondence amongst Men; *that* by which Countrys, as well as private Familys, flourish and are happy'.[50] Shaftesbury writes with a sense of the continuum between 'Countrys' and 'private Familys'. Although he gives no conjectural or historical account of the origins of society, it is clear that he believes it to have evolved as an extension of the natural ties and affections between men, women and their children. Human beings, he argues against Locke, in 'An Inquiry' are inherently sociable, and the instinct for self-preservation, far from bringing them into savage competition with one another, causes them to coalesce and act for the common good. There is no moment of social contract in Shaftesbury, no point at which human beings have to decide to stop competing for survival and delegate authority to someone who can hold them together as a society.

To a degree, Shaftesbury posits a seamless moral integration of inner, familial and public life: to be morally active in one sphere is to contribute to the good of the whole. There is little evidence that women readers found this an especially empowering alternative to Lockean contract theory. However, there is abundant evidence for female enthusiasm for Pope's *An Essay on Man*, a poem which, though in many respects very different from Shaftesbury's works, combines a similar, naturalistic account of social origins with a moral philosophy linking public virtue to the private, self-regarding passions. In the *Essay*, Pope explains how the self-loving passions act as a stimulus to virtue, as individuals make the imaginative transition from personally beneficial relationships, such as parenthood or friendship, to a general love of mankind: 'Self-love thus push'd to social, to divine,/Gives thee to make thy neighbour's blessing thine./Is this too little for the boundless heart?/Extend it, let thy enemies have part.'[51] In the fourth book of the poem, Pope gives a long conjectural history of the origins of political government, from a state of harmonious nature, to meritocratic paternal kingship, to tyranny, and, finally, to a contractual restoration of benevolent patriarchal government. Pope's theory of government derives neither from Filmer nor from Locke since he characterises social contract as part of the natural, evolutionary process towards a form of government obedient to the dictates of enlightened self-love.[52] He argues, rather, that society grows naturally out of family ties, and that it is instinct, including the instinct to propagate and rear children and the urge to seek safety in numbers, rather than contract, that propels men and women into complex societies and defines their mutual obligations. Like Shaftesbury, Pope does not confront the question of women's civil identity, and, in this poem, women disappear into Pope's account of God's adaptation, through the mechanisms of instinct, of different persons to different social ends. Yet, given the immense popularity of this work with women readers, it seems likely that they found something congenial in Pope's Shaftesburian endorsement of a private, instinctive kind of virtue in which personal relationships can form the basis for broader social ties, and of a 'close system of Benevolence' in which God has assigned a part to every man and woman.[53]

CATHARINE COCKBURN ON ETHICS, REASON
AND BENEVOLENCE

Whatever the extent to which Shaftesbury's philosophy was mediated by Pope's *Essay*, there is no doubt about the impact of his work on the philosophers of the Scottish Enlightenment and their discussions of the ethical conduct and social roles associated with women. In the English context, Shaftesbury's work helped to further debate about the ethical significance of affections and actions in private life, the internal or external means by which moral rules are engendered and enforced, and the origins and nature of community. Within the Latitudinarian wing of the Church of England, Shaftesbury was one source, and the theologian Samuel Clarke was another, upon which women writers drew to address or temper the problem of Locke's alleged voluntarism and ethical relativism. This was the case with Catharine Cockburn, one of the first and most accomplished defenders of Locke's *Essay*. Cockburn (her married name from 1708) was a successful playwright, and a sufficiently prominent member of the Whig Marlborough circle to merit satirising as 'Daphne' by Manley in the *New Atalantis* (1711), as well as rebuke for her allegedly hypocritical prudery in Manley's autobiography, *The Adventures of Rivella* (1714). Born Catharine Trotter, and originally of Protestant Scottish descent, she was for some years a practising Catholic until her reconversion to Anglicanism in 1707. Her *Defence of the 'Essay of Human Understanding', written by Mr. Lock* (1702) brought Trotter (as she was then) to public attention as a leading defender of the rational female intellect, gained her the notice of Locke and Masham, and through them the friendship of the Bishop of Salisbury, Gilbert Burnet, a figure at the heart of Whig, Latitudinarian Anglicanism. Her *Defence* is an extensive reply to Thomas Burnet, the natural philosopher, headmaster and author of a highly critical series of *Remarks* (1697–99) on Locke's *Essay*. Like Burnet, Cockburn is concerned primarily with the implications of Locke's empirical epistemology for morality and for the truth of revelation.[54] Her *Defence* is less a vindication of Locke, more a creative clarification and elaboration of this aspect of his work. She refutes accusations of voluntarism and seeks to rescue him from the charge that his empiricism does not provide a firm basis for morality. In the dedicatory epistle she urges Locke to write on ethics, something she here implicitly does for him. Her central argument, conducted by way of a rigorous, point-by-point refutation of Thomas Burnet, is that our innate knowledge of God is not cognitively prior to our knowledge of good and evil, but, rather, 'It must be then by reflecting upon our own nature, and the operations of our minds, that we come to know the nature of God.'[55] This, she claims, is the burden of Locke's view (sketchy, at best, in the *Essay*) of the law of nature, the unalterable rule of morality laid down by God. The fact that, unlike the Cambridge Platonists, Locke thought that God did not implant that unalterable rule in our hearts does not make morality any less real or obligatory: 'the nature of man, and the good of society, are *to us* the reason and rule of moral good and evil; and there is no danger of their being less immutable on this foundation than any other, whilst man continues *a rational and sociable creature*'.[56]

For Cockburn, both the Platonist and voluntarist accounts of the origins of the principles of right and wrong made the mistake of abstracting morality from the thinking, rational agent. What appeals to her in Locke's work is his emphasis upon the *process* by which moral agents arrive at moral codes through reason, and on the source of moral obligation, not just in God's commands, but in the way in which certain actions appear fitting to our nature.[57]

Her defence of Locke drew a complimentary response from him, and she later defended his work against charges of heresy levelled at him by an Oxford Anglican divine.[58] Nevertheless, Cockburn should not be regarded as solely, or even mainly, a defender or disciple of Locke. Her engagement with Locke's epistemology provided her with a starting point for a wide-ranging, independent investigation of the questions that most preoccupied her, both as a literary writer and as a philosopher. These were primarily questions of ethics, and in her subsequent works she spent many years considering the true source of our ideas of right and wrong, the relationship between rationality and virtue, and, above all in her later works, the sources of moral obligation in human beings' intrinsic (but not innate) benevolence.

Cockburn subsequently addressed all of these questions within the framework of Latitudinarian Anglicanism, adopted by her after her conversion from Catholicism in 1707. Her conversion was guided and very publicly endorsed by Gilbert Burnet, and her connection with him and with his wife Elizabeth swiftly opened intellectual and social doors previously closed to her.[59] Burnet has gone down in feminist history as the cleric who probably discouraged Queen Anne from adopting Astell's scheme for a female educational retreat, earning from her the thinly veiled rebuke, in Part II of her *Serious Proposal*, that certain men (i.e. Burnet) had wilfully misrepresented the proposed retreat as a Catholic nunnery.[60] The story is more complicated than this, since Burnet himself advocated, in his *History of His Own Time* (1724, 1734), the creation of 'Monasteries without Vows' to give otherwise vapid young women 'a due Measure of Knowledge and a serious Sense of Religion'.[61] Burnet was one of a number of senior, liberal Anglican clergymen of this period (like Thomas Secker and Joseph Butler after him, as we will see below) who gave encouragement both to female learning and to learned females, seeing this as an integral part of their intellectual and pastoral mission. All three of Burnet's wives were exceptionally clever and educated women (and rich, also), especially his third wife Elizabeth. His fond memory of her after she died in 1709 certainly prompted his advice to men, in the *History*, that, in choosing a wife, 'A good Understanding, good Principles, and a good Temper with a liberal Education, and acceptable Person are the first things to be considered: And certainly Fortune ought to come after all these.'[62] In point of fact, Elizabeth brought a great deal of money on her marriage to Burnet in 1700, although he did allow her to retain control of it. He benefited in other ways from her great political astuteness, a quality he famously lacked. Burnet's later career owed a great deal to her visit (allegedly on health grounds) to the Electress's court in Hanover a few years before the death of Queen Anne, and she was throughout her marriage an assiduous lobbyist for the Whig interest, as well as a friend and correspondent of Locke and of influential Anglican divines, including

Locke's opponent Edward Stillingfleet. Very little has been written about her life and writings (many of which survive in manuscript in the Bodleian Library), yet she must have seemed to her contemporaries the very personification of a publicly active, intellectually influential Latitudinarian woman. At very least, this is how she is presented in the biography prefixed to the second, posthumous edition of her *Method of Devotion* (1709). The biography is attributed to Timothy Goodwyn, but was probably dictated by Burnet himself.[63] It presents Elizabeth as a model of tact and self-discipline in a world of turbulent high politics and intellectual controversy, but it does give a glimpse of the effective tactician and manipulator behind the self-effacing piety. For example, it claims that she talked with leading divines 'as if she had equally studied the same Subject with them', but that in other company 'she made no appearance of Knowledge above the common Rank'.[64] She clearly managed to present her political lobbying as a kind of benevolence: 'She entered into Friendship with some Persons of the greatest Quality, which made no other alteration in her, than the increasing her Zeal of doing more Good.'[65] Above all, she embodied the Latitudinarian ideal of a deeply held, yet sociable and tolerant, never enthusiastic form of religious belief: 'Her Design indeed, was to render a Strictness in Religion as agreeable to all Companies, as was possible, and to shew that it did not take off from that easiness and freedom which is the Life of Conversation.'[66] Elizabeth's *Method of Devotion* itself gives ample evidence of that strictness with its prescriptions for a daily routine of early rising, prayers, theological reading (Clarke's works are recommended) and charitable activity. Her work also gives some hints to its women readers about how to develop both a self-appraising inner voice and a practical rationality: 'Some time in the Evening, as most convenient, call over the past Day, going over in your Mind all the Time since your last Examination . . . Permit not your Passions to put false Glosses on your Actions, or to excuse their own Rebellion; but consider impartially how far Temptations have been yielded to . . .'[67]

Elizabeth Burnet may have seen in Catharine Cockburn a woman of similarly strenuous and self-critical rationality, as well as theological and educational interests. At Locke's prompting, Elizabeth Burnet befriended Cockburn, and later put her in touch with Samuel Clarke. Cockburn was greatly influenced by Clarke's two famous series of Boyle lectures (an invited lecture series given annually at St Paul's) of 1704–5, *A Demonstration of the Being and Attributes of God* and *A Discourse concerning the Unchangeable Obligations of Natural Religion*. In these sermons, Clarke expounded a theology that was to have a huge impact on eighteenth-century Latitudinarian Anglicanism. He argued that the truths of Christianity were scientifically demonstrable propositions, including the proposition that the eternal principles of right and wrong do not depend upon the fiat of God, but are antecedent to his will and law, and accord with the order of creation. There were enough similarities between Clarke's theology and Locke's work – their tendency to treat natural and revealed religion as separate entities, their belief in the freedom of the will, and, above all, their emphasis upon the accessibility of religion to human reason – for them to have been closely identified in the minds of contemporary liberal Anglicans. Cockburn's biographer asserts that she was one of those who conflated the two as part of her own attempt to work out a Christian ethics grounded in natural religion.[68] My own view is that, having defended (and experienced the difficulties of defending) Locke against the charge of voluntarism, Cockburn found in Clarke's work a different and more secure basis for her own ethical theories. In particular, Clarke's ascription to God of eternally fixed attributes antecedent to his decrees, gave her a way of thinking about the metaphysical permanence of the distinction between right and wrong. She repeatedly stated her admiration for Clarke's 'sense of *antecedency*', as she put it: which means the idea that moral distinctions and our obligation to act in accordance with them are anterior to rewards and punishments (which merely reinforce these distinctions and obligations).[69] She also constantly defended Clarke's Christian orthodoxy, even though his *The Scripture-Doctrine of the Trinity* (1712) had, in the eyes of a majority of readers, exposed him as an Arian (that is a person who believes that Christ is a secondary divinity, created by God and not coeval with him).

Clarke's work helped Cockburn to find a whole new philosophical vocabulary for dealing with those questions of moral obligation which she may well have felt were not adequately addressed in Locke's *Essay*. Her fullest engagement was in her *Remarks upon some Writers in the Controversy concerning the Foundation of Moral Virtue and Moral Obligation* (1743), in which she deals in some detail with Clarke's work, and which she prefaces with the highly Clarkean declaration, 'I think . . . that the obligation to *moral virtue* is ultimately founded on the *eternal and immutable nature of things*.'[70] Elsewhere in her works, Cockburn uses Clarke's moral theory as a point of philosophical orientation, rarely citing or discussing it at length, but taking as read his demonstration of the independent existence of moral obligations, and the duty of all human beings to recognise them. Clarke is an authoritative, though discreet, presence in her later *Remarks upon the Principles and Reasonings of Dr. Rutherforth's Essay on the Nature and Obligations of Virtue: In vindication of the contrary principles and reasonings, inforced in the writings of the late Dr. Samuel Clarke* (1747). This work is a critique of *An Essay on the Nature and Obligation of Virtue* (1744) by the Cambridge academic Thomas Rutherforth, but it is also her most fully worked out statement on ethics.[71] Rutherforth's work, as Cockburn was quick to recognise, brought something new to the scene of moral philosophy, namely a utilitarian argument – offered as an alternative to the rationalism of Clarke, the hedonism of Mandeville and the disinterested view of virtue held by Shaftesbury – that human beings are motivated to act virtuously out of a desire for their own pleasure, and that God makes them virtuous by rewarding them with happiness. Against this, Cockburn gives her own version of the Clarkean argument that moral obligations arise naturally from the differences and fitness of things: 'Hopes of reward, or fears of punishment, may indeed excite to good actions, or restrain from evil; but *of themselves*, without a sense of duty arising either from the fitness of acting suitably to the nature, which God has given us, or of obedience to his will, they can never make a virtuous or a religious man.'[72]

Cockburn's refutation does not end with a restatement of Clarke's ethics since these alone do not cope adequately with Rutherforth's claim, in his *Essay on Nature*, that human beings are fundamentally self-regarding, and that self-regard is implicated in all the virtuous deeds that they perform.

In other works, she had seen off the argument, associated with Hobbes and Mandeville, that 'the natural tendency of moral virtue to the happiness of mankind' is reason enough to regard it 'as a mere invention of politicians, to keep the several societies of men in good order'.[73] However, Rutherforth's Christian utilitarianism posed a more serious challenge since he gave the impression that it was God, not the politicians, who had made virtue pleasurable as a way of keeping mankind in order. Cockburn was astute in spotting the significance and potential of this kind of theological reasoning, as it would enjoy considerable currency for the rest of the century, culminating in the work of William Paley. Cockburn replied with what, by this point in her career, had become a characteristic insistence on the disinterested nature of virtue and the natural benevolence of human beings:

a disinterested benevolence and approbation of virtue are *natural* to man, and given him as proper excitements to good actions; that tho' these may be misapplied or misguided, he has it in his power to regulate them, by the obvious *relations and nature of things*; (for I take our consciousness of right and wrong to be the result of some perception, that every rational mind necessarily has of the essential difference between good and evil) . . .[74]

The above quotation shows Cockburn folding Clark's metaphysics ('the obvious *relations and nature of things*', 'the essential difference between good and evil') into her own theory of benevolent human nature as the source of all moral obligation. It also shows how she combines elements of moral irrationalism (we are motivated to virtue by instinctive benevolence) with a continuing commitment to human reason as virtue's watchman (our instincts can misguide us, but the 'rational mind' can consider more deeply the law of nature and correct our actions).

Clarke's work gave Cockburn the basis, in her later writings, for her own, differently worked out theory of benevolent ethics, and enabled her to defend that theory, not only against those who held a view of mankind as fundamentally self-interested, but against those wanting to downplay the role of the rational mind in virtuous action. In this project, she was very much Masham's legatee, as well as a forerunner of the Bluestocking writers who shared both her high regard for Clarke and her aspiration to reconcile benevolence and reason. This aspiration seems to have been deeply held by her as a woman writer. The examples she provides of mankind's natural benevolence almost always come from domestic life, especially the love of mothers for their children. As she pointed out in the *Remarks . . . concerning the Foundation of Moral Virtue*: 'The connection of her [a mother's] happiness with that of her child must be owing solely to her kind affections, an association of *nature's* forming, quite different from that, which Mr. *Locke* has observed of the ideas *accidentally* united, that have *no connection in nature*.'[75]

For Cockburn, Locke's model of a pleasurable association of ideas does not account for women and men's most instinctive feelings of love and loyalty towards others. She insists upon the importance of these instincts, but says that this does not mean that human beings have innate moral principles, but that they have the 'seeds' of 'social or benevolent affections . . . implanted in their nature'.[76] These seeds grow inside people along with: 'a moral sense or conscience, that approves of virtuous actions, and disapproves the contrary. This plainly shews them, that virtue is the law of their nature, and that it must be their duty to observe it, from whence arises *moral obligation* . . .'[77]

She is very careful, however, to insist that her idea of a moral sense has nothing to do with Shaftesbury whom she considered merely an infidel and an aesthete.[78] The most important point for her is that the moral instincts and the moral sense 'are all resolvable into *reason*, and are undeniably cultivated and improved, by making a right use of our faculties'.[79] The moral sense is the secondary faculty that enables people to reflect rationally upon their actions; it is not the source of their moral obligations, but the means by which they come to understand the obligations imposed by their nature.

Cockburn constructed a rational, theologically orthodox account of morality that gave due place to the instinctively affectionate and altruistic nature of man. Her conception of the ethical human being can certainly be exemplified by (and is in some ways geared to) the idea of the intelligent, affectionate mother, sister or wife. The posthumously printed works include a long and fascinating series of letters to her niece Anne Arbuthnot. Collectively, they amount to a guide to eighteenth-century philosophy thus far, and an educational programme for women. The highest commendation is reserved for Pope's *Essay on Man*: 'You will find in it the foundation of all ethics, with a beautiful vindication of the order of nature.'[80] In Pope's *Essay*, Cockburn found an emotionally compelling account of human benevolence, the congruence of self-love and altruism, and the mysteries of the law of nature, and she dedicated her *Remarks . . . concerning the Foundation of Moral Virtue* to him.

BLUESTOCKING THEOLOGY

More than anyone else, Cockburn served as an honoured example to the next generation of female writers seriously concerned with questions of femininity, morality and religion. There were personal points of connection (Elizabeth Montagu's close friend James Beattie lodged for a time with Anne Arbuthnot, Cockburn's intelligent niece and correspondent), but there was also a strong sense of intellectual continuity, of shared influences and moral vision.[81] Chief among those influences were Pope and Clarke. The young Elizabeth Montagu (Robinson, as she was before her marriage) wrote in her letters of her excitement of reading both of these writers for the first time, and for her Clarke was the 'man who so well demonstrated the being of a god, and set forth the truths of the gospel, and enforced moral obligations by every argument'.[82] There was also a new element, the writings of Joseph Butler with their searching investigation of the role of reason, conscience and benevolence in human ethical life. These had struck Cockburn as highly significant, and also entirely congruent with her own views on reason, free will and benevolence, but they probably came a little too late for her to address fully.[83] For the younger generation, it was Butler, one of the greatest moral philosophers of his age, who provided the way forward from the seeming impasse of the opposing ethical perspectives of Locke and Shaftesbury, and an appealing alternative to the pseudo-scientific rationalism of Clarke. Catharine Talbot and Elizabeth Carter had close personal ties to Butler, indeed, the Bluestockings as a group might plausibly be termed the female Butlerians. Modern commentators have recognised the importance of Latitudinarian Anglicanism to this group, but only as a practical, socially orientated kind of piety, not as a theology.[84] Yet Carter and Talbot in particular, and, to an extent, the younger Montagu, engaged seriously with the questions that most preoccupied the theologians and moral philosophers of their day. They all constructed for themselves a non-dogmatic, anti-voluntarist kind of Christianity. It was serious but flexible; it was less important to adhere to the orthodox doctrine of the Trinity, for example, than to believe that men and women have reason enough to decipher the laws of nature and discover the truths of religion for themselves. Like Cockburn before them, they preferred this idea of reason to Shaftesbury's idea of the moral sense. They considered freethinking and deism (of the Shaftesburian or of any other variety) highly undesirable. For this reason, they admired Butler's anti-freethinking polemics and his work on the ways in which human beings assent to beliefs in the unseen and unknown on the basis of reasonable probability.

Elizabeth Carter met Joseph Butler through Catharine Talbot's patron and guardian Thomas Secker. Secker and Butler attended the same Dissenting academy in Gloucester before conforming to, and rising within, the Church of England. Secker became Bishop of Oxford, and then Archbishop of Canterbury in 1758, and Butler became Bishop of Bristol in 1738, and of Durham in 1750. Butler first gained public prominence through his published correspondence with Samuel Clarke over matters of divine necessity, and Clarke became his generous patron and friend. Butler also came to know Catharine Talbot's father Edward while studying at Oxford. When Edward Talbot died, Secker took Catharine and her mother into his household, where Catharine remained until her death in 1770. Carter and Catharine Talbot seem to have adored Butler, and his writings had a huge bearing on their own Latitudinarian Christianity.[85] Both were avid readers of Clarke's works, but still more influenced by the ways in which Butler sought to depart from his rationalist kind of Anglican apologetic, and to construct a theory of moral

obligation based upon an empirical understanding of the facts of human
nature, and upon the notion of reasonable probability, rather than absolute mathematical certainty, as the very 'guide of life'. Butler's most
celebrated work, his *Analogy of Religion, Natural and Revealed, to the
Constitution and Course of Nature* (1736), was a highly original defence
of Christianity against the challenge of the deists, particularly deists of
the Shaftesburian kind, who held that the only metaphysical certainties
are those which can be rationally deduced from the order of nature. The
Analogy explores, not the proofs of Revelation, but the kinds of evidence
that, in ordinary life, people require before they assent to and live by
propositions of religious truth. Butler argued that Christianity, no less
than deist systems of natural religion, offered reasonable probability, and
a secure basis for moral action. Carter was greatly influenced by Butler's
apologetic method and by his common-sense view of the capacities and
limits of human reason. In his posthumous edition of Carter's letters,
Montagu Pennington included an exchange between her and 'Vittoria',
a lady supposed to be in danger of losing her Christian faith and lapsing
into natural religion. The influence of Butler's *Analogy* on Carter's thinking is clear from her replies to Vittoria's doubts, and when she explores
the real nature of 'conviction' and makes the case for revealed Christianity
on the grounds of its reasonable probability: '[we are] reasonable creatures, whose assent is to be determined by reasonable arguments, and not
to be kept in eternal suspense by refusing to admit the most probable side
of a question, only because it cannot solve all the difficulties with which
every question . . . must be attended'.[86]

Conviction, in the area of 'moral truths', is something that comes to us
through a careful and rational sifting of the evidence. We cannot rely on
the law of fashion or private censure to give us an adequate idea of
morality ('if we look no farther than the moral behaviour necessary to
be observed in society, our virtue will make a very inconsiderable progress'), but nor can we expect an instant 'irresistible impulse', a throbbing
of the moral sense.[87] Rather, we must accept that moral truths 'in their
very nature can rest only on probable and reasonable proofs'.[88] For Carter,
Butler's apologetic method, and his recognition of the role and limits of
empiricism in the formation of our moral ideas, represented a significant
step forward from the work of Locke. Butler's work enabled her to form
and defend an idea of female rationality, exercised and developed in the
conduct of everyday life, but equal to the task of discovering a truly
Christian morality. As important as the *Analogy* to the Bluestocking
writers were Butler's writings on ethics, the *Fifteen Sermons Preached at*

the Rolls Chapel (1726). In these sermons he argued that virtue consists in following nature, and for the central importance of conscience as a faculty implanted by God. He agreed with Shaftesbury that we are naturally affectionate and sociable in orientation, but added that it is only the faculty of conscience (he steered clear of Shaftesbury's 'moral sense') that allows people to evaluate their moral actions and to become self-conscious moral agents. Subordinate to conscience are the human principles of self-love and benevolence, both of them distinct yet complementary kinds of affections that lead people to take care of themselves and of others. Butler writes with great sophistication of benevolence as an impulse fundamental to the workings of human society, yet sometimes misleading and at odds with the dictates of conscience. His theory of human nature takes meticulous account of the existence and validity of self-regard (as well as benevolence) without ranking self-love as the prime motivational principle of human action, as Hobbes and Mandeville had done.

As we will see below, the Bluestocking writers were in deep agreement with Butler's portrait of human nature as judiciously self-regarding yet naturally sociable and self-reflectively ethical in orientation. They may well have welcomed the more orthodox Christian treatment he gave to moral themes tackled by Shaftesbury, and all of the Bluestockings agreed with him that Christianity could and should be compatible with an acceptance of human nature as it is. They rejected schemes of philosophy or theology which demanded unreasonable asceticism (such as classical Stoicism) or an eschatological concern for the next life, rather than for the life lived on earth. Elizabeth Montagu's thoughts on this question were prompted by a theological work entitled *A Moral Proof of the Certainty of a Future State* (1725), in which its author, Francis Gastrell, argued that our only purpose on this earth is to prepare for the life hereafter. Montagu deeply disapproved of the way that Gastrell attempted to inculcate a self-interested, future-orientated morality; she felt that he ignored our natural partiality to this life ('Our nature may be restrained, but never can be subdued'), and underestimated the ways in which benevolence in this life brings its own satisfactions: 'hope is the spur of diligence; if we believe there is happiness in virtue, and that . . . all her paths are peace, we shall endeavour to make a progress in this road'.[89] She cites Alexander Pope as giving support to the idea that man is part of the divine order in this world, and that the natural order is imbued with God's providential purpose.[90] Carter, too, disapproved of perverse asceticism, and, as she told Montagu, she was suspicious of those who 'think they may substitute the voluntary infliction of external sufferings, instead of that true Christian mortification, which consists in correcting the internal disorders of the heart'.[91] Carter, as we will see, had reservations about the other-worldly, humanly unattainable demands of the Stoic morality propounded by Epictetus, even though she admired its lofty conception of virtue. In a paper she wrote for Samuel Johnson's periodical *The Rambler*, she described a dream vision in which a terrifying, wrinkled figure, dressed in black, admonishes her to fly 'from the fatal Enchantments of Youth and social Delight' since 'every Enjoyment is an Offence to the Deity, who is to be worshipped only by the Mortification of every Sense of Pleasure, and by the everlasting Exercise of Sighs and Tears'.[92] However, another dream figure, Religion, soon appears to contradict this counsel of lonely self-denial, insists that 'Religion is not confined to Cells and Closets, nor restrained to sullen Retirement: these are the gloomy Doctrines of Superstition [the true identity of the first figure], by which she endeavours to break those Chains of Benevolence and social Affection, that link the Welfare of every Particular with that of the Whole.'[93] True religion, Carter argues in this essay, neither requires deliberate suffering ('Suffering is no Duty') nor precludes pleasure of the kind which naturally arises from the practice of virtue ('to reject [Virtue and Obedience], merely as the Means of Pleasure, is pitiable Ignorance, or absurd Perverseness').[94]

Carter's *Rambler* essay gives some hint of the deeper consideration of the relationship of virtue to both pleasure and suffering that would feature so fully in the notes and introduction to her translation of Epictetus, published eight years later in 1758. Her vision of religion as something residing in the everyday, pleasurable practice of virtue and benevolence is a far cry from that of Astell, but it has cautious, selective affinities with that of Shaftesbury. It is Shaftesbury to whom Carter alludes in the phrase 'Religion is not confined to Cells and Closets': Shaftesbury famously made a similar assertion on behalf of Philosophy ('We have immur'd her (poor Lady!) in Colleges and Cells').[95] Carter certainly had no quarrel with his idea that society was the most important domain both for philosophy and for the exercise of moral behaviour, as in the remark, cited earlier, that society was the true sphere of human virtue.[96] She shared Shaftesbury's confidence in the virtuous import of the natural affections, although she was more mistrustful than he of the emphasis of classical Stoic philosophy upon the need to suppress and quash the affections and passions. In this she had more in common with Pope when, in his *Essay on Man*, he dismisses the Stoic view of the passions ('In lazy Apathy let Stoics boast/Their Virtue fix'd'),[97] and celebrates a divine scheme in which all human passions and affections are part of a higher purpose. Back in 1739, commissioned by Edward Cave, proprietor of *The Gentleman's Magazine*, she translated a prominent and hostile *Examination* of Pope's *Essay* by a Swiss academic, Jean Pierre de Crousaz. This translation has often been construed as a declaration of hostility to Pope's work, yet in the few footnotes Carter supplied, she consistently defends Pope against Crousaz's inaccuracy (he was working from an imperfect French translation) and misrepresentation.[98] Certainly, both Carter and her friend Talbot shared Pope's belief that the emotional and spontaneous side of human nature had its place in the divine scheme of things, and they were both quite suspicious of any philosophical scheme, whether Christian or pagan Stoic, that demanded their repression.

On this subject, Carter and Talbot entered into an intensive correspondence during the run-up to the publication of the Epictetus translation. Talbot expressed her dislike of the emotional asceticism of the Stoics:

Every now and then I am shocked at the pride and harshness of the Stoic doctrines. *If affections make me suffer I renounce them* . . . No! poor Epictetus! If laudable affections give me pain, I humbly submit to it as the due lot of frail and fallen human nature. If the giving a due check and restraint to those affections is a difficulty, I thankfully and cheerfully undertake it.[99]

Carter was similarly uneasy about Epictetus' account of the natural affections, and, in many of the notes to her translation, she supplies Christian correctives to his pagan point of view. For example, in one of the discourses, Epictetus counsels his pupils to bear the loss of friends with the same emotional indifference as the breaking of a pipkin (a cooking utensil). Carter intervenes with an indignant footnote:

This is a wretched Idea of Friendship; but a necessary Consequence of the Stoic System. What a fine Contrast to this gloomy Consolation are the noble Sentiments of an Apostle! Value your deceased Friend, says *Epictetus*, as a broken Pipkin; forget him, as a Thing worthless, lost, and destroyed. St. *Paul*, on the contrary, comforts the mourning Survivors; bidding them, *not sorrow, as those who have no Hope* . . .[100]

Similarly, she finds the advice in his *Enchiridion* ('manual') for eliminating the pain of bereavement out of step with human nature: 'Natural Affection prompts us to grieve for a Wife or a Child, and to sympathize with the Griefs of others.'[101] She allows that Epictetus' limitations as a philosopher are due to the fact that he had no knowledge of Christianity.

There was some debate about this at the time of Carter's translation, since Epictetus lived during the first and early second centuries after Christ, but she felt sure that he could not have knowingly encountered and ignored Christian doctrine, especially the doctrine of rewards and punishments after death.

Given the corrective, even on occasions hostile tone of Carter's foot-notes, readers did and still do wonder what drew her to Epictetus in the first place, and why she devoted so many years of her life to translating his works. The project would inevitably have appeared to a contemporary readership as somewhat Shaftesburian in conception. Shaftesbury was himself a great admirer of Epictetus and cited him copiously in his private notebooks. Shaftesbury in turn figured in the public mind as the supreme example of a modern-day pagan Stoic.[102] Catharine Talbot foresaw immediate popularity for Carter's translation but warned her that, 'Fine gentlemen will read it because it is new . . . Shaftesburian Heathens because Epictetus was an honour to Heathenism, and an idolater of the beauty of virtue.'[103] Carter herself did not deny that there was something true and appealing about the Stoic and neo-Stoic aesthetics of virtue. She wrote in her long introduction to the translation 'That there is an intrinsic Beauty and Excellency in moral Goodness; that it is the Ornament and Perfection of all rational Beings . . . are Positions, which no thinking Person can contradict.'[104] For her, Epictetus' writings, with their lofty conception of virtue and exaltation of human reason, represented the highest level of moral philosophy that it is possible to attain without the aid of revelation on the one hand, or a modern, empirical understanding of human nature on the other: 'The Stoics every-where testify the noblest Zeal for Virtue, and the Honour of God: but they attempted to establish them on Principles, inconsistent with the Nature of Man, and contradictory to Truth and Experience.'[105]

For Carter, the Stoics are an example to modern readers of both the enormous capacity and the limits of human reason in the moral sphere. In their pagan world, they did not have access to the revealed truth of a future life in heaven, and their works show how narrow, even perverse moral philosophy can be without this all-important dimension. Carter admires Epictetus' struggle, as a former slave who suffered all his life from physical disability and poverty, to rise philosophically above his circum-stances. From a Christian perspective, his life seems to her an admirable example of the divinely implanted instinct for moral striving. Carter would not have said the same of Shaftesbury, nor of other eighteenth-century deists and sceptics who revived and revised Stoic philosophy whilst wilfully ignoring Christian revelation. She spent over a page of her introduction to the translation attacking those modern unbelievers found 'rejecting the Doctrines of the New Testament for those of the Portico'.[106] Claudia Thomas, in an article on Carter, has speculated that 'Epictetus became Carter's opportunity to oppose the "false Enlightenment" she observed in her culture. Convinced of the resemblance between the late Stoics and contemporary deists, Carter felt compelled to "take a pedantic turn"' for the sake of Christianity.[107] To this might be added Carter's broader social concerns. She knew that late Stoicism, however valuable its moral teachings in times of paganism, was essentially an elite moral philosophy, very much like the aristocratic philosophy of Shaftesbury. Carter observes 'how little the Doctrines of this Sect were fitted to influence the Generality of Mankind', adding, 'But indeed, about the Generality of Mankind, the Stoics do not appear to have given themselves any kind of Trouble.'[108] Furthermore, Stoicism fails her ultimate test of philosophical truth: that is, whether it is in accordance with our rational sense of the nature of things. Christianity, by contrast, instantly commands our rational assent.

Carter's translation of Epictetus presented its readers with a hugely impressive display of deep classical learning, and she had the self-confidence to indicate her sole authorship on the title page.[109] During the preparation of the translation, she received a great deal of advice from Thomas Secker, who was Bishop of Oxford at the time, and was promoted to Archbishop of Canterbury the year the work came out. Secker made lengthy comments on matters of linguistic accuracy and tone, and also urged her to add discursive notes to the translation.[110] He later claimed that, having 'suggested many Notes', he 'wrote a considerable Part of the Preface' to the translation, although there is no further evidence for this.[111] Carter had a witty way of deflecting the pressure of advice from Secker and his ward Talbot. On one occasion she told them that she and Epictetus 'are determined to go peaceably blundering on; he in being translated till I cannot understand him, and I in translating till nobody can understand me'.[112] Whatever the degree of Secker's involvement, he certainly considered Carter's translation relevant to the wider project of learned, broad, charitable Whig Anglicanism to which they both adhered.[113] There was room, in their world, for a degree of latitude on matters of doctrine. Carter herself appears to have held unorthodox (though certainly not Unitarian) views about the Trinity, and she expressed these in an anonymous pamphlet entitled *Remarks on the Athanasian Creed*, published in 1753. The pamphlet was a response to a sermon by the Reverend Randolph, a vicar local to her neighbourhood in Kent, and is robustly dismissive of the 'Jargon of School-Divinity' he used to air his views about Christ's dual divine and human nature: 'If this be your Doctrine, speak it out fairly, and endeavour to prove it', she demanded.[114] Notwithstanding the Creed in the Anglican liturgy, Carter states in plain language her doubts about Christ's consubstantiality and co-eternity with the Father. She argues that the evidence from her reading of scripture and her own reason is that Christ is divine, but subordinate to the Father. In a wider sense, the pamphlet is a defence of scripture-based faith, of rational enquiry and of plain speaking in matters of doctrine. It also makes the implicit claim that debate about theological matters is too important to be confined to an abstruse, male academic and professional arena.

Although Carter's pamphlet was unattributed and unacknowledged during her lifetime, she did address the question of a theology for everyday living in her translation of Epictetus, and no doubt admired the way he illustrated his philosophy with homely analogies and anecdotes. The question of an everyday theology was also one that she explored in close collaboration with her friend Catharine Talbot. After Talbot's early death in 1770, Carter published her works, thereby bringing this exploration into a public arena that Talbot had previously shunned. Talbot's posthumous works, *Reflections on the Seven Days of the Week* (1770) and *Essays on Various Subjects* (1772) presented the public with the ruminations of a young woman struggling to create a morally and spiritually purposeful life for herself. This struggle is conducted in the light of her intellectual commitment to key theological tenets such as the freedom of the will, the need to express one's faith through good works, and the duty to find meaning and happiness in the world given new meaning by the Incarnation, even while preparing for the next. Unlike Elizabeth Burnet's *Method of Devotion*, Talbot's *Reflections* offered its readers not a set of prescriptions for a holy life, but the inner voice of someone going through the often difficult process of making her life fit those prescriptions. Both the *Reflections* and the *Essays* are haunted by an acute sense of the pointlessness of the writer's constricted female existence. Yet Talbot often manages to render that sense of pointlessness emblematic of the wider Christian condition:

To complain of the Insignificancy of our Employments, is but another Name for repining at that Providence, which has appointed, to each of us, our Station . . . But whence then, is this constant Dissatisfaction of the human Mind; this

Restlessness, this perpetual Aim at something higher and better, than, in the present State, it ever can attain? Whence, but from its celestial Birth, its immortal Nature, framed for the noblest Pursuits . . .[115]

It must surely have been Talbot's peculiar gift for conveying so acutely her own female predicament, and for generalising beyond her own narrow experience, that gave her essays and reflections such enormous popular appeal. Intellectually, these works are thin gruel, especially when compared to Talbot's learned, incisive and witty letters, not published until the early nineteenth century. Yet, the *Reflections* went through thirty-five separate editions between 1770 and 1861 and the *Essays* five editions between 1772 and 1839. More than any other writer of her circle, Talbot carried into the nineteenth century the Bluestocking theology of good works, and their moral philosophy of active, amiable sociability balanced by intellectual self-cultivation and reasonable self-love. Talbot was at one with Carter and Montagu in her moderate Christian Stoicism, and in her belief that a cheerful, sociable life diversified by innocent indulgences was in accordance with God's will: 'Uncommanded Severities, that are of no apparent Use, but to torment ourselves, and sour our Natures, and shorten our Lives, can never be acceptable to our gracious Maker.'[116] She was also in agreement with her fellow Bluestockings and with her friend Joseph Butler in thinking that true self-love lies neither in Mandeville's selfishness nor in Stoic asceticism. In her essay on this subject she remarks that:

The same tie [of self-love], that so closely binds us down to our own interest, makes us sympathize, in the fortunes of our fellow-creatures. By self-love we learn to pity in others, what we dread, or fear for ourselves . . . Self-love endears virtue to us by the tenderness it gives us, for whatever degree of it we perceive in ourselves: and in the same way, makes us look with a peculiar charity on those, whose faults are of the same kind with ours.[117]

Talbot goes on to quote Pope's *Essay on Man* on self- and social love, but her essay, in its attempt to reconcile, rather than to conflate, self-love and benevolence owes much more to Butler's sermons and, no doubt, to conversations with Butler himself. Transplanted by Talbot into essays and reflections on everyday living for women of leisure, Butler's moral and theological ideas take on a new colour. His ideas underpin Talbot's Bluestocking conviction that self-denial, retirement and social and intellectual submission are morally detrimental courses of action for a woman. Publication may have seemed a step too far for Talbot herself, but she certainly lived and wrote according to what Norma Clarke has called the 'bluestocking ideal' of 'self-realisation through intellectual cultivation'.[118] She was ever convinced that women and men were capable of personal progress. As she wrote to Carter, 'I have the highest notions of those noble improvements [human nature] is capable of.'[119]

The latter part of this chapter has explored the Latitudinarian theological fabric of the Bluestockings' ideas of intellectual self-cultivation and female social action, and their roots in the work of Clarke, Cockburn and Butler, as well as, more remotely, in Masham's response to Astell's work. Later in this book it will also be possible to trace continuities and differences between this Latitudinarian approach to theological, ethical and social questions, and the radical approach articulated in the work of Catharine Macaulay (an unconventional Anglican) and Mary Wollstonecraft (an unconventional Dissenter). The gap between these two radical writers and the Bluestockings may at first seem very wide, but there are nevertheless important similarities of religious vision that lie behind a genuinely shared allegiance to the idea of female rationality. Macaulay's theology will be discussed more fully in chapter 4. Wollstonecraft, in her semi-autobiographical novel *Mary, A Fiction* (1788), cited Butler as an early influence in favour of rationally considered Christian belief and religious toleration: 'Mary thought of . . . Romish tenets, and the deistical doubts; and though not a sceptic, thought it right to examine the evidence on which her faith was built. She read Butler's Analogy, and some other authors: and these researches made her a Christian from conviction, and she learned charity, particularly with respect to sectaries.'[120]

Cockburn was the subject of an admiring portrait by Wollstonecraft's friend and fellow radical Mary Hays in her *Female Biography* of 1803.[121] The strain of Christian Platonism running through Clarke's work into Cockburn, Carter and Talbot's discussions of human love and benevolence comes to the surface in Wollstonecraft. Barbara Taylor has discerned in Wollstonecraft's early work a Christian Platonist, passionate idea of reason, never enthusiastic, but indirectly reminiscent of Astell in its intensity and in its subordination of earthly to divine love.[122] The political inferences that the Bluestockings and radical writers such as Macaulay, Wollstonecraft and Hays drew from their theological and ethical beliefs were, in many instances, diametrically opposite. Notably, they responded very differently to the French Revolution, viewing it, respectively, as a threat and as an opportunity for male and female emancipation. Yet, as John Robertson has argued, it is surely right to

see these women writers as part of the same, broad English Enlightenment: one that responded ambivalently to Locke but warmly to Butler,
that encompassed both conservative and radical political beliefs, yet
emanated from a common commitment to religious toleration, the cultivation of women's free will and reason, and the social efficacy of
benevolence.[123]

CHAPTER 2

From savage to Scotswoman:
the history of femininity

We have seen how women writers participated in English philosophical debate about the implications of Locke's empirical epistemology for the derivation of religious beliefs, and also for the source of the obligation to be virtuous. In the wake of the work of Shaftesbury and Butler, women writers of an emerging, Bluestocking tradition elaborated and defended a view of men and women as fundamentally benevolent (in a self-cultivated and rational, rather than irrational, spontaneous way), and as realising their nature in the voluntary exercise of benevolence. Explicitly or implicitly, they opposed conventional and expedient accounts of morality, such as Mandeville's or (as his detractors would wrongly have it) as Locke's, on the grounds that such views were amoral and antipathetic to the idea that women's good actions could have wider social benefits. This chapter turns to Scotland in order to assess the impact of these debates, particularly as they were prompted by Mandeville and Shaftesbury, on the moral philosophers and social and economic thinkers of the Scottish Enlightenment, and their implications for the Scottish conception of women's nature, capabilities and place in the world. It begins with the pioneering work of Francis Hutcheson, who held the Chair of Moral Philosophy at Glasgow University from 1730 until his death in 1746. As a writer and a teacher, Hutcheson exerted an enormous influence upon a younger generation of academics, Adam Smith among them, who contested many aspects of his account of the sources of human morality, but who nevertheless endorsed and elaborated his view that the family was the site where moral norms and the sense of justice necessary to civil society were constructed and rehearsed.[1] Men's treatment of women in the domestic context, and women's role as wives, mothers and educators of children were thus important topics within a wider consideration of the network of moral obligations, duties and rights that made up society as a whole.

Both Hutcheson's and Smith's moral philosophy was developed within an academic tradition, particularly strong in Scotland, of 'natural jurisprudence' or the study of the duties and rights prescribed by the law of nature for the preservation of the individual, the family and society. The tradition of natural jurisprudence, derived from seventeenth-century jurists such as Samuel Pufendorf provided a strong sense of social life as natural to man, and of the underlying nature of society as a structure of mutual obligations. In this tradition, moral agency consisted in the discernment and performance of the duties prescribed by natural law. The question of moral perception was, therefore, a pressing one for moral philosophers, and it had an important bearing on the conduct of social and political life as a whole. Rights, in traditional natural jurisprudence, were derivative in the sense that they followed on from the performance of duties, and were often a matter of civil rather than natural law: marriage, for example, was generally regarded as something prescribed by natural law, but the right of husbands to govern their wives sprang from their mutual and voluntary entry into a contract of marriage regulated by the civil law. Some rights and duties originated, according to natural law theorists, in voluntary contracts such as marriage, but many of the major familial and civic duties did not originate in free, individual choice, but came about, over a long period of time, through the developing moral life of the community. In order to understand those duties, one had to understand tradition and history.

Thus history had an important informative and educative role for many moral philosophers of the Scottish Enlightenment such as Francis Hutcheson, Thomas Reid and James Beattie, and for the many moralists, such as Lord Kames and Adam Ferguson, who wrote extensively on historical matters. For other Scottish Enlightenment thinkers, however, natural jurisprudence and history offered very different intellectual possibilities. For Hume, Smith and Smith's pupil John Millar history was, as Knud Haakonssen has written, 'essential to moral theory, because moral consciousness, moral judgement, and moral institutions were formed by the accommodations reached at a given stage of society and in a given type of government'.[2] Smith and Millar gave the natural law tradition a particularly empirical twist, and they adduced a wealth of anthropological and historical evidence to help them distinguish between those rights and duties that were natural to man, and those that had come about, as a matter of convention, in relation to changing systems of property ownership or of divisions of labour. Smith, Millar and Hume all rejected the juristic idea, advanced by Locke, Pufendorf and others, of an original

social contract, and instead located the origins of society in the spontaneous formation and coalescence of families.[3]

The historical investigation of human sociability (known in its time as
'conjectural history') became, from the 1760s and 1770s, ever more central
to the understanding of natural and civil rights and duties, with questions
of marriage, family life and the relative status of women in different ages
occupying a position of unprecedented centrality in moral-philosophical,
legal and historical writings. Women were ubiquitously cited as an insight
into a society's economic system, its degree of social leisure, its moral
values and, above all, its cultural practices (or 'manners'). There were
Scottish works, notably William Alexander's *History of Women* (1779)
discussed below, devoted exclusively to women, but, in the main, the
history and social geography of women formed part of an evidential base,
not an end in itself. Nevertheless, the historicist turn in Scottish moral
and legal philosophy, pioneered by Smith and Hume, and developed in
different ways by Millar, Alexander, William Robertson and others, had
enormous, unintended consequences for the understanding of women's
position both north and south of the Scottish border. The Scottish
Enlightenment effectively created a sociological and economic vocabulary
with which to describe women, not as unchanging natural or moral
entities, but as social agents. The intertwining of questions of women's
natural and civil rights, history and manners in Wollstonecraft's
A Vindication of the Rights of Woman, for example, would make little
sense without reference to the influence of conjectural history. Well into
the nineteenth century, Scottish Enlightenment writing continued
to motivate comparative and historical considerations of the plight of
women in different places and ages, up to and beyond Engels's *The Origin
of the Family, Private Property and the State* (1884).[4]

There has been, and will continue to be, considerable debate as to how
far the historical investigation of women's status and role, in the Scottish
Enlightenment, enhanced their position in the eighteenth century or
contributed to the case for civil rights. This is a question to which I will
return, but first I offer below an analysis of the different kinds of Scottish
Enlightenment writings in which the position of women was addressed.
The discussion distinguishes between those writers who saw history as
simply illustrative of moral philosophical and natural jurisprudential
arguments about man and society, and those more historicist thinkers
who, in probing the relationship between morality and law, opened up a
new discursive space for a comparative history of women. Greater weight
is given to the latter, but it is nevertheless important to bear in mind that,

ultimately, it was a moralised, rather than an economic, version of this comparative history of women that had gained the most ground by the end of the century. The reasons for this are explored in the brief discussion of the influence of Kames, John Gregory and James Beattie on Elizabeth Montagu and her Bluestocking circle, and then again in chapter 3. This emergence, towards the end of the century, of a gendered, moralised conjectural history took place in the context of a wider, disciplinary separation of moral philosophy from economics – a separation that Hume, Smith and Millar did not promote or endorse. As we will see in the next chapter, such a moralised, increasingly nationally specific history made sense and proved serviceable to writers who made the case for women's education and social influence at moments of conservative retrenchment – after the outbreak of the American Revolutionary war, for instance, or during the anti-Jacobin backlash of the 1790s. Yet it left the question of women's economic agency, as producers rather than as consumers or as bearers of children, in long suspense, even while it provided women writers with a language with which to connect female benevolence, social progress and improved education for women.

THE OFFICES OF WOMEN

The institutional changes that motivated the Scottish Enlightenment enquiry into men and women's natural moral sentiments and capacities, and its creation of a human science of law and history, were similar to those that engendered the Latitudinarian reformulation of Anglicanism in England some years earlier. The Church of Scotland, established in 1688–9, once intolerant and strictly Calvinist, underwent a period of liberalisation. From the early eighteenth century a faction of so-called 'Moderates' emerged from within its clerical ranks, and they gradually gained ascendancy to the point where, by the second half of the century, they came to dominate its intellectual life. The Moderates tended to play down the Calvinist doctrine of predestination (despite the fact that it was enshrined in the Kirk's Westminster Confession of Faith) in favour of an emphasis upon human reason and the need for practical morality and social improvement. They were able to institutionalise their values of improvement and (within limits) religious toleration by means of their control of academic appointments in the country's major universities.[5] More generally, university men such as Hutcheson and Smith wrote in an atmosphere heightened by a sense of growing freedom of expression (the last execution for blasphemy in Scotland, in 1697, seemed far behind), and of the economic and intellectual opportunities offered, if often far from realised, by the Union of 1707. Hutcheson openly promoted the work of Shaftesbury and of pagan Stoics such as Marcus Aurelius and Epictetus to his young students. Moreover, he brought an unusually democratic sensibility to bear on his reinterpretation of Shaftesbury's idea of the moral sense, that he made applicable, not just to a spiritual elite, but to men and women of all classes. This was of a piece with his republicanism and his background as a Northern Irish Presbyterian who seems to have dissented openly, in his early life, from the chief tenets of Calvinism.[6] He is of interest here partly because his views on women and marriage were progressive by the standards of his day, and partly because, along with Shaftesbury and Butler, he was an influential moralist on behalf of the idea of intrinsic human benevolence. Like them, he attacked those writers who considered morality to be partly or wholly a matter of the law of private censure or to be based in man's self-love and self-interest. Virtuous motives, Hutcheson replied, are natural to human beings, and we all have an innate moral sense that observes and approves of virtue and benevolence in others, as well as a faculty of reason that allows us to reflect on people's motivation and the effects of their actions.

Much of Hutcheson's early work was devoted to challenging Mandeville's notion of the selfish origins of social behaviour. 'Our *Love* either of *Esteem*, or *Benevolence*', he observed, 'is not founded on *Self-Love*, or views of *Interest.*'[7] He rescued the notion of 'honour' from the social contingency of Mandeville's *Fable*, and linked it instead to a '*Sense* of *moral Virtue*, both in the Persons who confer the Honour, and in him who pursues it.'[8] There is, in Hutcheson's early works, no explicit discussion of female honour beyond some slightly priggish remarks on the compromising effects of male gallantry for women.[9] It was not until he published *A Short Introduction to Moral Philosophy* (Latin 1745, English 1747), originally delivered as lectures in Glasgow, and later expanded as *A System of Moral Philosophy* (1755), that Hutcheson first gave serious attention to the place of women. This forms part of his consideration of the origins, in common moral consciousness, of the network of private and public relations which make up civil society. In the study of moral philosophy, women were traditionally comprehended in general discussions of ethics, but only accorded separate treatment under sub-sections of the heading of 'oeconomicks' (the household sphere). Hutcheson's specific discussion of women in the *Introduction* is thus limited to the chapter on marriage, which comes under the heading of 'The Principles of Oeconomicks and Politicks' (in the *System* 'Of Civil Polity'), although reference to women can be legitimately inferred from many other discussions of man's rights and duties. 'Oeconomicks', Hutcheson explains in the *Introduction*, 'treat of the rights and obligations in a family.' Within the family, marriage constitutes 'an equal friendly society' bringing obligations, on the part of both partners, to sexual fidelity (Hutcheson argues strongly against the double standard).[10] Specifically excluded from the rights of partners is the 'right of commanding, vested in either of the parties', a departure from traditional natural law theory which usually asserted the right of man's dominion over his household.[11] The duties and rights of men and women in marriage are both equal and reciprocal. The foundation of all marital rights and obligations lies in the providential dispensations of nature which have 'implanted vehement affections between the sexes' as well as a 'strong parental affection' in order to create lasting and procreative families.[12] Female chastity is necessary to guarantee men's natural interest in their own progeny, an idea elaborated in the *System of Moral Philosophy*, where Hutcheson also discusses the 'moral machinery' of the instinct for parental and sexual love, and claims (*pace* Mandeville) that love is more, not less, natural than lust.[13] In the *System*, Hutcheson also expands upon the natural jurisprudential idea of monogamous, faithful, affectionate marriage as the natural moral underpinning of society 'in all ages and nations', and lays still greater emphasis upon the need for a 'state of equal partnership or friendship' without which divorce should be permitted.[14] Hutcheson never explores the disparity between the equality which nature requires in marriage and the state of affairs in his own times, and the egalitarian tenor of his argument is tempered by an argument for separate economic spheres: 'Domestick matters indeed seem to be divided into two provinces, one fitted for the management of each sex.'[15] The argument applies indefinitely since Hutcheson has no sense of history as anything other than tradition, illustrative of the past and prescriptive for the future. Yet his unusually egalitarian account of rights within marriage must also have seemed, in its time, like a call for reform.

In the longer term, Hutcheson's insistence that society could not function without public-spiritedness, and his identification of the family as the site for political socialisation, pointed towards a new idea of republican motherhood – an idea which would take root in post-Revolutionary America.[16] In terms of Hutcheson's more immediate influence on the study of women, however, what most interested subsequent Scottish moral philosophers was his idea of the moral sense, his insistence that disinterested benevolence is an empirical fact, that benevolence is consistent with self-love, and that civil society is an institution for the moral improvement of mankind. In Scotland, the writer who most elaborated upon this relationship between the moral sense and civil society was Henry Home, Lord Kames. Kames (1696–1782) was a prolific writer and judge, a friend of Hume and Smith, the patron of Millar, and, in many ways, the godfather of the Scottish Enlightenment. His early work, *Essays on the Principles of Morality and Natural Religion* (1751), caused a storm of controversy when it elaborated, from a religiously unorthodox point of view, Hutcheson's notion of the moral sense and its operations in social life. The *Essays* offered some criticisms of Hutcheson, first (following Butler) by identifying the moral sense more firmly with conscience, and secondly by rejecting Hutcheson's attempts to base all morality upon benevolence.[17] Kames considered human beings to be naturally sociable, rather than purely self-interested, but thought that this sociability could be compromised by our anti-social passions of selfishness and malevolence. The jurist in Kames argued that human beings need legal and political institutions to overcome their selfish dispositions and to realise their natural sense of justice. This, as he went on to say in subsequent works, is something that can only happen over time, and history can supply examples of the ways in which natural human moral propensities towards justice and benevolence slowly unfold and develop. Kames elaborated the historical side of his moral philosophical argument some years later in his *Sketches of the History of Man* (1774, revised 1778). The *Sketches* are concerned with man's natural progress from savagery to a just and well-regulated civil society, and also, conversely, with the effect of geographical, political and social variables upon the generic aspects of human nature. This is history *a priori*: historical processes are deduced from the final cause of providence (Kames thought that human beings really only have the illusion of free will), and from the intermediate cause of the moral sense. In all this, women feature prominently as illustrations of natural and social processes, as well as warning instances of the dangers to public morality of excessive modern luxury.

The sixth sketch, on the 'Progress of the Female Sex', traces 'the gradual progress of women, from their low state in savage tribes, to their elevated state in civilised nations'.[18] This progress to refinement, which Kames equates with the rise of monogamous, faithful marriage, brings about the actualisation of natural moral tendencies in women, including chastity ('a branch of the moral sense') and modesty ('by nature intended to guard chastity').[19] The consequences, for Kames, of this social materialisation of the moral sense are twofold: the increased prestige of women resulting from greater sexual self-restraint, and the civilising of men through more frequent hetero-social exchange:

Conversation is their [women's] talent, and a display of delicate sentiments: the gentleness of their manners and winning behaviour, captivate every sensible heart. Of such refinements, savages have little conception: but when the more delicate senses are unfolded, the peculiar beauties of the female sex, internal as well as external, are brought into full light . . .[20]

Although the luxuries and indulgences of mixed society bring new moral dangers, Kames argues that women play an important role in enabling men to realise the potentialities of their moral sense, and, hence, of their public spirit and patriotism.

Kames's expansion of Hutcheson's idea of the female moral sense into the area of women's history lacks coherence (it ends, disconcertingly, with an appendix 'Concerning the Propagation of Animals, and Care of Progeny'), and conflates female progress with social feminisation. Much of the latter part of the *Sketches* is taken up with polemic against the dangers of commerce, luxury and sexual immorality, a subject on which he had strong views since Kames himself banished his own daughter after her husband had divorced her for adultery two years before the publication of this work. Kames's framing perspective for his remarks about the position of women remains very much that of moral philosophy. Unlike the contemporary work by Millar, Smith and Robertson, there is little sense of the possibility of a gendered science of culture that might explain or ameliorate the varieties of female subordination. Nevertheless, Kames's work on the history of women had some impact south of the border partly through his personal and intellectual connection to the Bluestocking circle, who shared his preoccupation with the problem of luxury, and with the need for more self-restrained, benevolent women to improve the behaviour of men. Elizabeth Montagu first met Kames during a trip to Edinburgh in 1767. Kames was soon writing to her, at first recommending Adam Ferguson's recently published *Essay on the History of Civil Society* ('to wean us from selfishness and luxury, the reigning characteristics at present of all commercial nations'), and then suggesting his own *Essays on the Principles of Morality* (she was not too scandalised).[21] Montagu's introduction to Kames came from her escort, the Aberdonian doctor John Gregory. He was later posthumously famous as the author of *A Father's Legacy to His Daughters* (1774), a best-selling conduct book that was premised on a paradoxical idea of social evolution, very similar to Kames's own, as both the realisation and distortion of women's natural moral capacities.[22] Kames and Montagu continued to correspond during the composition of his *Sketches of the History of Man*, and he asked her advice when writing the chapter on women:

My present work is a general history of the human race in its gradual progress towards maturity; distributed into many articles, Religion, Morality, Manners, arts, commerce with many others. I have in particular one curious chapter viz. Progress of the female Sex from their lowest Savage stage to their highest State among refined nations. I want to levy contributions from my friends . . . There is variety in plenty for Mrs Montagu's pen . . .[23]

There was also a lengthy exchange of letters between them, quoted in the next chapter, on women in the ancient Highlands recorded by the poet Ossian, and the stage of civilisation implied by their high status.[24]

For all her encouragement of Kames's work on the moral progress of the female sex, Montagu felt that he needed to change his views on the subject of innate human benevolence. On one occasion she wrote to him: 'You observe very justly, that the pleasure of doing good never decays, but on the contrary strengthens by exercise. As we love those to whom we do good, we grow more affectionate to our fellow-creatures, in proportion to the extent of our benevolence.'[25] Her remarks on this occasion may have been prompted by the memory of a recent letter from another close Scottish friend, James Beattie. Beattie had written her a disapproving letter on the subject of Kames's *Sketches*:

A man [i.e. Kames], who reads thirty years, with a view to collect facts, in support of two or three whimsical theories, may, no doubt, collect a great number of facts, and make a very large book. The world will wonder when they hear of a modern philosopher, who seriously denies the existence of such a principle as universal benevolence; – a point, of which no good man can entertain a doubt for a single moment.[26]

Beattie's objections to Kames were mainly to do with his unorthodox natural religionism, though in other respects he shared his basic commitment, following Hutcheson, to the idea that men have the mental capacity for moral knowledge, and that, over time, they may arrive at a high degree of certainty about the intrinsic moral order of the world. Beattie was the principal conduit through which Scottish 'Common Sense' moral philosophy, science of mind and ideas about the moral and civil progress of society, reached the Bluestocking circle. His personal connection to that circle ensured that the version of the Scottish Enlightenment they discussed and disseminated was a relatively conservative one: hostile to Hume's scepticism and to Locke's critique of innate ideas (Montagu was suspicious of Locke who, she told Carter in 1772, had been 'much more admired that he deserved to be'), and inclined to moralise the notion of historical progress as a problem of luxury.[27] It was Gregory who drew Montagu's attention to Beattie's *Essay on the Nature and Immutability of Truth* (1770), a philosophical attack on Hume's scepticism that made him, partly through her offices, a London literary celebrity, and soon after the subject of a portrait by her friend Joshua Reynolds.[28] Beattie essentially popularised the epistemological and moral philosophy of his former Aberdeen Philosophical Society colleague Thomas Reid in arguing that the mind possesses a natural power (or 'common sense') to perceive the objective existence of the external world and its self-evident truths (including the truth of a divine author, and of good and evil). Like Reid, and like Kames and Butler before him, Beattie asserted that we do have a moral faculty, or conscience, that has the final say in matters of morality. Unlike Butler, however, Kames, Beattie and Reid saw the insights of conscience as intuitive, not a matter of reflection, although Beattie and Reid (if not Kames) assigned an important role to free will and to reason, that enables people to pursue and grasp more complex, abstract ideas. It seems likely that Montagu and her circle would have found Beattie's philosophy highly acceptable, particularly as it developed Butler's ideas into a synthesis of intuitive common sense, reflective reason and free will. Certainly, Beattie was in turn convinced of the potential intellectual parity of men and women ('were they to have the same education and opportunities, the minds of the two sexes would be found to approach more nearly to equality'), and of the close connection between sexual equality and social progress.[29] As he wrote in the section 'Of Economics' in his *Elements of Moral Science* (1790, 1793): 'the more the sexes approach to equality, the more will society be civilized. Savages are tyrannical to their women. In polite nations, it is otherwise; and the superiority vested by law in the men is compensated to the women by that superior complaisance which is paid them by every man who aspires to elegance of manners.'[30]

Beattie's notion of equality is, of course, limited to the social terms on which he thinks men and women can now converse with one another, terms he had no doubt readily accepted in Elizabeth Montagu's salon. Neither Beattie nor Reid departed from the natural law framework, deployed by Hutcheson, in which women were held to be obliged to perform certain moral duties, as wives and mothers, for the good of the whole community. Reid, in writing in his *Essays on the Active Powers of Man* (1788) on the 'benevolent affections', reiterated the familiar point that 'Nature has assigned different departments to the father and mother in rearing their offspring . . . The parental affection in the different sexes is exactly adapted to the office assigned to each.'[31]

MORAL PHILOSOPHY IN HUME AND SMITH

The dominance, in Scotland, of the moral philosophical line stretching from Hutcheson and Kames to Reid and Beattie was consolidated with the appointment, in 1785, of Reid's pupil Dugald Stewart (1753–1828) to the Chair of Moral Philosophy at Edinburgh. Stewart (discussed later in this study) instructed and encouraged women writers, most notably Elizabeth Hamilton, to apply his Common Sense philosophy to the question of women's education.[32] Ultimately, this line encouraged those who wished to analyse the respective social position and duties of the sexes to focus upon the evidence of nature, rather than that of history. Yet, it did not, as intended, curtail or contain the influence of another, altogether more sceptical Scottish philosophical line, that of Hume, Smith and Millar: one that set firmer limits to man's powers of moral cognition, that saw moral consciousness itself as a historical formation, and history itself as essential to the understanding of how moral, legal and political rules come about and gain their obligatory force. This line, particularly as it was developed by Millar and by the historian William Robertson, was not only concerned with the duties of women prescribed by moral philosophy and natural law. From their work, it became possible for readers to deduce that womanhood, far from being a stable category of nature, was subject to wide geographical and historical variations, and that these variations could be accounted for in social and economic terms. It must be said that this analysis of femininity was not a product of historical materialism since the natural law framework remained significant. Particularly in the case of Smith and Millar, history enabled them to show how societies come about and evolve in order to protect natural rights, especially a man's natural right to his property. Changing forms of property (livestock, land, commodities, luxuries and so on) require different kinds of social and legal organisation in order to be protected, and the condition of women provides a window on to that process of historical change. But those natural rights must first be understood in a moral philosophical context as arising, not from our moral sense or common sense, but from our capacity to form objective moral rules and rules for justice out of our natural sympathy (i.e. imaginative engagement) with the motives and actions of others. Women are thus an incidental, illustrative feature of the Scottish Enlightenment investigation of the relationship between morality, history, economics and the law. Even the progressive Whig Millar did not suggest political rights for women. Yet, as we will see later in this study, the work of these Scottish Whigs did much to introduce the idea that women in general – not just a few celebrated female 'worthies' – did have a history, even, in some respects, an influence upon the course of male history, and that this history was bound up with the evolution of natural rights and justice.

In order to understand the roots of the Scottish conjectural history of women, we must first say something about its genesis in the moral philosophical work of Hume and Smith. Although they were acquainted with Hutcheson (Smith was his pupil) and shared his hostility to Mandeville's idea of intrinsic human selfishness, they both criticised his theory of the moral sense and his teleological view of the natural order of things. They rejected his view (and, indeed, those of Shaftesbury and Clarke) that the particular moral actions of individuals contribute to the overall good of society by virtue of the ultimately purposeful design of God's creation. Their sense that private virtues are not, in a seamless way, public benefits had some bearing on their discussions of specifically female virtues, as well as on their general treatment of the nature and limitations of individual benevolence. Women readers of Shaftesbury, Clarke or Hutcheson would have felt, with some justification, that these philosophers implicitly included female benevolence in their analysis of the ways in which personal moral conduct contributed to the common good of the community. By contrast, the explicit tendency of Hume and Smith's work was to narrow the compass of female moral action, and to exclude it from their philosophical accounts of how societies construct and enforce moral rules outside the intimate sphere. Like Hutcheson, Hume's starting point for the consideration of women was his concern with the family as the site for the practice and internalisation of moral rules, but unlike Hutcheson he thought that there was no objective natural law and no inherent moral sense to enable human beings to form those rules in the first place. He argued, in his earliest major philosophical work, *A Treatise of Human Nature* (1739–40), that human beings have a number of natural virtues (such as benevolence, moderation and human-ity) that tend to promote the good of society, but that these are usually localised in effect, and do not explain how societies come to create and expect codes of conduct from people and to institutionalise those codes in the law. Natural law theorists explained the genesis of these codes by reference to the rights and duties arising from contracts. Hume, by contrast, gave a highly original account in the third book of the *Treatise* of the workings, outside the intimate sphere, of what he called the 'artificial virtues', that is, those virtues, such as justice, the keeping of contracts and so on, that have meaning and obligatory force only in the context of an artificially constructed set of social institutions and laws. People internalise and act according to these artificial virtues because they are useful and they enable society to work. The rules, practices and institutions of human society are thus not, in any straightforward way, an enlargement of the rules governing family life, although Hume does say that the family group is in part a kind of imaginative rehearsal for social life.[33]

Hume and Smith subsequently became deeply interested in the origins and historical development of social practices and institutions, along with the artificial virtues that support them, and it is mainly in this context that women enter their discussions as the casualties or beneficiaries of the practice of those virtues. It is significant to note here that, in the *Treatise*, female chastity is listed as an artificial virtue under the general heading 'Of Morals' and under the sub-heading 'Of Justice and Injustice'.[34] Most philosophers of Hume's time considered chastity one of the 'offices' of women, whereas chastity for him is neither a natural virtue nor rooted in any other natural virtue such as modesty. Indeed, Hume insists that female modesty arises merely 'from education, from the voluntary con-ventions of men, and from the interest of society'.[35] Society encourages women to internalise the virtues of modesty and chastity, not because they are in some way essential to the natural order of things, but because men need to have cast-iron assurances of the legitimacy of their offspring in order to feel motivated to care for them. A combination of education ('Education takes possession of the ductile minds of the fair sex in their infancy') and the law of private censure enforces a strict regime of female chastity: 'There seems to be no restraint possible, but in the punishment of bad fame or reputation.'[36] The qualified libertinism of Hume's treat-ment of female chastity and modesty has similarities with that of Locke, who also discussed the 'bounds which the received opinion of her [a woman's] country or religion, and not nature or reason, have set to modesty'.[37] Hume's *Treatise* was not widely read on first publication, and the discussion of chastity was not transplanted into his *Enquiry concerning the Principles of Morals* (1751). But it did bear further fruit in his discussion of the (socially and historically contingent) male creation of what he called the 'rules of justice' governing women's lives. He wrote that in 'barbarous' societies, women are, quite simply, outside all rules of justice, and are subject to male tyranny. In 'civilised' societies, however, women gain public rights and a measure of justice through a process of sexual negotiation. Civilised men are sympathetic and susceptible to women: 'such are the insinuation, address, and charms of their fair companions, that women are commonly able to break the confederacy, and share with the other sex in all the rights and privileges of society'.[38]

Hume expressed similar views in the essay 'Of the Rise and Progress of the Arts and Sciences' (1742), where his starting point is the physical and mental superiority of men:

As nature has given *man* the superiority above *woman*, by endowing him with greater strength both of mind and body; it is his part to alleviate that superiority, as much as possible, by the generosity of his behaviour, and by a studied deference and complaisance for all her inclinations and opinions. Barbarous nations display this superiority, by reducing their females to the most abject slavery; by confining them, by beating them, by selling them, by killing them. But the male sex, among a polite people, discover their authority in a more generous, though not a less evident manner; by civility, by respect, by complaisance, and, in a word, by gallantry.[39]

Male benevolence – towards women and others – may be, for Hume, one of the natural virtues, but it is mainly in a civilised social context that it becomes institutionalised as a set of conventions governing relations between the sexes, and internalised by men as a sense of moral obligation.

Like Hume, Smith rejected Hutcheson's notion of an inner moral sense, along with his idea of an objective moral realm and of natural law, with implications for the way he saw the relationship between private moral conduct and the public realm. In his *The Theory of Moral Sentiments* (1759, revised 1761, 1790), Smith gave an influential account of the ways in which people form moral rules by observing and then entering imaginatively (through 'sympathy') into the moral motives and actions of others. It is sympathy, the principle of imagination – extensively elaborated by Smith in social, psychological and moral terms – which, through his device of the 'impartial spectator', accounts for the norms of propriety. In answer to Hume's preference for the humane virtues, Smith draws a sharp distinction between those virtues of which we most highly approve as perfect and those that we regard as simply excellent. The humane virtues of benevolence, gentleness and sympathetic insight are excellent, but the most perfect virtues require self-control and the conquest of the impulse of self-love:

It is not the soft power of humanity, it is not that feeble spark of benevolence which Nature has lighted up in the human heart, that is thus capable of counteracting the strongest impulses of self-love. It is a stronger power, a more forcible motive, which exerts itself upon such occasions. It is reason, principle, conscience, the inhabitant of the breast, the man within, the great judge and arbiter of our conduct.[40]

Those higher virtues (prompted by 'the man within') really do belong to men and men alone. 'Humanity,' Smith explains, 'is the virtue of a woman, generosity of a man.' Humanity is a fine virtue, but 'the most humane actions require no self-denial, no self-command, no great exertion of the sense of propriety', and it is this self-denial that lifts virtue on to a higher, generally more masculine plane.[41] There is also the implication that what is required for the exercise of the higher virtues is active participation in the public world, something largely denied to women. Smith does not regard the connection between private benevolence and the public good as automatic or inevitable. Rather, he implies that the progress of society plays a part in the development of both the perfect and excellent virtues, and that, in the civilised world, the intimate sphere of mothers, wives and friends provides the moral education needed for those more demanding acts of public generosity.[42]

THE IMPACT OF MONTESQUIEU

Hume and Smith's discussion of the process by which men and women form and internalise moral rules opened out new historical territory both for themselves, in their subsequent works, and for other Scottish writers. In Scotland there followed, in the second half of the eighteenth century, the most extensive sociological and historical enquiry into the lives of women ever undertaken in Western intellectual history. The major forerunner here was Montesquieu, a French Enlightenment thinker widely read and admired in Scotland. Both Hume and Smith were deeply familiar with Montesquieu's masterpiece, *De L'Esprit des lois* (1748), translated as *The Spirit of Laws* in 1750.[43] This huge and influential work gave unprecedented analytical prominence to women as part of a philosophical investigation of the forms and functions of human laws, and, after long neglect, has recently been accorded a place as a seminal text for the discussion of French female cultural identity.[44] Montesquieu's purpose was twofold: to provide the foundations for a social science of human law, and to make a polemical case on behalf of the rule of law and against despotic tendencies in laws and governments. He adduces numerous historical examples by way of evidence, but his aim is not to provide an account of the evolution of laws, but to look at scientific and polemical questions synchronically through a cross-section of different kinds of polities. *The Spirit of Laws* is a work in the natural law tradition insofar as it begins with notions of natural law (the law of self-preservation) and justice, both of which, Montesquieu feels, precede and ought to determine the process of law-making.[45] Women are conspicuous in his discussions of nature and justice, though not of citizenship, and he gives them fullest consideration as an essential part of the cultural climate which determines the effectiveness of particular laws.

Montesquieu classifies governments according to three types of political organisation: monarchies (in which one man rules according to established laws), republics (subdivided into two kinds: government by the many, i.e. democracies, or government by the few, i.e. aristocracies), and despotisms (where the only law is the whim of the ruler). Each form of government has its own actuating 'principle' ('*principe*'): in monarchies that principle is honour, in democratic republics it is virtue, in aristocratic republics it is moderation, and in despotisms it is fear. The principles of virtue, moderation, honour and fear, which lie behind the laws of republics, monarchies and despotisms, have gender-specific applications, as Montesquieu makes clear in Book VII, 'Consequences of the different principles of the three governments with respect to sumptuary laws, luxury, and the condition of women'. Throughout, Montesquieu analyses the kinds of laws – constitutional, criminal, civil and ecclesiastical – generated by, and geared to, each form of government, and evaluates their effectiveness with scientific detachment. His detachment is nevertheless circumscribed by his larger polemic against despotism both as a political system and as a tendency in other constitutional forms of government. The work as a whole stands poised between descriptive and normative modes of analysis, and, among other problems, this makes the moral standpoint of its discussion of the role of women in despotisms, monarchies and republics difficult to gauge. Montesquieu does not examine the status of women as citizens, but focuses instead on their social status as an *effect* of different political arrangements. In the case of despotisms, much of what Montesquieu has to say recalls his earlier, enormously popular novel about life in the harem, the *Lettres persanes* (1721), especially the claim that despotisms make no distinction between political and domestic government.[46] He has the Eastern example in mind when he states that, 'the slavery of women is perfectly conformable to the genius of a despotic government . . . Thus at all times have we seen in Asia domestic slavery and despotic government walk hand in hand with an equal pace.'[47] By contrast, the personal freedom of women, which Montesquieu associates with monarchies and republics, is the result of a more reticulated legal system in which different kinds of laws govern different spheres of life. Book xxvi of *The Spirit of Laws* explores the applications and limitations of different sets of laws: constitutional, civil, criminal, canon and (what he again calls) domestic. Montesquieu associates freedom with the strict limitation of each set of laws to its proper sphere of operation, and builds, throughout the work, a liberal case for limiting the intrusion of public laws into the private sphere.[48] Women's rights as such, in matters of divorce, property, succession to the throne and so on, are nevertheless held to be relative to the particular form of government. Thus, although despotism functions as the negative pole in Montesquieu's discussion of women's rights, these rights are not presented as a matter of absolute justice, and he remains philosophically committed to a notion of the 'natural dependence' of women.[49]

The Spirit of Laws gives a highly sophisticated turn to the traditional association between female behaviour and luxury, citing and elaborating Mandeville's work in the process, and according an influential role to women's desires, including the desire for luxury goods, in the economic functioning of the state. In order to maintain economic equality in republics, Montesquieu argues, women's consumer and sexual behaviour must be regulated, either formally by sumptuary laws and a public censor, or by the laws of private censure: 'In republics women are free by the laws, and constrained by manners; luxury is banished from thence, and with it corruption and vice.'[50] Despotisms coerce female desires in different, more oppressive ways since women 'do not introduce, but are themselves an object of luxury' offered for the instant pleasure of men who have too little faith in their future to seek richer, more delayed forms of gratification.[51] Only in monarchies, such as those of Britain and France, is luxury 'absolutely necessary'. Not only does it support the differential display of wealth necessary to the ethos of honour, but it also creates a sphere of personal choice free from the interference of governments and censors.[52] This is, specifically, the sphere of female liberty, which is more extensive in monarchies than in any other form of government: 'the liberty of women [is naturally connected] with the spirit of monarchy'.[53] Montesquieu's British readers, Hume and Smith among them, were influenced by his notion that female liberty is an *effect* of the distinctions of wealth and rank incidental to monarchy, rather than its aim or deliberate creation. They were also influenced by his pioneering account of political culture and its gender ramifications. In Book xix, 'Of Laws in Relation to the Principles which form the general Spirit of the Morals and Customs of a Nation', Montesquieu examines the degree of influence which laws can have over what are called 'mœurs' and 'manières' (what we might call social norms and culture). These have their origins in the nation's physical environment, history and system of government, but, once established, are highly resistant to legal intervention and, in many respects, exert a more powerful influence over people's lives than laws and statutes.[54] 'There is this difference', Montesquieu argues, 'between laws and manners, that the laws are most adapted to regulate the actions of the subject, and manners to regulate the actions of the man.'[55] He does not subdivide 'man' into men and women, but it is clear that, for women, manners are more relevant than laws to the conduct of their lives. For Montesquieu, it is this domain of manners which governs the civil existence of women, and under which their citizenship is subsumed. By a kind of compensatory process, it is here, too, that women exert greater influence than men. In despotic regimes women 'have no influence in society', but in other kinds of state they are a major force for cultural flexibility and change: 'In other countries where [women] live with men, their desire of pleasing, and the desire men also have of giving them pleasure, produce a continual change of customs. The two sexes spoil each other, they both lose their distinctive and essential quality; what was naturally fixt becomes quite unsettled, and their customs and behaviour change every day.'[56]

In monarchies and republics, women are emancipated from the purely sexual character attributed to them in despotisms, and help to shape a culture in which gender identities are fluid. Thus, although Montesquieu does suggest, at several points in *The Spirit of Laws*, that femininity has some natural content, including modesty ('*pudeur*'), capriciousness and weakness, he is more interested in the ways in which this is modified through the processes of cultural self-fashioning. In the context of his conception of '*mœurs et manières*' as a realm which constrains and shapes the activities of governments, this constitutes a significant case for the feminisation of politics. The domain of manners to which he consigns women, in monarchies and republics, is not simply a private or domestic sphere, but one in which women are accorded a significant measure of cultural and political influence. Montesquieu conceived of the distribution of power within states in terms of force-fields, each attracting and resisting the magnetic pull of the other. Female influence within the cultural field can, he feels, define the limits and possibilities of constitutional, civil, criminal and religious law.

CONJECTURAL HISTORY AND THE SEXUAL SURPLUS

Unlike the Scottish Enlightenment writers who read his work, Montesquieu was not primarily interested in how cultural habits are acquired and change over time. Despite the many historical examples cited, along with the lengthy closing section on early medieval France, the primary aim of *The Spirit of Laws* is to provide a comparative rather than an evolutionary study of laws. Montesquieu's portrait of the sexual equality and flirtatious *politesse* of European high society must have seemed scarcely recognisable to many of his Scottish readers, living, as they did, so far in space and time from London and Paris. Hume had spent some early, formative years in France and was attracted then, and during his later celebrity visit to Paris in the 1760s, to the dazzling, mixed gender salon culture of the French capital.[57] Smith also spent part of the 1760s among France's intellectual elite before returning to Scotland for good. The metropolitan cultures of mid eighteenth-century Edinburgh and Glasgow were differently configured from those of Paris and London, revolving as they did around the institutional life of the Kirk and universities, and diversified socially by the mainly male clubs and societies.[58] Even so, Montesquieu's Parisian ideal of mixed gender sociability had its attractions, and was often cited as the very apex of civilisation in Scottish accounts of the progress of society, along with Montesquieu's warnings about the dangers of luxury and sexual corruption in modern life. It is to this historical model of the progress of civilisation that we now turn, and its enormous implications for the understanding of the position of women in contemporary Scotland and England.

The 'conjectural' or 'stadial' history first developed by Smith, Kames, Millar and William Robertson generally described the process of historical change in terms of four major stages universally experienced by all societies, measured according to their economic way of life (or 'mode of subsistence', as it was called).[59] Societies that rely on hunting and gathering as their mode of subsistence belong to the first stage; those based on a nomadic life herding and tending livestock belong to the second, pastoral stage; settled, agricultural societies are at the third stage; and modern, commercial societies represent the fourth, most advanced stage. Scottish historians and philosophers were interested in the interplay between the mode of subsistence and the political institutions, legal systems and cultural practices arising at each stage of history, and they examined the ways in which any one of these elements could shape or transform all the others. Conjectural history was deployed for a variety of interpretive ends by different Scottish writers, and historians today continue to debate its purpose and meaning.[60] It served, first of all, in Millar's words, 'to illustrate the natural history of mankind in several important articles', and to flesh out the Scottish study of the relationship between morality and the law.[61] It functioned as an interpretive grid in the study of natural jurisprudence, enabling legal theorists to show the different ways in which natural rights are enshrined or voluntarily exchanged for civil rights in different societies. In this context, conjectural history thus furnished an empirical enlargement of the debates in moral philosophy and civil law conducted in Hutcheson's *System* and in Smith's *Theory of Moral Sentiments*. Scottish writers drew eclectically upon histories and travel writings as a means of illustrating points about natural law or the origins of natural rights. Yet, in many Scottish works of moral philosophy or jurisprudence, the illustrative material seems to provide something more than empirical corroboration. Particularly when discussing variations in sexual practices and female roles, a kind of sociological impulse overtakes the writer, and historical difference, rather than natural law or rights, becomes a prominent part of the enquiry.

Conjectural history also furnished a narrative of political and moral change whose end-point and object of explanation was modern, commercial society. Among other issues, the conjectural model of history enabled Scottish writers to investigate the fate of older kinds of civic virtue in the commercial world. A particular concern was the way in which the commercial mode of subsistence, and the legal rules, political institutions and cultural norms associated with it, enhanced or constrained man's moral and political capacities as a citizen. Scottish writers were, variously, ambivalent or optimistic on this question of the moral and political consequences of the commercial stage. They approached the question in terms of the links between economic and institutional developments in history, and changes in the human personality. As J. G. A. Pocock observed: 'They were able furthermore to relate the historicisation of property to social personality; as man moved through these successive phases of relationship with his environment, his social, political and cultural needs and aptitudes, and with them his intellectual and imaginative capacities, changed accordingly. A historical science of culture now seemed possible.'[62]

The anecdotal information to be found in travellers' tales or in history – the religious beliefs of the Aztecs, for instance, or the warlike behaviour of Celtic women – could now be integrated into a science of culture. Social and cultural data gained new interpretive legibility as part of an integrated account of economics, institutions and the changing human personality, with gender data supplying important source material in comparative investigations of the origins and nature of commercial modernity. In many conjectural versions of history, the figure of the woman functioned as a barometer of social evolution, revealing the deep structure of each stage of development. As the Edinburgh doctor William Alexander stated in his *History of Women, from the Earliest Antiquity to the Present Time* (1779): 'the rank . . . and condition, in which we find women in any country', mark out to us with the greatest precision, the exact point in the scale of civil society, to which the people of such [a] country have arrived'.[63] In the work of most practitioners of conjectural history, this notion of a female barometer of historical change took precedence over any overt interest in gender difference as such, but nevertheless yielded up a rich sense of the varieties of female experience. A broad spectrum of comparative data led, almost inevitably, to a highly contingent sense of what is natural to women, although this was often tempered by jurisprudential ascriptions of 'naturalness' to the historical process itself, or to a sense of underlying uniformity in the way that different societies experience each stage. For example, Scottish writers almost all (with the exception of Smith) equated the sexual and political subjection of women with early, barbarous phases of development, and good treatment of them with the advancement of civilisation.

Whether their main preoccupation was with natural law or the political consequences of commercial development, Scottish writers incorporated into their conjectural histories a narrative of female emancipation from the hunter-gatherer to the commercial stages. This narrative also included an account of psychological evolution. They regarded the division of labour and the more elaborate social stratification that occurs during the agricultural and commercial stages as both an effect and cause of the evolution and diversification of the human passions. The emancipation of women is, in most versions of conjectural history, a by-product of those changes in personality and passions that led to the invention of romantic love, male–female friendship and the familial affections. This emancipation is certainly rather a limited affair, giving women only the benefits of enhanced social prestige rather than citizenship, although Scottish writers were certainly correct to assume that there is no inevitable connection between the expansion of male political participation brought about by commerce and increased political status for women. They did make a number of assumptions, the first of which was to equate female progress with liberation from work, especially onerous domestic work, brought about by the division, and extension into new areas, of male labour. In this, Scottish writers may have either spotted or anticipated a tendency, in the later eighteenth century, for women of the middling sort to withdraw from many areas of paid and heavier domestic labour, and a growing association between this withdrawal and the assertion of a polite, middle class identity.[64] Secondly, they assumed that the progress of civilisation, far from dissipating sexual desire, brings about an introjection of sexual energy into social relations, and they saw the arousal and deferral of the gratification of desire (we would now call this 'sublimation') as a motor for social change. Rousseau's Emile is civilised by being obliged to wait two years before he can consummate his love for Sophie. In a similar way, encounters between men and women in the sexualised, yet carefully regulated, public sphere of agricultural and commercial societies enable them to practise the self-restraint, mutual co-operation and polite negotiation essential to civilised exchange economies. For this reason, Scottish writers all assumed, as a third point, that the progress of women equates with greater public visibility. As commerce flourishes, Millar observed, women 'are encouraged to quit that retirement which was formerly esteemed so suitable to their character, to enlarge the sphere of their acquaintance, and to appear in mixed company, and in public meetings of pleasure'.[65] A fourth and central assumption was that women, as well as being barometers, are also agents in the process of civilisation. In this reading of history, women, who are, according to some writers (not including Smith) largely powerless at the hunter-gatherer and pastoral stages, gain considerable influence as soon as the social conditions exist for them to excite and manipulate male desire. Publicly visible but sexually inaccessible, women play a key role in the formation and maintenance of morals, social norms and 'manners'. Their extensive influence thus depends upon a heightening, rather than attenuation, of gender difference as civil society advances. The commercial stage and the progress of women are associated with an intensification of femininity, and economic surplus is allied to surplus sexuality. The metonymic connection between sexual surplus and surplus economic production was also explored in ways that carried forward Mandeville's arguments in favour of luxury, but also incorporated Montesquieu's warning about its dangers for female morality.

SMITH, MILLAR AND THE VARIETIES
OF FEMALE EVOLUTION

The first major public appearance of conjectural history occurred in Smith's lectures on jurisprudence, which were delivered at Glasgow University in the 1750s and early 1760s, and are known today through two surviving sets of students' notes. In the Scottish university curriculum of the period, jurisprudence was treated as an aspect of moral philosophy,

and it related to those aspects of morality that had to do with the human
sense of justice, and with the theoretical foundations of politics in justice.
Smith described jurisprudence as 'the theory of the rules by which civil
governments ought to be directed', and proceeded to apply his jurisprudential theory to areas of public law (relating to government and to man's
rights as a citizen), domestic law (relating to man's rights as a member
of a family) and private law (relating to man as a property owner, and
including criminal law).[66] Most of the material relating to women and
their civil rights comes under the heading of domestic law (which is
incomplete in the fuller, 1762–3 set of notes), although there are also
discussions of female property rights, rape and female political succession
under both the private and public headings.[67] The structure of Smith's
lectures, with his constant application of criteria of natural justice to
diverse legal practices, was not inherently unusual, but he brought to
the subject an original and exceptionally broad sense of history. Early on
in the lectures he set out the 'four distinct stages which mankind pass
thro', insisting throughout that these four stages arise from accident and
improvisation, rather than from any kind of social contract.[68] As Smith
examines 'the theory of the rules by which civil governments ought to be
directed' through the lens of conjectural history, he also generates a
secondary account of 'the natural progress which men make in society'.[69]
He gives no separate account of the natural progress of women through
the four stages of society, but it is possible to discern the outline of a
conjectural history of women, particularly from the second, slightly later
set of student's notes. From the agricultural to the commercial stages,
improvements in women's lives are linked to the evolution of the
passions, the invention of romantic love, and the institutionalisation
of permanent, affectionate marriage (something which Smith thinks is
natural, but which has often been derogated by corrupt societies such as
the Romans, or by polygamous, eastern societies).[70] Romantic love at first
provokes nasty bouts of male jealousy, but is eventually favourable to
women once the transition to commercial modernity brings them out into
the public domain: 'As mankind became more refined, the same fondness
which made [men] shut up women made them allow them liberties.'[71]

   Smith entertains no doubts about the superiority of modern marriage,
yet his history of the progress of women and sexuality, though briefly
sketched, remains complex and contradictory. He worries that modern
female liberty will bring about the kind of sexual licentiousness currently
prevalent in France. He also warns that modern female liberty is dependent upon a benign but inherently changeable 'prejudice of manners'

which accords women status mainly as 'objects of pleasure'.[72] Smith contrasts this with the genuine social prestige enjoyed by women at the hunter-gatherer and pastoral stages:

Tho' there was little or no regard paid to woemen in the first state of society as objects of pleasure, yet there never was more regard paid them as rational creatures. In North America, the women are consulted concerning the carrying on of war, and in a very important undertaking. The respect paid to women in modern times is very small. They are only put to no trouble for spoiling of their beauty.[73]

Elsewhere, when describing early feudal societies, Smith remarks that 'the women of all barbarous nations are intrusted with a considerable share in all their deliberations'.[74] He does not try to downplay the brutality suffered by women in many primitive societies, but the conflicting sense of simultaneous advancement and decline in his conjectural history of women is often at odds with his history of the 'natural progress which men make in society'.

Smith did not publish his lectures on jurisprudence, but they are significant here because they exerted a very considerable influence upon his contemporaries, both through his network of intellectual contacts, and through the writings of his pupils. Adam Ferguson, the author of the Scottish Enlightenment's most ambivalent theoretical history of social progress, *An Essay on the History of Civil Society* (1767), reiterated Smith's observations about the invention of romantic love, though he could only reluctantly bring himself to admit that this rendered modern societies superior to ancient ones.[75] Elizabeth Montagu, for one, found Ferguson's particular take on conjectural history too favourable to the ancient world.[76] Many more of Smith's insights, along with some of his reservations about the moral and political consequences of commerce, were developed in the work of his student, the Glasgow professor John Millar. Millar's *The Origin of the Distinction of Ranks* (1779), first published in 1771 as *Observations concerning the Distinction of Ranks in Society*, was deeply indebted to Smith's work, and contained the most extensive discussion of the cultural role of women so far attempted in Scotland. In terms of its genre, it is an enigmatic text which has been variously described as a study in natural law, sociology or the 'oeconomicks' of the household.[77] *The Origin* grew out of Millar's law lectures at Glasgow University from the early 1760s, and his focus was trained, as his biographer John Craig pointed out, on 'the changes produced on the several relations of society, by the gradual progress of civilization and improvement'.[78] *The Origin* resembles *The Spirit of Laws* in that it takes a particular set of laws and institutions (in this case 'ranks'), gauging the ways in which they are shaped by sub-political kinds of human activity (in this case, manners, customs and conventions). Millar's order of analytical priority is clear from the title of chapter 5, 'The Changes Produced in the Government of a People, by their Progress in Arts, and in Polished Manners'. Other chapters discuss the power of fathers over children, the authority of chiefs and sovereigns, and of masters over slaves. Millar's focus upon the stratum of manners and customs in society makes women peculiarly central to his argument, and so, in the first and most substantial chapter, he writes 'Of the Rank and Condition of Women in Different Ages'. As in the rest of *The Origin*, Millar's discussion of women is largely confined to the domain of manners: 'It is not intended . . . to consider those variations, in the state of women, which arise from the civil or religious government of a people', but rather those which 'are chiefly derived from the progress of mankind in the common arts of life [which] therefore make a part in the general history of society'.[79] This entails the recognition that it is culture, almost as much as civil law, that determines women's familial and social 'rank'. By 'rank', Millar understands something more complex than 'class' or social position. He uses the term quasi-scientifically to denote status and authority in different areas of private and political life, but he is also interested in the discursive function of rank as a form of social ascription. It is only by ascription that women, who do not possess a class identity separate from that of their husbands or fathers, can be said to have their own 'rank' in the world. 'Rank', as we will see, also pertains to the position of women in relation to the history of the passions, and it is this which largely determines their status within and outside the family unit.

Although his work is thematically arranged, Millar's approach is more evolutionary than that of Montesquieu. His examination of the distinction of ranks in society uncovers a gradual historical process of diversification of forms of authority as society advances. For women, as in most other cases (with the notable exception of modern colonial slavery), this diversification is associated with increased personal liberty. Like Smith, Millar uses a four-stage taxonomy of society partly as the basis for a natural history of humanity, and partly as a means of illustrating general ideas about rank and authority. Each stage is associated, by Millar, with particular types of personality and passions, as well as modes of subsistence and forms of government. Over and above this general taxonomy, Millar amasses a range of (often dubious or anecdotal) ethnographical evidence to suggest wide geographical and historical variations in the social experience of each stage. The first chapter, on women in different ages, charts a slow historical process of improvement, albeit one which takes place only at the sub-political level, since the extension of citizenship to a wider section of society, associated by conjectural historians with the commercial stage, does not apply to women. Millar mainly links improvements in the social position of women to the history of the passions, and he claims that the emotional complexities associated with life in more advanced societies are broadly favourable to women. Even so, Millar, like Smith, is ultimately ambivalent about the looser sexual mores brought about by the heightened passions and social opportunities of modern times.

In tribes at the hunter-gatherer stage, Millar argues, there are few hierarchies or differences of wealth to separate people from each other, and therefore only crude and personal ideas of authority. This has two consequences for women. The first is that women, who make up most of the servant class in tribal societies, are property-less, and placed under the direct governance of their menfolk. As the 'servants or slaves of the men' they are: 'degraded below the other sex, and reduced under that authority which the strong acquire over the weak: an authority which, in early periods, is subject to no limitation from the government, and is therefore exerted with a degree of harshness and severity suited to the dispositions of the people'.[80]

The second consequence is that, paradoxically, they are disadvantaged by not being the objects of male sexual attention. A lack of a distinction of ranks means that women and men have unlimited access to each other, and that this ease of access diminishes, rather than excites, the men's sexual interest in women: 'He must have little regard for pleasures which he can purchase at so easy a rate.'[81] Routine sexual gratification and a lack of romantic sensibility in men leads, in turn, to a low regard for female virtue, and female chastity is not prized.[82] Millar adduces a number of (rather far-fetched) examples of the casual promiscuity of primitive societies. Sexual urges and romantic desire are, then, two distinct aspects of the history of the passions, and it is only when they can manipulate the latter ('the passion between the sexes') that women can begin to acquire 'rank and dignity'.[83]

There are exceptions to this pattern, notably the matriarchies that occur in tribal societies where marriage ties are weak or non-existent. Millar devotes the second section of the chapter to this subject, but, unlike Smith, regards the political prestige of women as a great rarity at the early stages of society. The 'refinement of the passions of Sex', as Millar phrases it, really begins at the pastoral stage when greater differences in relative wealth stratify society, and 'interrupt the communication of the sexes'.[84] This, along with increases in leisure time, leads to an 'indulgence of those indolent gratifications' of romance, while, at the same time, more limited male access to women fosters a 'degree of tenderness and delicacy of sentiment' on the subject of sex.[85] The advent of the agricultural stage accelerates this dual process of physical separation and emotional entanglement between the sexes. Extreme inequalities of wealth, arising from the new forms of property in land, separate one family from another. The inaccessibility of women from wealthy families has 'a manifest tendency to heighten and improve the passion between the sexes', a feeling given sublimated cultural expression in the conventions of courtly love, which, in turn, serve to 'divert the attention from sensual pleasure' and to generate an elaborate cult of female chastity.[86] Courtly love was an aristocratic invention, but, Millar observes, it was diffused across the social scale, gained 'stability from custom', and carried on shaping sexual 'manners' right up to modern times.[87] This point about the enduring influence of chivalry is an important one, though not unique to Millar, and would be elaborated and contested by subsequent writers. What is notable about Millar's account of courtly love – an especially harsh and elaborate system of sexual restraint – is the ease with which he thinks it was internalised by medieval men and women. In an earlier passage, Millar describes the process by which men (he later includes women) learn sexual self-restraint by the example of others, and acquire 'sentiments of modesty' through a process of voluntary self-tutoring.[88] This, as Michael Ignatieff has pointed out, is a far less coercive account of sexual socialisation than the hard lessons in shame described by Mandeville; there is no violent self-denial, no pining and wasting away for the sake of appearances.[89] Millar's notion of learned restraint is consistent with the Scottish notion of the sexual appetite as a social production, alternately awakened and culturally regulated, rather than as a brute instinct of nature. Paradoxically, his conjectural approach reveals the historical contingency of the categories of romantic love, chastity, modesty and delicacy, yet demonstrates the capacity of women to internalise those categories as though they were prescribed by nature.

This paradoxical aspect of Millar's work can be seen most clearly in the section on the condition of women in the commercial age. Women at this stage are in the best position to manipulate the culture of romantic love to their own advantage: 'Possessed of peculiar delicacy, and sensibility, *whether derived from original constitution, or from her way of life,* she is capable of securing the esteem and affection of her husband' (my italics).[90]

The ambivalence of Millar's account of women resides in the 'whether . . . or' formulation above. Do women have an innate, natural capacity for sexual delicacy, or is it something produced by economic and social progress? This unresolved question is overlaid with the ambivalences of Millar's attitude to commerce in its beneficial and degenerate manifestations. The transition from the agricultural to the commercial stage creates a greater plurality of social interactions and more subtly ramified distinctions of rank, which in turn put an end to the segregation of women, and promote a 'free intercourse of the sexes'.[91] Women benefit from the 'greater variety of transactions' between the sexes, since they cease to be the cloistered objects of 'romantic and extravagant passions'.[92] The increased public visibility of women inevitably results in some cooling of male desire, although now that sexual restraint has been fully internalised by all members of society, it does not herald a return to the sex-object woman of tribal society. Internalised sexual restraint, and the forms of desire which it engenders, create opportunities for women to engage in social negotiation. Whereas women in primitive societies find it 'impossible [to] procure esteem by such talents as they are capable of acquiring', commercial women have no difficulty making their presence felt, and 'securing the esteem' of their husbands.[93]

Commerce, however, is a double-edged sword: one the one hand, it brings a division of labour, distribution of wealth and extension of citizenship; on the other, it leads to excess luxury, concentrations of wealth in few hands and the loss of civic culture. Its benefits are associated with the companionate, esteem-securing wife described above, but its degenerate side brings a powerful and alluring, but less respectable, kind of courtly woman. In the final part of the first chapter of *The Origin*, Millar discusses the ways in which the advent of 'refinement and luxury' in the most advanced states of modern Europe has enhanced the public visibility of (middle to upper class) women. Relieved of domestic duties, they participate in a mixed public domain: 'They are encouraged . . . to enlarge the sphere of their acquaintance, and to appear in mixed company, and in public meetings of pleasure.'[94] They exert considerable influence over their social environment as they 'cultivate those talents which are adapted to the intercourse of the world', and 'excite those peculiar sentiments and passions of which they are the natural objects'.[95] This happy state of affairs is, however, vulnerable to corruption and political decline, and may eventually threaten women with the loss, through careless social mixing, of the elevated rank that gave them their freedom in the first place: 'The natural tendency, therefore, of great luxury and dissipation is to diminish the rank and dignity of the women, by preventing all refinement in their connection with the other sex, and rendering them only subservient to the purposes of animal enjoyment.'[96] It is one of the ironies of history, for Millar, that primitive poverty and luxury have similar consequences for the condition of women by rendering them lust-objects, undifferentiated by class or accomplishments.

In his closing reflections on the consequences of luxury for women, Millar thus goes well beyond the usual jeremiads on excessive consumption, sexual depravity and effeminacy, and expresses concern for the loss of female social status and power. This concern is certainly consistent with what is known, biographically, about Millar's progressive Whig political views, and about the way Millar fostered the intellectual life of his own daughters and other women of his circle.[97] Millar establishes, in the final section of this chapter, a semiotic equivalence between sexual relations and commerce: at the commercial stage, men and women engage in 'transactions', output of consumer goods and romantic passions is increased, and economic surplus, or luxury, is associated with the over-production of sexual appetite. Millar is exploring what would now be called the 'commercialisation of sexuality', and its detrimental effects upon the status or 'rank' of women (the penultimate paragraph alludes to the contemporary 'encouragement given to common prostitution').[98] This is innovative material, and can be read in the context of the more overtly antagonistic accounts, in the ensuing chapters, of power and exploitation in the class domain, as well as in connection with Millar's wider jurisprudential investigation of civil society as a mechanism for guarding the natural rights of both men and women.

GENDER AND ETHNOGRAPHY FROM THE FRENCH TO THE SCOTTISH ENLIGHTENMENTS

Millar's work had an immediate effect on his Scottish contemporaries, and through their writings, a longer-term impact on the sociology of woman. Kames's *Sketches of the History of Man*, which followed hard on the heels of Millar's work in 1774, has already been discussed as a work that attempted to assimilate conjectural history to moral sense philosophy. The clergyman John Logan provided a simplified, accessible account of conjectural history, including remarks on the position of women, in his *Elements of the Philosophy of History* (1781), incorporating them into a general survey of world history.[99] William Russell included sections of *The Observations concerning the Distinction of Ranks*, along with extracts from Adam Ferguson, in his *Essay on the Character, Manners, and Genius of Women in Different Ages* (1773). The *Essay* is a translation of the *Essai sur le caractère . . . des femmes*, a popular work by the French historian Antoine Léonard Thomas, which Russell tried to adapt, through interpolation and expansion, to the Scottish model of conjectural history.[100] Thomas himself was very much the product of the French salon culture – specifically, the intellectually serious salon of Suzanne Necker – and his work is a lively but conventional performance which combines traditional praise of brave and learned women with a call for greater recognition of their role as softeners and polishers of society ('Society to them is like a harpsichord, of which they know the touches').[101] There are historical elements to Thomas's argument, including an account of the effects of early Christianity on women's lives (a subject conspicuously absent from Scottish conjectural history), and of the high status of women in primitive tribes: 'Among men who have made few advances in civilization . . . women have naturally, and must have, the greatest sway.'[102] Russell supplements Thomas's work with his own material and extracts from Millar, and appends his own, competent account 'Of the Progress of Society in Britain, and of the Characters, Manners, and Talents of the British Women'. This follows Thomas's pattern of praising illustrious women (including Astell, Masham, Chudleigh and Elizabeth Montagu), and, in line with Thomas's preoccupation with the decay of female manners, expresses the fear that 'our British ladies, once so remarkable for modesty, chastity, and conjugal fidelity, will soon equal their sisters of France in impudence, levity, and incontinence'.[103]

Thomas's *Essai* gains from Russell's interpolations of his own and Millar's work, but remains a conventional and somewhat incoherent work of gallantry rather than a plea for reform. It did have its British admirers, among them Jemima Kindersley, who also translated the work in 1781. In her introduction, she welcomed Thomas's arguments on behalf of female education, and claimed that her sentiments were so similar to his that, having read the work, she thought she would translate it before bringing out her own essays on the female mind. Her new project was now 'to consider the character of women in different countries, of different religions, and under different forms of government', and she appended to her translation two portions of the proposed essays.[104] Kindersley is a notable example of a female English disciple of Montesquieu who also appears to have absorbed some elements of Scottish conjectural history. In the first

essay she explores the (in her view, inverse) correlation between severe
laws and lax manners in relation to women, and vice versa. Citing the
contrasting cases of Muslim countries and of modern Holland, she argues
that, where women are excessively restricted by the laws (as in eastern
countries) they establish compensatory cultural influence, but have less
influence when the laws are more favourable to them. The second essay
glances briefly (and autobiographically) at the situation of widowed
mothers and other women not dependent upon men in contemporary
Britain. The first essay is of a piece with her earlier, successful work, a
travel account of her journey to India (published in 1777), in which she
cites Montesquieu's *The Spirit of Laws* in the original, and uses his
analytical methods to assess the predicament of Indian men and women
under a despotic system of government.[105] Kindersley's work is of particular interest because it gives some insight into the question, posed at the
beginning of this chapter, of the appeal and serviceableness of Scottish
conjectural history to progressive women thinkers. For Kindersley,
at least, a geographically and historically comparative vocabulary of
laws and manners is a potentially powerful tool of collective female self-
understanding, and, as she argues in the introduction to her translation of
Thomas, the first step on the road to a new theory of female education.[106]
It is regrettable that her comparative essays on the female character were
never published.

The impact in Britain of both Montesquieu and the Scottish conjectural historians was enhanced and qualified by the ways in which their
work intersected with contemporary anthropology, or, as it was termed,
the 'natural history of man'. The nature, gender order and religious
practices of primitive peoples were, of course, subjects of intensive investigation in the eighteenth century, particularly as new discoveries in the
North American interior and in the South Seas enlarged the available
evidence base.[107] To eighteenth-century writers generally, the hunter-
gatherer stage represented what we would now call a 'pre-historic' phase,
and was explored through often competing discursive models ranging from
cultural antiquarianism (the precursor of modern-day archaeology), conjectural history, and the materialist anthropology pioneered in eighteenth-
century France. When mentioning the primitive stage, Millar generally
had in mind Native American tribal society, but, like other conjectural
historians before and after him, he was mainly concerned with this stage
as the point of origin and negative pole of the civilising process. Like most
other British writers of his time, he discussed primitive society in terms of
its economic and social organisation, and largely set aside the determinist

climate theories that held greater sway with French writers such as Montesquieu and Voltaire. French natural historians laid great emphasis upon the physical inter-dependence of man, especially primitive man, and his environment, and in the sphere of natural history no author exerted greater European influence than the comte de Buffon. His massive *Histoire naturelle, générale et particulière* (1749–88) was readily available in Britain, and an authorised, nine-volume translation was published in Edinburgh in 1780, of which volumes two and three were concerned with the natural history of man. In volume two, Buffon surveys the natural progression of man from infancy to old age. He discusses women separately and in detail throughout, but with very little emphasis upon their difference from men over and above basic biological functions. Rather, Buffon aims to dispel a number of myths surrounding the female body. To this end, he explains how the age of female puberty relates to nutrition and climate, argues that female circumcision and infibulation are 'ridiculous and cruel operations' springing only from a male 'desire of monopolizing natural pleasures', and asserts that virginity cannot be medically ascertained, and female celibacy is unhealthy.[108] Buffon's review of the abuses and superstitions associated with the female body leads him to the conclusion that women are generally oppressed in primitive nations, and that 'it is only among people highly polished that women have obtained that equality of condition which is due to them'.[109]

Having provided the biological justification for the view, also adopted by Scottish thinkers, that the civilising process is favourable to the position of women, Buffon moves forward, in the third volume, to his famous essay 'Of the Varieties of the Human Species'. Here he gives an overview of the physical appearance, customs and sexual mores of the nations of the globe with the aim of revealing the material basis of human existence, and the close interrelationship between geography, the body and human culture. Throughout, he gives separate consideration to the female component of each group or nation, although some of the information he provides reads like a sexual tourist's guide to the women of the world. In even greater detail than the men, the women are described in terms of their physical appearance, dress and sexual behaviour. Bengali women, for instance, are 'the most lascivious in India', while Senegalese women are 'generally handsome, gay, active, and extremely amorous: They are peculiarly fond of white men, whom they caress with ardour'.[110] Buffon adopts a rhetoric of scrupulous neutrality on the subject of sexual mores across the globe, but his prurient details and racial stereotyping appear, to a modern reader, highly prejudicial. The climax of Buffon's argument comes near the end of the third volume of the *Natural History*, when he clinches his case for the unity of the human species by arguing that Native Americans were originally migrants from Tartary. There was considerable debate among eighteenth-century intellectuals, in France, Scotland and elsewhere, as to whether the different races of the human species derived from a single origin (as the Bible teaches) or from several, separate points of origin (as Voltaire and Kames thought).[111] Buffon's migration theory was decisive in favour of the single-origin theory, but gained instant notoriety on account of his assertion that Native Americans, having crossed from Asia to America, degenerated physically, becoming weak and slow to procreate. Buffon's notion of the sexual indolence of these hunter-gatherer peoples flew in the face of the many contemporary travel works which described, sometimes in lurid tones, the hot sexual appetites of primitive tribes, although it gained support from works such as Cornelius de Pauw's *Recherches philosophiques sur les Américains* (1768) and Guillaume Thomas Raynal and others' *Histoire philosophique des . . . deux Indes* (1770, revised 1774, 1780), both of which told a similar tale of enfeeblement.[112]

Buffon's anthropological work confirmed, and in many cases, supplied the basis for, the Scottish conjectural-historical account of the primitive stage. The environmental determinism of his account of human social development also introduced, or accentuated, a tension in Scottish work of this kind between determinist natural history and comparative sociology. This is particularly evident in accounts of women, and of the ways in which social evolution ameliorates, without fundamentally altering, natural gender roles. As Jenny Mander has shown in a valuable essay on the female figure in French Enlightenment anthropology, this tension also goes to the heart, and to an extent lies at the origin, of the 'noble savage' debate of the later eighteenth century.[113] For Diderot's response to Millar's work on women, first rehearsed in his contributions to Raynal's *Histoire philosophique*, and later incorporated into his essay *Sur les femmes*, coincided with his writing of the *Supplément au Voyage de Bougainville* (1773, revised 1774). In this Diderot famously defended, through the mouth of a Tahitian chieftain, the innocence and nobility of tribal life, and mounted his scathing attack on the pretensions of European civilisation, including its claims to accord higher status to women.[114] Other, particularly British, writers were less inclined to rethink the conjectural model of gender progress in terms of the historical distortion of nature, but were nevertheless inclined to use the category of 'natural' womanhood as a yardstick with which to measure some of the abuses of civilisation: straight-lacing, wet-nursing intead of feeding one's own babies, licentious public behaviour and so on. This is the case in Gregory's *A Father's Legacy to His Daughters* (1774) which was, as Mary Catherine Moran demonstrates, one of the means by which Scottish thinking about the progress of civilisation and its implications for women reached its widest public.[115] It was certainly famous enough to warrant an extended attack in Wollstonecraft's *Vindication*. Gregory incorporated Montagu's advice and ideas when he drafted the book in the early 1760s, but he also drew upon his current work as a natural historian of the human and other animal species.[116] His conduct book engages, as Moran argues, in a simultaneous naturalization and historicisation of the female sex, and communicates a double perception of civilisation as both a partial distortion and yet, also, a positive effect of the energy and sociability of women.

The tension between natural and conjectural history, below the surface of Gregory's *Father's Legacy*, is far more apparent in the work of another important exponent of Scottish social theory, William Robertson, a leading Scottish clergyman, Principal of Edinburgh University and friend of Millar, Smith and Hume. Robertson's *History of America* was published in 1777, and shows the influence of Buffon's *Natural History* and of Millar's *Observations concerning the Distinction of Ranks* (1771), as well as some traces of de Pauw and Raynal. His prestigious and influential work allows us to see how, particularly in the case of Native Americans, the apparent universalism of Scottish four-stages theory came into conflict with the racial taxonomies of French materialist anthropology, as well as the implications of this conflict for an emerging view, in late eighteenth-century Britain, of women as the carriers of a nation's ethnic or racial heritage. In the fourth book of his *History*, Robertson interrupts his narrative of the Spanish conquest of America in order to provide a systematic evaluation of Native American life at the hunter-gatherer stage, from its material base to its institutions, forms of property, religion, family and gender roles. Whereas Smith and Millar relied selectively on ethnographical anecdotes and traveller's tales, Robertson tried to make sense, within a conjectural framework, of empirical data gathered in the form of questionnaires sent to friends in the Americas.[117] These included questions about family relations in the different tribes, sexual behaviour, property and other matters relating to the role and status of the women. Robertson's presuppositions about women in primitive societies – that they are brutally oppressed, arouse passing lust but not sexual desire in their men and play little part in the public life of the tribe – indicate a broad acceptance of Millar's analytical approach, but also of Buffon's sense of women as the markers of a nation's inherent racial characteristics.

The setting of Robertson's analysis differs from Millar's, since the book on Native Americans (along with another, subsequent chapter on the Aztecs and Incas) forms an anthropological interlude in an otherwise linear narrative. Instead of taking place within an analysis of the natural history of man, Robertson's account of the Native Americans is presented in binary contrast to the Europeans in the history. The main focus of Robertson's *History of America* is the origins of modern European civilisation in the sixteenth century, and the role that the discoveries and colonisation played in its development. Thus, not only do Native Americans offer a hypothetical image of how Europeans might have lived at their earliest stage ('In America', Robertson remarks, 'man appears under the rudest form in which we can conceive him to subsist'), but their primitive way of life also throws into relief the intermediate civilisation of early modern Europe as well as the advanced state of modern times.[118] The tribes represent, in other words, both the dawn and the opposite of civilisation. In this way, the portrait of savage women as exploited 'beasts of burden', enslaved to lazy and pitiless husbands, provides both a pre-history and counter-image of the modern ideal of liberated womanhood:

In every part of the New World the natives treat their women with coldness and indifference. They are neither the objects of that tender attachment which takes place in civilized society, nor of that ardent desire conspicuous among rude nations . . . To despise and to degrade the female sex, is the characteristic of the savage state in every part of the globe.[119]

Robertson argues that there are powerful social reasons for this indifference and degradation, and these arise from the absence of any delays to gratification (although Robertson does not acknowledge any contradiction in his argument when he asserts that native women marry late to avoid the exhaustion of excessive child-bearing).[120] Tribal life for men consists of brief spurts of hunting activity followed by long periods of indolence. For women, however, the division of labour is such that they are, in effect, a servant class, and carry out all the domestic labour: 'A wife', Robertson remarks, 'among most tribes, is no better than a beast of burden, destined to every office of labour and fatigue.'[121] This crude division of labour separates the women from the men, and prevents the production of desire which occurs through the exercise of sexual restraint in mixed company. Romantic passions can never be awakened in primitive life, as they are in at the commercial stage of society: 'In a state of high civilization, this passion, inflamed by restraint, refined by delicacy, and cherished by fashion, occupies and engrosses the heart. It is no longer a simple instinct of nature; sentiment heightens the ardour of desire, and the most tender emotions of which our frame is susceptible, soothe and agitate the soul.'[122]

Hunter-gatherer women are deprived of the means of negotiating an improved social position for themselves since, without a compensatory system of manners, their biological weakness renders them helpless. Throughout his analysis, Robertson is careful to generalise from the race to the stage, and insists that cold and brutal treatment of women is not peculiar to America, but typical of all societies at the hunter-gatherer stage: he treats the tales of free love and uncontrollable lusts among savages, reported by geographers and French explorers such as Bougainville and embellished by Diderot, as pure fabrication. Yet the impression of innate biological difference lingers, particularly when he attributes the lack of female sexual power in this society to a specifically *ethnic* physical feebleness in native American men, reading their beardlessness as a sign of 'a defect of vigour'.[123]

THE GRADUAL SEPARATION OF CULTURAL HISTORY FROM LAW, ECONOMICS AND POLITICS

Robertson's account of Native Americans gave wide currency to conjectural notions of the evolution of femininity. Yet he lacked the conceptual breadth of Smith and Millar, and tended to reduce their taxonomies of primitive and advanced societies to a kind of moral opposition – an opposition which simultaneously gave impetus to the racial denigration of Native Americans to be found in Buffon's work and elsewhere, and strengthened the prescription, in Millar's work, for improvements to the condition of modern women. For Robertson could hardly have been unaware that, in many areas, the segregation and domestic exploitation of women characteristic of primitive societies persisted in his own day. There is, for instance, some (possibly intentional) irony in Robertson's indignation at the way in which native American marriages are conducted as property transactions ('the marriage-contract is properly a purchase. The man buys his wife of her parents') which may point towards contemporary abuses.[124] His work gives some indication of the paradoxes of conjectural history for women as, at once, a normative (at times, admonitory) account of modern commercial society, a prescription for future liberation, and a naturalistic, even ethnically specific, account of European female sensibility. These paradoxes, productive of considerable analytical complexity in the work of Millar and Smith, caused well-meaning inco-herence in the one Scottish Enlightenment work devoted exclusively to the conjectural history of women, William Alexander's *History of Women, from the Earliest Antiquity to the Present Time* (1779). This substantial and reasonably successful work (it went into its third edition in 1782) applied the conjectural history of women to questions of their education and civil rights. Alexander's book allows us to see the potential of conjectural history for arguments in favour of the legal and political improvement of the status of women, but still more, the ways in which, from the later eighteenth century, histories of female and male 'manners' often became detached from the legal and economic theory that gave them real analyt-ical and political force. The work does have a long middle section on the condition of women in the four different stages of society, as well as in specific periods of European history, and Alexander makes use of a diluted version of conjectural theory by which he understands the 'progress of manners'. This is preceded by a discussion of the history of women's education, and followed by a volume on marriage and the rights of women under British law, including a final chapter 'Of the Rights, Privileges, and Immunities of the Women of Great Britain'. The *History* is a logical extension of the work of Smith, Kames, Millar and Robertson, and might, had Alexander been capable of following his arguments through, have engendered specific recommendations for women's domes-tic and civil rights. Alexander, however, was a writer of limited abilities, and fundamentally complacent about the condition of women in modern society, and he lacked Smith's or Millar's sense of the complex interrelat-edness of the condition of women with the history of forms of property and of legal and political rights. His history of women is, in essence, a history of politeness *to* women, designed to brush up the manners of his male readers, and to reassure his female ones. Lacking a conceptual frame-work within which to connect polite manners to good laws, Alexander is not able to translate his dissatisfaction with the legal disadvantages suffered by English and Scottish women into a programme for reform.

The *History of Women* begins with an overview of the progress of female education in different periods and places. Alexander links these improvements to a loosely conjectural argument about the growing regard which man has 'when he becomes civilized' for the 'qualities of [woman's] mind'.[125] He then embarks upon conjectural history proper, with a series of chapters 'Of the Treatment and Condition of Women . . . in savage and civil life'. This series of sketches of the evolution of kinder attitudes to women precludes the sense of female agency in history more evident in Millar's work. He deploys all the latest ethnographic information (about Tahiti, for example) to prove that, in savage life, women are 'destitute of every thing by which they can excite love, or acquire esteem', and then goes on to describe improvements at the pastoral stage.[126] Alexander becomes more historically specific when writing about the agricultural stage in ancient Rome, the Germanic dark ages and medieval Europe, in ways which confirm but also complicate his conjectural scheme. The idea that ethnic culture may be a more powerful determinant of gender relations than the mode of subsistence seems to be hinted at in Alexander's chapter on the exceptional virtue and prestige of early Germanic women, but is not developed here, as it would be by subsequent writers discussed in the next chapter.[127] There are also observations on female virtue considered, not as an intrinsic quality, but as something called into existence through moral action. This leads to the shrewd gloss on Pope's remark, in the *Epistle to a Lady*, that most women have no characters at all: 'As the circle of female action is commonly more narrow and circumscribed than that of the other sex, so their good or bad character is also, for the most part, comprised under fewer virtues and vices.'[128] This essentially civic humanist idea of virtue as something created by public action was rarely applied to women, and carries with it the implication that women, whether primitive or civilised, could be deprived of a moral identity if wholly confined to private life. Unfortunately, Alexander goes no further in terms of linking a morally accountable public identity to female citizenship, and, if anything, retreats from this position in a subsequent, conventionally moralising chapter, 'Of Delicacy and Chastity'.

Having separated questions of female agency from his history of polite manners, Alexander reintroduces the subject in a chapter 'Of the Influence of Female Society'. Women, he asserts, have a civilising impact on society: 'Of all the various causes which tend to influence our conduct and form our manners, none operate so powerfully as the society of the other sex.'[129] He links women's escape from drudgery and confinement to progress, but still does not succeed in integrating female agency into history. Robertson and Millar showed how women's sexuality and sociability acted as stimuli to historical change, and how the withholding or delay of sexual gratification gave them the power to shape or even restructure social relations. But Alexander, by making the stimulus of female society a postscript to his main historical argument, is reduced to saying only that women's power lies in their ability to please.[130] Unlike his predecessors, Alexander makes the female-influenced domain of 'manners' discontinuous with society's economic, political and legal structures. This, in turn, makes it logically difficult for him to make the transition, in the second volume, from the cultural history of 'manners' to a cogent critique of English and Scottish law. He does make the case that common law protection for British women – against rape, forced marriage, beatings and so on – affords much better protection to women than polite manners: 'Such privileges and immunities as the French and Italian women derive from the influence of politeness, the British derive from the laws of their country.'[131] Yet he also defends coverture, and takes it for granted that women are, in the main, very well legally protected in modern Britain.

In many respects, Alexander's distillation of Scottish history as the progress of polite manners exposes the weakness of conjectural theory as a potential basis for feminist argument. Vivien Jones's critique of the limitations of Alexander's work could be applied, with similar trenchant force, to conjectural history as a whole: in this argumentative framework, 'the enlightened feminine subject is a structural impossibility'.[132] This is, in the end, unanswerable, although it did not prevent subsequent feminist writers from making use of Scottish methodologies in their explorations of the geographical, historical and class dimensions of femininity. Priscilla Wakefield (discussed in the last chapter), for example, welcomed the way in which, after Adam Smith, womanhood 'has become a branch of philosophy, not a little interesting, to ascertain the offices which the different ranks of women are required to fulfil'.[133] The historical context-ualisation of women's status, pioneered by Scottish Enlightenment writers, remained until well into the nineteenth century the dominant methodology for the analysis of women's social position. Jane Rendall has argued for the continuing relevance of the language of conjectural history to nineteenth-century feminism, citing as an instance of this an article by one of Millar's granddaughters on 'Woman and her Social Position' written in 1841.[134] Similarly, Kathryn Gleadle has argued for the relevance of Scottish social theory for radical and feminist reformers in the early nineteenth century, and we will see, particularly in the case of Lucy Aikin, the continuing usefulness of this theory in providing a vocabulary that linked improvements in the status of women to social progress as a whole.[135] Yet this theory was in need of a good deal of refinement, particularly on account of its narrow focus on middle- to upper-class, non-working women, and of the way in which women's work was equated with oppression. Wakefield's *Reflections* discusses the limitations of the Scottish association of progress with a lack of economic opportunities for women, limitations clear in the near total absence of references to women in the century's pre-eminent work of political economy, Smith's *Inquiry into the Nature and Causes of the Wealth of Nations* (1776). Like other Scottish Enlightenment writers, Smith had no truck with Mandeville's idea of women as stimulators and consumers of luxury, yet his argument (implicitly here, and explicitly in the *Lectures on Jurisprudence*) that women's influence was long-term, cultural and not rooted in their vices, paradoxically deprived them of a place in his analysis of economies. Smith's *Wealth of Nations*, as Kathryn Sutherland has argued, downplayed the national economic contribution of women's labour, and thereby bolstered the late eighteenth-century tendency to imagine women, not as economic agents, but as the inhabitants of privatised, leisured spaces that supplied men with a temporary, reinvigorating retreat from productivity.[136] Sutherland's influential essay may not do justice to Smith's work as a whole, since, as we have seen from his *Lectures on Jurisprudence*, he was in fact uneasy about the tendency of commercial economies to assign an adjunct, facilitative role to women as homemakers and consumers, rather than as active social participants and decision makers. To a far greater extent than Smith or Millar, it was the next generation of political economists that hived off the moral investigation of commercial society from economic analysis, and, with this, Smith and Millar's urgent sense of the relevance of sexuality, gender relationships and the 'oeconomics' of the household. As we will see, even in the emerging new economic science of population, there was a tendency to downplay the sexual agency of women and the involvement of their reproductive capacities in networks of familial and social relations. The triumph in Scotland of the Common Sense moral philosophy of Thomas Reid, James Beattie and Dugald Stewart coincided with the curricular institution of political economy, and tended to consolidate this separation of moral and economic analysis. As Knud Haakonssen has argued, the Common Sense philosophers demonstrated that the moral problems of commercialisation no longer had to be understood historically, and that they might, indeed, be solved.[137] The question became a more pressing one of education, for men and women, and education seemed to them a potentially decisive intervention in the processes of history, even as they purveyed a more restricted sense of the cognitive and moral powers with which man constructs and interprets that history.

Scottish conjectural history thus came under assault from those who, particularly in the politically repressive climate of the Scotland of the 1790s to early 1800s, preferred to treat historical change as moral progress.

It also came under pressure from those wanting to reinstate the specificity of history, above all European history, over and above the generalised, stage-by-stage categories of conjectural analysis. The seeds of a more particularised history of European manners had been sown by Smith, Kames, Ferguson and others – feudalism seemed to them a peculiar manifestation of the agricultural stage, and Celtic societies, with their lofty manners, a remarkable instance of the pastoral stage – but they did not anticipate the way in which this new European history would swell from a trickle to a flood in the late eighteenth century. As a postscript to this chapter, and in anticipation of chapter 3, I will examine briefly one example of the way in which this new history emerged partly out from under conjectural history, and partly as a critique. My example is that of a Scottish Common Sense philosopher, James Dunbar, the author of a fine series of *Essays on the History of Mankind in Rude and Cultivated Ages* (1780). Dunbar (d.1798) was Professor of Philosophy at King's College, Aberdeen, a subscriber to Hutcheson's idea of benevolence and a disciple of Reid, and he lectured on moral philosophy, philosophy of mind and political economy. His essays take a sceptical, intelligent look at the theoretical vocabularies of Scottish history and their implicit assumption of modern European superiority, concluding that 'Europe, in modern times, boasts a pre-eminence that seems to insult the rest of the world.'[138] In his essay 'Of the Criterion of Civilized Manners', he asks, what do we understand by barbarous and civilised, and why should civilised necessarily be taken to mean anything more than 'warm and steady affections in private life'?[139] He refutes the notion that mankind necessarily passes through a particular succession of stages, and this allows him to reinstate the idea that, in early societies such as the Gauls, Northern Celts and Britons, women enjoyed great political power.[140] What Dunbar calls 'moral influences' are, he argues in the essay 'Of the Hereditary Genius of Nations', often just as powerful as economic or geographical causes in determining the lives and destiny of particular peoples. Nations transmit cultural characteristics from parents to children, gradually becoming more distinctive in the process: 'is there not reason to expect', he asks, implicitly rebuking the conjectural theorists, 'that some general inheritance may be derived in a course of ages, and consequently, that a greater or less propensity to refinement, to civility, and to the politer arts, may be connected with an illustrious, or more obscure original?'[141] Different ethnic inheritances, he argues, bring different kinds and levels of civility which cannot be adequately described along a conjectural trajectory of history. Manners, though not a matter of economics, law or politics in

Dunbar's work, go to the heart of national culture as it is transmitted and internalised in families, and have explanatory force for the exceptional, if not necessarily superior, nature of post-classical European civilisation. They are also the arena in which the cultural and moral influence of women is at its greatest, an arena that can now be accounted for outside the analytical frameworks of natural law, economics or politics, definitive of a separate and feminine historical sphere.

CHAPTER 3

Roman, Gothic and medieval women: the historicisation of womanhood, 1750–c.1804

James Dunbar's work provides an instance of the ways in which Scottish conjectural history gave rise to broader, less systematic investigations of 'manners'. Dunbar treated manners, as did many later eighteenth-century writers, not so much as a feature of particular economic stages, but more as a manifestation of the cultural or ethnic personality of a society, transmitted within families and often at odds with, or resistant to, the modernising processes of history. This chapter examines the diversification of the Scottish study of manners, both north and south of the border, into questions of cultural and ethnic heritage in ways that enlarged the scope of conjectural history, but that also loosened it from its original moorings in natural law and political economy. Some of those who contributed new work on manners, notably Edward Gibbon, gave greater cultural depth to the Scottish account of the progress of society in Europe. Some took a sceptical approach to the very notion of 'progress', and explored the manners of ancient European cultures (as, to some extent, Adam Smith and Adam Ferguson had done), and drew attention to those features of society, such as spontaneous creativity, martial independence and respect for female courage, which were lost or rendered obsolete in the process of modernisation. Many of the later eighteenth-century writings on manners were diffuse and anecdotal, but almost all continued to give weight, similar to that of the Scottish conjectural histories, to the status and role of women. There was also a new element: a growing attention to the connection between the social mores of the past and the social reflexes and habits of the present, as well as a speculative interest in the deep roots of those habits in Britain's distinctive ethnic heritage.[1] By the end of the century, there was a widely diffused sense of the historical basis of everyday social exchange, and it was possible, even usual, to feel that some social acts, especially polite conversation, flirtation and courtship, were in part reprises of time-honoured roles and rituals. This pervasive 'historicisation of everyday life', as Mark Phillips has termed it in his profound study of 'manners' in this period, concentrated discursively upon women, or upon social interactions involving women.[2] A developing sense of women as the carriers of the nation's cultural and ethnic inheritance was crucial to the wider process of historicisation we now associate with Edmund Burke and the Romantic writing that took heed of his work.[3]

The historicisation of femininity was, I will argue, essential, even prerequisite, to Britain's altered sense of its relationship to its own past in the late eighteenth to early nineteenth centuries. A revived interest in chivalry, its golden age famously lamented in Burke's work, and in the persistence of medieval chivalric codes in modern courtship, was an important part of this historicising process. But this was in turn symptomatic of a wider re-evaluation of the significance of civilised manners, not as the expression of a particular stage of economic and political development, but as the very pre-condition for development and prosperity. Of central relevance here is Burke's argument that, as J. G. A. Pocock has paraphrased it, 'commerce is dependent upon manners, and not the other way round'.[4] In Burke's account as in many others, women are assigned a particularly important role as the creators and guardians of civilised manners, even though women themselves are imaginatively positioned as historically prior to, and socially at one remove from, the economic sphere. In many instances, the idea of women as guardians of manners also implied that societies do not develop along a single, modernising trajectory, but that they contain internal temporal variations, traces or residues of history made visible in the conduct of women. This idea, as we will see in chapters 5 and 6, underscored the new and (by the early nineteenth century) growing prominence of women themselves as historians in certain kinds of fields. It also helps to explain the eventual triumph, in my reading, of a 'Gothic' account of British femininity over other competing accounts in wide circulation in the late eighteenth century. The triumph was a slow one and, for much of the period, both classical and post-classical historical accounts of femininity were variously cited as exemplary or explanatory for modern manners. Among these, the Roman matron, the ancient British Celtic or Gothic tribeswoman and the medieval courtly lady were most commonly referred to as the cultural or ethnic ancestors of modern British women. Each type of ancestor was given new prominence, respectively, by the neo-classical revival, the Ossianic vogue and the Gothic revival of the later eighteenth century.

This chapter will examine the role that each of these female ancestors played in later eighteenth-century attempts to anchor modern manners in an imaginatively accessible, culturally serviceable past. It will indicate the contribution of women themselves, as translators, scholars and imaginative writers, to these endeavours. It will also point up the ways in which the study of historical manners was linked to an emerging ethnic conscious-ness in Britain. Interest in women accelerated the separation of previously blurred and confused Gothic and Celtic ethnic pre-histories, paving the way for a new idea of medieval culture as distinctively Teutonic in character. Historians have speculated about the nationalist reasons for the articulation of a new historical and ethnic consciousness in Britain in this period – one that placed particular emphasis upon the cultural role of British women – and have pointed to the imperial warfare in the years 1756 to 1783, and, in particular, the radical agitation, national self-doubt and 'gender panic' (as Dror Wahrman has termed it) provoked by the American crisis.[5] Others have traced the flowering of neo-classicism as a political idiom in the 1750s–1770s to the wartime leadership of William Pitt the Elder, and have linked this to a revival of the ideal of patriotic Roman matronhood.[6] Yet it is also important to look beyond the national context, and to bear in mind the European, cosmopolitan dimensions of both the neo-classical and Gothic revivals. Classicism had long been the cultural idiom of the European aristocratic elite as well as, in its radical republican version, of the counter-culture of the European and transatlantic common-wealth tradition.[7] The investigation of post-classical western cultures and ethnicities – of those obscure and intermingled barbarian tribes who overran the Roman Empire – was also a pan-European phenomenon, and, as Colin Kidd has shown in his definitive study, not simply explicable in terms of a nationalist search for racial origins.[8] Indeed, it is plausible to regard the Gothic revival as a logical extension of Enlightened cosmopolit-anism – perhaps even as a bourgeois answer to the classical cosmopolitan-ism of the aristocratic grand tourists and neo-classical revivalists, as well as an alternative to the radical appropriation of Roman republican imagery. The investigation of Gothic manners, as Kidd points out, did not so much enhance Britons' faith in their own uniqueness as give them a sense of the progressive differentiation, not of absolute difference, of European peoples from each other.[9] From this, many British commentators came to feel that there was something unique about European history that meant that the four stages of development occurred in a very particular way, not likely to be repeated in other parts of the world. In all of this, women came to define what was specific and superior about European culture, and represented a point of connection to the best aspects of the past, whether barbarian, medieval or Roman.

THE ENGLISH 'MATRONA ROMANA'

In 1770, the *London Magazine* reproduced a painting by Catherine Read of Catharine Macaulay 'in the character of a Roman Matron lamenting the lost Liberties of Rome'. The painting, as Kate Davies points out in an illuminating discussion, is strongly reminiscent of Cornelia, the daughter of Scipio Africanus and mother to the two reforming Roman republican statesmen, the Gracchi.[10] According to Plutarch, Cornelia was an effective, behind-the-scenes guardian of Roman republican liberties, a role self-consciously reprised by Macaulay herself in what she saw to be her own age of declining freedom. In this, and in several other Roman self-representations, Macaulay asserts an important civic role for women and also gives evidence of the attempt by radical reformers of the 1760s–1770s to appropriate classical imagery and ideas to their cause. This took place in the wider context of the neo-classical revival of the late eighteenth century, a period that witnessed a flowering, across the political divides, of Roman republican political symbols, and that marked, as Philip Hicks has argued in a valuable article, the 'high-water mark' for the prestige of the Roman matron.[11] Hicks provides abundant evidence for the late eighteenth-century fascination with Roman matrons, from paintings by Benjamin West and Gavin Hamilton, to Wedgwood medallions or to Sarah Siddons's celebrated portrayal of Veturia in Shakespeare's *Coriolanus*. He explains this fascination in relation to an intensified public concern with civil liberty and with the common good of the realm, ideas both bitterly contested during the Wilkes agitations of the 1760s, and by opponents of state attempts to tax and subdue the American colonies. In these debates, and especially in the context of the imperial warfare of 1756–63 and 1775–83, republican Rome represented a potent example of a state that had expanded and maintained its territory through the military efforts of its citizen-soldiers. In Rome public service was a way of life for all, and a man's very identity was bound up with his country.

The Roman Republic was an ideal, a warning and an image of unenviable austerity. British people knew that, in its most successful phase, its citizens went voluntarily without the comforts and luxuries of life, their women were subject to strict sumptuary laws, and private desires had to be subordinated to the common good. In the end, it was thought, Rome was the victim of its own success. Military over-expansion led to the loss of the kind of public cohesion and commitment only possible in a small state, and the Republic was diverted from its original purpose by wealth, luxury and foreign habits and indulgences. The institutionalisation under

Augustus of the Principate heralded the end of Rome's austere way of life, and the beginning of a protracted period of tyranny, effeminacy and decline. This was the version of early Roman history that eighteenth-century readers would have encountered through their history books. It was available in sophisticated form in Montesquieu's *Considérations sur les causes de la grandeur des Romains et de leur décadence* (1734), in Laurence Echard's successful *Roman History* (1695), Thomas Blackwell's *Memoirs of the Court of Augustus* (1753–63), Gibbon's *The Decline and Fall* (1776–88) and, later, in Thomas Bever's academic *History of the Legal Polity of the Roman State* (1781) and Adam Ferguson's *The History of Progress and Termination of the Roman Republic* (1783).[12] In the arena of popular history, the standard work for most of the century was Charles Rollin's *Histoire Romaine* (English translation 1739–50), later replaced by Goldsmith's updated and accessible *Roman History* in 1769.[13] Alongside accounts of male Roman patriotism, all of these histories recorded the fierce sense of personal investment that Roman women would have felt in the fortunes of their country, notwithstanding the harshness of the legal restrictions placed upon their property and freedoms. 'Roman history', Rollin points out towards the beginning of his work, 'has already supplied us, and will further supply us, with many examples of the zeal of the ladies for their country.'[14] Roman civic culture fostered and rewarded female patriotism, and many aspects of private life were imbued with a sense of civic obligation. Marriage was highly regarded in the Republic as a moral training ground for men, and consequently the role of wife represented a great deal more than that of private adjunct to a public man. Blackwell describes how Roman youths were 'moulded to modesty and moderation' for the glory of the state, and how women were 'regular and abstemious: they drank no wine, admitted no Visits, nor went to any Spectacles without their Husband's permission'.[15]

Certain female exemplars predominated in the later eighteenth century. As Hicks points out, these were not always, or even mainly, mother figures, but women who had made heroic gestures of self-sacrifice in order to uplift or maintain the morale of the Republic: Lucretia, whose suicide was instrumental in its founding, was constantly cited. So was Arria, who showed her husband the way to honourable suicide ('Paete non dolet') and who (along with Portia and Octavia) featured in one of George Lyttelton's *Dialogues of the Dead* (1760). There was also Attilia, brave daughter of the Roman general Regulus, who, in Hannah More's successful play *The Inflexible Captive* (1774), reconciles herself to his honourable surrender to Carthaginian captives with the words, 'A Roman virgin should be something *more*—/Shou'd dare, above her sex's narrow limits—/And, I *will* dare.'[16] Also notable was Hortensia – the name Macaulay used for her fictional addressee in her *Letters on Education* (1790) – who broke with Roman custom by making a speech in the Forum against a proposal of the triumvirs to impose a new tax on women, and who was singled out for special praise by the author of *Woman. Sketches of the History . . . of the Fair Sex* (1790).[17] Then there was Portia (the pen name of Mary Robinson) who demanded to share in the knowledge of her husband Brutus' plot to assassinate Caesar, and who proved herself worthy of his trust by her discretion and by her suicide.[18] Octavia was a woman of legendary forbearance and courage, sister of Augustus, the broker of a peace treaty, and the subject of a biographical account by Sarah Fielding.[19] And, from the post-Republican era, Agrippina the Elder, Augustus' granddaughter, who defied the tyranny of Tiberius, was painted by Gavin Hamilton and Benjamin West, and was the subject of Elizabeth Hamilton's *Memoirs* (1804).[20] All of these women played an active part in public life either directly, by acting as a stoical support to male family members, or by achieving a symbolic role around which the state could rally.

Despite their currency, these and other Roman female exemplars circulated in a cultural climate of historical revisionism in which commentators both idealised Rome and yet distanced modern Britain from ancient republics and the kind of political liberty they offered. Central to the British evaluation of the usefulness of Roman models (and with a considerable bearing on the image of the Roman matron) was the question of the role of commerce and luxury. It was commonplace that luxury – financial over-consumption and a lack of self-discipline on the part of men, and financial and sexual indulgence on the part of women – was the main reason why the Roman Republic declined into imperial despotism. Rome, wrote Goldsmith in his *Roman History,* was a state that 'had risen by temperance, and fell by luxury'.[21] Many eighteenth-century historians followed Cato the Censor (as reported by Livy), Juvenal, Ovid and other Roman writers in blaming female luxury and debauchery for political decline. Blackwell remarks of the late first century BC, 'Ovid says, that the Virtue of Chastity began to decay in *Rome* . . . To what a Pitch of Dissoluteness must they have come during all the confusions intailed on the State by the Civil Wars!'[22] Renaissance historians were convinced of the connection between female behaviour, male effeminacy and the decline of republics (the best-known example is the chapter 'How States are Ruined on Account of Women' in Machiavelli's *Discorsi*). However, following the sophisticated Scottish investigation of the role of both commerce and sexuality in stimulating social and political progress, there were other historians, notably Ferguson and Gibbon, who rejected this version of Roman decline, and queried its simplistic account of Roman women as either virtuous matrons or decadent strumpets. Yet in order to give a more nuanced, less luxury-centred version of the story of Roman decline, historians like Ferguson and Gibbon had to confront the more general problem as to whether conjectural history could make any sense of the story of Rome. From a stage of agricultural republicanism, Rome appeared to have entered a protracted phase of decadent, commercial luxury without there ever having been time in between for a polished, commercial society to emerge and flourish. If women had rapidly transformed from extreme virtue to extreme decadence, this could be read, not so much as their fault, but as a symptom of the truncation of the evolutionary process of society.[23] For Ferguson, the decline of social restraints on sexual gratification, in the period after Tiberius, was symptomatic of political decline: 'Love was no more than the ebullition of temperament, without the allurements of elegance, or the seduction of affection or passion.'[24] In *The History of the Decline and Fall of the Roman Empire* (1776–88), Gibbon famously addressed the reasons for Rome's skewed pattern of development and decline, as well as its impact upon women and sexual morality. He speculated about the ways in which the demise of the Republic might have affected the lives and behaviour of women, particularly, as we will see, in the legal arena, but he never entertained the idea that women's vices played any causal role in the decline of Rome.

There were wartime polemicists, such as John Brown (author of a famous fulmination against British luxury and effeminacy, *An Estimate of the Manners and Principles of the Times*, 1757), who blamed Britain's 'decline' on luxury, female debauchery and male effeminacy. However, most writers accepted the distinction, most memorably made by Hume in his essay 'Of Luxury', between politically corrosive classical luxury and economically productive modern luxury.[25] There was little genuine nostalgia, among either male or female writers, for the austere economic self-discipline of the Roman matrons, their suicidal tendencies or their forbidding refusal of male attention. Both Machiavelli and Montesquieu had shown the paradoxical weakness of states that over-invest in female purity. Better, Montesquieu suggested, to live under a modern monarchy where a little female flirtation oils the wheels of politics and commerce, rather than in an ancient republic where men are continually fighting in defence of female honour. Furthermore, popular historians showed what intolerable demands the Roman Republic placed on women's lives as the price of their personal and symbolic involvement in the *res publica*. Echard, Rollin and Goldsmith all retell the story of Virginia, whose father, as Eachard puts it, 'Dragg'd her hanging about him to a Butchers Stall hard by' and stabbed her in public rather than surrender her to dishonour at the hands of the decemvir Appius Claudius.[26] This horrifying story gained currency through its inclusion in a popular *Historical Miscellany* (1771), as well as through Frances Brooke's play *Virginia* (1756), in which the girl's tragedy is heightened by the inclusion of a desperate suitor.[27]

Eighteenth-century readers were increasingly aware of the different and often harsh legal restrictions governing Roman women's lives. Millar mentioned, in his *Origin of the Distinction of Ranks*, the despotic legal power Roman fathers had over their daughters and sons, and the steps taken, in the post-Republican era, to reduce this.[28] In a similar spirit, Gibbon provided a detailed analysis of Roman law as it changed from Republican to Roman Imperial to Byzantine times. Chapter 44 of *The Decline and Fall* is devoted to the *Corpus Juris Civilis*, the monumental compilation of Roman law undertaken, towards the middle of the sixth century AD, by the Emperor Justinian. This body of laws provides a record of nearly a thousand years of Roman history, including the remnants of the laws of ancient Rome (including the Twelve Tables, the law code of the early Republic). Gibbon's analysis enables him, as he puts it, 'to breathe the pure and invigorating air of the republic'.[29] Yet, despite inhaling this wholesome air, Gibbon shows little nostalgia for the severe and primitive republican legal system. One important object of his attention in this chapter is the changing legal status of Roman (and Byzantine) women that, far from declining or falling, presents a clear picture of improvement. From legal subjugation under the Republic, Gibbon sees Roman women steadily achieving a degree of legal liberty and protection far greater than that possessed by the British women of his own day. Early on in the discussion, there is a section on the legal relations of husbands and wives that opens with the (Scottish-sounding) reflection that 'Experience has proved, that savages are the tyrants of the female sex, and that the condition of women is usually softened by the refinements of social life.'[30] With palpable indignation, Gibbon depicts the republican form of marriage as a move from frying-pan into fire, as women exchange complete filial bondage to their fathers for conjugal servitude: 'so clearly was woman defined, not as a *person*, but as a *thing*, that, if the original title were deficient, she might be claimed, like other moveables, by the *use* and possession of an entire year'.[31] Gibbon's account of the severity of early Roman marriage is somewhat exaggerated, and there is no mention of the less restrictive form of marriage (without *manus*, i.e. without the formal authority of the husband over the person and property of his wife) available to women from the time of the Twelve Tables.[32] Gibbon is equally indignant on the subject of divorce. The fact that Roman men, during the first five hundred years AD, chose not to exercise their right to divorce, cannot, he insists, be taken as evidence of their reliability as husbands. Where Blackwell praised Roman men for their reluctance to exercise their right to divorce, Gibbon comments acidly that this fact merely 'evinces the unequal terms of a connection in which the slave was unable to renounce her tyrant, and the tyrant was unwilling to relinquish his slave'.[33] Eventually, Gibbon reports, Roman matrons did become the 'equal and voluntary companions of their lords', and initiated divorces themselves.[34] However, following an essay of Hume, Gibbon does not consider the right of women to divorce as evidence of real liberty, since it merely weakened the security of marriage, and lowered the moral standards of the women concerned: 'the matron, who in five years can submit to the embraces of eight husbands, must cease to reverence the chastity of her own person'.[35] Here Gibbon is in agreement with Blackwell, who asks: 'Can we imagine that the Fair-One, who changed her Husband every Quarter, strictly kept her matrimonial Faith all the three months?'[36]

Gibbon is particularly appalled by the Roman system of guardianship according to which adult women required the authority of their *pater familias*, nearest male relative (*agnate*), or (in a *manus* marriage) husband to perform any legal transactions. In practice, as Gibbon certainly knew, this system of guardianship was generally honoured in the breech. Nevertheless, he uses the occasion to inveigh against this legal affront to the rational autonomy of women: 'Women were condemned to the perpetual tutelage of parents, husbands, or guardians; a sex created to please and obey was never supposed to have attained the age of reason and experience. Such at least was the stern and haughty spirit of the ancient law, which had been insensibly mollified before the time of Justinian.'[37]

The changing rights of Roman women in matters of property owner-ship and inheritance reflect a similar process of improvement, from the Voconian law of 169 BC which 'abolished the right of female inheritance', to the rules of equal inheritance for male and female relatives in the age of Justinian.[38] Here, Gibbon offers some reflections on the English common law which, in this respect, seems to him inferior even to republican property laws. For before the Voconian law changed the rules, the Twelve Tables provided for sons and daughters to share equally in their deceased father's estate. In this matter, Gibbon observes, 'the jurisprudence of the Romans appears to have deviated from the equality of nature, much less than the . . . English institutions'.[39] Throughout the history of Rome, 'the insolent prerogative of primogeniture was unknown: the two sexes were placed on a just level; all the sons and daughters were entitled to an equal portion of the patrimonial estate'.[40] In England, as Gibbon's readers would all have known, the case was very different: male primogeniture was prescribed by common law, and the vestiges of the more equal Roman property law, for many centuries preserved in canon law, had long since been expunged.[41]

Gibbon provided eighteenth-century Britain with its most prominent account of the unjust legal restrictions placed upon Roman republican women, without saying that the civil rights of modern English women were any better protected. This may come as a surprise to those accustomed to think of Gibbon as a conservative political sceptic with few progressive opinions to offer on the subject of women. Yet Gibbon had a high regard for female rationality, and had once wanted to marry the woman who became the prominent Paris salonnière, Suzanne Necker, and he always approached the question of women with the same intellectual independence as he did any other subject, including the Christian church. There are elements of *libertinage* in Gibbon's attitude towards women reminiscent of Bayle or Mandeville, especially when it comes to his attack on the early Christians for their perverse or hypocritical sexual abstemiousness. He records one incident in which some 'virgins of the warm climate of Africa' put their vows of chastity to the test when they 'permitted priests and deacons to share their bed, and gloried amidst the flames in their unsullied purity'.[42] Gibbon is bemused by this kind of asceticism, and he remarks with dry humour that 'insulted Nature sometimes vindicated her rights'.[43] His note to this passage cites a similar incident at a later period in history, and he observes that 'Bayle has amused himself and his readers on that very delicate subject.'[44] Throughout *The Decline and Fall*, Gibbon is well disposed towards Roman women exercising power as queens, consorts, empresses or regents. He expresses admiration for female philosophers and scholars, and sympathy or tolerance for women of questionable sexual virtue.[45] He prefers women and men of great energies and passions to bloodless, repressed figures, and is suspicious of fanatical ascetics, such as monks and saints.

Nevertheless, there were those who felt that Gibbon did not do justice to Roman female heroism, notably Elizabeth Hamilton, who justified her decision to write her semi-fictionalised biography *Memoirs of the Life of Agrippina* (1804) with this statement: 'It is asserted by the historian of "The Decline and Fall of the Roman Empire", that as "female fortitude is commonly artificial, so it is seldom steady or consistent." Agrippina is one of the many thousand instances which may be adduced as proof that the assertion is unfounded, and the conclusion false.'[46] Hamilton qualifies this statement by conceding that 'Active courage belongs not to the female character; when it occurs, it is an exertion beyond the strength, and may therefore deserve the epithet of artificial; but the nobler virtue of enduring fortitude seems to be the gift with which nature has peculiarly endowed the sex.'[47] The story of Agrippina (the Elder) is indeed one of enduring fortitude, and Hamilton's biography traces her steadfast 'indignation against injustice', her defiance of Tiberius, her refusal to be cowed, even when she is imprisoned ('no sigh, no tear betrayed the anguish of her soul') and her decision to commit suicide.[48] Hamilton's insistence on the female heroism of endurance, rather than of active political intervention, gives some indication of her ambivalence about the ideal of the Roman matron. During an overview of the 'manners' of the Roman women, she comments:

[The Roman woman's] country was no less dear to her than to her husband . . . The strength of mind inspired by this principle does not accord with our ideas of female amiability . . . we shall rather applaud than condemn the heroism which taught her to impress upon the minds of her sons, that it was better to die with glory, than to live without renown.[49]

There is, for Hamilton writing towards the end of our period, something unamiable, even alien, about self-sacrificing Roman matronhood. Republicanism, and the republican ideals of liberty carried forward into the imperial period by figures like Agrippina, enforced a subordination of private, family feelings to the requirements of the state. For Hamilton, writing very much within the ambit of the Scottish Common Sense philosophical tradition, there is something suspect about a political philosophy that forces a choice between private affections and public duties. The Roman matron, even in her highest embodiment in Agrippina, is not ultimately a suitable or imitable figure for modern British women. Hamilton could be sure that Agrippina would be of contemporary interest, however, in that she provided the opportunity to tell the story of a life poised between different worlds: the new world of imperial tyranny and the old of republican patriotism, and also, the world of Rome and that of the barbarian, Germanic outsiders whom she encounters when she accompanies her husband Germanicus on his military campaigns. Hamilton's depiction of Agrippina's admiration for the Germanic people, their way of life, values and brave (but not 'unamiable') women shows the real extent of her debt to Gibbon. Like him, she is interested, not so much in ancient Rome alone, but in the interface between Roman and barbarian cultures, and the eventual absorption and transformation of the Roman heritage by the new migrants to Europe. Agrippina represents the last of an old, heroic Roman type of womanhood, but, as Hamilton makes clear, new forms of civilisation and new kinds of womanhood were, at that time, slowly taking shape to the east of the Rhine.[50]

THE DEVELOPMENT OF A GENDERED ETHNIC CONSCIOUSNESS

Rome provided late eighteenth-century writers and artists with a potent but highly ambivalent stock of female images. They understood their 'unamiability', self-harming proclivities and their state of legal bondage, as well as their incessant divorces and remarriages. All of this limited the salience of Roman matrons as models for British women seeking an iconography or a language of patriotic action. Moreover, Roman matrons, and the Republic generally, were in this period becoming increasingly associated with radical Whiggism, partly through the self-presentational strategies of Macaulay and her circle, partly because of a loss of confidence in British and Roman imperial analogies after the success of the American Revolution, and still more when Robespierre's Jacobin faction of French revolutionaries adopted Roman republicanism as their official iconography.[51] British neo-classicism did not of course disappear, but lingered on as a ubiquitous cultural reflex, often only as plaster-deep as a Nash façade. But as a mode of national self-understanding it was eclipsed by a new focus upon Europe's other ancestors, such as the Gauls, Celts, Germani, Angles, Saxons and Goths. This interest was facilitated by new philological scholarship into the Welsh, Gaelic and Anglo-Saxon sources for early British history. Edmund Gibson's monumental edition of Camden's *Britannia* (1695), along with the pioneering studies of Celtic Britain by the Welsh scholar Edward Lhuyd, expanded the range of this scholarship, and publicised new archaeological evidence.[52] A good deal of scholarship was devoted to working out the origins and ethnic taxonomies of the peoples who migrated across Europe during and shortly after the Roman Empire, and to creating familial ethnic ancestries for the modern European nations. This work, as Colin Kidd argues in his *British Identities Before Nationalism*, was less motivated by racial nationalism (which comes after this period) than by a desire to establish the longevity of constitutional liberty, the national church and European cultural customs.[53] The medium-term effect of this late eighteenth-century scholarship was certainly to create hard-and-fast ethnic distinctions between 'the pragmatic, freedom-loving Teuton and the mystical, sentimental, but improvident Celt', and to pave the way for the Romantic denigration of the peoples of the Irish, Highland and Welsh Celtic fringes.[54] But before this could happen, classical and other sources would have to be sorted and disaggregated, the nomenclature of Celtic, Germanic and Gothic would have to be clarified, and the pan-Celtic identity of Ancient Britons, Welsh, Irish and Gaelic-speaking Scots would have to be established. These groupings or distinctions were not clear by the middle of the eighteenth century, but they became increasingly so by the late nineteenth. In the period under discussion here, ethnicity was understood as the collective manners of a given tribal group, with the manners relating to women, as ever, a highly significant part of the cultural evidence. Eighteenth-century writers before and after Gibbon were particularly interested in the ways in which the manners of the barbarian tribes differed from those of the Romans. They became increasingly fascinated by the non-classical roots of their culture in the indigenous peoples of their island and in its post-Roman invaders. And, as we will see later in this chapter, they were quick to interpret the high moral tone and venerable status of modern women as the historical residue of age-old, native British tribal traditions.

ANCIENT BRITONS

Eighteenth-century readers read about their most remote ancestors, the Ancient Britons, in Caesar, Tacitus and other classical sources. Caesar's *De Bello Gallico* supplied brief ethnographic information about the inhabitants of Kent, including details of the men's hunter-gatherer way of life, their long hair and moustaches, and their woad-dyed, shaven bodies. Women, Caesar claimed, were held in common by groups of ten or twelve men ('Uxores habent . . . inter se communes'), although their children always belonged to the house in which the woman first took up residence.[55] The domestic arrangements and status of ancient British women greatly interested eighteenth-century commentators. Millar speculated that the communal arrangements described by Caesar might have reinforced a matriarchal system of lineage and power:

Among the ancient Britons we find . . . that the women were accustomed to vote in the public assemblies. The rude and imperfect institution of marriage, and the community of wives, that anciently took place in Britain, must have prevented the children from acquiring any considerable connexion with their father, and have disposed them to follow the condition of their mother, as well as to support her interest and dignity.[56]

It was thought that the Welsh were the remnant of the people described by Caesar, and that the ancient Britons were different from the Gauls and other tribes. Tacitus, in his biography (*c*.98 AD) of Agricola, the first-century governor of Britain, finds them quite distinctive as a people because of their remoteness from Rome and the recent date of their subjugation.[57] Female leaders were not uncommon since, to quote from Thomas Gordon's very popular translation of Tacitus' works, 'in conferring Sovereignty [the Britons] make no distinction of sexes'.[58] The story of the greatest female leader, Boadicea, and her rebellion against the Romans is told in book 14 of Tacitus' *Annals*. He presents her as a terrifying figure who leads her people and their confederates in an orgy of sacking and slaughter before she is defeated and kills herself with poison. She does all this, however, not merely for power, but to avenge the violated sexual honour of her daughters and the lashing she received from rogue Roman centurions. Tacitus puts into her mouth a troop-rousing speech in which she declares that she 'sought vengeance for the extirpation of publick liberty, for the stripes inflicted upon her person, for the brutish defilement of her virgin daughters . . .'[59] A later, less well-known source in Greek was Cassius Dio's *Roman History*, which is more preoccupied with the implications of Boadicea's sovereignty as a woman, but which paints her as an intelligent and similarly terrifying figure: 'she was very tall, in appearance most terrifying, in the glance of her eye most fierce, and her voice was harsh'.[60] Boadicea is a prophetess, a fiery orator and the instigator of terrible atrocities against Romano-British men and women. As a figure for liberty and female courage, but also as a site of British cultural ambivalence about female violence, Boadicea enjoyed considerable currency in the seventeenth and eighteenth centuries, and her legacy has been explored by Jodi Mikalachki and Carolyn Williams.[61] Richard Glover, an oppositional Whig poet, published *A Short History of Boadicea, The British Queen* (1754), in which she is portrayed as a glorious figure of

liberty struggling against foreign subjection.[62] The history was the basis
for a play in which Boadicea appears as heroic, but somewhat blood-
thirsty, and given to inflicting horrible torture on prisoners.[63] Boadicea
had, since John Fletcher's play *Bonduca* (1609) (adapted by George
Colman in 1778), long been a stage emblem for Britain's proud, non-
Roman cultural identity. There were other female figures in this
repertoire. In Ambrose Philips's tragedy *The Briton* (1722), another British
queen, Cartisand (Cartimandua) of the northern tribe of the Brigantes,
connives treacherously with the Romans. She justifies her actions to her
Roman ally, citing the difference between herself as a politically active
British woman and the more passive Roman women:

> Am I unfit to share in all your Counsels?
> Or, Is this Treaty no Concern of mine?
> What? Do you take me for a *Roman* Matron;
> Bred tamely to the Spindle and the Loom?
> Are these the Business of a *British* Queen? [64]

The subject of Cartimandua was revisited by William Mason in his
play *Caractacus, A Dramatic Poem* (1759), which (with input from
Thomas Gray) tells the story of Caradoc the Welsh king betrayed by
Cartimandua, and features a chorus of female Druids.

Boadicea enjoyed a vigorous afterlife, from the late eighteenth century
onwards, as a figure of national resistance and courage in adversity (not
least in William Cowper's famous poem 'Boadicea', 1782). In the eighteenth century, her military leadership linked her, both culturally and
to a degree ethnically, to other warrior women of the ancient non-Roman
peoples. These peoples, as Colin Kidd has explained, were seen as being
more closely connected than they were by Roman writers such as Caesar
and Tacitus, because seventeenth-century philologists had identified a
'Scytho-Celtic' language family, to which they thought nearly all of the
western European tongues belonged.[65] This led scholars to posit a
common ethnic origin and cultural identity for nearly all non-Slavic
Europeans, including the Gothic and Celtic peoples, and enabled them
to draw upon such diverse sources as Caesar's account of the Gauls
('Celtae') in *De Bello Gallico* and Tacitus' description of the Germanic
tribes in the *Germania* or of the Caledonians in his *Agricola*. Among the
modern scholars, one of the most important was the German Philippus
Cluverius, author of the *Germania Antiqua* (1616). His work set the tone
for others by devoting two chapters to the condition of women in ancient
Europe ('De conjugio, et amore fideque conjugali' and 'De mulierum

partu, liberorum educatione'), and was quite effusive on the subject of the traditions, handed down to modern times by some of the early Europeans, of female virtue and monogamous marriage.[66] This was followed, among many other subsequent works, by Simon Pelloutier's popular *Histoire des Celtes* (1750), which painted a composite picture of the ancient 'Celts' as blond, blue-eyed and heavy-drinking, with a passion for warfare and a love of liberty even stronger among the women than among the men ('encore plus ardentes à défendre la liberté').[67] Among the philologists, Lhuyd had discovered, in the very early part of the century, affinities among the Celtic language family of Welsh, Irish Gaelic and Scots Gaelic, but not until the work of Thomas Percy in the 1770s would this form the basis for differentiating them in terms of ethnic origin from Britain's Teutonic ancestors.[68] Earlier, however, there was some pressure, applied particularly after the Jacobite Rebellion of 1745, for a rudimentary account of the origins of the different peoples of the British isles, if only to explain ideological differences between them. One can discern the beginnings of this process in the *General History of England* (1747–55) by the Jacobite historian Thomas Carte, who accepted the 'Scytho-Celtic' formulation that the Germani were Celts in origin, but who nevertheless (and with differences between Highlanders and English Anglo-Saxons in mind) emphasised the ways in which the two ancient cultures had diverged. A telling point of divergence, for Carte, was the important public role accorded to women by the ancient Celts:

It was common to them . . . that their women, were as much distinguished for their courage as the men; accompanied them to the field; animated them to the combat; and often rushed themselves undaunted, though unarmed, into the midst of the battle, catching at the swords of the enemy: *But it was peculiar to the Celtic nations not to march, move, or fight, without the advice of the women*, to constitute them judges of the contraventions of public treaties and the laws of nations; to admit them to their councils of war; and to consult them on the most important occasions of public concern [my italics].[69]

Carte has in mind the ancient Caledonians, ancestors of modern-day Gaelic-speaking Highlanders, and his emphasis upon the status of women as a key point of difference between the ancestral peoples of Britain would find many echoes in the late eighteenth-century romanticisation of the Highlands.

Questions relating to the origins of the Highland people were given topicality by the '45, and imaginative depth by the publication, from the 1760s, of James Macpherson's Ossian poems. Macpherson's ethnic genealogies owed much to the work of his clansman John Macpherson, who, in his *Critical Dissertations on the Origin . . . of the Ancient Caledonians* (1768), argued that the Caledonians (and their descendants, the Picts) arrived in Scotland as a result of the migration of Celtic tribes from south Britain and ultimately from Gaul. Scotland, which he says was later invaded by the Scots in the ninth century, is thus a thoroughly Celtic, rather than a Germanic, country.[70] John Macpherson's work shows how contemporary Scottish conjectural theory could be harnessed to regional patriotism, as for example when he cites the fact that the ancient Caledonians were a pastoral people as sufficient evidence against the accusations of wife-sharing made by some historians: 'Chastity', he insists, 'is one of the great virtues of rude life: when the soul is active, it seldom sinks into shameful enormities.'[71] Chastity is certainly conspicuous among the virtues of the heroines of the Ossian poems, as well as female courage equal to that of Roman matrons. The public's first taste of the Ossianic literary corpus, the *Fragments of Ancient Poetry* of 1760, tells how Oscur, Ossian's son, tricks his mistress, the daughter of Dargo, into killing him with her bow and arrow, and how she commits suicide immediately afterwards: 'Oscur! I have the blood, the soul of the mighty Dargo. Well pleased I can meet death. My sorrow I can end thus . . .'[72] The success of the *Fragments*, some of which dramatised ancient Caledonian female voices, led to the publication of two full-length epics, *Fingal* (1761–2) and *Temora* (1765), along with other Ossianic pieces, all created by Macpherson from the raw materials of Highland oral tradition, and the Ulster and Fionn cycles of early Gaelic literature. All of these feature women of strong emotions and high courage, lamenting their dead, urging their men to battle, and, on many occasions, taking control of their destinies by disguising themselves, pursuing their lovers and befriending their enemies. *Fingal* features Agandecca, who falls for her enemy Fingal, warns him of a trap to kill him and is killed for her betrayal of her people. Inibaca wins Fingal's great-grandfather Trenmor, by dressing up as a warrior, challenging him to a fight, and then revealing herself: ' "I first will lay my mail on earth. – Throw now thy dart, thou king of Morven". He saw the heaving of her breast . . .'[73] In book four of *Temora*, there is the story of Sul-malla, who disguises herself as a warrior, follows her lover Cathmor, Fingal's enemy, to war, and tries unsuccessfully to persuade him to sue for peace, only to encounter his ghost at the end of the poem. In a separate poem, *Oithona*, the heroine is abducted and raped, but by disguising herself as a man contrives her own death during a revenge attack on her rapist and his forces.

Very soon after the publication of *Fingal*, the women, manners and men of the Ossianic corpus were influentially interpreted and rendered intelligible according to a conjectural-historical scheme by Hugh Blair in his *Critical Dissertation on the Poems of Ossian* (1763). Blair was an Edinburgh University colleague of Robertson and a friend of Hume and Smith. He soon revised the *Dissertation* to take account of *Temora*, and it was appended to most editions of Ossian thereafter. Blair's *Dissertation* offered both a literary discussion and a conjectural-historical analysis of the Ossian poems as emanating from the first, hunter-gatherer stage of society.[74] Blair shows how the hunter-gatherer context of the poems accounts for many of their cultural features, but he also overlays and complicates his four-stage scheme with an innovative examination of the relationship between tribal ethnicity and manners. He identifies the poems as the work of a distinctively *Celtic* people, kin to the Gauls described by Caesar but quite different from Gothic or Germanic peoples: 'the ancient Scots were of Celtic original . . . The Celtae, a great and mighty people, altogether distinct from the Goths and Teutones, once extended their dominion over all the west of Europe.'[75] The Ossianic corpus enables Blair, in advance of Percy's work, to distinguish the Celtic from other peoples hitherto conflated by scholars and philologists, and to attribute particular qualities to them, notably a love of poetry, and bravery tempered by tenderness and sensibility.[76] That sensibility provides the basis for the affecting love stories in the poems, and for the representation of female characters generally. Blair devotes a long section to the romantic stories of 'women who follow their lovers to war disguised in the armour of men', marvels at the way, even in the racier passages, the poems preserve a sense of 'tender and exquisite propriety' and speculates that chivalry had its origins in the works of the Celtic bards.[77] He contrasts this with the 'ferocity of manners' to be found among the Scandinavian people of that time, whom he identifies as specifically Teutonic, not Celtic, in origin, and of whom he remarks: 'even their women are bloody and fierce'.[78]

Despite Blair's efforts, the Ossian poems were mired in controversy from the outset. Part of the scepticism that greeted them related to what seemed to some observers the implausible propriety of the women that populated the poems. Elizabeth Montagu wrote to Lord Kames of her doubts as to whether the manners of the hunter stage could really have been as Ossian depicted them:

Can one imagine politeness of manners began before even agriculture? Does Nature operate in other modes in Scotland, than in the rest of the world? . . . – as to myself, I credited Ossian the more, because I do not see any thing in his poems inconsistent with uncivilized times. The heroes are brave in the field, hospitable and courteous at a feast. They were not cruel, as absolute savages are . . . I do not understand . . . how great delicacy of manners subsisted, where all men and women of a family undressed and slept in the same apartment.[79]

The same year as Montagu's sceptical letter, Macpherson published *An Introduction to the History of Great Britain and Ireland* (1771), a work that fleshes out Blair's ethnic speculations, and establishes the origins and ethnic character of the Celtic-Caledonian heroes and heroines celebrated by the bard Ossian. Building on the work of John Macpherson, he argued that the Scottish Gaels ('fierce, passionate, and impetuous . . . in private life plain and upright in their dealings') are the remnant of the earliest wave of migration from Celtic Gaul through England and into the north.[80] Macpherson, as Kidd has pointed out, drew eclectically from sources relating to the ancient Celts and the Germani (notably Tacitus). But he did also distinguish, in ethnic terms, between the Scottish people (of Caledonian descent) and the English Sassenach (originally of Gothic descent).[81] He was also, in my reading, more eager than Kidd allows to separate out the Celtic from the Gothic cultural heritage. To this end, he cited the magnificence of the Celtic-Caledonian women as evidence for their distinctive ethnic heritage: 'Their women did not yield to the men in stature, and they almost equalled them in strength of body and in vigour of mind . . . Their long yellow hair flowed carelessly down their shoulders, and their large blue eyes animated their looks into a kind of ferocity less apt to kindle love than to command respect and awe.'[82]

Moreover, he emphasised the active participation of Celtic women in the public life of the tribe in ways that not only complicated Scottish conjectural-historical accounts of the earliest stages of society, but that also implied that, in the modern world, one anaemic (mainly Anglo-Saxon) kind of femininity has been allowed to eclipse other, more assertive ones:

In modern Europe, a fictitious respect is paid to women, in the ancient they possessed real consequence and power. They were not chained to the distaff, or confined to the trivial cares of domestic life. They entered into the active scenes of public affairs, and, with a masculine spirit, shared the dangers and fatigues of the field with their husbands and friends . . . The picture we have drawn will not probably please the refined ideas of the present times. But the high spirits of the Celtic women gave them more influence over our ancestors than our modern beauties derive from all their elegant timidity and delicacy of manners.[83]

This is a stern rebuff to cherished contemporary notions of delicate and modest womanhood, and to the Lowland Scottish notion of culturally influential femininity. Macpherson's Ossian poems are sometimes regarded by modern critics as something of a sop to the eighteenth-century British appetite for a polite literature of origins, a nostalgic or sentimental safety-valve in a culture of modernisation.[84] But here, at least, is a decisive rejection of polite, modern femininity, and a Highland defence of women's active, civic participation.

Other Scottish writers followed Ossian's lead. In the same year as Macpherson's *Introduction*, another Scottish historian, Robert Henry, produced an account of Celtic manners and women that calls into question Roman allegations of polygamy or wife-sharing among the Celtic nations: 'These brave, rough, unpolished nations treated their women with much attention and respect, as the objects of their highest esteem and most sincere affection', he remarks before quoting Ossian extensively on the subject of 'high-bosomed' Caledonian maids.[85] Macpherson's argument that Britain's Celtic and Anglo-Saxon heritages were separate and culturally distinct, however indiscriminately sourced, was corroborated by the publication around the same time of Thomas Percy's *Northern Antiquities* (1770). Percy's work was a translation of a history of Denmark by the Swiss explorer Paul-Henri Mallet, written fifteen years earlier, but he added his own, ground-breaking preface, in which he argued definitively that the ancient Celtic and Germanic nations were entirely separate and had little in common.[86] Percy's work confirmed Macpherson's idea of Celtic difference, and did not challenge his passionately held conviction that the Scots were originally all one people. The challenge to this notion, and with it the beginnings of an ethnic ghetto for Scottish Gaels, came later, in the 1780s, from a Scottish antiquarian called John Pinkerton. Pinkerton had a great number of languages and source materials at his command, and was, for political reasons, intent on proving that the Pictish ancestors of the Lowland Scots were Germanic rather than Celtic. Pinkerton drew explicitly *racial* distinctions between the Gothic/Lowland and Celtic/Highland strains of the Scottish nation. He was one of the first British writers in the century to do so, and his work was to have important consequences for subsequent modes of racial analysis, as well as an incidental effect on the historical classification of women.[87] In his *Dissertation on the Origin and Progress of the Scythians or Goths* (1787), Pinkerton argues that the tribes known to the ancient Greeks as the 'Scythians' were, in fact, the ancestors of the northern peoples known to the Romans as the Germani. These 'Goths' were, he says, 'a distinct, peculiar, and marked people', known for their hospitality, generosity, courage and learning (he does not mention the stories in Herodotus about the blood-drinking, scalping, Amazon-slaying habits of the Central-Asian Scythians).[88] Europe, he claims, is descended from four original but unequal races, the magnificent Scythians, the Iberi, the Sarmatae and the inferior Celts 'who were to the other races what the savages of America are to the European settlers'.[89] In support of this assertion he adds, 'if any foreigner doubts this, he has only to step into the Celtic part of Wales, Ireland, or Scotland, and look at them, for they are just as they were, incapable of industry or civilisation'.[90] One sure sign of the racial inferiority of the Celts is the way they treat their women: 'the Celts were the only nation who despised women, as appears also from the Welsh and Irish histories, and their present practice; while the Germani, as Tacitus observes, paid such respect to the sex, as almost to adore them'.[91]

In defiance of many of the written sources, Pinkerton dismisses the notion of the high status or heroism of Celtic women. He later repented the virulence of his hostility towards the Celts. Yet his work allows us to see the centrality of gender ascriptions to the ever more strict enforcement of racial divisions between Anglo-Saxons and Celts that would occur in the next century, and the denigration of the latter.[92] Celtic women ceased to embody ideals of female bravery and public power, even though they retained Ossianic characteristics of tender feeling, romantic recklessness and tragic self-destructiveness.

GOTHIC WOMEN AND AFFECTIVE PATRIOTISM

The establishment, from the 1770s, of a separate ethnic identity for Britain's Gothic ancestors was highly significant, both for the country's evolving perception of its internal, regional hierarchies and for its sense of kinship with the peoples of Europe. The term 'Gothic' was used by seventeenth- and eighteenth-century writers as the collective term for the tribes who overran the Roman Empire during the third century AD, although they disagreed as to whether these originally issued from Scandinavia or Germany.[93] Their attitudes towards these Germanic peoples were complex and ambivalent, since they could be regarded as both the spoilers and inheritors of the much admired Roman Empire.[94] In political discourse, a favourable attitude towards the barbarian ances-tors of the English people was associated, from the early seventeenth century, with the defence of parliament against royal absolutism. The phrase 'Gothic [or Saxon] liberty' remained a mantra for oppositional or radical political groups, until it subsided, in the early nineteenth century, into orthodoxy.[95] Later in the eighteenth century, 'Gothophilia' also took on a variety of artistic forms, and a national predilection for things 'Gothick' was accompanied by an improved scholarly understanding of the history and culture of the Germanic peoples. As we will see, most eighteenth-century writers found in the classical sources evidence for the high status of women in Gothic societies, and from this they were able to produce a genetic account of British femininity from its origins in the northern forests to its present-day drawing-room splendour.

Most of the classical sources on the Goths (Procopius, Paul the Deacon, Isidore of Seville, Cassiodorus, Caesar, Tacitus and Jordanes) which we know today were read by eighteenth-century scholars, although many of them were imperfectly understood. They were available in separate editions or in compilations such as Hugo Grotius's *Historia Gotthorum, Vandalorum et Langobardorum* (1655), a work that featured a long prolegomenon drawing attention to, among many other things, these peoples' great reverence for matrimony.[96] Most of the sources recognised, to some degree, the virtues and courage of the northern peoples. Indeed, it was an article of Roman, and particularly of late Romano-Christian, political correctness to extol the sexual virtues of the Goths and to contrast them favourably with the moral turpitude of the imperial Romans.[97] The myth of Gothic uxoriousness and sexual virtue was most fully articulated in Tacitus' late first-century work known as *De Moribus Germanorum* or the *Germania*.[98] In Tacitus' account (here translated by Thomas Gordon) Germanic women are brave and goad their men into battle. Marriage itself accustoms them to a life of warfare:

That the woman may not suppose herself free from the considerations of fortitude and fighting, or exempt from the casualties of War, the very first solemnities of her wedding serve to warn her, that she comes to her husband as a partner in his hazards and fatigues, that she is to suffer alike with him, to adventure alike, during peace or during war.[99]

Chastity ('pudicitia') before marriage is strictly observed by both sexes. Marriage occurs relatively late in youth and is never treated lightly: 'the laws of matrimony are severely observed there; nor in the whole of their manners is aught more praise-worthy than this'.[100] Unlike Roman marriages, women bring no dowry. Rather, it is the husband who offers presents to his wife, though these are not 'adapted to feminine pomp and delicacy, nor such as serve to deck the new married woman', but practical items such as livestock and weapons.[101] Punishments for adultery and fornication are harsh, even barbaric. Fortunately, however, monogamous marriages require few legal sanctions since sexual virtue is strongly enforced at the cultural level: 'And more powerful with them are good manners [Gordon's translation of 'mores'], than with other People are good Laws.'[102]

Many eighteenth-century commentators were struck by the link between the monogamous, permanent, un-Roman form of marriage of the Germanic tribes, and the unusually courageous and chaste character of the women. Germanic women, it was generally agreed, were quite unlike Roman women: their virtue distinguished them from the decadent creatures of the Empire, but their self-discipline and active involvement also differed, in quality and kind, from that of Roman republican women. Republican women demonstrated their courage by subordinating, in an almost unnatural way, private feelings to the good of the state. The Roman woman who, on hearing that a battle has ended, was more likely to ask, not 'is my husband alive?', but 'did we win?' represented, to the eighteenth-century mind, a heroic perversion of feminine nature. For Germanic women, however, private feelings and public loyalties were one. According to Tacitus, they would come out to the edge of the battlefield to encourage their men as they fought, and in this way, family feelings and tribal loyalties interlocked and reinforced each other. This model of affective patriotism, which assigned to women a public role as the brave companions, helpmates and cheerers-on of men, proved far more attractive to eighteenth-century writers than the alternative models of Roman female heroism or Celtic female warriorship. Even before Germanic and Celtic ethnicities were clearly discriminated, the virtuous character of Germanic women was associated with a Saxon-Gothic myth of British nationhood and freedom.[103] A considerable challenge to the old myth of Gothic virtue might have come, in the mid eighteenth century, from the theoretical model of conjectural history, which assimilated the Goths and their gender relations to the harsh realities of the pastoral stage. Most of the Germanic and Gothic peoples described in the classical sources were herdsmen and hunters, but their mores, and in particular their treatment of their women, conformed very little to the eighteenth-century image of the pastoral stage. Some Scottish writers nevertheless tried to make these peoples fit into a conjectural model of social evolution. Millar insisted that the Germani were fundamentally similar to all other barbarian nations since they entertained 'the same notions . . . concerning the inferiority of the woman' as other people in a state of barbarism.[104] Others, however, made allowances for an unusual case. Kames, for instance, applauded Germanic sexual virtue as something quite exceptional among barbarians, although he put the difference down to the temperate northern climate: 'Among them, women were from the beginning courted and honour'd, nor was polygamy ever known among them.'[105] Alexander was, in his incoherent way, at a loss to account for the chastity which 'became almost an innate principle' in the German female mind; it unsettled his conjectural model of history, although it did not prevent him from expressing his distaste for the 'mixture of pride and ferocity' in the nature of the Germanic women which he considered 'not very consistent with that female softness and delicacy which the men in general so much admire'.[106]

The fullest consideration of the tension between conjectural and ethno-centric accounts of the Germanic tribes and their women came from Gibbon, writing very much in the Scottish tradition, but with a sceptical and libertine emphasis all his own. Gibbon devotes the ninth chapter of *The Decline and Fall* to 'The State of Germany . . . in the Time of Decius', before proceeding to a long narrative section on the ravages of the barbarians on the Roman Empire from the middle of the third century AD. The chapter derives almost all its information from the *Germania*, which is then subtly contextualised within a theoretical notion of 'the progress of civilisation'.[107] This theory of progress is partly indebted to, and partly critical of, Scottish ideas.[108] Gibbon also seeks to undermine the historical basis of the kind of politically motivated Gothicism which, in his own day, linked the origins of modern 'Gothic liberty' to the forests of the north. Goths and Germani, he observes dismissively, were essentially barbarians, and their way of life should not be moralised or sentimentalised: 'They passed their lives in a state of ignorance and poverty, which it has pleased some declaimers to dignify with the appellation of virtuous simplicity.'[109] In respect of their ignorance, poverty and hunter-gatherer mode of subsistence, Gibbon agrees with Millar and Robertson that the Germani were largely typical of tribes at the earliest stage of social evolution, especially in respect of their 'carelessness of futurity'.[110] However, Gibbon has to reckon with one aspect of Tacitus' account that could not be accommodated to the Scottish mode of sociological reasoning: the high status and chastity of the Germanic women. According to Smith, Robertson and others, deferral and sublimation of sexual gratification is one of the main mechanisms of the civilising process, bringing with it improvements in the sexual autonomy and, hence, status of women. Yet, because the Germanic tribeswomen were clearly not sex objects or slaves, this particular ethnic group, Gibbon concedes, did not conform to the normal progress of civilisation: 'The sentiments and conduct of these high-spirited matrons may, at once, be considered as a cause, as an effect, and as a proof of the general character of the nation.'[111] This is deliberately ambiguous, as though Gibbon is unwilling to reconcile his idea of refinement as a taste for deferred, rather than immediate, pleasures, with the fact of Germanic sexual restraint.

This ambiguity is linked to Gibbon's general unconcern about female purity, especially in those whom he admires, such as Julia Domna or the Empress Theodora.[112] At a more fundamental level, *The Decline and Fall* demonstrates that gender and sexual morality are historical variables which cannot be mapped, in a schematic way, on to the progress of society.[113] The Germanic people, women as well as men, are emphatically masculine, even super-masculine, and their women, although their courage could only be 'a faint and imperfect imitation of manly valour', exhibit more masculinity than femininity: 'Whilst they affected to emulate the stern virtues of *man*, they must have resigned that attractive softness in which principally consist the charm and weakness of *woman*.'[114] Scottish writers argued that the historical acquisition of attractive feminine qualities by women was the only means by which women could, in their phrase, 'acquire esteem' and hence a modicum of power. Gibbon agrees that femininity is an acquired female characteristic, but effectively refutes the notion that this is the only, or even the most effective, means to female power. The remark on the lofty stature of the Germanic women recalls Gibbon's comment, in a summary section at the end of the second chapter, that 'the Roman world was indeed peopled by a race of pygmies; when the fierce giants of the north broke in, and mended the puny breed. They restored a manly spirit of freedom . . .'[115] The northern incursions which hastened the downfall of the Roman Empire are imagined as a rape, or a brutal, yet ultimately fertile, encounter between the surplus masculinity of the men and women of the north and the deficient and diminutive masculinity and femininity of the south. Gibbon confirms that the 'most civilized nations of modern Europe issued from the woods of Germany, and in the rude institutions of those barbarians we may still distinguish the original principles of our present laws and manners.'[116] There is, then, a line of ethnic continuity between early, Germanic tribal society and modern Europe, albeit one that for Gibbon has entailed a decline in the power, prestige and, indeed, 'masculinity' of women.

Other writers before and after Gibbon sought to defend the notion that there was something exceptional about the Gothic ancestors of British women that did not fit with preconceptions about the earliest stages of society. Mallet's work on the ancient Scandinavians pointed the way forward. In a prefatory volume to his translation of the *Edda* and other Old Norse pieces, Mallet discussed the unique character of gender relations among Gothic peoples, their strict sexual morality and the 'naturally chaste and proud' behaviour of the women.[117] In Britain, one of the first writers besides Gibbon to consider the new northern antiquarian studies as a complicating factor for conjectural theory was Gilbert Stuart. Stuart was a Scot, but personally hostile to Robertson and his circle, and sceptical about the kinds of history they were writing.[118] His major work, *A View of Society in Europe* (1778), is, for the most part, an extended essay on the history of women in the Dark and Middle Ages (it is a measure of the importance accorded, by the late eighteenth century, to the gender dimension of history that Stuart felt able to claim that this did, indeed, constitute a 'view' of 'society' in Europe).

The work was moderately successful during and after Stuart's lifetime.[119] Stuart's main purpose was to mount a critique of the Scottish idea of social progress by providing an alternative, conjectural history of romantic love. In his historical scheme, the Middle Ages represents the high point of relations between the sexes, whereas the modern age bears witness to their subsequent decay. Stuart used the historical category of gender to subvert received Scottish wisdom about the progress of society, and posited instead a more ethnocentric reading of European history in terms of the distinctiveness and persistence of its Gothic heritage. In particular, a section of Stuart's *A View of Society*, entitled 'An Idea of the German Woman', takes issue with the Scottish Enlightenment idea that women are always locked away in pastoral societies. Germanic women, he argues, were well respected, and enjoyed a high degree of freedom and public influence: 'They went to the public councils or assemblies of their nations, heard the debates of the statesmen, and were called upon to deliver their sentiments.'[120] This influence proceeded from the unique form of Germanic marriage, which was based on the natural affections: 'The fidelity of the married women among these nations, and the constancy and tenderness of their attachment, express also their equality with the men and their importance.'[121] Reciprocal constancy and tenderness were elicited from the men by the 'reserve and coyness of [the women's] demeanour', and their unusual 'modesty'.[122] They were also, in times of peace, 'studious to recommend themselves by the performance of domestic duties'.[123]

These different aspects of the lives of Germanic women – their public influence, their affectionate, monogamous marriages, their coy modesty, and their primarily domestic role – might appear incongruous, but are linked by an underlying concept of Germanic affective patriotism. Stuart goes on to argue, in a section on the age of chivalry, that women's public influence continued to increase as their high status was formally institutionalised by the feudal system, and the respect paid to them by men became ever more exaggerated: 'Concerned in great affairs, they were agitated with great passions. They prospered whatever was most noble in our nature, generosity, public virtue, humanity, prowess.'[124] He then shows how the Gothic model of affective patriotism had tangible material benefits for women in terms of their property rights, and their ability to inherit and acquire wealth and social authority.[125] In this respect, Stuart was nearer the mark than many of his Scottish contemporaries, since the waning of the Middle Ages did, indeed, coincide with a deterioration in the legal rights, and material and social status of women.[126] However, Stuart's moralising tendencies get the better of his feminism when he argues, towards the end, that modern women's infidelity and licentiousness are the cause of their reduced power and influence. His work does not, finally, add up to a compelling case for female civil or property rights, but it tries to remind its readers of a deep vein of Germanic feminism in British culture that, he seems to hope, will be rediscovered and revived.

THE GOTHIC ROOTS OF CHIVALRY

Despite Stuart's enthusiasm, Gothic woman remained in the eighteenth century a somewhat ambiguous figure: a virtuous wife, yet active and courageous in the public life of the tribe, she represented Britain's growing confidence in the distinctiveness of its European heritage, as well as a degree of uncertainty about the appropriate national model of femininity. The high status and affective patriotism of Britain's Gothic female ancestors might have remained little more than a curiosity were it not for the fact that this phenomenon was so thoroughly integrated into an emerging new history of the Middle Ages. The contradictory aspects of Gothic woman were stabilised in the figure of her medieval descendant, the woman of chivalry. The woman of chivalry retained many of the best features of Gothic woman – her chastity, her high status as the repository of society's identity and values, the veneration she elicited from men – whilst outgrowing some of her more barbaric characteristics, such as physical strength and courage, or her sacramental role in pagan worship.

The story of the historical recovery and rising prestige of the medieval institution of chivalry, and, its eventual installation, in the Victorian period, as a major constituent of national historical consciousness may be a familiar one. But I will attempt, during the remaining part of this chapter, to place women at its centre both as a historical category and as writers, and to connect this new, gendered way of imagining past and present society with the developing British ethnic self-awareness described above. Walter Scott claimed in his famous *Encyclopaedia Britannica* article on chivalry of 1818 that 'the defence of the female sex . . . the regard due to their honour, the subservience paid to their commands' constituted 'the very essence' of chivalry.[127] Chivalry, as it was redis-covered and reformulated in the late eighteenth to early nineteenth centuries, was primarily and essentially an account of relations between the sexes that came to be seen as paradigmatic of social relations generally, including relations across the class divisions of the early industrial revolution, and those between metropolitan and peripheral British and colonial cultures. In the revived discourses of chivalry, we also see the beginnings of the rewriting of conjectural history, in the nineteenth century, as the domestic history of British liberty, and the disintegration of the Enlightenment connection between mixed-gender sociability and social progress.

Byron dismissed chivalry as one of the 'monstrous mummeries of the middle ages', but by the time he was writing the return of the Middle Ages was everywhere visible in art, architecture and literature.[128] The new age of chivalry reached its literary high-water mark in the 1820s with the publication of Scott's *Ivanhoe* (1820 [1819]) and *The Talisman* (1825) and Laetitia Landon's *The Troubadour* (1825), accompanied by historical works such as Charles Mills's *History of Chivalry* (1825) and Kenelm Digby's *The Broad Stone of Honour: Rules for the Gentlemen of England* (1822–3). The fascination with chivalry and chivalric activity did not fade, and as late as 1890 John Batty published *The Spirit and Influence of Chivalry*, equating chivalry with Christian self-sacrifice. Remarkably, Joseph Strutt's highly original *The Sports and Pastimes of the People of England* (1802), featuring large sections on medieval tournaments and ladies' pastimes, remained in print until the early twentieth century. The process of cultural and literary recovery started around the 1760s with the publication of the *Letters on Chivalry and Romance* (1762) by the clergyman and scholar Richard Hurd. Hurd presented a series of sketches of late medieval life, and tried to give his readers a sense of the coherence of the apparently disparate political and cultural practices associated with chivalry. Chivalry, Hurd argues here, was 'no absurd and freakish institution, but the natural and even sober effect of the feudal policy'.[129] If the 'institution' of chivalry, as Hurd calls it, had a logical political role, it was also the cultural expression of a society still in touch with its heroic, Gothic roots ('the resemblance between the heroic and Gothic ages is very great'), as well as of a certain kind of religious sensibility.[130] He claims that chivalry was the source of the 'Gothic manner' and of the romance tradition in English literature forged by Chaucer and others during the Middle Ages, and developed by Spenser and Milton. An important feature of Hurd's argument is that chivalry was, in origin, a northern, Germanic invention, and that its development went hand-in-hand with the refinement of the Gothic style of gender relations; 'the foundation of this refined gallantry', Hurd later wrote, 'was laid in the antient manners of the German nations'.[131] The ancient Germanic veneration for women and respect for chastity was formalised by the medieval knights as part of the chivalric code: 'Violations of chastity being the most atrocious crimes they had to charge on their enemies, they would pride themselves in the glory of being its protectors.'[132] The connection between the northern destroyers of the Roman Empire and the institutions of chivalry was by no means self-evident in Hurd's time, and there were many historians who believed that chivalry was originally imported from the Saracens or from the Roman *equester ordo*.[133]

On this important point, Hurd was emboldened by the work of his French predecessor, the pioneering French medievalist Jean-Baptiste La Curne de Sainte-Palaye. Sainte-Palaye was a prolific editor of medieval literary texts, the author of a study of the troubadours and of the enormously influential *Mémoires sur l'ancienne chevalerie* (1759). This work was first translated into English in 1784 by the medieval scholar Susannah Dobson, but it formed the basis of Hurd's and almost every other British account of chivalry well before then.[134] The *Memoirs* is a readable and discreetly scholarly account of chivalry as a training for knighthood, and as a sporting and military code of conduct. Sainte-Palaye drew upon a wide range of sources, both literary and factual, French and English, to create a vibrant portrait of aristocratic medieval life. Despite the emphasis upon the military and political aspects of chivalry in the title of the work, it is chivalry as an ideal and as a way of life which Sainte-Palaye communicates most engagingly.[135] He presents chivalry as a set of psychological inducements, inculcated in boys and girls from early childhood, to noble, generous actions in war and peace. Whatever its disadvantages, Sainte-Palaye insists that: 'It is certain that Chivalry . . . tended to promote order and good morals; and though in some respects imperfect, yet it produced the most accomplished models of public valour, and of those pacific and gentle virtues, that are the ornament of domestic life.'[136]

The process of education begins for pages with contact sports and with their deprivation of 'paternal tenderness', while girls learn to clean the boys' wounds and to cherish their own honour.[137] Once the page becomes a squire or a young knight, he takes part in tournaments, described by Sainte-Palaye in lavish detail. These occasions enable the trainee knight to rehearse his military skills, and, more importantly, encourage him to make a subconscious association between his martial and sexual impulses. It is the presence of women – publicly visible yet inaccessible – which holds the key to the meaning of the tournaments: 'the knights, at the sight of beauty, softness, and the enchanting tenderness of virgin chastity, filled the universe with their valour, and echoed the praise of their mistresses, till they had disarmed the rigour of the ladies, whom they thus served'.[138]

Slowly, the ladies 'uncloathe[d] themselves' as they hand out favours to the competitors, until, at the last tourney or 'lance of the ladies', the victors are granted a kiss.[139] The experience of the tournaments as erotic display is carried over by the knights into the conduct of war, a theatre in which the 'love of glory and of the fair sex' is 'employed with success'.[140] Women gain from all this as the objects of dedicated knightly protection and veneration, although ladies of bad reputation are publicly shunned.[141] Over and above the pleasures of antiquarian rediscovery, Sainte-Palaye had a conservative political purpose which was directed towards the moral regeneration of French aristocratic youth. He sought to remind the eighteenth-century French *noblesse d'épée* of their heroic Germanic and medieval ancestry, and so to renew their confidence in themselves as a governing class.[142] This aspect of the *Memoirs* would have been of little interest to British audiences, but they were receptive to Sainte-Palaye's general point about the Germanic (as opposed to Saracen) origins of chivalry and romance, and would probably also have welcomed his wider message of social moral renewal. Susannah Dobson commented in the preface to her translation of the *Memoirs* that she, too, was convinced of the benefits of the lessons of chivalry for 'the youth of both sexes'.[143] Dobson herself later gave a lengthy account of chivalry in her *Historical Anecdotes of Heraldry and Chivalry* (1795), citing Tacitus as evidence for its Germanic origins, and commenting favourably on its influence upon the morals of medieval society.[144]

An early British enthusiast for Sainte-Palaye's work was George, Baron Lyttelton, by the 1760s a semi-retired politician and close friend of Elizabeth Montagu. Lyttelton's *History of the Life of King Henry the Second* (1767–71) is a monumental work of scholarship, largely oblivious or hostile to Enlightenment methodologies, but receptive to antiquarian works such as the *Mémoires sur l'ancienne chevalerie*. Lyttelton's work was, for its time, a somewhat old-fashioned work of scholarly narrative, with very few of the usual mid eighteenth-century digressions on manners, customs and laws, except for a brief ethnographic section on the manners and marriage practices of the medieval Welsh and Irish peoples.[145] However, in the second volume, Lyttelton does give a detailed account of the origins and function of chivalry in which he credits the institution with the preservation of 'virtue and sense of humanity' in times of violence. He is refreshingly sceptical about how conducive chivalry was either to the 'improvement of the intellectual faculties' or to female chastity.[146] Even so, Lyttelton does believe (citing Sainte-Palaye) that the prestige of women was enhanced by the way that young knights were trained 'to make the passion of love an incitement to valour'.[147] Lyttelton's history was, in part, the result of intellectual collaboration with Montagu. She too was a little suspicious of modern philosophical history of the kind produced by Hume or Voltaire, and Lyttelton's work better conformed to her idea of serious history.[148] She had a long-standing, deep admiration for medieval chivalry, but, like Lyttelton, she was also sceptical about its moral tendencies.[149] She took note of Hurd's *Letters on Chivalry and Romance* as soon as it came out, but wrote to Carter of her continuing preference for the manners of the ancient world:

Mr Hurde supposes that Homer would have preferr'd the manners of the Western World in the days of Chivalry, to those of the age he wrote of: but I must own I cannot agree with him. Those who write from nature write for posterity. Those who describe men as form'd by customs, & inspired by some fanaticism, when those customs and opinions are worn out, seem to have follow'd the suggestions of their fancy, & the reveries of a wild imagination.[150]

Earlier, she placed much the same sentiments in the mouth of Plutarch in one of the *Dialogues of the Dead* (1760) that she contributed to Lyttelton's hugely successful publication of the same name.[151] Both Lyttelton and Montagu offered some resistance to what would soon become a gathering tide of enthusiasm for medieval models of womanhood. Like Montagu, Lyttelton was personally committed to an ideal of rational female education. Back in 1735 in his popular *Letters from a Persian*, he had written that 'in a Country, where the Women are admitted to a familiar and constant Share in every active Scene of Life, particular Care shou'd be taken in their Education, to cultivate their Reason, and form their Hearts, that they may be equal to the Part they have to Act'.[152]

Whatever Lyttelton and Montagu's doubts about the usefulness of chivalry as a model for modern virtue, she, at least, saw it as inevitable that after Hurd's publication 'the gothick Muses will be more honoured than of late'.[153] Percy's edition of Mallet's *Northern Antiquities* followed Sainte-Palaye and Hurd, and he celebrated chivalry as the historical fruition of the best aspects of Gothic manners:

the ideas of chivalry prevailed long before in all the Gothic nations, and may be discovered in embryo in the customs, manners, and opinions of every branch of that people. That fondness for going in quest of adventures, that spirit of challenging to single combat, and that respectful complaisance to the fair sex (so different from the manners of the Greeks and Romans) all are of Gothic origin.[154]

Percy was not greatly concerned with questions of medieval women beyond presenting them as scrubbed-up, toned-down versions of their Gothic ancestors. He was far more interested in chivalry as an explanatory framework for a new and revolutionary kind of literary criticism through which he aimed to reinstate non-classical genres and modes, such as romance, within the canon of British literature. Some eighteenth-century studies of Gothic as an aesthetic category, for example Clara Reeve's *The Progress of Romance* (1785), largely ignored the question of chivalry as a system of gender relations, even though they often gendered Gothic as a feminine, fantasy element in art.[155] By contrast, the great literary scholar Thomas Warton devoted a great deal of attention to the cultural conditions and gendered manners which gave rise to medieval literature. To the first volume of his *History of English Poetry* (1774), Warton prefixed a detailed essay 'Of the Origin of Romantic Fiction in Europe'.[156] His aim was to provide a scholarly context for courtly romance, which he regarded, not simply as a set of conventions, but as a window on to the medieval system of gender relations known as 'gallantry'. In the essay he approaches literature as a source of cultural information, and in this way he sees the extravagantly deferential demeanour of the knights towards their ladies in courtly literature as a mirror of medieval social conventions.

Warton does acknowledge that courtly romance was partly oriental in origin, but infers a more fundamental indebtedness to Norse saga from the cultural similarities between the Goths of the Dark Ages and the medieval

Europeans. Of these similarities, none is more indicative to him of this northern line of continuity than the treatment and status of women:

There is no peculiarity which more strongly discriminates the manners of the Greeks and Romans from those of modern times, than that small degree of attention and respect with which those nations treated the fair sex . . . No sooner was the Roman empire overthrown, and the Goths had overpowered Europe, than we find the female character assuming an unusual importance and author- ity, and distinguished with new privileges, in all the European governments established by the northern conquerors . . . This perhaps is one of the most striking features in the new state of manners, which took place about the seventh century: and it is to this period, and to this people, that we must refer the origin of gallantry in Europe.[157]

The high status and chastity of Gothic women are thus the fount of chivalry. Warton goes on to describe in detail the later, medieval ramifi- cations of the Gothic style of gallantry. For the man, 'the passion of love acquired a degree of delicacy', whereas, for the woman, 'conscious of her own importance, affecting an air of stateliness', it was her 'pride' to preserve 'her chastity inviolate' and to be approached only 'in terms of respect and submission'.[158] Warton does not draw attention to the fact that the medieval woman of chivalry, in attracting such inordinate quan- tities of 'respect and submission', lost the political and religious status which, he tells us, she enjoyed in previous Scandinavian and Germanic societies. For Warton, as for Hurd, Mallet and Percy, the woman of chivalry represents an attenuation of the more publicly active Gothic woman. After a process of evolution, she preserves her status as chaste cultural icon, but quietly relinquishes her religious and political role. Warton calls this process the 'general growth of refinement, and the progression of civilisation'.[159] He thus claims Gothic woman as part of Britain's cultural heritage, but implies that her more martial and barbaric qualities have been filtered out by the institutions of chivalry, and by a literary tradition which celebrates her as an allegorical figure of romance.

Following the first volume of Warton's literary history, James Beattie published *The Minstrel* (1777), a poem in Spenserian stanzas on the theme of a medieval bard. This was an enormous popular success, and helped to promote a species of poetry (including Scott's *The Lay of the Last Minstrel*, 1805), dedicated to the revival of romance. Beattie explained the nature of the enterprise in an essay 'On Fable and Romance' in which he gave an overview of current medieval scholarship, placing particular emphasis upon the sexual aspects of the culture of chivalry. Having discussed the peculiar 'attention to . . . women' characteristic of Gothic peoples, Beattie examined the women of the Middle Ages, and the courtly love which they inspired:

there actually did prevail, among the women of fashion in those days, a dignity, and even a stateliness, of manner, tending to inspire the enamoured beholder with a passion compounded of love and veneration. Hence the origin of Romantick Love: which, regarding its object as something more than human, forms extravagant ideas of perfection and happiness; a passion almost peculiar to latter times; and which, in antient Greece and Rome, as well as in Asia, where the sexes lived separate, and where the condition of the female was little better than servitude, could have no place.[160]

Beattie credits the civilising mechanisms of restraint and deferred sexual gratification with the creation of certain distinctive aspects of European culture. The woman of chivalry holds the key to Europe's distinctiveness, its difference from the ancient and eastern worlds and its unique literary traditions.

CHIVALRY AND ENLIGHTENMENT

Literary critics such as Hurd, Percy and especially Warton and Beattie were in the intellectual vanguard of their day in taking forward the cautious reappraisal of medieval chivalry by Enlightenment historians into a new area of cultural history. Many contemporary historians were grudging or dismissive of chivalry, such as the Scottish historian Robert Henry, who mentioned chivalry as something 'which is now an object of ridicule'.[161] In the two volumes of his *History of England* devoted to the medieval period, Hume alluded to chivalry only in passing, saying that its 'ancient affectations' did, at least, issue in 'modern *gallantry* and the *point of honour*, which still maintain their influence'.[162] Gibbon, in a brief digression on chivalry, praised its tendency 'to refine the temper of Barbarians', but, for him, as for Hume, chivalry is mainly indicative of the ritualised cruelty and social inequality of the Middle Ages.[163] Robertson's more positive assessment, however, was both original and influential: 'The wild exploits of those romantic knights who sallied forth in quest of adventures . . . have been treated with proper ridicule', he commented, '[but] the political and permanent effects of the spirit of chivalry have been less observed.'[164] For Robertson, these 'effects' were partly the result of contact between the Crusaders and the more sophisticated Arab and Byzantine civilisations, after which chivalry became, not merely the eccentric manifestation of Europe's feudal-agricultural stage, but a force for social cohesion and progress. In particular, he felt that the 'sentiments which chivalry inspired' (including the impulse 'to protect, or to avenge women, orphans, and ecclesiatics') had exerted 'a wonderful influence on manners and conduct' from the twelfth century onwards.[165] The hints in Robertson's work were developed by Millar as he explored the psycho-social effects of the concentrations of property that tend to occur at the agricultural stage. In *The Origin of the Distinction of Ranks* he argued that, in feudal-agricultural societies where a few families own most of the landed wealth, notions of family lineage and inheritance become highly developed, and their guarantor is women's chastity before and within marriage. This means that male access to women, at least among the higher social classes, is restricted, and that desire is sublimated into idealised kinds of love. The inaccessibility of young women, along with the new military ideal of the 'gentleman', had 'a manifest tendency to heighten and improve the passion between the sexes', creating a spirit of 'romantic love and gallantry, by which the modern nations of Europe have been so much distinguished'.[166] Thus, in scarcely resourced, highly competitive agricultural societies, men's economic and sexual longings coincide in ways that provide a wider personal and social education in self-control, self-sacrifice and the benefits of delayed gratification.

Millar thought that, although the knights' chivalry was primarily an elite affair, their behaviour did have a trickle-down effect both on literary culture and on the rest of society: 'their dispositions and manner of thinking became fashionable, and were gradually diffused by the force of education and example'.[167] Other writers were more forthcoming, not only about the wider social and cultural impact of chivalry, but also about its lasting effects. Among his Scottish contemporaries, Adam Ferguson gave the most striking account of chivalry as a cultural reflex that had outlasted its roots in medieval social conventions. In his *Essay on the History of Civil Society* (1767), having argued (in advance of Warton and Percy) that chivalry was of Gothic origin and founded on 'a marvellous respect and veneration to the fair sex', Ferguson claimed that this essentially literary invention has come to define what is peculiar to European nations:

What was originally singular in these apprehensions, was, by the writer of romance, turned to extravagance: and under the title of chivalry was offered as a model of conduct . . . *Warriors went forth to realize the legends they had studied;* princes and leaders of armies dedicated their most serious exploits to a real or to a fancied mistress.

But whatever was the origin of notions, often so lofty and so ridiculous, we cannot doubt of their lasting effects on our manners. *The point of honour, the prevalence of gallantry in our conversations, and on our theatres . . . are undoubtedly remains of this antiquated system: and chivalry, uniting with the genius of our policy, has probably suggested those peculiarities in the law of nations, by which modern states are distinguished from the ancient.*[168]

Ferguson contends that, from the Middle Ages onwards, chivalry entered the fantasy life of European nations and influenced not only their cultural tone, but also their (by implication, highly aristocratic) political systems. He does this with a rare feeling for the way that social behaviour is nourished by imaginative identification with an idealised self and an idealised past, and for the way that even minor social rituals are experienced as a re-enactment of time-honoured traditions. Ferguson's notion that the culture of chivalry is a defining feature of modern European civilisation, as opposed to the ancient or non-European worlds, gained currency in the work of subsequent writers, especially when amplified in Burke's *Reflections on the Revolution in France*.

The immediate context for Burke's famous lament that 'the age of chivalry is gone' and that 'that of sophisters, oeconomists, and calculators has succeeded' was, of course, his alarm at the legislative reforms of the French Constituent Assembly, but he was also mounting a wider argument about the historically sanctioned legitimacy of Europe's *anciens régimes*.[169] These hierarchical regimes, Burke writes, have been sustained by a 'generous loyalty to rank and sex' on the part of all, and a culture of voluntary and dignified obedience on the part of the governed in return for the submission of the ruler to the 'soft collar of social esteem'. He describes this culture of mutual loyalty between the different ranks and sexes as a 'mixed system of opinion and sentiment', one that:

had its origin in the antient chivalry; and the principle, though varied in its appearance by the varying state of human affairs, subsisted and influenced through a long succession of generations, even to the time we live in. If it should ever be totally extinguished, the loss I fear will be great. It is this which has given its character to modern Europe. It is this which has distinguished it under all its forms of government, and distinguished it to its advantage, from the states of Asia, and possibly from those states which flourished in the most brilliant periods of the antique world.[170]

J. G. A. Pocock has argued that this passage should be read as a significant development of Scottish ideas of the progress of civilisation towards commercial modernity, since, for Burke, 'a civilized society is the prerequisite of exchange relations, and the latter alone cannot create the former'.[171] Burke makes the case for the stabilising and economically enabling effects of cultural tradition: in modern Europe, he asserts, 'commerce, and trade, and manufacture' are the 'effects' of 'antient manners'.[172] Modern societies like Britain's, Burke believes, thrive on a tension between a chivalric style of social relations, reminiscent of an older, agricultural order, and the self-interested, exchange relations required by a commercial economy. The economy may collapse but, since it is the effect rather than the substance of civility, civilisation may endure. He regards the French revolutionaries as reprehensibly reckless because they have set out to destroy not only the French economy but also the system of civilised manners that sustained it. A touchstone of those civilised manners is the treatment of women, such as Marie-Antoinette, and the revolutionaries' failure to act chivalrously towards her is amply indicative of their unfitness to run a modern European economy.

The association in Burke's mind between women, civilisation and European distinctiveness was of long standing. In 1771, when speaking in the House of Commons in favour of a legislative move to restrict the right of divorced women to remarry, he argued: 'The foundation of all the Order, harmony Tranquility and even civilization that is amongst us turns upon two things the *Indissolubility* of Marriage and the freedom of the Female sex. To these we owe every advantage that Europe has over every state in the World.'[173]

What Burke meant by 'the freedom of the Female sex' is not clear. Manifestly, he did not envisage female sexual freedom (although he might have been thinking of the freedom and security conferred by indissoluble marriages), but he probably had in mind the Scottish idea of the progress of woman from oppression to modern courtesy. There is a hint here, and in the *Reflections* also, that there is something both peculiar and definitive about Europe's gender order, something that does not occur in other non-European societies undergoing similar stages of social evolution. For Burke, chivalry is not an Enlightenment sociological category applicable to all societies moving from the agricultural to the commercial stage. Women define for him, as for Ferguson, what is *local* to European culture rather than its broader developmental features. They carry the historical residue of that culture, and, far from being the barometers of progress, they remind the modern world of its debt to an older, finer cultural tradition. For Burke, societies do not simply progress in a linear fashion, but develop unevenly, so that it is possible, perhaps even instructive, to imagine different social groups and genders as occupying different temporal positions.

Just as, by the late eighteenth century, the Romantic juxtaposition of modern England and its Celtic periphery made it possible to imagine Britain in terms of co-existent yet incommensurable time-zones (the Highlands and wild Wales trapped in an obsolete but enticing past), so, after the chivalric revival, it became possible to imagine women occupying a different relationship to history from that of their male counterparts. Men might address themselves to women, or merely open a door or pick up a dropped handkerchief, with a sense that they were re-enacting a venerable historical part. An air of historical dignity seems to hang over the gentlemanly courtesy of Austen's Mr Knightley and his kind. Many commentators in the late eighteenth and early nineteenth centuries believed that chivalry was the true ancestor of modern politeness and benevolence. In Thomas Peacock's novel *Melincourt* of 1817, the likeable, if dewy-eyed, heroine, Anthelia, hopes for just such a knight at arms:

THE HONOURABLE MRS PINMONEY. And do you really expect to find such a knight-errant? The age of chivalry is gone.

ANTHELIA. It is, but its spirit survives. Disinterested benevolence, the mainspring of all that is really admirable in the days of chivalry, will never perish . . . To protect the feeble – to raise the fallen – to liberate the captive – to be the persevering foe of tyrants . . . it is not necessary to wind the bugle before enchanted castles, or to seek adventures in the depths of mountain-caverns and forests of pine . . . I believe it possible to find as true a knight-errant in a brown coat in the nineteenth century, as in a suit of golden armour in the days of Charlemagne.[174]

More earnestly, in his *View of the State of Europe during the Middle Ages* (1818), Henry Hallam praised chivalry for the politeness it had bequeathed to the modern world: 'The spirit of chivalry left behind it a more valuable successor. The character of knight gradually subsided in that of gentleman.'[175]

Hallam's history was the most influential account of medieval Europe in the first part of the nineteenth century, and it combined Scottish methods of conjectural analysis with a Burkean feeling for the enduring value of medieval culture.[176] Like his predecessors, Hallam was interested not only in the origin of the modern gentleman but also the modern lady, whose character he attributes to her Germanic ethnic heritage and to the very particular way that European society experienced its agricultural stage:

The German women were high-spirited and virtuous; qualities, which might be causes or consequences of the veneration with which they were regarded . . . The spirit of gallantry, which became perhaps the most animating principle of chivalry, must be ascribed to the progressive refinement of society during the twelfth and two succeeding centuries. In a rude state of manners . . . woman has not full scope to display those fascinating graces, by which nature has designed to counterbalance the strength and energy of mankind. Even where those jealous customs that degrade alike the two sexes have not prevailed, her lot is domestic seclusion . . . But as a taste for the more elegant enjoyments of wealth arises, a taste which it is always her policy and her delight to nourish, she obtains an ascendancy at first in the lighter hours, and from thence in the serious occupations of life.[177]

Hallam does not overstate the case for the morally improving effects of chivalry, and, marshalling an array of economic evidence, he notes its tendency to widen differences between the social orders. But he has no doubts about its long-term benefits for the moral conduct and social standing of the ladies.[178] The same year as Hallam's history, Scott enshrined a very similar view of chivalry as the progenitor of the modern lady in his *Encyclopaedia Britannica* article. Having argued that Germanic manners were 'amalgamated' into those of the Middle Ages, Scott claims that the sexual restraint imposed by chivalry was the reason for the comparative sexual equality of the modern age, and that this taught young women 'to regard themselves, not as the passive slaves of pleasure, but as the objects of a prolonged and respectful affection'.[179] 'From the wild and overstrained courtesies of Chivalry', he adds, 'has been derived our present system of manners.'[180]

One of the important lessons of Millar and other Enlightenment historians was that femininity was a kind of 'rank', as well as a biological category, and that the rank of 'lady' was the outcome of a long process of European civilisation. Acknowledging this insight, but deeply unhappy about its consequences, Mary Wollstonecraft protested that women are, by modern chivalric manners, '*localized*. . . by the rank they are placed in, by *courtesy*'.[181] At once morally restrictive and attractively *déclassé*, the word 'lady' came to imply, in the nineteenth century and beyond, an identity that all women, irrespective of their social origin, could either achieve or fail to live up to. The idea of the lady of chivalry meshed with Rousseau's appeal to women to reclaim their femininity across the class divide. It also positioned women at a remove from economic production and consumption, according them a role in the creation of the taste 'for the more elegant enjoyments of wealth', as Hallam does in the quotation above – that is to say, in the process by which consumerism is elevated into aesthetic preference. As I will argue in chapter 6, the intensified association between women and the medieval past may have lent support to the growing involvement of women in the writing of literary history, art history and history proper. Overall, the woman of chivalry gave late eighteenth- and early nineteenth-century Britain a point of contact with the moral resources of the Gothic tribes, and the moral idealism (uncontaminated by commerce) of the Middle Ages. Later eighteenth-century versions of history concurred that commerce had put an end to the extreme distinctions of ranks and the seclusion of the feudal age, but that the memory of medieval civilisation preserved a high tone in sexual relations in the modern world. This memory could bring ceremonial veneer and a provocative sense of submerged romance to the ordinary transactions of social life, and it could lend an air of national ritual to the smallest act of male gallantry.

CHIVALRY DECLINED

The idea of chivalry was appropriated, in the nineteenth century, to a variety of political causes, providing both men and women with a language in which to express social concern across the class divide. Some of those who used this language were Tory and paternalist, such as the Young Englanders, but others, as Clarissa Campbell Orr has argued of the mid nineteenth-century Langham Place circle, used it for feminist purposes.[182] Although it was flexible, the idea of the woman of chivalry had many detractors before, and especially after, Burke's *Reflections*. Barbara Taylor has written of Mary Wollstonecraft's bitterly hostile response to the eighteenth-century male cult of 'gallantry', a cult that acquired historical burnish through its association with rediscovered chivalry.[183] Before Wollstonecraft, Catharine Macaulay, in her *Observations on the Reflections of the Right Hon. Edmund Burke, on the Revolution in France* (1790), voiced her hostility to the 'methodized sentimental barbarism' of chivalry, and attacked Burke's obscurantist, medieval vision of the British constitution.[184] She made no explicit reference to women, yet in her root-and-branch demolition of Burke's underlying history of European manners she made clear her opposition to the very idea of the progress of civilisation. She particularly objected to the insidious tendency of Burke and other contemporary figures to make the minor improvements in the manners of the Middle Ages (which 'were indeed a proper remedy to the evils arising from *ferocity, slavery, barbarity,* and *ignorance*') the subject of nostalgia, veneration and imitation.[185] Her sentiments were echoed, a generation later, by Charles Lamb in one of his 'Elia' essays, 'Modern Gallantry'. Lamb's repudiation of the cult of gallantry is designedly stirring:

In comparing modern with ancient manners, we are pleased to compliment ourselves upon the point of gallantry; a certain obsequiousness, or deferential respect, which we are supposed to pay to females, as females.

I shall believe that this principle actuates our conduct, when I can forget, that in the nineteenth century of the era from which we date our civility, we are but just beginning to leave off the very frequent practice of whipping females in public . . . I shall believe in it when actresses are no longer subject to be hissed off a stage by gentlemen . . . I shall begin to believe that there is some such principle influencing our conduct, when more than one-half of the drudgery and coarse servitude of the world shall cease to be performed by women.[186]

Soon after, John Stuart Mill pointed out in a marvellous piece for the *Westminster Review* of 1826 how modern historians have reduced chivalry to a series of frivolous courtship rituals, and, indeed, how patronising those rituals were in the first place:

There is one feature in the chivalrous character which has yet to be noticed; we mean, its gallantry. And that we shall think it necessary to examine the more fully, because we are persuaded that nine-tenths of the admiration of chivalry are grounded upon it. We own it is hard to speak ill of men who could make vows to their lady-love that they would wear a scarf over one eye till they should have signalized her charms by some exploit . . . We trust, however, that without treason to the fair sex . . . it may be permitted to doubt whether these fopperies contributed much to the substantial happiness of women, or indicated any real solicitude for their welfare.[187]

Like Lamb, Mill writes against the groundswell in the 1820s of chivalric nostalgia, and disputes the complacent histories of civilisation that underwrite the contemporary affection for medieval manners. He does not deny that the 'good treatment of women . . . is one of the surest marks of high civilization' and he concedes that, 'if it could be proved that women, in the middle ages, were well treated, it would be so decisive a proof of an advanced stage of civilization'.[188] However, the evidence points in the opposite direction since good treatment 'does not consist in treating them as idols to be worshipped, or as trinkets to be worn for display'.[189] Mill then builds on an argument of 'Professor Millar, perhaps the greatest of philosophical inquirers into the civilization of past ages', in order to show that medieval women were treated very much as he imagines the secluded women of Asia to be, subject to domestic brutality, rapes and abductions.[190] The sentimental modern view of chivalry, he complains, takes no account of the treatment of lower-class women or of plain women who cannot excite male idolatry: 'it is the treatment of them', Mill adds unanswerably, 'and not that of their more attractive sisters, which is the test of civilization'.[191]

CHAPTER 4

Catharine Macaulay's histories of England: liberty, civilisation and the female historian

John Stuart Mill, Mary Wollstonecraft and Catharine Macaulay voiced their hostility to the idea that the chivalrous treatment of women was a true 'test of civilization', and their doubts about the very histories of civilisation from which such notions of chivalry were drawn. In the next two chapters, I will consider how far the latter two writers felt it necessary to rewrite those histories of civilisation in order to challenge the cult of chivalric manners, and the extent to which they deployed and adapted contemporary vocabularies of progress, civil society and commerce to their own ends. In the case of Wollstonecraft, we will see an intensely revisionist engagement, on the ground of moral philosophy, with Scottish ideas of the progress of society. In the case of Macaulay, no less deeply read than her younger contemporary in the historical and sociological works of her time, there is a defiant attempt to update older ideas of male and female freedom on the ground of history. In Mill's case, beyond the scope of this book, we see a thoroughgoing scepticism as to whether history can form a basis from which to argue against the subjection of women. Mill was doubtful about the value both of history and of Christianity as resources for the case for liberty. Macaulay and Wollstonecraft, however, drew considerable inspiration from their Protestant faith when seeking to reinterpret the past and imagine the future in the image of liberty. As we will see, their social vision for this Protestant faith and their theological ideas bore some similarities to those of the Bluestockings, as well as the Latitudinarian Anglican writers of the previous generation, even though their politics, notably their support for the American and French revolutionaries, were diametrically opposed. Studies of Wollstonecraft and Macaulay have often started with their close (in Wollstonecraft's case, confessional) ties to rational, radical Dissent, treating this as a world apart from the more conservative eighteenth-century mainstream.[1] Yet, just as it is productive to read their works as part of a dialogue with conjectural, Gothic and medieval accounts of manners, so it is illuminating to read them as parts of a Latitudinarian tradition emphasising benevolence, rational moral autonomy and female education as the means of integrating women into a reformed social order.

Of the two writers, Macaulay is certainly the most difficult to situate within the vigorous (and, for women, highly consequential) debates about femininity, manners and progress of the later eighteenth century. She boldly presented herself as an exceptional figure: as a last voice for freedom in an age of corruption and colonial warfare, as a Roman matron at a time when such creatures were seen as lacking in feminine softness, and as a great national historian when most other women writers stuck to novels and poetry. Recent work on Macaulay, notably Kate Davies's important study of the transatlantic contexts of her image and ideas, have probed her self-presentation with care, finding intractable contradictions between her Roman persona and her role as fashionable *salonnière*, woman of learning and astute commercial writer.[2] Allied to the Roman persona is the deeper question of Macaulay's republicanism. Most 'commonwealth' republicans of the eighteenth century advocated the strengthening and reform of Britain's mixed constitution of monarch, lords and commons, but few shared openly her outright hostility to monarchy in all its forms. Macaulay thought of herself as a pristine, unapologetically Roman kind of republican, and took Marcus Junius Brutus as her hero. Unsurprisingly, most accounts of Macaulay have wrestled with the question of how a woman writer and advocate of female property rights and education could have found congenial such an exclusively male model of politics and citizenship. Most recently, alongside Davies's painstaking analysis of Macaulay's (highly unstable) public image as a refined female republican, Philip Hicks has argued that, although she 'remained captive to republican paradigms reserving full political participation to males', she did remind women that 'they could be patriots without being citizens'.[3] Both of these accounts refine J. G. A. Pocock's argument that Macaulay was essentially gender-blind in her approach to writing, 'a woman wholly committed to the ancient ideal of active citizenship and wholly undeterred by its hyper-intense masculinity'.[4] Some of her contemporaries, it must be said, did regard her republicanism as a kind of male impersonation. Elizabeth Montagu, with whose circle Macaulay had a tangential and uneasy relationship, cut her altogether after her second marriage, blaming her for 'adopting Masculine opinions, and Masculine manners. I hate a woman's mind in men's cloaths as much as her person.'[5]

Macaulay's historical works themselves do not overtly purvey history from a woman's point of view do not pay great attention to the role of particular women in history and they do not engage at any length with contemporary discussion of the historical 'progress of women', the feminisation of manners, or the economic and intellectual advantages of a mixed-gender public culture. Macaulay's major statement on the failure of the 'progress of civilisation' to deliver improvements in women's lives and the need for much better female education came mainly in her final work, the *Letters on Education* (1790). Here, there is direct engagement with Gibbon on the advances made by European societies since the Dark Ages: 'Much has been said of the progress of modern civilization, but it certainly has so little tended to bring us back to classic simplicity, that we are every day departing more and more from it.'[6] In most respects, civilisation remains in a 'state of modern barbarism', little different in its manners from the barbarians Gibbon himself describes.[7] And here, also, is a complaint that the much vaunted modern cult of gallantry has done little or nothing to ameliorate women's legal position:

For with a total and absolute exclusion of every political right to the sex in general, married women, whose situation demands a particular indulgence, have hardly a civil right to save them from the grossest injuries; and though the gallantry of some of the European societies have necessarily produced indulgence, yet in others the faults of women are treated with a severity and rancour which militates against every principle of religion and common sense.[8]

Macaulay came to this diagnosis of the partial and inadequate nature of social progress – a diagnosis that, as we shall see in the next chapter, was accepted and amplified by Wollstonecraft – by way of writing history, and by hammering out in her histories and her pamphlets a set of political principles designed to expose and remedy those social ills. These principles were not, as we will see, straightforwardly a female adaptation of republican ideals. Rather, she attempted to synthesise the Roman republican ideal of men sharing in the life of the state with a liberal idea, derived from Locke, of the natural equality of men and women, and the contractual duty of the state not to interfere in the private concerns of the individual. In the *Letters on Education*, she explicitly located her politics as a happy medium between the classical tendency to 'make a deity of the society in its aggregate capacity . . . [and to sacrifice] the dearest interests of those individuals who formed the aggregate', and 'the most liberal of the moderns' who feel that 'governors have little else to do but to eat and drink' and to leave individuals alone.[9]

Macaulay's synthesis of republican and liberal politics was an unstable, even on occasions an incoherent one, but it was derived from a deep reading of the classic texts of political theory, including those by Hobbes (the subject of her first published piece), Locke and Harrington, and the major Roman authors.[10] This synthesis owed something to her involvement with American revolutionary intellectuals and their British supporters, who distilled abstract theories of liberty from the inherited languages of the freedom and political agency associated with Britain's classically balanced constitution and with the common law rights of Englishmen. Macaulay's politics were grounded in an Enlightenment reading of history as a process of accident and human improvisation against an unseen, swirling backdrop of economic and social change. But they were above all a politics for action, offering both her male and female readers a shared ideal of individual rationality, responsibility and patriotism (not for Macaulay the Gothic idea of female affective patriotism). Her ideal of the politically responsible individual – an ideal potentially applicable to either sex – lies at the heart of her politics and her vision of history. J. G. A. Pocock has suggested that Macaulay was 'primarily a woman who crashed her way into the writing of history, normally defined as a specifically masculine activity', but whose history did not have 'anything specifically female about it'.[11] My case will be the opposite: that Macaulay's histories embody an ideal, a fantasy almost, of meaningful personal responsibility, and a yearning to stand up and be counted which could only have issued from a woman writer never expected to have or do either. This clearly resonated with readers, among them unenfranchised English reformers, dissatisfied American colonists and French revolutionaries, who sought responsibility over their own political destinies. And it resonated with women writers – Mary Wollstonecraft most prominent among them – who saw the intellectual shock value of a female voice offered boldly, apparently even unreflectively, as the voice of self-evident reason.

MACAULAY, HUME AND THE HISTORICAL NATURE OF LIBERTY

Macaulay (née Sawbridge) came to national prominence in her thirties with the publication of the first volume of her *History of England* (1763), which covered the history of the early seventeenth century. Seven more volumes followed at intervals over the next twenty years, during which time she also wrote pamphlets on the subjects of electoral reform, copyright, constitutional theory and, in 1775, the crisis in America. In 1778, she took a break from her seventeenth-century history to finish and publish the first and only volume of her *History of England from the Revolution to the Present Time*, a work presented as a series of letters to her friend the Reverend Doctor Wilson. Before the public sensation of her marriage, at the age of forty-seven, to a young man of twenty-one, she enjoyed an unassailable position as the leading female radical Whig and *salonnière* of her day. Her acquaintance with leading radical intellectuals in Britain, France and America was wide, and her intimate social circle, as her biographer Bridget Hill has described them, included activists for constitutional reform, such as John Wilkes, and republican political theorists.[12]

A defining feature of Macaulay's eight-volume *History of England* is its long time-span of composition (from 1763 to 1783). Obliquely, and sometimes overtly, engaged with contemporary affairs, it constitutes a kind of intellectual record of the period from the end of the Seven Years' War (there are references to her hopes for and disillusionment with the leadership of William Pitt), to the crisis which followed Wilkes's election for a Middlesex parliamentary seat (Macaulay never wrote a pamphlet on the subject, but volumes IV and V amount to a very full consideration of the rights of parliament), to the events leading up to and including the American Revolutionary War. There was a long interval between volume V (1771) and volume VI (1781), during which she was pamphleteering and writing the 1778 history. The final three volumes are particularly well written, and far less dependent than the earlier ones on over-long quotations from primary sources. Their tone is alternately embattled and contemplative, reflecting a double sense of England's and her own personal setbacks. All of the volumes are in some way competitively engaged with the work of Macaulay's great predecessor in the field of seventeenth-century British history, David Hume, author of the *History of England* (1754–62). Macaulay set out to surpass Hume in point of scholarship, carrying out pioneering research into forgotten tracts, pamphlets and diaries of republican writers.[13] She covered the same chronological terrain as Hume, but where he had explored England's descent into and gradual emergence from dangerous religious fanaticism, she told the story of how the English briefly institutionalised (in the Commonwealth of 1649–53) and then lost their liberty. More generally, Macaulay's *History* mounted a powerful case against the cosmopolitanism, religious scepticism and political detachment of Hume's work.[14]

Yet even these substantial differences are deceptive. Both Hume and Macaulay's histories are Enlightenment histories of liberty as it was accidentally acquired by the English, and then progressively understood and implemented. Both set out to broaden the remit of traditional political history, by paying attention to the economic and social origins of political ideas and movements, as well as to more general questions about the customs and culture ('manners') of the people. Such general discussions, in Hume's work, are usually fleshed out in appendices, and Macaulay follows suit by including a number of summary chapters. For example, she concludes her account of events up to the Stuart Restoration with a 'Dissertation' in which she reviews the economic and social changes, from Tudor times to 1660, which brought about the momentous events of the mid seventeenth century. She explores the economic developments that permitted commoners to enrich themselves, often at the expense of the nobility. This shifting economic balance in England, which gave the commons an 'appetite for Liberty' under James I, precipitated 'an entire change . . . in their manners, from the immediate commencement of Charles's government'.[15] Thus far, Macaulay borrows heavily from Hume's account, but she develops this idea of an abrupt change in the 'manners' of the English political class as a partial explanation of their failure to foist their puritan republicanism on the population as a whole: 'as the true love of Liberty is founded in virtue, the Parliament were indefatigable in their endeavors to reform to a state of possible perfection the manners of the people'. A mistake, of course, and one for which they were 'ridiculed', since manners cannot be transformed without economic change or redistribution.[16]

Moreover, in spite of her overriding commitment to retrieving moral and political certainties from history, Macaulay retained a sophisticated and distinctively Humean sense of history as a process of accident, coincidence and unintended outcomes. She acknowledged that the very values for which she claimed historical transcendence – liberty, natural rights, the right of resistance to tyranny – had been stumbled upon by chance during the course of history. For Macaulay, as for Hume, liberty was an instinct, and a reaction to provocation (not based 'on any enlarged notions of government'), long before it could be politically theorised. It was bound up with customary and common law notions of secure possession of one's property and privileges, and was thus quite narrow in compass: 'Liberty, in an enlarged sense, was never a general principle of action among the English.'[17] In the summary chapter on the 'State of civil and ecclesiastical government of England at the accession of the Stewart

Family', at the end of the first book, Macaulay explains how a more classical understanding of liberty was the outgrowth of the broader intellectual transformations of the English Renaissance: 'noble principles had taken deep root in the minds of the English people, that the progress of more enlightened reason would bring . . . to perfection'.[18]

This rediscovery of the idea of liberty was part of an ongoing historical process, far from complete in Macaulay's own more enlightened age. She writes as though from a modern, enlightened vanguard, better able than her less insightful contemporaries to recognise the real merits of seventeenth-century advocates of liberty: 'the praise due to the illustrious champions of the public cause . . . is a theme of delight among the few enlightened citizens [of her time]'.[19] For her, the origins of the modern notion of liberty among 'enlightened citizens' lay in the early seventeenth century. This was a point in history when the Commons refashioned classical ideas of liberty in the image of their own political, social and religious aspirations, and this set them on a collision course with, first, James I, then Charles I, kings hopelessly committed to inherited notions of royal prerogative: 'the short-sighted James was unable to account for the inconsistence he found between the theoretical and practical government of England'.[20] Here, again, there is a considerable debt to Hume, who gives a similar, though much more sympathetic account of James I and Charles I's stubborn, misguided adherence to notions of royal prerogative. The moral conclusions Macaulay extrapolates from her analysis of the political deadlock of the early seventeenth century have none of Hume's fine balance. Her directness is refreshing: James I was so 'surrounded by flatterers [that] he snuffed up continually the incense of his own praise'.[21] She praises the heroes and excoriates the enemies of liberty: Cromwell's *coup d'état* 'fixes an indelible stain on the character of the English, as a people basely and incorrigibly attached to the sovereignty of individuals, and of natures too ignoble to endure an empire of equal laws'.[22] Not for her the alternately sentimental and satirical registers used by Hume to direct his readers' sympathies towards the Stuart kings and away from religious and political enthusiasm. Macaulay demonstrates throughout a radical republican's wariness of sentiment and irony. She ignores the contemporary trend, among both Tory and Whig historians, to sentimentalise the story of Charles I as the sacrilegious judicial murder of a good father and husband. Instead, she tells the story of his trial with clinical brevity, and reserves the emotive vocabulary of sacrilege, not for the king, but for her idol Liberty. Charles is the desecrator of Liberty and she is horrified, 'that he [Charles I] should be able to persuade men to lift their impious hands against the altars of Liberty, and drench their country in blood, to support him in a power he had abused'.[23] She faced such intense public pressure on the point of Charles's martyrdom that she had to climb down, and assume a more sentimental authorial tone: returning to the *History* after a ten-year interval, she opened Volume VI with the claim that she had, in fact, 'shed many tears' over Charles's fate.[24]

A SCIENCE OF POLITICS

Bridget Hill has discussed Hume's touchy reaction to the (initially very stiff) competition to his *History* presented by Macaulay's work.[25] Macaulay had covered the same chronological ground, adopted a similar methodology, taken a similarly historicised view of liberty, and yet had come to diametrically opposite conclusions about the legitimacy of the English monarchy in the past and in the present. Her exchange of letters with Hume on the writing of history, later published in the *European Magazine*, reveals both their ideological differences and methodological similarities. Both saw history as the servant of (what Hume called) the 'science' (i.e. philosophy) of politics. Hume's observation that 'I look upon all kinds of subdivision of power . . . to be equally legal if established by custom and authority', drew from her the response that 'Every kind of government may be legal, but sure all are not equally expedient.'[26] Macaulay's science of politics is, like Hume's, historical in character, but this, as Hume hints in his remark above, is not to say that she thought that the historical origins and longevity of particular political arrangements made them any more suitable ('expedient'), even if it made them, from some points of view, 'legal' and legitimate. There is a practical, historically evolutionary side to Macaulay's political thinking with which she is not often credited. Most commentators (including Caroline Robbins and J. G. A. Pocock, but not including Hume) have tended to see Macaulay's political philosophy as peculiarly abstract and a-historical.[27] Others, notably Lynne Withey, have emphasised the basis of her political thinking in the idea of an ancient, liberal Saxon English Constitution, although this, in itself, was quite compatible with relatively abstract republican thinking in this period.[28] Neither of these characterisations fully captures the modern and evolutionary cast of her political thought. Traditional classical politics posit a tension between republicanism and commerce, and more particularly between the qualities of self-denial and public dutifulness needed for the state to protect and maintain itself, and the acquisitive, peace-loving and self-interested qualities encouraged by commercial activity. Yet Macaulay was more positive about the benefits of commerce to the state than most of her radical associates. She highlighted, throughout both her histories, the social benefits of the growth of trade. She absorbed and put to good use the new approach to questions of luxury and trade developed by Mandeville, Hume and other writers, notably the distinction which Hume made, in his essay 'Of Refinement in the Arts', between 'vicious' and 'innocent' or 'beneficial' luxury.[29] Her *History of England from the Revolution to the Present Time* (1778), with the contemporary world in mind, draws clear distinctions between properly managed, beneficial commerce (the 'improvement of commerce, my friend, may undoubtedly be reckoned among the arts of peace'), and the kind of self-indulgent, ruinous luxury ('vicious luxury') which results from corrupt schemes such as the sale of South Sea stock (when 'the increase of luxury and vice kept more than equal pace with the imaginary increase of riches').[30] She berates some ministries for their neglect of Britain's imperial interests, and welcomes the steady progress of commerce stimulated by the financial revolution of the 1690s. Although strongly opposed to slavery, she supports the notion of a British sea empire, and even praises James II for his efforts in this arena: 'he cherished and extended the maritime power of the empire, and his encouragement of trade was attended with . . . success'.[31]

Macaulay's notion of an ancient English constitution was similarly modernised and handled with the same practical, evolutionary historical insight. It is true, as Withey argues, that Macaulay makes a number of references to a Saxon constitution, destroyed by the Norman Conquest, but lingering below the surface of English politics. There was (and still is) a bust of King Alfred displayed outside her house in Alfred Street in Bath, and both of her histories feature phrases like 'constitutional rectitude'. Yet, to a degree unusual among her radical Whig contemporaries, Macaulay treats the hypothetical existence of an ancient, free constitution merely as a moral buttress for her case for a much more modern reformulation of the ideological underpinnings of English politics. The central question which she poses herself (with the parliamentary revolt against Charles I at the front of her mind, but the case of the American colonists never far behind) is, to which set of rights and principles should a people appeal when they are no longer being governed in their own best interest? Her answer is a sophisticated one, without reference to the Saxon constitution, and it emerges from her long and intense reflections on the justice of Charles I's execution: 'The parliament, on the principles of self-defence, on the principles of equity and reason, *without respect to constitutional forms*, had a right to oppose the tyrant to the utmost' (my italics). The case for the execution of ('utmost' opposition to) the king could not, and cannot, be made on ancient constitutional grounds (or, as she says earlier, 'on the narrow bottom of constitutional forms').[32] Rather, it seems that the regicides enunciated, almost involuntarily through their actions, the true principles of natural rights and legitimate government which ought, if properly adduced from the laws of God and nature, to have normative force in all states. Paraphrasing (and considerably embellishing) the case made by the regicides, she spells out her own political creed:

That government is the ordinance of man; that, being the mere creature of human invention, it may be changed or altered according to the dictates of experience, and the better judgement of men; that it was instituted for the protection of the people, for the end of securing not overthrowing the rights of nature; that it is a trust either formally admitted, or supposed; and that magistracy is consequently accountable . . .[33]

The telling phrase here is 'dictates of experience'. The 'rights of nature' may exist in the abstract, but they become intelligible and enforceable only in the light of historical experience. Far from being entirely abstract or centred on an unchanging model of the ancient English constitution, Macaulay's politics are part of a continuous, open-ended practice of historical interpretation, one which certainly allows for the modernisation of republican politics in her own age.

In the long quotation above, as elsewhere in her work, Macaulay is substantially and openly indebted to the second of Locke's *Two Treatises of Government* (1689) for her idea of government as a contract made by the people with their rulers, designed to preserve their security and natural (i.e. inherent) rights. Her work appeared towards the beginning of a major revival of interest in Locke's work, which would deeply inform subsequent best-selling works by radical associates, such as Richard Price's *Observations on the Nature of Civil Liberty* (1776) and Major John Cartwright's *Take Your Choice!* (1776). Yet, in important respects, Macaulay tried to transform Locke's idea of the social contract, and, in particular, of the right of resistance that, for Locke, was something which the people may exercise only *in extremis*. In her hands, the idea of resistance becomes an active principle requiring the citizen continually to monitor *and extend* the bounds of civil liberty. At some moments this might involve a complete change of government, as under the English Commonwealth, but at others, it necessitates a transformation of the constitution from within. The originality and radicalism of Macaulay's take on Locke lies not so much in abstract political theory as in her application of these ideas to the historical experience of one political event, the Revolution of 1688–9. By the later eighteenth century, nearly all commentators agreed (Jacobites excepted) that the foundation of English liberties lay in the Glorious Revolution, and that the expulsion of James II in favour of William III and Mary II had amounted to a reassertion of the principles of the ancient constitution against tyrannical abuses of power. Yet Macaulay was adamant that this event was neither Glorious nor a Revolution; worse than a missed opportunity, it had actually made an oligarchic and oppressive constitution more difficult than ever to resist.

THE INGLORIOUS REVOLUTION

Macaulay's view of the events of 1688–9 evolved slowly during her writing career. In her 1778 *History of England from the Revolution to the Present Time*, she voiced her scepticism about the value of this venerated moment in British history. She conceded that the accession of William III had introduced the idea of a social contract ('the people, instead of being considered as beasts of burthen, and live stock on a farm . . . were now looked up to as the only legal source of sovereign authority'), but nevertheless insisted that the Revolution settlement was a botched affair that was quickly betrayed or forgotten, even by the Whigs, and that had, if anything, increased the powers of the king.[34] The Glorious Revolution served to demonstrate that the political lessons of the Commonwealth had never been properly learned or applied since it failed to 'admit of any of those refinements and improvements, which the experience of mankind had enabled [its authors] to make in the science of political security'.[35] Most commentators cited the events of 1688–9 as a cardinal instance of Britain salvaging positive lessons from the mistakes of the past, but for Macaulay, it represented a failure to bring 'the experience of mankind' to bear on the science of politics. Bridget Hill, in an article on Macaulay's attitude to the Glorious Revolution, records how even John Wilkes was a little scandalised by all this, and how, like others, he worried that she would cut too much ground from under radical Whig feet.[36]

In the eighth, and final, volume of *The History of England from the Accession of James I* Macaulay revisited the subject, this time with more radical results, supported by a more deeply considered theory of government. The volume was published in the year 1783, at a point when

Macaulay's popularity had waned considerably, yet it has a good claim to be the most accomplished and original of all the volumes. Macaulay covers the period from the reign of James II to 1689, and her writing is strongly coloured by the end of the American War, marking the success of one major act of resistance to the British government. James II was usually portrayed as the villain of the Revolution story, even in accounts, such as Hume's, which took a sceptical approach to Whig history, so Macaulay confounded expectations when she presented him with sympathy and insisted upon his place as the nation's then rightful monarch. If James entertained an 'exalted idea . . . of the royal office', it was because parliament, 'by an unprecedented servility, helped to confirm' him in it.[37] If he fled the country and turned to the French king, rather than stay and face his enemies, he was no worse than 'the generality of mankind [who] would, in James's situation, have sought shelter in the proferred generosity of a trusted friend [Louis XIV], from personal insult, personal danger'.[38] His religious bigotry had unintentionally beneficial consequences, in that it made it impossible for him to consolidate royal power to the extent that he desired.[39] In view of his legitimacy and relative political impotence, Macaulay argues (with palpable relish of the unconventional revisionism of her position) that William and Mary should never have been called in. A better, and far more radical, solution would have been to force James into a new constitutional settlement. The route taken in 1688 – a simple change of royal dynasty – could never have amounted to a real advance for freedom: 'because the extinction of power in a particular reigning family, has often been effected by the impatience of slaves; whereas the asserting the authority of the people over the power of a reigning sovereign, has never been effected but by free nations, and is the highest triumph of popular liberty'.[40]

Most modern-minded Whigs of the eighteenth century, including Hume, emphasised the innovative character of the constitutional settlement of 1688–9.[41] Macaulay replied that it was, in fact, a highly conservative solution to the age-old problem of royal tyranny, and one which was largely motivated by greed on the part of 'those who expected favours from William'.[42] The settlement had no commercial benefits for the country since its consequence was 'to involve [Britain], contrary to the interest of a commercial maritime power, in expensive land armaments' as part of William's continental war against Louis XIV.[43] It was, in essence, an aristocratic coup, masquerading as restoration of popular liberty, which subjected the people to a mercantile Whig oligarchy: 'under the specious appearance of democratical privilege, the people are really and

truly enslaved to a small part of the community'.[44] The most pernicious
aspect of the whole process was that the framers of 1688–9, unlike the
earlier parliamentary opponents of Charles I, had at their disposal a
body of political experience and thought (greatly enhanced by James
Harrington, Algernon Sidney and other republican intellectual heroes)
which should have enabled them to implement the fundamentals of
liberty and popular sovereignty. The settlement was made 'without
adding any new trophies to the altar of liberty, or even of renovating
those sound principles in the constitution, which, in the length of time,
had fallen a sacrifice to the lusts and the opportunities of power'.[45]

A THEOLOGY OF INDIVIDUAL RECTITUDE

We can conclude from Macaulay's bold reinterpretation of the Glorious
Revolution that she did not consider mere constitutional change, even if
progressive in some respects, as an end in itself. The processes and
motivations of liberty are, for her, as important as the result. She had
no theory of the 'general will' of the people, no clear idea as to how the
sovereign people could convey their will to greater freedom except via
limited political representation. Yet she communicated a strong sense
that, in order to survive and improve, political communities must engage
in a constant process of self-renovation at both the intellectual and
practical levels. Occasional and drastic resort to their Lockean right of
resistance is not enough; the striving must take place within, and as an
integral part of, any constitutional arrangement. Of course, this insistence
upon the need for an active, vigilant political culture is, in its contours,
classically republican, but it shades into a more liberal notion of the need
for individuals to assert their natural rights. Macaulay had a relatively
narrow notion of what the political, voting community should be, and it
is worth emphasising here that she never proposed a universal franchise or
any kind of franchise for women. Indeed, when, in 1767, she wrote her
own *Short Sketch* for a good 'Democratic Form of Government', she
made no provision for votes for women, although she did suggest the
provision of independent annuities for women in lieu of dowries.[46] This
would not be surprising for its time, except for the fact that the *Short
Sketch* was addressed to the Corsican leader, Pasquale Paoli, and that
Corsica's constitution of 1755, adopted shortly after Paoli led Corsica to
independence from Genoa, gave the vote to all women over the age of
twenty-five, on an equal basis with men. Macaulay was either unaware of
this or chose to ignore it, but she did consider that natural rights are

possessed by all, even those outside the political community, and that it is important for the good of the whole that individuals constantly stand up for and defend them. Macaulay's thinking thus synthesises the republican idea of active citizenship with a broader conception of the role of assertive individuals, endowed with rights, outside the formal political process. By formulating this synthesis in these terms, we are able to see where she, like any other unenfranchised woman, might fit into her model of the political nation. We can also see the orientation of her political thought around the idea of the individual. Both methodologically and ethically, this is her main concern. Macaulay's histories are intensely preoccupied with the moral conduct of individuals, and the ways in which their moral choices affect the fate of liberty. As Lynne Withey points out, 'individual morality lay at the heart of Macaulay's method of writing history'.[47]

Macaulay's idea of the political priority of the individual was shared with, and no doubt considerably influenced, the reforming and radical political circles in which she moved. Much is known about her connections with such groups as the Club of Honest Whigs (comprising such figures as James Burgh, Richard Price, John Cartwright and Granville Sharp), and the Society of Supporters of the Bill of Rights (including her brother John Sawbridge, Horne Tooke and other friends of Wilkes).[48] The extent to which these groups, and other like-minded reformers and dissenters, articulated a radically new theory of government has been compellingly argued by Peter N. Miller in his study, *Defining the Common Good*. Miller argues that, particularly after the American Declaration of Independence shattered public consensus about the nature and purpose of the British imperial state, reformers redefined the relationship between the subject and the state in ways which rendered the individual philosophically and morally paramount: 'Individuals, defined by their possession of certain natural rights, were to be sovereign within their political communities.'[49] Natural rights, in this context, encompassed the idea, derived from Locke, of freedom of thought, as well as self-preservation; political communities ought to be arranged so as to accommodate the demands of truth and justice placed upon them by rational individuals. Miller pays far less attention to Macaulay than to her acquaintances Burgh, Sharp, Cartwright and Price, but his argument greatly illuminates her thought, especially when it comes to the relationship between liberalism, republicanism, ethics and metaphysics. Like her contemporaries, she was a moral realist, believing that a standard of truth existed independent of men, which all political agents needed to recognise and act upon. This was the true source of moral obligation for the

individual, and moral responsibility for women as well as men is thus not
a function of citizenship, but a theological given, no matter what the
political circumstances in which one finds oneself.

Macaulay thought deeply about the theological implications of such a
notion of individual moral responsibility, and published the fruit of her
thinking as *A Treatise on the Immutability of Moral Truth* (1783), the same
year that she completed her *History*.[50] This is undoubtedly her most
perplexing work. Ostensibly written to counter 'the decline of rational
religion' in her day, and in particular the association, in the works of
Scottish Enlightenment moral philosophers, between moral virtue and
'mere sentiment', it also continues the project of her histories by seeking
to add moral improvement to the other, more superficial ways in which
the 'human species have . . . been improving in [the] modes of civilization'.[51] Thus, while 'commerce has been celebrated as a Deity, whose
universal influence on the happiness of man is felt in present enjoyment',
Macaulay tells her readers that 'the present times have no reason to boast
of having made any progress in that higher part of civilization, which
affects the rational interest of man'.[52] Like the histories, Macaulay intends
her *Treatise* to contribute to a raising of the level of moral civilisation,
by countering what she and Joseph Priestley call the 'corruptions of
Christianity' muddying the waters of eighteenth-century Protestantism.[53]
Macaulay does this by refuting at length deism and scepticism, as represented in the works of Lord Bolingbroke. She does not attack Shaftesbury,
whom she excuses as a warm friend to virtue and as not necessarily an
'antichristian', and she is full of praise for Stoics such as Epictetus,
known to her through the translation of the 'very learned and judicious
Mrs. Carter'.[54] The greater part of the treatise is devoted to attacking
the voluntarist theology of the Irish Archbishop William King. King's
theodicy was set out in *De origine male* (1702), a work still popular in
Macaulay's day and one that argues for the reality of moral evil, which
arises from human free will and in some measure lies outside of the power
of God.[55] Macaulay's own position is in many respects very similar to that
of Catharine Cockburn and her Bluestocking heirs, and derives ultimately
from Samuel Clarke, which is that there is a moral order in the universe
and eternally fixed distinctions between right and wrong that cannot be
reduced to the 'arbitrary productions of the divine will'.[56] These 'essential and eternal discriminations of moral good and evil' are discoverable
by our senses and our reason, and this discovery constitutes the source of
our moral obligation to act rightly, even before the question of eternal
rewards and punishments arises.[57]

Thus far, Macaulay stakes out a familiar Lockean epistemology of sense impressions and reason, and a Latitudinarian theology of salvation for all. Her theology, as she acknowledges, owes a great deal to Clarke, and, as Sarah Hutton has pointed out, can be located upon the very considerable common ground between the Anglicans and dissenters of her circle, such as Richard Price and James Burgh.[58] There is a generous notion here of human rationality, including female rationality, as our means of understanding God's universal benevolence, and a potentially large place for philanthropic social action as part of Macaulay's conception of the world as a trial of virtue and a seed-bed for the soul.[59] Yet it is on this very point of benevolence that Macaulay takes a surprising turn away from her Latitudinarian predecessors and contemporaries, and argues passionately that 'the doctrine of philosophical liberty is hostile to every rational idea which can be formed of a perfect benevolence and perfect wisdom'.[60] In the closing section of her refutation of King, she mounts a long, bravura argument against the Arminian idea of the freedom of the human will, and in favour of what she calls 'moral necessity'.[61] Against King's and others' idea of the 'absolute freedom of will', Macaulay asserts that the human mind, in perceiving the 'essential difference which lies in the nature of things', has no choice but to desire the good and reject the bad, 'else why have we schools to train our youth in knowledge, and in habits of virtue?'[62] We experience moral necessity as a cognitive process, but this can, Macaulay argues, be reinforced at the level of education and of psychological inducements to good behaviour: the child who is taught that he (or she) has no choice but to do good is much less likely to err than the one who is taught that he has complete freedom to choose.[63] Like the modern-day member of Alcoholics Anonymous who must first acknowledge that he has no power over his addiction before taking the twelve steps to recovery, Macaulay thinks that the child is more likely to follow a good path if he accepts that it is not one of his own free choosing. To the common objection that necessitarianism makes us give up trying to be good or rational, Macaulay replies that it in fact makes us *more* morally active: 'where a rational interest is once thoroughly understood, the very law of our nature forbids that supineness which is supposed to take place in this instance'.[64] Education plays an essential role in enabling us to determine our true 'rational interest'. Indeed, Macaulay's theory of the will was fundamental to her theory of education, so much so that she included most of the *Treatise* in the third part of her *Letters on Education*. Adapted to the epistolary format of the letters, cut up into smaller sections and the specific references to King largely replaced by more generalised references to 'free-willers', the *Treatise* provided the epistemological and metaphysical underpinning of her theory of public education.

Macaulay's psychologically naturalistic updating of the old Calvinist idea of providential predestination might, at first sight, seem surprising in the context of her intellectual investment, in all her other writings, in the causes of political and education reform. Yet it should not be regarded as a private religious idiosyncrasy on Macaulay's part, or even as an instance of a writer carrying Clarke's idea of an objective moral realm, antecedent to God's commandments, to its logical extreme. Calvinism of a kind was undergoing something of a revival in Macaulay's day, and the theological issues of free will and necessity were in fact highly topical in the 1770s and 1780s, within the Methodist wing of the Church of England, and also among the Anglo-American dissenting community.[65] Macaulay alludes to this in her introduction to the *Treatise* when she praises Priestley and the great American theologian Jonathan Edwards for proving that moral necessity is 'consistent with the freedom, power, and infinite perfections of God, and the rational agency of man'.[66] She almost certainly had in mind Edwards's inquiry on the *Freedom of Will* (1754), in which he argued that such freedom was not essential to moral agency. Bridget Hill found evidence from a contemporary source that Edwards was 'a favourite author with her' and that she was seen reading 'Edwards on the Will'.[67] Macaulay was selective in her adaptation of Edwards's modernised Calvinism, but she certainly shared his view that a cultivated reason was necessary to co-operate with God's benevolent purpose for this world. History furnished her with many examples of men and women failing to cultivate this reason, and failing to respond to God's offered grace. She did not use the theological language of election to describe those historical agents who did act in conformity with God's providential purpose for human liberty, but she clearly regarded the politically responsible individual as in some way divinely chosen.

It follows from this that, in any given historical situation, individuals are not bound by customs and traditions (for example, allegiance to a bad sovereign) to act against the requirements of divine goodness, but are obliged to follow what their understanding tells them to be the right course of action. In Macaulay's *History of England*, this idea of a higher political responsibility is embodied in only a very few individuals: one important instance is the republican martyr Algernon Sidney who dominates virtually the whole of volume VII. John Hampden, despite some reservations on Macaulay's part, is another. Both exhibited what she praises as 'those generous sentiments of independency' which she counts as the 'the only characteristic of a real gentleman'.[68]

It is clear from the outset of the *History* that Macaulay is also presenting her authorial self as another such embodiment of autonomy or 'independency', in the ethical sense in which she uses the word, with rare confidence in her own rectitude. Macaulay's writing style is unique among eighteenth-century historians: wittily forthright to the point of colloquialism, she could also handle the language of political theory with sustained control, and yet despatch an opposing viewpoint in a single epigrammatic sentence. Unlike Hume before or Gibbon after her, irony was not her medium, and she was suspicious of the kind of rococo stylistic elaboration which Gibbon, in particular, made his own (as she observed, 'the flights of poetic fancy are too wild for the exercise of subjects bound within the limits of rationality, fitness, convenience, and use').[69] No other historian could match her assertive daring, or the panache with which she dismissed whole sets of ideas and swathes of history. Reviewing the eighteenth century, towards the end of her epistolary history, she delivered one of her customary dismissive flourishes:

Indeed, my friend, the history of England is at this period so little entertaining, that it puzzles me how to arrange the annual revolution of the same unavailing arguments on one side, and the same profligate venality on the other, in a manner as shall not render the detail of the abuses in our government as irksome in the reading as it is painful in the reflection.[70]

The confidence in her voice derives partly from her sense of her own exemplary rational independence, partly from the knowledge that she is aligned with the truth: her liberal creed will, she asserts, 'meet with little contradiction in a country enlightened with the unobstructed rays of rational learning'.[71] Since 'rational learning' is still obstructed by ignorance, she is content to appear as a living embodiment of a rationality ahead of her time. The fact that her embodiment is inescapably female does not stand in her way: 'The invidious censures which may ensue from striking into a path of literature rarely trodden by my sex, will not permit a selfish consideration to keep me mute in the cause of liberty.'[72]

Those who have written about the relationship between Macaulay's sex and her seemingly gender-neutral notions of rationality, liberty and

republican virtue have puzzled over remarks like that above. In one of
the best essays on Macaulay, Susan Wiseman makes the case that, 'In
Macaulay's own writing, republican commitment takes priority over
gender'.[73] It is not a puzzle which is easily resolved, but another way to
look at the question of the gender implications of republican history is
through the lens of the republican idea of qualification. In republican
political theory, not all are citizens; some are excluded from citizenship
(slaves, foreigners, children, women), others are potential citizens in the
sense that they may qualify (through property ownership, public service
etc.) for full, active membership of the polis at a point in the future.
Macaulay's histories are directly and indirectly engaged with this republican notion of qualification, and she ponders the virtues of independence,
rational self-control and financial autonomy which might qualify some
individuals as potential British citizens. Propertied independence is,
certainly, one qualification for citizenship, but intellectual and moral
qualities are also very important. One inference from her reflections on
the personal conditions for citizenship that seems warranted is that there
are women – herself included – who exhibit qualities of potential or what
we might call 'proto'-citizenship under the present arrangements.
A significant example she supplies of this idea of qualification and
potential public leadership is that of Mary II, wife of William III.
Macaulay makes it clear that, from the point of view of intelligence and
abilities, Mary was qualified to assume, on the abdication of her father
James II, a role in government equal to, or greater than, her husband.
Yet Mary fails to assume the leadership for which she is qualified, deterred
by an exaggerated respect for the authority of husbands:

Had Mary always exerted that independence of conduct which reason authorises,
and principle exacts, her virtues would have been sullied with as small an alloy of
frailty as is perhaps compatible with the human character; but as the whole tenor
of her conduct seems to have been directed by the blind rule of an indiscriminate
obedience, she cannot be classed among the illustrious characters which have
done the highest honour to the human race, except by those who imagine that
passive obedience to husbands stands the foremost in the list of female duties,
and is the highest virtue to which any woman can aspire.[74]

Mary is censured for her reluctance to push herself forward, when, in
all likelihood, 'she would have filled the throne with an equal degree of
dignity . . . as any one of the most boasted successors to the Norman
Conqueror'.[75] In Macaulay's modernised version of republicanism,
women should assume the responsibilities for which they are qualified
at the point when their country makes a call upon their active service.

There is an implicit contrast here between Mary's failure to act for her country and Macaulay's own refusal to keep mute in the cause of liberty.

The notion of qualification defines the borderline between Macaulay's idea of universal natural rights and her republican idea of selective citizenship. It makes sense in the context of her ideal of a vigilant, constantly resistant political culture, and of her individualism. Any male or female individual, qualified by intellect and rational independence, may find themselves in a time and place where their country needs their active participation. At that point, it is for them to read the runes of moral necessity, and to act for the public good. Macaulay's authorial persona seeks to exemplify the political vigilance, the independence from vested interests, parties and elites prerequisite to citizenship. Of course, her claim to speak in the public service has nothing to do with any idea of a special relationship between femininity and history, or of women as relics and reminders of the high ideals of the age of chivalry. Her own unequivocal sense of her qualification to speak, and cajole, on behalf of national liberties comes from her education, scholarship and independence of mind, with independence of fortune playing some part in all of these. What is also clear, from her histories and from the overt intellectual egalitarianism of her *Letters on Education*, is that she believed that greater influence for women should not come about merely as a by-product of the progress of refinement. If such refinement and politeness created a space for women to address more authoritatively domestic, moral and social matters, Macaulay chose not to speak out about it. Not for her the kind of 'progress' which only served to intensify notions of gender difference, and to isolate woman as a sociological rather than a political category of analysis.

Macaulay does not merely aspire to speak on an equal footing with men, but, rather, asserts her own discursive equality with a select band of men who have properly understood God's preordained providence and truth, their natural rights and the best principles of government. Her histories breathe the atmosphere of this elect and elite, virtual coterie, the historical counterpart of her own mixed radical circle with its self-consciously neo-classical radical style. Harriet Guest has written of Macaulay's status as a figure of fashion, noting how commentators such as Samuel Johnson and Horace Walpole suggested that 'Macaulay's reputations as a fashionable woman and as a republican historian may be interchangeable'.[76] Her reputation for preposterous fashionableness was certainly the downside of her self-conscious attempts to modernise the republican political tradition, to free it from images of aggressive, ascetic masculinity and self-lacerating, heroically loyal femininity. She writes as one whose higher obligation to herself as a rational being naturally and inevitably coincides with political right thinking. Such right thinking is, as I have argued, not simply the product of her reading of classical republican and early liberal texts; it derives from her insight that historical experience, moral realism and rational theology must constantly inform and transform both the practice and the ideals of politics. There is room here for the contemporary commercial world of Macaulay's family and friends, and there is room for a politically influential role for suitably qualified women. No reader can reach the end of Macaulay's histories without sensing how deeply held an aspiration the latter point really was for her. Macaulay writes history with the intensity of engagement and judgemental directness of one who feels that, had she been there and able to act, things might have turned out for the better. All the more intense, perhaps, because of the knowledge that, under any historical circumstances, her sex would have excluded her. All the more judgemental because the failed avatars of national liberty had power and opportunities which someone of her own calibre might have been far better qualified to use. Contemporary historians such as Hume and Gibbon wrote with a coolness and scepticism which proceeded, in part, from a sense of what their own fallibility might have been, if faced with the dilemmas and choices confronted by others in the past. Macaulay's histories could only have come from the pen of a woman who made her own political exclusion an imaginative source of strength, judgemental infallibility and superior historical insight.

CHAPTER 5

Good manners and partial civilisation in the writings of Mary Wollstonecraft

In her final work, the *Letters on Education* (1790), Catharine Macaulay turned, for the first time, to the matter of the current state of the progress of society and the ways it can be seen in the low educational level of the young. She offered a historically informed critique of modern manners, and suggested a remedy in an ambitious programme of identical education for girls and boys. This work, coming from a writer who had demonstrated a lifelong commitment to progressive political principles, had a profound impact on Macaulay's younger contemporary Mary Wollstonecraft. This chapter will endeavour to show how Wollstonecraft realised the potential of that critique of modern manners, from a similar radical political standpoint, for a feminist intervention in the course of social progress. Like Macaulay, Wollstonecraft engaged very critically with the cult of medieval chivalry and its degenerate manifestation in modern gallantry, but she was far more convinced than Macaulay of the value of the social analysis of the Enlightenment as a means of advancing the cause of male and female rights.[1] Wollstonecraft can also be placed more squarely than Macaulay within an eighteenth-century British tradition of Latitudinarian religious thought that bridged the gap between Anglicanism and Rational Dissent, with its undogmatic emphasis upon God's benevolence, upon the free will and rationality of the human subject, and upon the public duty to promote the welfare of all members of society.

In giving prominence to the British intellectual lineage of Wollstone-craft's thought, this chapter builds upon the recent, important study, *Mary Wollstonecraft and the Feminist Imagination* by Barbara Taylor, on Gary Kelly's earlier account of her ideas, as well as the many new insights generated by Janet Todd's biography of 2000.[2] Prior to Taylor's work, many studies of Wollstonecraft and her times, particularly those focusing upon the problem for feminist writers of the covert male gendering of abstract, universal rights, tended to press Wollstonecraft into a French mould; her preoccupation with manners was taken as the sign of her evasion of the fundamental problem of the male gendering of citizenship in the liberal thought of the period.[3] There was also a tendency to play down the religious dimensions of her thinking, or to see her faith as either idiosyncratic and heterodox or a radical rejection of the Anglican mainstream, following her husband and biographer William Godwin's depiction of it as a largely irrational, enthusiastic matter.[4] It is now possible to interpret Wollstonecraft's religious and moral sentiments in the context, not only of the rational dissenting intellectual milieu of which she was a part, but also of the productive cross-fertilisation of that milieu and broad church Anglicanism despite the increasingly adversarial relationship between those two religious tendencies in this period.[5] None of this is to downplay the power and originality of Wollstonecraft's intervention in the Enlightenment debate about women. Rather, this chapter aims to bring to the fore her remarkable intellectual fertility and eclecticism in deploying the vocabularies of that debate to radical and feminist ends. In all this, the work of Macaulay played a significant part. In her long review of Macaulay's *Letters on Education*, Wollstonecraft drew attention to Macaulay's argument that there is '*no characteristic difference in sex*', commenting that 'the observations on this subject might have been carried much farther, if Mrs M.'s object had not been a general system of education'.[6] Macaulay's treatise offered simultaneously a programme of education for the young, an account of moral motivation and a diagnosis of the social roles ascribed to men and women. Wollstonecraft's *A Vindication of the Rights of Woman* (1792) analyses the social and psychological conditions governing women's lives that make such a programme necessary in the first place. In doing so, she makes her own culture's stubborn insistence upon the reality of a 'characteristic difference in sex' a measure of its incomplete state of civilisation.

MACAULAY, EDUCATION AND THE HIGHER MORALITY

Macaulay's *Letters on Education* are divided into three parts, and addressed to a fictional correspondent, 'Hortensia'. The first part begins with the care of children's bodies, and moves from physical education to the cultivation of their imaginative, moral, social and spiritual capacities (the latter to be applied only to older children). It then reflects upon sexual differences, concluding that most of these are a matter of social ascription only, and ends with remarks on the class-based nature of contemporary education. Most of the remarks on women are directed towards preparing them to be rational wives and mothers, but always with the sense that Macaulay would like them to aim higher. The second part considers education in a wider political context, with historical observations on the educational practice of ancient civilisations, and reflections on the role of the modern state in promoting 'a more general Civilization' through public education.[7] The final part reprints, with some specific names removed, Macaulay's earlier *Treatise on the Immutability of Moral Truth*. The three-part structure of the *Letters* embodies Macaulay's fundamentally political and theological, rather than social, understanding of human agency. Readers might have been tempted to skip past the long theological section of the *Letters*, but Macaulay's idea of virtue as the rational co-operation with God's moral necessity is, in fact, central to her case for a better female education. One instance of this – perhaps echoing Masham's distinction between virtue and the law of private esteem – is her argument that girls should be taught to disentangle genuine virtue from mere public opinion. Under the present, defective system of education, Macaulay claims, 'reason loses its energy, and becomes no more than the echo of the public voice'.[8] Rather than being merely the servant of public opinion, women's reason must be cultivated so that their will is compelled to take the virtuous course of action. As Macaulay explains, 'God, in the same extent as he gave the privilege of reason, and allowed to this privilege its free course, necessarily subjected the volitions of the creature, to the necessity of being determined by that which the rational principle perceived to be the best.'[9] Society's obsession with 'necessary appearances' deadens the mind to the point where it understands only rigid and worldly ideas of virtue. One example of this, Macaulay argues with considerable daring, is the equation of female virtue with total chastity, which 'gives rise to the trite and foolish observation, that the first fault against chastity in woman has a radical power to deprave the character'.[10] This need not be the case since women are quite capable of moral resilience and growth even after a sexual lapse: 'The human mind is built of nobler materials than to be so easily corrupted; and with all the disadvantages of situation and education, women seldom become entirely abandoned till they are thrown into a state of desperation by the venomous rancour of their own sex.'[11]

At first, Wollstonecraft thought that this was taking the idea of adherence to a higher morality a little too far; she wrote in her review: 'The reflections on female chastity are just; but they required further explanation; for till the minds of women are more enlarged, we should not weaken the salutary prejudices which serve as a substitute, a weak one we own, for rational principles.'[12] However, by the time she came to write the

Vindication of the Rights of Woman, Wollstonecraft felt sufficiently emboldened by Macaulay's disregard for society's obsession with female chastity to endorse and elaborate upon this passage.[13]

In the review Wollstonecraft struggles with Macaulay's theology, finding that she takes a laudable anti-voluntarism to extremes ('she . . . thinks . . . that moral necessity extends to God'), as Samuel Clarke had done, and that she has caricatured 'free-willers' as those who believe that the understanding can arrive at moral insights and yet choose not to act upon them.[14] However, she does entirely concur that a higher morality is impossible without a good education. The hidden element in Wollstonecraft's disagreement with Macaulay is probably their different understandings of the ideas of David Hartley. Hartley is certainly one of the 'modern metaphysicians' credited by Macaulay in her preface to the *Letters* as one of those who have shed light on the 'operations of the mind', especially in relation to the 'power of association' by which the mind builds up ideas into moral habits.[15] Hartley's *Observations on Man*, originally published in 1749, was still current in the 1790s, having been edited by Joseph Priestley in 1775, and then republished in its entirety by Joseph Johnson in 1791.[16] Hartley was a necessitarian to the extent that he believed that 'Free-will is inconsistent with the infinite power of God', and this underpins his determinist, materialist account of man's psychological development. He argued that, although we have free will in the popular and practical sense, in 'the important Actions of our Lives or the strong Workings of our Affections' we do not have real 'philosophical Liberty' since all of these are 'determinable by previous Circumstances'.[17] Neither Macaulay nor Wollstonecraft followed Hartley's utilitarian emphasis upon pleasure and pain as the basis for moral associations, but they do seem to have espoused his view of the human mind as highly malleable, and of the acquisition of morality as an essentially cognitive process.[18] Macaulay concurred with his observations about 'philosophical liberty', especially as they rendered a good education morally imperative: as she writes, 'we must be esteemed passive agents in the collection of by far the greater number of the ideas lodged in the storehouse of the brain; and the purity of the mind must chiefly depend on the discretion of those with whom we are entrusted in our youth'.[19] Education becomes a kind of moral programming, and its goal is the creation of morally autonomous, benevolent human beings strong enough to retain their purity of mind even after lapses in chastity, and kind enough to pardon moral frailty in others.

This idea of human malleability forms the basis of Macaulay's case for a comprehensive system of national education, funded by public taxation, and designed to include all ranks and both sexes. The social consequences of this system are explored in Part II, where Macaulay develops some of the ideas, raised in her histories, about the effects of politics on education and manners. She sets out a kind of conjectural history of education and its role in the shaping of national manners, including discussions of ancient Greece and Rome. She combines a Montesquieuan sense of the relationship between education and the general spirit of individual societies, with a classical belief in the state as the instrument of social education. There is a culminating letter on the 'Duty of Governments towards Producing a general Civilisation' which places utopian faith in the state to educate people's sympathy through wise laws and by carefully regulating their physical and spiritual environments. Ever the political theorist, Macaulay is conscious that such a regulation implies an intervention by the state in private life, something, she says, that might be confused with the 'power . . . of interfering with all private as well as public concerns' usually claimed by despots and by strict republican governments.[20] Such objections notwithstanding, she says government must do something more than 'act the part of a good constable in preserving the public peace', and she then seems to grope her way towards a welfare model of the state as she argues that individuals must recognise that it is in their interest for the state to promote their happiness and interest through policies of social uplift.[21] From this we may infer that the goal of such a government would be to create an educated public and to realise the potential of each individual for citizenship. Economic progress alone, she insists, will not deliver an advanced state of society, but the 'refinement in morals' that comes with state education is necessary to the real progress of civilisation.[22]

The kernel of Macaulay's argument is in part I of the *Letters* where she explores the practical ways in which children should be educated into a state of moral and rational autonomy sufficient to inoculate them against the prejudices of society, and to transform that society in the longer term. The argument here is given intellectual bite by her engagement with Rousseau, an author whom she seems to have encountered quite late in life. She follows Rousseau's *Emile* (1762) in regarding the ideal education as one that develops a child's natural moral instincts in an arena segregated from the social world, but she objects strenuously to the fact that he assigned an ancillary role to the female character in his novel, Sophie – objections aired in two letters, number 22 ('No characteristic Difference in Sex') and number 23 ('Coquettry'). Rousseau's assertion of innate and hierarchical sex difference would not have been surprising or exceptionally enraging either to Macaulay or to Wollstonecraft were it not for the fact that it formed part of what was, in other respects, a progressive programme for political reform. Macaulay counters Rousseau by denying that 'Nature intended the subjection of the one sex to the other', and also engages, in a more sophisticated way, on his own terms, with his contradictory argument for differentiated sex roles.[23] The domestic subordination of men to uneducated, coquettish women, she points out, can only have bad consequences for society ('[it] must produce confusion and disorder in the system of human affairs').[24] She admits that this is an 'objection' which Rousseau did try to anticipate, but 'in order to obviate it', he 'has made up a moral person of the union of the two sexes, which, for contradiction and absurdity, outdoes every metaphysical riddle that was ever formed in the schools'.[25] For her, Rousseau's politics depend upon the idea of women and men as morally incomplete and lacking in ethical autonomy, and in this he can be said to degrade both sexes. For Rousseau, it was a matter of women contributing to male self-actualisation, preparatory to their public role. He was more concerned, as Penny Weiss has argued, with the *effects* than with the causes of sex differentiation, and with the ways in which basic biological difference might be nurtured and institutionalised for the good of the political realm.[26] For him, the domestic symbiosis of the sexes – the woman sexually and domestically all-powerful, the man intellectually superior – formed the ethical basis for an (all male) political community. Sex difference is thus, in part, for Rousseau, a strategically inculcated experience of the self; after all, a child 'does not perceive himself to be of any sex or any species; man and woman are equally unknown to him'.[27] The same is true, in Rousseau's *Discourse upon . . . Inequality*, of the civilising process in general, where behavioural differences between the sexes, which are not much in evidence in primitive tribes, only surface with the invention of property and civil society: 'it was now that the Sexes, whose way of Life had been hitherto the same, began to adopt different Manners and Customs'.[28]

For Macaulay, however, as later for Wollstonecraft, it made little difference whether such differentiation between the sexes was innate or strategic since both sexes were diminished by it. The diminution of the female mind was already a reality, one that Macaulay admits, 'fully justifies the keenness of Mr. Pope's satire on the sex', and that only compounds their 'total and absolute exclusion' from 'every political right'.[29] That exclusion was in no way mitigated by what Rousseau and many writers of the Scottish Enlightenment saw as women's compensatory sexual power: a power, Rousseau claimed in the *Discourse*, that women are keen to retain: 'Now it is easy to perceive that the moral Part of Love is a factitious Sentiment, engendered by Society, and cried up by the Women with great Care and Address in order to establish their Empire, and secure Command to that Sex which ought to obey.'[30] Women, Macaulay retorted, 'will be glad to give up indirect influence for rational privileges; and the precarious sovereignty of an hour enjoyed with the meanest and most infamous of the species, for those established rights which, independent of accidental circumstances, may afford protection to the whole sex'.[31] This forceful point formed the core of Wollstonecraft's argument against Rousseau's advocacy of a moral complicity between the sexes, and it crowns Macaulay's case for educating boys and girls together so that women will seem less mysterious in the eyes of men, and that girls will be preserved 'from the bane of coquetry'.[32]

The impact of Macaulay's *Letters* upon Wollstonecraft was great, and is attested by Wollstonecraft's review, as well as by a recently discovered correspondence in which the two women express mutual admiration and exchange copies of their replies to Burke's *Reflections*.[33] Macaulay's death in 1791 put an end to the possibility of friendship between them, but Wollstonecraft continued to feel the impact of her work, and was saddened by the loss of an ideal reader.[34] The intellectual similarities between the two women were grounded in their Protestant belief in the potential moral purposefulness of the social order, and in the idea that virtue and benevolence, rather than mutual self-interest, were the only viable basis for social co-operation. Both differed fundamentally from Rousseau in their view of man as a naturally sociable being, although they did not wish to jettison his idea that childhood should be a genuinely pre-social stage of human development, and not a parody of adulthood (like Mandeville's pert little Miss learning to curtsey).[35] Neither of them shared Rousseau's hostility to commerce, only to the hyper-feminised breed of female and abject kind of male which commerce tended to produce. Both were thoroughly familiar with the role which commerce played in Scottish ideas of the progress of society; and, while they rejected straightforward ascriptions of progress to modern history, they accepted and extended, for the purpose of feminist cultural analysis, many of the descriptive categories created by Scottish sociology (Macaulay only belatedly). Their reception of the Scottish Enlightenment was coloured by the reworking of conjectural history in Burke's *Reflections*, and by the advent, in the later part of the eighteenth century, of the new cultural Gothicism that prescribed, for women but not for men, a prolongation of the feudal stage. Through Burke, they learned one of the most important lessons of Millar's work: that, since feudal times, gender had become a form of rank, and that rank was analogous to gender. In Wollstonecraft's work, this idea was to become a sharp, double-edged critique of the distinction of (social and sexual) ranks in society. The idea makes an appearance in Macaulay's *Letters*, although she only scratches its surface, as a critique of class subjectivity. The first part of the *Letters* ends with 'Hints towards the Education of a Prince', a letter that, at first, seems anomalous, but that makes sense once Macaulay makes clear that her interest lies in the warped subjectivity engendered in young people by too early and too great an attention to their social position. 'A being, treated with ceremonies which from their nature must destroy every just idea of self' is bound, she says, to become a capricious and flattery-dependent king.[36] Macaulay then goes on to denounce the 'idle debauchery' and servility of courtly culture in ways which anticipate Wollstonecraft's own attack on courtliness.[37] She does not make any explicit link between the 'idea of self' instilled into princes by flattery and the perverted selfhood of those domestic princesses, modern women. Yet the germ of *A Vindication of the Rights of Woman* is here, and there can be no doubt that Wollstonecraft would have noticed it.

THE RADICAL USES OF MANNERS

Both Macaulay and Wollstonecraft had common intellectual and/or personal affinities with 'commonwealth' radicals on both sides of the Atlantic, such as Richard Price, James Burgh and Joseph Priestley, and they have often been read as giving a female turn to English dissenting radicalism.[38] But, as Taylor has argued, Wollstonecraft adapted and diluted the residually classical elements of dissenting radicalism without espousing their particular strain of natural rights arguments.[39] In recent years, more attention has been paid to the relationship of Wollstonecraft's writings to the canonical works of the Enlightenment – works which, after all, engaged explicitly with questions of women's history, social position and rights. This is the case in Sylvana Tomaselli's introduction to her edition of the two *Vindications*, and especially in Jane Rendall's seminal work on Wollstonecraft's *Historical and Moral View of the French Revolution*.[40] Wollstonecraft's early familiarity with Scottish and French Enlightenment texts is evident in an educational work which she compiled for young girls, *The Female Reader* (1789), which includes extracts from Robertson, Hume, Voltaire and Addison.[41] A review for the *Analytical* indicates her familiarity with Montesquieu's *Persian Letters*, and probably also with *The Spirit of Laws*, and she makes reference in other works to Pope, Mandeville, Smith, Locke and Shaftesbury.[42] In the light of this intellectual lineage, it is possible to read Wollstonecraft's non-fictional works, from the two *Vindications* to the history of the French Revolution, as an ambitious and constantly evolving attempt to adapt Enlightenment history and sociology to a radically critical analysis of modern culture. Her focus, in other words, was trained upon the sub-political stratum of society, the arena of 'manners', and her aim was to extend or revise existing categories of cultural and historical analysis for the purposes of practical reform. She believed that reform could only follow from a proper understanding and implementation of the cultural pre-conditions for change, such as higher standards of personal morality, the re-education of women or the transformation of political culture. Indeed, as we will see, she was increasingly alert to the dangers of trying to effect political change too quickly, and without the prerequisite reformation of manners.

Wollstonecraft's first polemical work, *A Vindication of the Rights of Men, In a Letter to the Right Honourable Edmund Burke* (1790), inaugurated her investigation of the relationship between manners and politics. Written as a reply to Burke's *Reflections*, its title seems to promise a liberal defence of natural rights in the manner of other contemporary radicals such as Thomas Paine. After all, the Lockean language of rights, which lay dormant for much of the eighteenth century, had recently been revived in England by dissenting radicals and proponents of constitutional reform.[43] Yet Wollstonecraft shows little interest in deploying or developing this new vocabulary of rights; indeed, it was not until the *Historical and Moral View of the Origin and Progress of the French Revolution* (1794) that she gave a clear statement of her belief that freedom is the 'natural and imprescriptible right of man' under the social contract.[44] Instead, she offers a diagnosis of modern manners, and of the warped social norms and cultural tastes of which Burke, with his 'real or artificial affection, for the English [medieval] constitution', is both a defender and a symptom.[45] Like Macaulay, in her attack on Burke, Wollstonecraft ridicules contemporary medievalist reverence for all things Gothic, and examines the cultural roots of long-established habits of political submission in Britain. These habits, she complains during a lengthy evaluation of modern manners, have fostered either libertinism or 'unmanly servility' in men, and coquettishness and vanity in women.[46] As Janet Todd has argued, 'she could not be straightforwardly revolutionary like Paine, who wanted society transformed through a change of institutions; instead she sought a basic psychological and personal reform that must come from change in individual attitudes'.[47]

Rather than giving a lengthy defence of the French Revolution or of the rights of man, Wollstonecraft sets out to reverse the Enlightenment tradition of sociological irony in which manners are judged according to their effect rather than by their moral content. For Montesquieu, Hume, Mandeville and even to a limited extent for Burke, a people's manners, even if they are a little frivolous, must be evaluated in the light of their effect upon economic prosperity and political stability. A person's moral actions may be less important to the good of the whole than the general tendency of the social conventions to which he or she adheres. It is this vein of irony in the social thought of Burke's predecessors which explains Wollstonecraft's repeated assertions, in both *Vindications*, that manners and morals have become confused: 'The civilization which has taken place in Europe has been very partial, and . . . refines the manners at the expence of the morals.'[48] In the first *Vindication*, she uses the example of women as part of her critique of what she sees as the Enlightenment de-moralisation of manners. The 'laxity of morals in the female world', she warns, is a direct consequence of the European 'refinement' so strenuously defended by Burke, which, in reality, 'lessens [male] respect for [female] virtue, by rendering beauty, the grand tempter, more seductive'.[49] She tackles directly Burke's complaint about the French Revolutionary disregard for the special sanctity of monarchy, citing his remark that, 'On this [the Revolutionaries'] scheme of things a king *is* but a man; and a queen *is* but a woman' – a phrase which struck a deep chord with her and to which she would return in the second *Vindication*.[50] This, she points out, is to subordinate a king or queen's humanity to their rank, something which happens at all levels of modern society when people internalise the social persona expected of them, and come to believe it is their real self. Wollstonecraft's sense of a tension between men and women's innate humanity and their socially ascribed identities is indebted to Rousseau's distinction between 'amour de soi' and 'amour propre'. But there is also the kernel of a more original argument that inequalities of property and distinctions of rank are uniquely unfavourable to the humanity of women: women have the most to lose, in both moral and practical terms, from being forced into social identities such as 'the fine lady', the strumpet or the lowly governess, and being (literally) classed by male gallantry as a venerated yet subordinate group.

Soon after the first *Vindication*, Wollstonecraft corresponded with Macaulay, reviewed her *Letters* and read her *Observations* on Burke's *Reflections*. Macaulay's work no doubt encouraged Wollstonecraft to think more deeply about the connection between sexual difference and ideas of medieval chivalry. Wollstonecraft's *A Vindication of the Rights of Woman* appeared two years later, and developed Macaulay's attack on Burke's medieval genealogy of modern manners and politics. Here, as in the first *Vindication*, Wollstonecraft characterises modern Europe as at once feudally retarded and hyper-civilised. In the arena of gender relations, she saw this as being epitomised in the new cult of male gallantry, once dismissed as Frenchified and silly by Shaftesbury, but modernised by Enlightenment thinkers, and given fresh historical burnish by proponents of the new medievalism.[51] Both modern women and pre-Revolutionary France (which she describes in her *Historical View* as the sick woman of Europe) are symptomatic of the depraved state of European civilisation, and neither can be reformed quickly or easily. Macaulay's political hostility to constitutional medievalism thus becomes, in Wollstonecraft's later works, part of a broader diagnosis of the malaise of European culture.

Wollstonecraft's second *Vindication* inaugurated that diagnosis with, as its subtitle indicates, 'Strictures on Moral and Political Subjects', but it did not contain an overt or detailed programme for political or legal reform in the manner of, say, Paine's *Rights of Man* (1791). She stated, in the advertisement to the *Vindication*, that she planned a second volume containing specific proposals for the reform of the 'laws relative to women', but this never appeared, and the surviving notes towards it suggest that her interests continued to be mainly psychological and cultural.[52] The work has strong similarities with the second part of Macaulay's *Letters* in that it examines the ways in which contemporary culture influences, or rather deforms, women's education, but unlike her predecessor, Wollstonecraft doubts whether even the best, Rousseauan education can ever protect the young from the influence of a bad society: 'I do not believe that a private education can work the wonders which some sanguine writers have attributed to it. Men and women must be educated, in a great degree, by the opinions and manners of the society they live in.'[53]

In terms of its content and methodology, the *Vindication* approximates most closely to a Scottish-style study of the origin of the distinction of gender in society, structured, like Kames's *Sketches of the History of Man*, as a series of closely interrelated sketches of (middle-class) female manners, but aiming at systematic argument. In the introduction, Wollstonecraft declares her aim to provide a 'treatise' on 'female rights and manners'.[54] The account of manners stems, as she says in the opening sentence, from 'considering the historic page', and from her observation that 'the civilization which has hitherto taken place in the world has been very partial'.[55] By diagnosing female manners under the present, partial state of civilisation (mis-called by others the 'commercial stage'), and by disentangling manners from morality, Wollstonecraft is able to mount a critique of Enlightenment history on its own terms. She challenges the ironic and instrumental view of female morality implicit in her predecessors' depiction of social interaction as a kind of sexual sublimation. 'Manners and morals are so nearly allied that they have often been confounded,' she warns, and women are unfortunately taught to 'acquire manners before morals'.[56] Wollstonecraft prescribes a moral education for women which would promote their mental and spiritual welfare, and would disentangle female morality from questions of social expediency. In order to achieve this, she argues in chapter six that we must analyse, not only the defects of modern education, but the deep psychological roots of sexual subjectivity – those early sense impressions which 'give a sexual character to the mind', and, in chapters seven and eight, those pervasive cultural influences which teach women to be slaves to the laws of private esteem.

Polemicism aside, Wollstonecraft's characterisation of the modern, commercial stage of society as peculiarly perilous for female sexual morality has much in common with Millar and Smith in their more anxious moments, and she does recognise, as they did, that female morality and manners are functionally related to the economic life of society as a whole. Where she differs sharply from many of her Scottish Enlightenment predecessors, and has more in common with Price and Priestley, is her insistence upon the explanatory precedence of individual morality as a means of evaluating the workings of society and of politics. She reiterates at the very end of the *Vindication* a point she makes throughout that 'public virtue is only an aggregate of [the] private', and this points to an underlying, continuity theory of individuals and the state.[57] There is a Shaftesburian (and emphatically anti-Mandevillean) component to her belief that 'public affections, as well as public virtues, must ever grow out of the private character'.[58] But, whereas Shaftesbury assumed a natural and inevitable connection between private virtues and the public good,

Wollstonecraft points out that, in the case of women, the connection is ruptured because their lack of civil and political rights reduces their moral stake in the good of the commonwealth: for women's 'private virtue' to become 'a public benefit, they must have a civil existence in the state, married or single'.[59] Denied a public dimension to their moral choices, women have little incentive to act virtuously: 'the private duty of any member of society must be very imperfectly performed when not connected with the general good'.[60] A realignment of private female virtues and public benefits could be effected by a dual process of legal reform and moral regeneration; improved civil rights would thus have a civic purpose. This is not liberalism in the modern sense, although many critics have said so, because, unlike liberal theorists such as Paine with his claim that 'society is produced by our wants, and government by our wickedness', Wollstonecraft seeks to promote a realignment, rather than a liberal separation, of public and private domains.[61] And, unlike Paine or Smith, she does not see the pursuit of economic self-interest ('our wants') as the basis of social cohesion. Indeed, one of the political theorists with whom she felt some affinity was the French finance minister, Jacques Necker (husband of Suzanne), whose religious reservations about liberal individualist views of society she seems to have absorbed and partly shared. Although she later became disillusioned with Necker's political conduct, Wollstonecraft was sufficiently impressed by his treatise *On the Importance of Religious Opinions* to translate it at her own initiative in 1788.[62] Necker's work is a curious blend of political pragmatism and Protestant conviction, and amounts, in effect, to a religious critique of the liberal idea of society as multiple pursuits of private interests. Private interest, Necker argues, is no basis for community. All societies need the moral cement of religious belief: 'We are then under a great illusion, if we hope to be able to found morality on the connection of private interest with that of the public; and if we imagine, that the empire of social laws can be separated from the support of religion.'[63] Religion, for Necker, as well as being an inner light, is also a mode of public opinion which influences people to make private moral choices in public-spirited ways. He does not make specific reference to women, but Wollstonecraft might have inferred that he envisaged a place for them in the ethical life of the public sphere.

Necker's work may have provided Wollstonecraft (as it certainly did his daughter Germaine de Staël) with a starting point for thinking about the connection between female morality and the public good within the general framework of her religious belief. Religious belief is fundamental to Wollstonecraft's advocacy of a higher private morality and its integration into reformed public life, and it is the religious framework of *A Vindication of the Rights of Woman* that gives particular force to her key vocabularies of virtue, benevolence and reason. Wollstonecraft's religious views, set out by Taylor in a pioneering chapter entitled 'For the Love of God', were in many ways unconventional.[64] She shared with Unitarians, such as Richard Price, the minister at her local chapel, an antivoluntarist theology of a benign God, accessible to reason and private judgement, offering the hope of heaven but not the threat of hell, and a view of Jesus – bordering, in Wollstonecraft's case, on distrust – as a human teacher, not as a part of the Godhead. She combined this Unitarian outlook with a highly personal, passionate, rapturous and, in later life, distinctively Romantic devotion to a God immanent in the natural world. As Taylor argues, Wollstonecraft's twin emphases upon reason and love have a Christian Platonist ancestry, something mediated through the work of Price, himself indebted to Cudworth and Clarke.[65] She probably read or knew a great deal about Price's *Review of the Principal Questions and Difficulties in Morals*, first published in 1758 and revised in 1769 and 1787. In this work, Price built upon Butler's idea that reflection is the cardinal principle of religious and moral life, in order to demolish more recent arguments, advanced by Hume and Smith, as well as by Hutcheson before them, that morality is a matter of sentiment, affection or instinct. Instead, Price advanced what Isabel Rivers has called 'the fullest and most convincing defence in the mid-eighteenth century of the rationalist account of the foundation of morals', insisting that the basis of a virtuous person's action must always be in reflection and reason, and not in feeling alone.[66] To argue otherwise, Price insists, is to deny that right and wrong have an objective reality, and to say that the moral agent is not responsible for his or her actions.

With these ideas Wollstonecraft entirely concurred, and her second *Vindication* is punctuated with remarks such as '*God is Justice itself*', that virtue 'has only one eternal standard' and that '*every being may become virtuous by the exercise of its own reason*'.[67] She seems to have admired Butler's *Analogy*, but was far less interested than Price or Macaulay in theological specificities, although she does state that it is a part of our rational devotion to want to 'scan the attributes of the Almighty'.[68] Her main interest was in the *processes* of moral cognition, and in how a re-educated woman reflects on the pain and moral errors of her life, and comes to a better understanding of the standard of virtue set by God: '[God] wounds but to heal, says reason, and our irregularities producing certain consequences, we are forcibly shewn the nature of vice; that thus learning to know good from evil, by experience, we may hate one and love the other, in proportion to the wisdom which we attain.'[69]

Once we come to this higher level of moral understanding and grasp the divinely created reality of virtue, we have no choice but to act virtuously: 'Rational religion . . . is a submission to the will of a being so perfectly wise, that all he wills must be directed by the proper motive – must be reasonable.'[70] Price, too, wrote of how an agent, as soon as '*moral good* appears to him', has no choice as to how to act, but 'is tied in the most strict and absolute manner, in bonds that no power in nature can dissolve'.[71] Like Clarke before them, Price and Wollstonecraft were committed to the idea of the free will of the human agent to do what he or she thinks is his or her duty, and they stopped short of the 'philosophical necessity' espoused by Macaulay and Priestley. Indeed, Price engaged in a lengthy correspondence with Priestley on the subject, later published as *A Free Discussion of the Doctrines of Materialism and Philosophical Necessity* (1778). Wollstonecraft takes this freedom for granted as she spends the greater part of the *Vindication* analysing and denouncing the defective education and social influences that cloud the judgement and pervert the will of most women. In chapter 13, she even shows how such influences produce woolly-brained superstition in the women who resort to hell-fire preachers, mesmerists, 'magnestisers' and other spiritual quacks (and there is a hint that Jesus may have been one of them).[72] Her commitment to the notion of free will lies behind her sense of the social sphere, not, as it was for Macaulay, as something to be transcended through the practice of moral rectitude, but as a sphere of moral cognition, experience and probation. From this perspective the case for a reformation of manners is more pressing than ever.

THE ORIGIN OF THE DISTINCTION OF THE FEMALE RANK

Much of the second *Vindication* is concerned with analysing and deploring the current system of manners, and in showing how they emanate from class and sex roles, since from the perspective of cultural analysis the 'distinction of sex' and the distinction of rank are functionally similar.[73] Wollstonecraft's central argument about ascribed class and gender identities develops from Burke's complaint that, in Revolutionary France, 'a king is but a man' and 'a queen is but a woman'. In Britain's hierarchical society, Wollstonecraft complains, 'a king is always a king – and a woman always a woman: his authority and her sex, ever stand between them and rational converse'.[74] The ranks of king or woman, although they confer power, subsume the person within their role, and cut them off from rational human interaction. Wollstonecraft is troubled, like Macaulay before her, by the distorted 'idea of self' that this engenders, but she is equally concerned with the moral consequences for society as a whole of this description of 'woman' as a role. She compares women to noblemen, and maintains that, like women, men of rank are morally diminished by the social identity forced upon them: 'may it not be fairly inferred that their local situation swallowed up the man, and produced a character similar to that of women, who are *localized*, if I may be allowed the word, by the rank they are placed in, by *courtesy?*'[75] She derives her characterisation of noblemen and kings from Smith's *Theory of Moral Sentiments*, which she quotes at length, but also takes her cue from Rousseau's remark, in *Emile*, that 'men are not naturally opulent, courtiers, nobles or kings'.[76] Yet he also contended, in the same work, that women, unlike men, are permanently localised in their gender identity, partly by their biology, but far more by the needs of the state. Wollstonecraft, by contrast, denies that there is a civic purpose behind the distinction of gender as currently constituted. The exalted yet hollow prestige of women, like that of kings and aristocrats, is merely the result of degenerate manners and a rotten constitution. Wollstonecraft thus puts together, in an original way, previous critiques of the system of ranks with an Enlightenment sociology of women, and then offers an alternative in the form of her famous and seemingly outlandish 'wild wish':

A wild wish has just flown from my heart to my head, and I will not stifle it though it may excite a horse-laugh. – I do earnestly wish to see the distinction of sex confounded in society, unless where love animates the behaviour. For this distinction is, I am firmly persuaded, the foundation of the weakness of the character ascribed to woman.[77]

This wild wish has been influentially interpreted by Cora Kaplan as proceeding from a sexual puritanism in Wollstonecraft, 'a violent antagonism to the sexual . . . [which] betrays the most profound anxiety about the rupturing force of female sexuality'.[78] The containment of that rupturing force may only be achieved at the price of women's strenuous self-desexualisation: a high price, it would seem, for the recovery of their self-respect and status in society.[79] This interpretation has led to a productive preoccupation, among modern commentators, with the split between the apparent hostility to female sexuality in the *Vindication* and the valorisation, in Wollstonecraft's fiction, of women's sensibility and desires, and the importance of expressing them.[80] However, one way of approaching this split is to look closely at the eighteenth-century intellectual genesis of notions such as the 'distinction of sex' and ascribed 'character'. 'Distinction', in the sense that Wollstonecraft uses it (like Millar before her), means the special social consideration and rank afforded to women at certain, higher stages of social evolution. Distinction is also a matter of tradition, and of the role assigned to women within the social structure. To wish that such distinctions might be confounded is, indeed, wild, but as much because it would entail a radical rethinking of history and politics as because it would require the neutering of women.

Scottish Enlightenment history enabled Wollstonecraft to think about gender in evolutionary terms, even though she did not share the presumption of many Scottish thinkers that the modern, commercial world had found a perfectly adapted form of femininity in the woman of sensibility. Indeed, Wollstonecraft singles out for censure the Scottish conduct book writers John Gregory and James Fordyce, not least because their prescriptions and complacencies were underwritten by Scottish Enlightenment notions of the evolution of femininity.[81] Far from being adapted to the commercial age, Wollstonecraft maintains, modern woman is a relic of an earlier phase of history, and to this extent she agrees with Burke and other contemporary medievalists. Historically derived distinctions of sex and 'characters' are, Wollstonecraft implies when she writes of 'courtesy', merely the residue of feudalism, and in this she agrees with the conclusions, if not the values, of the eighteenth-century medievalists. Thus, whereas for Burke the time lag between modern manners and the current stage of economic development helps to provide stability in an era of commercial and imperial change, Wollstonecraft sees feudal manners as a brake on progress: 'in short,' she writes, 'women, in general, as well as the rich of both sexes, have acquired all the follies and vices of civilization, and missed the useful fruit'.[82]

Wollstonecraft's attack on courtly women and her 'wild wish' for an end to distinctions of sex and rank thus belong to a wider philosophy of history. Only the bare bones of this philosophy are present in the second *Vindication* (she declares her intention not to 'go back to the remote annals to trace the history of woman'), but it later came to the fore in her account of the French Revolution. Wollstonecraft differs from other Enlightenment writers, and from Mandeville, in that she does not engage extensively with the notion of consumerism as a sublimation of sexual desire, or of female sexuality as a stimulus for commercial activity.[83] Like

Macaulay, she writes as though the 'fruit of civilization' – a politically reformed, commercial kind of society with its attendant modes of masculinity and femininity – has yet to arrive. Wollstonecraft's middle-class women inhabit a pseudo-medieval world of courtly decadence rather than a commercial one of voracious consumerism: 'gentlewomen,' she observes, 'are softened rather than refined by civilization'.[84] This is a world which also resembles late imperial Rome – at least as the Scottish historians represented it – with its advanced artistic culture, despotic government, sophisticated but degenerate manners, lack of morals and lack of any general social distribution of the benefits of commerce. In the first *Vindication*, Wollstonecraft describes ancient Rome in much the same terms as she describes Britain in the second *Vindication*, and as she would later describe *ancien régime* France: 'their civilization must have been very partial, and had more influence on the manners than morals of the people'.[85] 'Partial' civilisations, with their ritualised forms of courtship, mobilise women as sexual objects through a combination of display and delay.[86] Wollstonecraft, as her fiction clearly demonstrates, is not hostile to female sexual self-expression itself, only to the kinds of hyper-femininity produced by partial states of civilisation.[87] Hyperfemininity is, for Wollstonecraft, the sign of women's subordination to the social priorities of decadent or pseudo-feudal societies such as France, Britain or ancient Rome. Her contention that contemporary constructions of female morality and sexuality are the product, not so much of consumer culture but of an immature, unevenly developed commercial modernity, is thus part of an as yet under-developed historical argument.

A VIEW OF THE FRENCH REVOLUTION

Pre-Revolutionary France provided Wollstonecraft with a particularly compelling example of uneven social development. It had a culture of luxury and of highly refined modern manners frothing on top of a feudal system of economic injustice, and a highly sexualised and polarised set of gender roles that made real love almost impossible. In 1790, Wollstonecraft made these points in a review of a book entitled *La Galérie des Dames Françoises* in which she observed that:

in a state of society, where politeness destroys the great outline of character, the fine shades of manners will ever be caught, and artfully diversified . . . when the two sexes constantly associate, sentiment and gallantry imperceptibly take place of passion, and the desire of being thought *amiable* in the circle, soon makes vanity domineer over the more natural and laudable inclinations of the heart.[88]

A few years later, the writing of her history of the French Revolution provided her with an opportunity to test and explore these observations, and to gauge the effect of political revolution upon a hyper-civilised society. The *Historical View* certainly represents the culmination of her analysis of manners, gender roles and morals, which she now considers in the context of their relationship to the history of political culture. She told her sister Eliza that she was 'writing a great book'.[89] Its full title, *An Historical and Moral View of the Origin and Progress of the French Revolution; and the Effect It Has produced in Europe*, announces that the work is not a chronological history or political tract, but a philosophical and historical 'view', in the sense of Robertson's 'View of the Progress of Society in Europe', of the relationship between manners, history and political institutions. The nature of Wollstonecraft's philosophical ambitions was well recognised by contemporary reviewers, many of whom evaluated the work in the light of its preoccupation with political culture.[90] Modern critics are understandably disappointed by Wollstonecraft's lack of overt interest in the consequences of the French Revolution for women, by the absence of an emphatically female narrative voice, and by her attitude – critical, even by the standards of the other contemporary histories – towards the female participants in the events described. Rather than dwell on female historical agents, Wollstonecraft tends to use notions of gender as an interpretive tool. The French, she insists time and again, 'may be considered as a nation of women', and, like Pope's women, they have no characters at all ('a frenchman, like most women, may be said to have no character distinguishable from that of the nation').[91] This is not merely an insult to the French. Wollstonecraft uses a sociological vocabulary to argue that the French of the *ancien régime* occupied roughly the same cultural position as the British women in the second *Vindication*, both having succumbed to the debilitating effects of the hyper-feminisation that occurs at particular phases of social development. One major question for Wollstonecraft is whether, and how quickly, political revolution can put them on course for cultural reformation.

Wollstonecraft first came to Paris in December 1792, not long after the September Massacres. Initially, she adopted a cracking-eggs-to-make-omelettes attitude towards the violence of the Revolution, but she soon became disillusioned, and was moved by the plight of the king and queen.[92] Apart from letters home, her first written account of events seems to have been a letter 'Introductory to a Series of Letters on the Present Character of the French Nation', dated 15 February, 1793, but not published until after her death. The fragment suggests that she may have been planning a work along the lines of her friend Helen Maria Williams's *Letters written in France* (1790). Wollstonecraft's letters give her first impressions of the frivolousness of the French, and then ponder the likely fate of the Revolution in relation to France's level of social development ('I wish calmly to consider the stage of civilization in which I find the French').[93] The letters, as Gary Kelly pointed out, are clearly 'presented as Enlightenment sociology'.[94] Wollstonecraft wonders whether France is on a path towards a new social phase in which refinement and virtue might be combined. At first, she writes, she thought that Revolutionary France had already reached this stage: 'Before I came to France, I cherished, you know, an opinion, that strong virtues might exist with the polished manners produced by the progress of civilisation.'[95] A few weeks in the country were enough to cure her of such optimism, and to bring her back to the view that there is an inherent tension between civilisation and moral 'purity of manners'.[96] A nation's moral fibre, she acknowledged, must inevitably be slackened by the progress of refinement. The difficulty for France is that, having reached an advanced stage of cultural development under the *ancien régime*, it has played host to a revolution that must rely, for its survival, on the moral fibre of its citizens. Wollstonecraft's letter does not go on to explore this point, but this does look forward to the argument of the *Historical View*. She started writing this work in the summer of 1793, by which time France and Britain were at war, and soon after Wollstonecraft was living in comparative safety as the 'wife' of the American entrepreneur and writer Gilbert Imlay. Her social and intellectual ties were to the defeated Girondists, and, by the time she completed and published her work in 1794, she had become deeply disaffected with the Revolution. 'My blood runs cold', she wrote to her friend Ruth Barlow in July, 'and I sicken at thoughts of a Revolution which costs so much blood and bitter tears'.[97] The result of this disillusionment was a bleak account of the French and the French Revolution, and the *Historical View* records the events of May to October 1789 from the perspective of the Revolution's eventual failure. Wollstonecraft's version of the Revolution is full of enraged disappointment, over and above that of the other radical historians writing at the same time.[98]

Wollstonecraft was accused in one review of relying too heavily upon the synoptic account printed in the *New Annual Register*, but a careful cross-examination reveals very few borrowings and little similarity with the constitutional Whiggism of that work's support for the early reforms of the National Assembly.[99] Other contemporary narratives have few points of similarity with Wollstonecraft's *Historical View*, and most lack its philosophical quality. Mackintosh's royalist *Historical Sketch* shares her outrage at the attack on the palace of 6 October 1789, while Rabaut Saint-Etienne's *Précis historique* anticipates her interpretation of events in France as, first and foremost, a revolution in public opinion, but not her conviction that the Duc d'Orléans was responsible for much of the mischief.[100] There are similarities between the *Historical View* and the Scottish evolutionary sense of history apparent in the *Letters on the Revolution of France* by Thomas Christie, the editor of the *Analytical Review*, although she does not concur with his (almost De Tocquevillean) view that the Revolution occurred partly because the *ancien régime* had started to liberalise.[101] There are also similarities of approach with the radical *Histoire de la Revolution de 1789*, which places the same emphasis as Wollstonecraft on the role of Enlightenment ideas in the run up to the Revolution, and has her feeling for events as an exciting yet terrifying outburst of popular frustration.[102] Wollstonecraft was less concerned than most of these authors to supply new factual information, yet few of the French or British accounts strove for the same degree of philosophical generality or tried, as she did, to integrate a sociology of the French national character into an explanation of the Revolution.

Having decided to discontinue the letters on the character of the French nation, Wollstonecraft's choice of a non-epistolary, philosophical-historical format for the *Historical View* served her well. After the success of Williams's *Letters*, this format must have seemed less commonplace, and it avoided the gendered intersubjectivity and circumscribed perspective of the foreign woman writing home. Wollstonecraft's frame of reference is European, with France acting as both a case study and a warning to other nations. A combination of Enlightenment cosmopolitanism and Protestant providentialism forms the basis for her commitment to gradual political change. She acknowledges that providence has yet to deliver a higher stage of civilisation, but puts forward her own distinctive version of the idea of the progress of society in which she envisages a stage beyond the stage of commercial refinement when manners and morals will converge and political justice will be done. Civilisation in modern Europe, she argues here as in the *Vindications*, though it has made many advances, is still 'partial', and consists 'almost entirely in polishing the manners' at the expense of morality and a proper science of politics.[103] The purpose of the book is thus to discover why France was not able, through revolution, to make the transition to that final, advanced stage of society. Wollstonecraft's answer to this question is similar to Scottish Enlightenment explanations for the demise of Rome: both France and Rome were essentially agricultural states, with a wealthy and cultured aristocracy, which proved too unstable to last, and too backward to regenerate themselves.[104] There is, at one point, the rudiment of an argument, later developed in the *Letters Written . . . In Sweden*, about the greater evolutionary potential of commercial countries like England (with its 'monied interest, from which political improvement first emanates'), but this is not greatly developed, and she mainly focuses upon the ways in which cultural refinement actually inhibits political progress.[105]

The *Historical View* opens with an overview of the partial progress of civilisation, and the development of French courtly culture from the Middle Ages to the eighteenth century. Wollstonecraft argues that the *ancien régime*'s courtly ethos, with its elaborate system of deference and gallantry, suffused the culture of the French people to the point where reform became almost impossible. Revolutionary upheaval was doomed to replicate, rather than transcend, its inhumane frivolity. This is her perception of the Revolution from the hindsight of the September Massacres and the Terror:

The character of the french, indeed, had been so depraved by the inveterate despotism of ages, that even amidst the heroism which distinguished the taking of the Bastille, we are forced to see that suspicious temper, and that vain ambition of dazzling, which have generated all the succeeding follies and crimes . . . The morals of the whole nation were destroyed by the manners formed by the government. – Pleasure had been pursued, to fill up the void of rational employment . . . so that, when that changed their system, liberty, as it was called, was only the acme of tyranny . . .[106]

The point that the manners of the French limited the efficacy of the Revolution is made repeatedly in the *Historical View*, and this is linked to a general taxonomy of savage and advanced societies, as well as to a gendered account of national character. Over the centuries, she says, the French have acquired female characteristics such as a love of novelty and pleasure, an inability to think of anything beyond immediate gratification and a propensity for 'sudden transitions from one extreme to another'.[107] They have developed rigid social hierarchies at the expense of their humanity and have never had the political education to change their circumstances in a rational, gradual way. The feminised state of French culture is certainly not something which can be resolved by separating the public lives of the men, as Rousseau recommended as part of the social contract, from those of the women.

Wollstonecraft's account of the unsustainability of the French Revolution clearly has something in common with the traditional commonwealth idea of luxury feminising and corrupting a nation to the point where it becomes paralysed and incapable of regeneration.[108] This is, however, heavily overlaid, not only with a more nuanced account of gendered social identities, but also with an Enlightenment account of the impact of accelerated ideological change. Like the Reformation, as it is described by Robertson in the *History of Charles V* (1769), the French Revolution demonstrates the exhilarating, yet violent, effects that sudden influxes of ideas can have upon the calm sea of manners. The Revolution begins, for Wollstonecraft, with the transformation of middle- and lower-class attitudes brought about by the ideas of the Enlightenment. The *philosophes* (who 'twinkled their light into every circle') initiated a process of mental emancipation from all the old habits of submission: 'the people, who at this period dared to think for themselves, would not now be noosed like beasts', yet 'Ideas so new, and yet so just and simple, could not fail to produce a great effect on the minds of frenchmen [who were nevertheless incapable of . . .] ever considering, that it was a much easier task to pull down than to build up'.[109]

Wollstonecraft then conveys a powerful sense of the destructive momentum of the Revolution, as the impetuous French people loose their moorings once they are no longer contained by the old political structures, and shapes the inexorable processes of Revolution into the plot of a tragedy.[110] The Revolution is an energy, rather than a deliberative process. Even the decisions of the National Assembly (which other British works, such as the *Annual Register*, portrayed as the French equivalent of the Convention Parliament, rationally redesigning the nation's constitution) seem peripheral to the forces outside. She is contemptuous of the Assembly's new constitution with its single chamber and royal suspensive veto; these show only that it lacked either the courage to depose the monarch or the pragmatism to adopt a bicameral, constitutional monarchy. Wollstonecraft seems to incline towards the pragmatic as she argues that the new constitution is out of step with the wider nation (oppression having 'left the great bulk of the people . . . worse than savages'), and that a true republic could only work 'when civilization has arrived at a much greater degree of perfection'.[111] As it was, the Assembly contained too many ambitious and vain politicians, and lacked 'deep thinkers' who might have understood that the best way to achieve reform is gradually, with due regard to people's prejudices and their need for political stability:

And if they [deep thinkers] find, that the current opinion, in overturning inveterate prejudices, and the decayed walls of laws, that no longer suit the manners, threatens the destruction of principles the most sacred; they ought firmly to wait at their post, until, the fervour abating, they could, by diverting the stream, gradually restrain it within proper bounds. – But such patriotism is of a slow growth . . .[112]

On the score of culturally adapted reform and the unproductiveness of flouting popular prejudices, Wollstonecraft does seem to have learned some things from Burke. The failure of the Revolutionary leaders to reckon with the corruption of the elite and the barbarity and ignorance of the common people is most grimly apparent in early October 1789 during the mob attack – incited, in her account, by the Duc d'Orléans – on Versailles, and it is here that Wollstonecraft is at her most surprisingly Burkean. Her narrative of quasi-sexual violation, particularly of the queen's apartments ('the asylum of care and fatigue, the chaste temple of a woman'), is, as commentators have pointed out, strikingly similar to Burke's *Reflections*, although where he bemoans the reduction of a queen to a mere woman, Wollstonecraft claims that she pities the queen 'only as a [woman]'.[113] The women and men of the Revolutionary mob exemplify the dangers of a lack of political education. Wollstonecraft's belief in the importance of education is thus linked to her rhetoric of political gradualism and culturally adapted social reform.

AN AMERICAN VIEW OF THE FRENCH REVOLUTION

In writing of the National Assembly's ill-conceived and badly timed political reforms, and the mob violence which resulted from its lack of leadership, Wollstonecraft had before her a counter-example of revolutionary success in the shape of the American Revolution. In her *Analytical* review of the American historian David Ramsay's *History of the American Revolution* (1789) she expresses her admiration for the American achievement: 'The American revolution seems to form a new epoch in the history of mankind; for amidst the various changes, that have convulsed our globe, it stands forth as the first work of reason, and boasts of producing a legitimate constitution, deliberately framed, instead of being, like all other governments, the spurious offspring of chance.'[114]

Ramsay's history – the finest, by far, of the early accounts of the American Revolution – struck a chord with Wollstonecraft. Committed to the ideals of the Revolution, yet deeply ambivalent about violence and mob behaviour, Ramsay's history was, above all, a study of American political culture and its difficult transition from revolutionary upheaval to financial and constitutional stability. Wollstonecraft particularly admired in Ramsay's work the 'philosophical reflections which unobtrusively illustrate the subject'.[115] America was on Wollstonecraft's mind during the composition of the *Historical View*, not least because of her relationship with Gilbert Imlay. Imlay's influence was intellectual, as well as personal. She would certainly have read his *Topographical Description of the Western Territory of North America*, published in London in 1792, which was a prospectus written to entice European settlers to the area, presented in the form of letters and enlivened by descriptions of flora, fauna and the native and immigrant inhabitants of the Kentucky area. The work might have appealed to Wollstonecraft as a study of the connection between geographical location, manners and political culture, since Imlay's work turns on the contrast between the 'simple manners, and rational life of the Americans', and 'the distorted and unnatural habits of the Europeans'.[116] He presents the American backcountry as a place of regeneration in which inhabitants can learn to 'feel that dignity which nature bestowed upon us at the creation; but which has been contaminated by the base alloy of meanness, the concomitant of European education', and where they can form sympathetic communities.[117] Imlay was convinced that the virtuous simplicity of backcountry manners, as he idealised them, was owing not merely to geography but to good laws. The idea that people could be morally purged and politically re-educated by good laws was a commonplace in early American thought, and was a question with which Wollstonecraft wrestled in the *Historical View*.

Imlay did not discuss the impact of post-American-Revolutionary manners on relations between the sexes, although this also interested Wollstonecraft. In her review of the *Nouveau Voyage Dans Les Etats-Unies* (1791) by the Girondin leader Jacques Pierre Brissot, she compared the manners of American and French women: 'The simplicity conspicuous in the manners of every class [in America], particularly the innocent frankness that characterizes the American women, and the consequent *friendly* intercourse that subsists between the sexes, when gallantry and coquetry are equally out of the question, must have surprised a Frenchman, who could not instantly forget the sensual effeminacy of European manners.'[118]

Wollstonecraft cites the American Revolution, with its beneficial consequences for relations between the sexes, throughout the *Historical View* as an inspiration and unattainable goal for France, and the American Federal Constitution of 1787 provides her with the major example of a successful 'experiment in political science'.[119] Unlike the French Revolution, the American Revolution happened at a time when the people were sufficiently divested of their prejudices to absorb and make the most of drastic political change. 'America', Wollstonecraft observes: 'fortunately found herself in a situation very different from all the rest of the world; for she had it in her power to lay the first stones of her government, when reason was venturing to canvass prejudice'.[120] France was not so fortunate. The early goals of the French Revolution were praiseworthy, but the implementation was naive or reckless, and the people were as ill prepared for sudden political improvement as silly, uneducated women for rational choices and responsibilities. The short-term despair, medium-term pessimism and long-term optimism of the *Historical View* derive from Wollstonecraft's overall belief in the utopian potential of history to deliver a rational and just social order, as well as the perils of trying to accelerate its progress. America has shown that a sustainable revolution can be achieved once a society has reached a high enough level of political education and an advanced stage of social development. Like Macaulay, she was not reticent about presenting herself as a potential female citizen of such a rationally reformed state.

After completing the *Historical View*, Wollstonecraft continued to apply the lessons of political gradualism to other social subjects. In an essay, attributed to her, 'Of Public Charities' (1795), which appeared in a radical Norwich journal called *The Cabinet*, she may have argued that, ideally, charity schools should be abolished in favour of state education, but that since 'a very long time will probably elapse before society arrive at so desirable a state, as, that particular *charities* shall subsist no longer', interim reform was the best option at present.[121] In her last completed work, *Letters Written . . . in Sweden, Norway, and Denmark* (1796), Wollstonecraft had some words of caution for over-ambitious social reformers: 'An ardent affection for the human race makes enthusiastic characters eager to produce alteration in laws and governments prematurely. To render them useful and permanent, they must be the growth of each particular soil, and the gradual fruit of the ripening understanding of the nation, matured by time, not forced by an unnatural fermentation.'[122]

She applied the lessons of sustainable revolution to the more backward societies of Scandinavia, finding that these, too, were sorely in need of political reform, but not in a way that would 'force' prematurely the 'growth of each particular soil'. During her Scandinavian journey, on business for Imlay, Wollstonecraft became an ever more discriminating and sympathetic observer of manners, recording each 'state of society' as she passed through the towns and villages of Sweden, Denmark and Norway.[123] 'The more I see of the world', she concluded, 'the more I am convinced that civilization is a blessing'; the 'cultivation of the arts and sciences', criticised by Rousseau, really does promote 'delicacy of feeling', and 'refines our enjoyments'.[124] She had no truck with the idea that luxury and civilisation inevitably bring a slackening of moral fibre and political decline. Economic progress brings freedom, as well as the comforts of a cultivated outer and inner life: 'England and America owe their liberty to commerce, which created a new species of power to undermine the feudal system.'[125]

As a sociologist and literary describer of manners, Wollstonecraft can be placed firmly within the Enlightenment account of the progress of society, albeit as one for whom male and female rights were the ultimate goal. She dedicated *A Vindication of the Rights of Woman* to the revolutionary cleric Charles Maurice de Talleyrand-Périgord, upbraiding him for not having urged fellow drafters of the Declaration of the Rights of Man to extend those rights to women. In France in the early 1790s, there were feminists such as Olympe de Gouges, Condorcet and other members of the Cercle Social who challenged the male bias of the Revolution's universalist language of citizenship.[126] Condorcet himself published an article urging the government to give political rights to women, and it is possible that he was in touch with Wollstonecraft during her time in France.[127] Like Wollstonecraft, Condorcet thought about the question of women's civil and political rights in the context of an evolutionary idea of history, albeit one that differed considerably from hers. In his *Esquisse d'un Tableau historique des progrès de l'esprit humain*, 1795 (published the same year in translation by Joseph Johnson and therefore very probably read by Wollstonecraft), Condorcet gave a progressive account of history – indebted to but instructively different from that of the Scottish Enlightenment – as the steady 'march', through time, 'of the human mind', and as the gradual unfolding of universal human rights.[128] Through the primitive, pastoral, agricultural and commercial 'epochs', and from the time of the Greeks and Romans to the Reformation and, at last, to the founding of the French Republic, he adduces the laws of nature as evidence for the gradual progress and infinite potential of human rationality. In all this, Condorcet accepts uncritically the conjectural historical version of female emancipation: women are politically 'excluded' in the first epoch, looked upon as 'companions' in the agricultural epoch, and benefit from the 'mildness, decorum, and dignity' of manners in the age of 'chivalry'.[129] Women ultimately disappear into Condorcet's utopian and abstract reworking of the Enlightenment idea of the progress of society and manners, which becomes the story of the emancipation of the genderless human mind from the distortions of culture and language. His revolutionary outline of universal progress incorporates the older, Enlightenment history of women, without explaining how a history of ever greater male kindness *to* women is going to shade into one of equal rights *for* women. Wollstonecraft's reading of history, in the *Vindications*, the *Historical View* and the *Letters Written . . . in Sweden*, posed a more fundamental challenge to that Enlightenment version of progress, and to its late eighteenth-century adaptations. By contesting this reading of history on its own theoretical ground of manners – the cultural milieu within which gendered identities are constructed and negotiated – she was able to provide a radical, and disturbing, sociology of gender upon which a less naive theory of rights might be built. Her vocabularies of 'manners', 'moral' and 'partial civilisation' can sound a little stiff and repetitious at times, but she was attempting to realign morals and manners in ways that would give the rational, self-respecting woman of integrity a secure place in the modern world. She was therefore also struggling to define and bring into being a stage of society beyond the stage of commerce when wealth and political power would be more equally distributed, and when women would cease to be either stuck in the past or fatuously obsessed with the present moment, and live more fully for the future.

CHAPTER 6

The history women and the population men, 1760–1830

This chapter explores the aftermath and legacy of Wollstonecraft's critique of the Enlightenment idea of the progress of society during the turbulent years of the French Revolution and Napoleonic wars. It is in two parts. The first part is concerned with the models of social progress at work during the first real flowering of women's history in the early nineteenth century, and looks forward to the enduring involvement, throughout the rest of the century, of women historians with historical subgenres such as biography, literary history and art history. The second part considers the enormous challenge to advocates of female progress posed by Malthus's theory that population growth (pre-eminently an issue of female fertility) might set limits to historical development. It explores Malthus's own, complex articulation of the interrelationship between the biological nature and social status of women, and the tendency of populations to grow beyond their means of subsistence. It also considers the engagement by early nineteenth-century women writers with population theory and political economy, and the ways in which they promoted history and economics as, in themselves, a progressive form of female education. The concluding part of the chapter asks, ultimately, whether the Whig, Latitudinarian and Enlightened vision of social progress survived into the nineteenth century; and, if so, how it met and withstood the challenge, not only of Malthusian pessimism, but also of a new force, Evangelicalism, that harnessed the Enlightenment idea of female rationality and social influence to an aspiration for the spiritual and social uplift of poor women and their families by their more fortunate and educated sisters.

Both parts of the chapter are concerned, in different ways, with the critique of the idea of the progress of civilisation in the later eighteenth century that became ever more plausible after the descent of the French Revolution into violence, and during a period in Britain in the 1790s and early 1800s of harsh political repression and of government failure to heed calls for progressive reform in areas such as the franchise, Catholic emancipation, the abolition of the slave trade, the repeal of the Test and Corporation acts or more vigorous supervision of the East India Company. It was a period during which nothing was done to improve the legal position of women, despite their growing prominence in campaigning for these and other humanitarian reforms. As we saw in the previous chapter, Wollstonecraft dubbed her own age one of 'partial civilisation': she acknowledged that some commercial progress had been achieved, yet without anything being done to remedy the historical polarising of male and female identities, or the reduction of women to a purely instrumental and ornamental role. She called for a revolution in female manners, for moral progress to catch up with economic development, and for the extensive political re-education of the people as a prelude to gradual root-and-branch reform. As well as providing an incisive critique of contemporary female manners, she set out to reverse what she saw as the Enlightenment tendency to refine 'manners at the expense of morals'. Her project for moral and political reform was historically informed, to the extent that she believed that it could not be achieved without due regard to the stage of society a people have reached, or without some concession to the anachronistic social conventions and mind-worlds they continue to inhabit.

A number of women writers, under Wollstonecraft's influence, also argued for improvements to women's condition by way of a critical engagement with Enlightenment theories of social change. Among these was Lucy Aikin, a prominent member of the Warrington circle of dissenting intellectuals, historian and author of the poem *Epistles on Women, Exemplifying their Character and Condition in Various Ages and Nations* (1810). Aikin's declared purpose was 'to mark the effect of various codes, institutions, and states of manners' upon women during the different stages of social evolution, and (notwithstanding the pre-emptive cringe in her introduction to the effect that the sexes never can be 'placed in all respects on a footing of equality') she traces these through savage oppression to modern refinement.[1] Her conjectural history, however, differs markedly from many of her Enlightenment predecessors in that, after some conventional couplets on the high status of Germanic women ('revered, sublime, on Virtue's throne,/Judge of his honour, guardian of her own'), she depicts the age of chivalry as a kind of Norman yoke for women.[2] She continues with a witty attack on the farce of chivalry in the modern age ('Learn, thoughtless woman, learn his arts to scan,/And dread that fearful portent . . . kneeling Man!'), and ends with a plea for men to promote female education: 'unbind/Your barbarous shackles, loose the female mind . . .'[3] Like Wollstonecraft before her, Aikin identifies the lack of female education as a major instance of the incomplete, if not irretrievable, progress of civilisation in her own era.

PART I

HISTORY AND FEMALE EDUCATION

Not all women writers making the case for female education deployed and adapted the idea of the history of civilisation in the same way as Aikin and Wollstonecraft, but many found the writing of history a productive means of exploring women's relationship to public culture and of articulating their aspirations for greater female prestige, education and rights. The growing public association of women with history, from the late eighteenth century, certainly facilitated the rise of the commercially viable woman historian, and contributed to women's self-knowledge as a social group. The notion, nurtured in the early nineteenth century by Walter Scott and other historical novelists, that society contains internal temporal variations and that women had an instinctive affinity with tradition and cultural heritage, enabled women historians to claim special insight into certain aspects of history of value to the culture as a whole. At first sight, some of those insights might appear to have been restricted to a less than serious sphere (to a modern way of thinking), since most women's histories of the period from 1790 to 1830 – including those by Aikin and by Wollstonecraft's protégée Mary Hays – were biographies of queens or great ladies from the Renaissance or classical antiquity, or works that concentrated thematically in areas such as court life, medieval chivalry or elite society. Yet, it will be argued, these histories made a significant contribution to a wider shift in the conception of the relationship of the history of manners to lived, inward experience – to the historical articulation, in other words, of the individual life within a richly imagined social texture. These works reflected intelligently upon the nature and limits of personal moral agency in a world where, for most men and nearly all women, history was seen as something that simply *happens* to a person. The interest for the historian was to uncover the human ways of seeing and states of feeling, and to enter into the subjective experience of particular phases in the history of manners. Thomas Babington Macaulay defined his ideal work of history as one in which 'the character and spirit of an age is exhibited in miniature . . . Men will not merely be described, but will be made intimately known to us. The changes in manners will be indicated, not merely by a few general phrases or a few extracts from statistical documents, but by appropriate images presented in every line.'[4] Mark Phillips has argued that the historical culture of the period under consideration here can be characterised, in the way that Macaulay suggested, as one of deepening interest in the imaginative, affective and experiential aspects of history.[5] There was renewed interest in the individual life both as historical exemplum and as a point of imaginative mediation between the present and past. This was, in turn, the product of the social yearning for heroic figures in the years of the Napoleonic wars, of a sense, at this time, of living through a period of historical upheaval, and of a greater generic approximation, as Phillips describes it, of history to biography, memoir and fiction. Women's history, and (as we will see) new ideas of female heroism, played their part in this broadening of the thematic concerns and generic formats of history, as well as in the particularising of the individual life and the national culture within, and sometimes against the grain of, the social evolutionary history inherited from the eighteenth century.

Above all, women historians helped to push forward a new model of female agency that downplayed the idea of unintended sexual influence in favour of a spiritual and moral influence emanating from the domestic sphere to the wider world beyond.[6] This became most clearly evident in the cultural canonisation, in the nineteenth century, of certain heroines from the past, notably Rachel Russell and Lucy Hutchinson, who were thought to have combined Christian piety with a far-sighted, ultimately consequential commitment to the liberties of the British people. In Scotland, this model of female agency was bolstered by the academic and popular triumph of Common Sense philosophy that emphasised the capacity of ordinary men and women to grasp their world and make valid moral choices. This marked a break with the conjectural history of earlier decades, since more emphasis was now placed upon the ability of thinking agents to construct and improve their society, and upon the priority of intellectual and moral over economic and institutional progress. Building upon the work of Thomas Reid and James Beattie, the Edinburgh University professor Dugald Stewart extended the epistemological insights of Common Sense philosophy into the arenas of political economy and educational theory, arguing the need for women's education to enable them to fulfil their social obligations and to contribute to the progress of society as a whole.[7] Stewart was a mentor to Elizabeth Hamilton and significantly influenced her views of education and history, and he also cultivated and influenced Maria Edgeworth, herself a proponent of the view, as she put it in *Practical Education,* that history is 'a necessary accomplishment in one sex, and an essential part of education in the other'.[8] In England, Anna Laetitia Barbauld, another friend of Stewart's (as well as being Lucy Aikin's aunt), devoted a part of her public career to making the case for women's education in the interests of wider social improvement, and argued that the study of history was essential to the cultivation of their intellectual powers: 'to be ignorant of history,' she asserted, 'is not permitted to any of a cultivated mind'.[9] Barbauld linked women's mental cultivation to their sense of a stake in their country and in the wider world; history eliminates the 'clownish sneer of ignorance at every thing in laws, government or manners which is not fashioned after our partial ideas and familiar usages'.[10] Barbauld was a prominent and radical Dissenter, and, like many of the Latitudinarian women writers discussed in this study, she approached the question of mental self-cultivation from a standpoint of theological commitment to Arminianism and rational enquiry.[11] She was also, from the time of her early essay 'Thoughts on the Devotional Taste' (1775), deeply interested in the role of affect, as opposed to abstract philosophical reasoning, in motivating a person's quest for self-cultivation and piety and fostering a sense of national belonging.[12]

BLUESTOCKING BIOGRAPHY

Barbauld was more concerned with women's reading than writing of history, and largely interested in history as a means of fostering women's sense of belonging to a civic and Protestant public sphere.[13] In this respect, she wrote very much in the wake of Bluestocking writers who were committed to the reading and writing of history as a mode of personal and national education. Hester Chapone's *Letters on the Improvement of the Mind addressed to a Young Lady* (1773), for example, set out a dauntingly ambitious programme of historical reading for its young recipient (including Rollin, Pufendorf, Vertot, Voltaire, Hume, Robertson and many more). This programme was designed to dispel the 'shameful degree of ignorance' that most women have about ancient history, to teach them the 'laws, customs and politics' of the modern world and also, less reassuringly, to acquaint them with the 'shocking barbarity' of European behaviour towards the native populations of America, India and Africa.[14] The extraordinary success and multiple editions of Chapone's work attest to the growing public consensus about the female need for history, and it may have heightened the awareness of historians themselves of the importance of the female portion of their readership.[15] One work that answered Chapone's call for a history for women full of information about British 'laws, customs and politics', yet forthright in its criticism of their abuses, was Charlotte Cowley's *The Ladies History of England* (1780). Radically Whiggish in tone, sympathetic to Dissenters and to the cause of the American Revolution, Cowley's history of English liberty and its abuses has similarities with Macaulay's work, but it is also a history that declares its ambition to present the past from an avowedly female point of view: as she states in her prefatory poem: 'Mine be the Task to swell th'Historic Page,/And paint my Sex's Worth in every Age.'[16] The history does contain female-centred anecdotes (the story of the perjurer Elizabeth Canning, for example), but the appeals to a female readership are most clearly made in the discursive footnotes and in the lavish engravings, including scenes of pathos such as the 'final parting between Charles I and his Children', or of the widow of Edward IV taking her leave of her young son.

Aside from Cowley, however, Catharine Macaulay remained almost a unique figure for the rest of the century as a writer of grand narrative history. As Mary Hays remarked dryly in her biographical article on Macaulay: 'A female historian, by its singularity, could not fail to excite attention: she seemed to have stepped out of the province of her sex . . . Her talents and powers could not be denied; her beauty was therefore called into question.'[17] Readers were not aware of the female authorship of three notable works of history by Elizabeth Montagu's sister, Sarah Scott, published pseudonymously, and rarely discussed until very recently.[18] These works are instructive, nevertheless, for the instance they provide of a woman historian exploring, as did Cowley and Macaulay, Protestant-ism at moments of historical crisis, as well as of the exemplary and affective potential of modern historical biography. Scott admired the first volume of Macaulay's history, and met her in the late 1760s. Her own three works of history, *The History of Gustavus Ericson, King of Sweden* (1761), *The History of Mecklenburgh* (1762) and *The Life of Theodore-Agrippa D'Aubigné* (1772) were assumed by reviewers to have been written by a man, and, according to Betty Schellenberg, regarded as part of 'the British Enlightenment project of writing a refined, socially responsible, pacific and honourable Protestant public sphere into being'.[19] Of the three, *The History of Gustavus Ericson* is the work in which Scott most successfully sustains an independent, critical distance from the source material (in this instance, Vertot), as she relates the story of the early sixteenth-century Protestant reformer and elected king of Sweden, Gustav I. The result is a fast-paced, highly engaging telling of Gustav's courageous liberation of his country from Danish domination, and his attempt to reform and civilise its war-ravaged people.

In the preface Scott states the case for historical biography, not so much in terms of its traditional exemplary value, but as a means of exploring the complex interactions between individual character traits and the larger forces of history. She acknowledges that the value of biography as a means of exploring human nature must be set against its limitations as a somewhat narrow window on to history: it gives only 'detached pieces of history . . . like redoubts in fortification', and she says that this must be remedied by the historian supplying 'line[s] of communication' in the form of broader contextual narrative.[20] At the time of writing, the debate about the educational and affective value of historical biography was highly topical. Scott's contribution to this debate was to demonstrate that an individual life such as Gustav's might provide a coherent organising principle for history without skewing the factual data, and without sliding into the old kinds of 'secret history' (like Manley's) of trivial sexual intrigue behind great political events. Scott is clear-sighted and unsentimental about the politic thinking that motivated some of Gustav's more generous acts (his kindness towards the previous Swedish king's widow and sons, for example), and about the forces predisposing him to his conversion to Protestantism: 'he was half persuaded of their [the Lutheran doctrines'] truth, by his wishes that they might be true; and he who desires to be convinced is seldom far from conviction'.[21] Yet her aim is not to demystify public events, in the manner of secret history, nor to expose the pathological drive for individual greatness within the military hero, in the manner of Johnson's portrait of Charles XII of Sweden in *The Vanity of Human Wishes*. Gustav is an admirable Enlightened despot in the making, very much like Voltaire's contemporary portrait of Peter the Great, who uses military means to bring about civilised ends, and who is wise enough to recognise the limits imposed by popular feeling to the pace of civilisation and reform.[22] There are few details of Gustav's personal life in Scott's biography. This is partly the product of the scarcity of such information in the primary sources, but it also implies that Scott's notion of biography is not to affirm the value of the minute details of daily life, in the way that Johnson recommended in the sixtieth paper of *The Rambler*, for example, and that others would follow. Rather, she finds in biography a means of conveying the texture of public history, and the limitations and opportunities for action it imposes on those who pursue, deliberately or accidentally, the cause of Protestant civility.

Scott's next historical work, *The History of Mecklenburgh*, was, as the 'anon.' author acknowledged in her preface, a 'hasty performance', designed to catch a wave of public interest in the home principality of George III's new bride, Charlotte of Mecklenburg-Strelitz, herself an emerging figurehead for Enlightened, rational domesticity.[23] Even so, Scott gave evidence of the robust political intelligence that made her first history such a compelling work.[24] Ten years later she returned to historical biography with a life of the sixteenth-/early seventeenth-century French Protestant leader and poet, Théodore-Agrippa D'Aubigné. D'Aubigné's life provides Scott with an organising focus for a wider history of the French civil wars, but she also sees him as a subject of great significance in his own right, since, Scott observes, 'a brave and honest man must always be an interesting object; and the contemplations of great virtues, even of a sort the least suited to the fashion of the times, will ever warm the heart'.[25] The biography, however, is a leaden collage of sources, including D'Aubigné's own account of his life recently edited by Jean Dumont, that gives very little sense either of the man or of the drama of events such as the St Bartholomew massacre.[26] Scott was discreet about her authorship of her historical works, but the subject of the value of historical biography was nevertheless likely to have been much discussed in Bluestocking circles. Montagu wrote to Lyttelton's young son recommending the reading of great historical lives ('to raise the genius and to mend the heart, one should place in view examples of heroic virtue of which modern times are not so well furnished'), and sent him a list of recommended authors, reflecting her own very extensive reading of history from classical historians to Voltaire and Hume (she had reservations about the last two).[27]

The Bluestockings may also have known of or read Sarah Fielding's *Lives of Cleopatra and Octavia* (1757), published, like Scott's *History of Gustavus Ericson*, by Andrew Millar. This was presented through the voices of the two protagonists, and designed, in the case of Octavia, to 'excite a more lasting Sensibility of Pity or Relentment, than can be indulged from the most pathetic Descriptions of Romance'.[28] A younger member of Johnson's circle and theirs, Ellis Cornelia Knight, produced a fictionalised historical biography of a Roman soldier caught up in the disastrous defeat, in 9 AD, of the Roman army by the Germanic leader Arminius. Knight's novel, *Marcus Flaminius* (1792), dedicated to Horace Walpole, is informed by her considerable classical learning, and tells the story, as a series of letters, of Marcus' captivity by the victorious Cherusci tribe, and his eventual return to Rome. Knight uses the fictional device of Marcus as an internal observer, first as a Roman among Germanic people, and then as an exile returning to the unfamiliar and corrupt Rome of Tiberius, as a fresh way into the social and cultural history of the ancient world. The result is a more rounded, intimate history of manners than those to be found in conventional histories of this period. Knight has Marcus reiterate at length Tacitus' remarks about the fidelity and bravery of the Germanic women, but is also able to elaborate upon the source material by showing what they in turn think of Romans (they are very suspicious of Marcus and think that all Romans are seducers of women).[29] Knight is mindful of the historical legacy of the Germanic respect for chastity and liberty, and, at the point when the Cherusci are defeated, has a prophetess look forward to a future when 'the inhabitants of some island, blessed with a love of liberty, should form a government resembling ours'.[30]

Elizabeth Hamilton in her *Memoirs of the Life of Agrippina* (1804) followed Knight both in her choice of the age of Tiberius, and in her fictional use of an internal, Roman observer of Germanic manners. By depicting an individual sensibility at the interface of two worlds (that of the Romans and the Germani, and also that of republican Roman virtue and incipient imperial decadence), the two writers were able to show how 'manners' shaped everyday human interaction, how they were shaped by cross-cultural contact and how they were experienced and internalised in ordinary life. Marcus perplexes his Germanic captor by telling him that he cannot give up all hope of freedom. His captor, living a day-to-day existence in a nomadic, warrior culture, cannot understand this kind of hope since he 'had no conception what happiness would arise from illusion', whereas Marcus, who comes from a more sophisticated culture, feels the need to imagine his life in the dimension of the future.[31] Both Knight and Hamilton wrote in a culture that recognised similarities between history and fiction at the point of consumption, and which, even before the appearance of Walter Scott's historical novels, accepted that fictional and factual elements could co-exist within the same text without cross-contamination.[32] More generally, they took advantage of a growing interest in stories of individual lives as a point of access to history; as Mary Hays later argued, 'History . . . can be interesting and amusing only in proportion as it is biographical.'[33] Earlier eighteenth-century commentators had tended to distrust history written from, or organised around, a subjective point of view, and to regard history as an entity external to the perspectives and experiences of its agents. But later readers, who had grown up with novels and the newer kinds of memoir, were more inclined, as Mark Phillips has argued, to accept that 'every individual plays a part and enjoys an interest' in the 'vast and almost uncontainable domain of manners, material life, and social opinion'.[34]

By the end of the century, that domain seemed more uncontainable than before. The new histories of Gothic and medieval manners had had a partial solvent effect on Enlightenment narratives of progress. The persistence of chivalry – whether it was seen in a Burkean light as a stabilising force or, by Wollstonecraft, Aikin and others, as an impediment to change – demonstrated the unevenness of progress and the residual presence of tradition. As a social form that had been enshrined in poetry and music, chivalry also provided a powerful example of the role of art in the civilising process. This was a point developed by Susannah Dobson in her lengthy preface to her translation of Sainte-Palaye's *Literary History of the Troubadours* (1779), a preface that attracted especially warm notice from the reviewers.[35] Dobson emphasised the role of the troubadours in bringing about the culture of chivalry, and so effecting a historical transition between 'a state of ignorance and barbarism, to that of cultivation of manners, of reason, and of talents'.[36] The troubadours harnessed the power of art to '[awaken] Europe from its ignorance and lethargy; they re-animated the minds of men; and, by amusing, they led them to think, to reflect, and to judge'.[37] Their art, and literary history generally, thus provides not merely data for the history of manners, but clues to the expressive life of the emotions, or, as Dobson memorably phrases it, 'many interesting details towards a history of the heart'.[38] More than a translator, Dobson exemplifies the commitment made by other writers of her age – Burke, Horace Walpole, Montagu in her *Essay on the writings and Genius of Shakespear* (1769) and Clara Reeve in her *The Progress of Romance* (1785) – to the notion that literary and art history could deepen and transform an understanding of social development. The great success of Montagu, in particular, paved the way for the continuing involvement of nineteenth-century women writers, such as Maria Graham, Anna Jameson and Julia Cartwright, in literary history and art history.

A FEELING KNOWLEDGE OF THE NATIONAL PAST

The refurbishment, in the late eighteenth century, of historical subgenres such as memoir, biography, dialogues between historical characters, anecdotes and edited collections of letters, reflected a new awareness among writers of the affective possibilities of history. Whereas Johnson had lamented the inability of conventional history to engage the emotions ('Histories of the downfall of kingdoms, and revolutions of empires, are read with great tranquillity'), later eighteenth-century historians borrowed strategies from novelists for enlisting reader identification and imaginative sympathy.[39] For historians, this was partly a matter of emotional indulgence, and partly of manipulating readers' feelings in particular political directions, but it also signalled a growing confidence in sympathetic identification as a mode of historical cognition.[40] This cognition was both epistemological and moral: the reader's imaginative identification with a particular character promoted a deeper knowledge of the events and social fabric of the past; and the traditional idea of the moral or heroic exemplarity of particular historical figures was amplified to include the moral benefits to the reader of seeing the past through their eyes. All of this tended to legitimate the pervasive tendency of late eighteenth- to early nineteenth-century history towards what I will refer to below as inferential emotional colouring: the speculative attribution of private motivations and feelings to characters who appear largely as public figures in the primary sources. It also underwrote a new emphasis upon the moral and cognitive benefits for the reader to be gained from entering imaginatively into the lives of less significant historical personages, or, at least, of those who acted in only supporting roles to the truly great and famous. This emphasis certainly made it easier for writers to defend and make claims of exemplarity for biographies of women, as Elizabeth Hamilton's biographer Elizabeth Benger did in her preface to her *Memoirs* of her life: 'In a life devoted to quiet and seclusion, there may have occurred revolutions of opinion and vicissitudes of feeling, which, to those who would study human nature, are no less curious, and even more interesting, than the eventual changes of fortune which popularly arrest attention.'[41] In a more far-reaching way, readers' expectations of edifying affect allowed certain kinds of biographical history to flourish in which the central, organising figure was a woman. Indeed, the female historical figure – brave, perhaps, even heroic, but rarely in control of events – became a popular means by which history could be mediated through an intelligible, individual sensibility, and so provide a point of entry into the past.

In many historical works of the early nineteenth century, women played a central role, both as writers and as subjects of historical enquiry. One strikingly important factor in this was the publication, in 1806, of Lucy Hutchinson's previously unknown memoirs of her husband Colonel

John Hutchinson, along with an autobiographical fragment. John Hutchinson was a senior military figure on the parliamentary side of the Civil War and a signatory to Charles I's death warrant, and his descendants had for many years been reluctant to remind the world of their radical ancestry. Julius Hutchinson, the family member who eventually edited and published the memoirs, reported in his preface that his uncle Thomas 'had been frequently solicited to permit [the manuscripts] to be published, particularly by the late Mrs. Catharine Macaulay', but had stood firm against it.[42] Julius himself, having taken the decision to publish them, presented them with great tact and skill as an exemplary kind of historical biography eliciting sympathetic reader insight into one of the darkest corners of the national past. He acknowledges the 'alarum' that readers might feel at Colonel Hutchinson's political views, and he encourages them to see his actions in context before diverting attention to the real selling-point of the book, Lucy herself.[43] First, he establishes her exceptional good faith as a historian: the fact that she was writing privately, after her husband's death in prison, for the edification of her children guarantees her honesty ('a faithful, natural, and lively picture, of the public mind and manners'), as does the fact that she comes over in the *Memoirs* as a highly intelligent, patriotic woman, as well as a courageous and devoted wife and mother.[44] He then dwells upon the special value of biography – particularly a biography written by a woman, and highly attentive to the feelings of women caught up in historical events – as an imaginative way into history. Lucy Hutchinson, he observes, added 'to the vigour of a masculine understanding, the nice feeling and discrimination, the delicate touch of the pencil of a female', and the reader cannot fail to feel him- or herself 'a party in the transactions which are recounted'.[45] Julius supplies an engraving of Lucy with her son, and a number of footnotes, and reproduces the memoir, in its original spelling, to convey the impression of a writer from the past who was artistically and intellectually gifted, yet self-effacing (she refers to herself, in the third person, as her husband's 'faithful mirror' and his 'shadow').

Julius thus served up cooked in his edition of Hutchinson's *Memoirs* what Catharine Macaulay had presented raw in her *History of England*: one of the most disruptive moments in English national history. At a time when memories of Jacobin radicalism were still fresh in the public mind, Lucy Hutchinson's *Memoirs* gave nineteenth-century readers a means of coming to terms with its political and religious divisions. Seen through the eyes of a loyal, courageous woman, the civil wars of the seventeenth century were, in part, redeemed as a story of private dilemma and suffering. Rediscovered in the early nineteenth century, Lucy Hutchinson rapidly became an ideal both of the female historical agent, and of the female historian. Francis Jeffrey reviewed the edition warmly in the *Edinburgh Review*, praising Hutchinson for possessing a 'masculine force of understanding, a singular capacity for affairs' without compromising the 'delicacy and reserve of her sex'; and, in her *Epistles on Women*, published four years later, Lucy Aikin referred to her as a 'high-souled helpmate at the patriot's side'.[46] Some years later, the historian Mary Berry cited Lucy Hutchinson as an instance of women's judicious lack of direct involvement in the civil wars, since she kept her writings and opinions out of the public domain until after her death:

[Women] appeared in their only appropriate sphere of action, as the friends, helpmates, and companions of the families to whom they belonged. No woman started out of her sphere into unseemly notice. No heroine excited a momentary enthusiasm at the expence of the more difficult virtues of her sex. The distinguished abilities of Mrs. Hutchinson were not unveiled to the public eye, till above a century after she died, and we may fairly suppose that many other females, whose natural endowments were not inferior, and who acted not less honourable parts, remain unknown to us.[47]

Such an assertion was, in itself, an extraordinary feat of historical revisionism, and one that allowed Berry and other female historians of her generation to make the case for women's intellectual and spiritual influence, emanating from within but radiating far beyond the private sphere, as against direct political interference. Others, such as the historical biographer Elizabeth Sandford, elaborated this point by citing 'the quiet and gentle influence' of superior women such as Lucy Hutchinson and Lady Jane Grey: 'The influence of such women', Sandford wrote, 'has not been confined to domestic life, but has often embraced and adorned an ampler sphere.'[48] The question of Lucy Hutchinson's intellectual and spiritual influence was particularly interesting because it had been renewed, beyond the scope of her life and family, by her rediscovery as a writer of affecting, conciliatory history. A similar case was the seventeenth-century noblewoman Lady Rachel Russell, many of whose letters were published for the first time in the nineteenth century. Russell's second husband, the Whig hero William, Lord Russell, was executed for treason in 1683, and she had been celebrated in her own day, and in Gilbert Burnet's *History of His Own Time*, for her intellect, devotion to her husband and children and her tireless campaign on behalf of her husband during his last days in prison. Rachel Russell had long been in the pantheon of heroic wives when Catharine Macaulay celebrated her as a superior modern Arria who showed her husband and family the way to stoic fortitude without stooping to suicide, and when Aikin praised her in her *Epistles on Women* as one who 'shone a heroine, for she loved, a wife'.[49] But it was Berry's biography of 1819 that first made available her letters to her husband in the period immediately before his death, and allowed Russell to become her own historian, revealing, Berry claims, 'a character whose celebrity was purchased by the sacrifice of no feminine virtue'.[50] Berry recreated Russell as an icon of domestic heroism, downplaying the political role she played after the Glorious Revolution in favour of an image of her as a dutiful and inspirational wife and mother, possessed of a heart 'in which her friends, her country, her religion all found a place'.[51] Berry's scholarly representation of her life helped to ensure that her husband's tragedy, and, in particular, his final farewell to his wife and children, became a touchstone of Whig and Liberal political allegiance in the nineteenth century.[52] Historians' preoccupation with Lady Russell facilitated the domestication of William Russell in ways that deflected attention both from his political radicalism and from his dealings with Louis XIV, and paved the way for his place on the Victorian roll of moderate Whig martyrs.

Mary Berry herself was, by intellectual affiliation, a second-generation Bluestocking whose circle included Edgeworth, Germaine De Staël, Francis Jeffrey, Dugald Stewart and, in the 1820s, Thomas Babington Macaulay. Her closest associate was Horace Walpole, who provided a point of connection to Montagu's circle, encouraged her historical interests and chose her to be the editor of his posthumous works. Having published her account of the life of Rachel Russell, Berry continued to make capital out of the idea, first elaborated in the eighteenth century, that women have a special affinity with the social and cultural aspects of European history. In other respects, however, her work allows us to see how a nineteenth-century woman writer, with personal ties (through Walpole, especially) to the dazzling, elite social culture of Enlightenment France and England reckoned with its legacy, and distanced herself from its model of female influence. In 1828, she published *A Comparative View of the Social Life of England and France*, with a follow-up volume in 1831, taking the story to 1830. In the first volume she gives an account of the cultural life of England from the late seventeenth to the late eighteenth centuries. Her goal, as she sets it out in the preface, is to produce an intimate history of manners. The comparative focus and choice of recent history allow her to gauge the 'occasional, accidental ebbs and flows in the morals as well as in the manners of private life', to see how national manners were lived at home, and how they formed the characters of public individuals.[53] Berry's work is scholarly in terms of its sources, but deliberately unsystematic and impressionistic in its recreation of the social atmospheres of the recent past. The best section of the *Comparative View* is on English life immediately after the Restoration, taking in its literature, court culture and forms of sociability, and including a chapter on the 'Effect of the Restoration on Female Manners and Social Existence'. Here Berry continues the revisionist assault, started in her section on Lucy Hutchinson's era, on the notion of women's political empowerment through their sexual influence. She argues that the English people's deeply embedded cultural preference for virtuous, companionate marriage proved largely resistant to the libertine ethos of the Restoration court: 'we shall acknowledge with pride, as well as pleasure, that domestic felicity, founded on mutual and voluntary preference, was already dom-iciliated in England'.[54] Moreover, she writes, the Restoration culture of libertinism did nothing to enhance either the daily lives of women or their influence on the tone of public life: 'There can hardly be a stronger proof that women have never obtained any considerable influence on the national manners of England, than that even during the first popularity of a reign distinguished for its gallantry and devotion to women, the sex in general seemed to have gained little or nothing on the score of social enjoyment.'[55]

Berry thus joined the chorus of those women writers, in the early decades of the nineteenth century, who decisively rejected the Enlighten-ment notion that women can only gain power and some measure of autonomy in a respectfully flirtatious social environment. In the second volume, she gives an ambivalent account of the political activities of Georgiana, Duchess of Devonshire, ending with a plea for 'the political influence of women in England [to] be exerted in the much more dignified and more efficient line of confirming and encouraging their husbands and brothers in every independent sentiment'.[56] Her work, both here and in her life of Lady Russell, shows how far women writers were instrumental in writing out of history the political power of courtly ladies, and in promoting the notion of wifehood and motherhood as forms of rank and social entitlement in their own right. This was something other than an advocacy of female domestication. Indeed, Berry is often amusingly scathing about the fashion among women, especially in the later eighteenth century, for domesticity and ostentatious motherhood (too many of them read Rousseau and then 'maternal love became as much a fashion as soon afterwards balloons and animal magnetism'): Englishwomen in this period, she argues, went too far in their adoption of a domestic persona at the expense of cultivating their minds:

in much the same time which raised the Frenchwoman to the rank of an intelligent social being, the Englishwoman too often sunk into a gossiping housewife. Neglecting all the smaller graces of life, she boasted that she cared for nothing on earth but her husband and children, considered ignorance of the world as a proof of superior virtue, and narrow-mindedness as a qualification of her sex.[57]

Berry is concerned to historicise not only elite politicking women like the Duchess of Devonshire but also the sentimental domestic creatures of the late eighteenth century. In this, she anticipates the work of Victorian historians such as Hannah Lawrance who were concerned to retrieve from the past women's solid achievements especially in the cultural sphere. Lawrance published a pioneering history of early medieval women in England, emphasising the enormous role they played as patrons of the troubadours and numerous other artists and scribes: she claims that ultimately 'to woman's patronage, England owes the introduction of printing', and places great emphasis upon the 'silent and . . . gentle influence' of chivalry in creating favourable conditions for educated, intelligent women.[58]

IMAGINING ONESELF AS A QUEEN

Berry's *Comparative View* coincided and indirectly engaged with intensified public interest, in the 1820s, in the history of chivalry and gallantry. She was uneasy with the notion of male gallantry as enabling female influence. But she, like Lawrance after her, was clearly happy with the notion of femininity, advanced by revivers of chivalry, as an entitlement to a certain kind of public voice and as a site of historical continuity. The 1810s to 1820s were decades peculiarly preoccupied with questions of legitimate and illegitimate female power. Around the same time as Queen Caroline's notorious failed attempt to take her rightful place at George IV's coronation in 1821, and her death soon after, it became clear that the presumptive heir to the throne was female. Victoria's impending and eventual accession fuelled an extraordinary outpouring of histories of queens and princesses, written mainly by women writers, and aimed at a growing popular market for history. Most of these works took the form of 'lives' or 'memoirs', rather than political narratives, of female sovereigns, offering a window on to the manners and emotional environment of their times. The most celebrated and prominent women historians of the nineteenth century made their name in this kind of writing, notably Agnes Strickland (author, with her sister Elizabeth, of the twelve-volume *Lives of the Queens of England*, 1840–8, and further lives of Scottish queens and English princesses), the literary and art historian Anna Jameson (the author of, among many works, *Memoirs of Celebrated Female Sovereigns*, 1831) and Mary Anne Everett Wood (later) Green, author of the *Lives of the Princesses of England*, 1849–55. Along with other women historians such Lawrance (who also wrote *Historical Memoirs of the Queens of England*, 1838–40), Julia Pardoe, the historian of French court life and of Spanish queens, and Kate Norgate the medieval historian, these writers can, as Rosemary Mitchell has argued, be seen as the forerunners of the feminist historians of women of the late nineteenth and early twentieth centuries.[59] They were, as we will see, preceded by Mary Hays, Lucy Aikin and Elizabeth Benger, all to some degree preoccupied with the interface between women and the world of political power. However, their shared preoccupation may, in the short as well as very long terms, have been less consequential than the peculiar character that royal female biography gave to British popular history as a whole. In our own time, the British best-seller lists and film and television media continue to give a generous place to the wives of Henry VIII, to Mary, Queen of Scots, Elizabeth I and to princesses and elite women from the past, while paying far less attention to most of the male monarchs. The reasons for this enduring fascination with queens thrust by fate into the halls of power, suffering royal brides and betrayed female sovereigns, are a matter of conjecture, but historians who have reached a wide audience in our own time certainly see continuities between their work and eighteenth-century conceptions of the role of personality in history. In a recent article, Stella Tillyard, the author of an absorbing and widely read biography of the Lennox sisters, defended popular history of the kind practised by historical biographers of elite women such as Antonia Fraser, Elizabeth Longford, Amanda Foreman and Alison Weir, as 'emotional history', combining sophisticated scholarship, literary awareness and 'an original authorial voice'. 'Popular history', she argues, 'has few theorizers and practitioners' and it 'very often relies on ideas about character that in the eighteenth century found acceptance in all branches of literature, but which are more often now confined to the novel.'[60] Citing Oliver Goldsmith's remark that 'no one can properly be said to write history but he who understands the human heart', she defends the inferential and authorial emotional colouring of such works in terms that echo Dobson's call for history to supply 'many interesting details towards a history of the heart'.

The fact that so many historical biographies, from the late eighteenth century to the present day, have been concerned with elite or royal female lives may well have more to do with the opportunity they provide for emotional colouring than with non-elite class curiosity or aspiration. Stories of women of destiny can effectively dramatise the encounter between personal inwardness and the intractable public world of responsibility and power. They present both female and male readers with an accessible model of a private subjectivity that is forced to inhabit the ill-fitting clothes of a public persona, and that seeks to survive and negotiate its own happiness in a world it cannot control. Certainly, it was and remains the case that the most readily imaginable historical subjectivity is very often female, and that female historical characters have been accorded a privileged role in the mediation of the British past, particularly as it was experienced emotionally. In the early nineteenth century, an added attraction of elite women as a subject for historians was the fact that they provided a means of writing about publicly significant female lives without the need to generalise their case as feminist argument. This is to say that queens and princesses provided instances of how a female life might, by its very nature, be endowed with public significance, and hence, as a subject for history, they permitted the historian to make an indirect contribution to the wider debate about the civic role of the domestic and the feminine. Born to social prominence, queens and princesses embodied an idea of innate and socially incontrovertible human value that did not have to be earned by struggle or compromised by ambition. Female readers who identified with Mary, Queen of Scots or Elizabeth of Bohemia could imagine themselves in a position of great consequence without having breached any decorum in getting there. They could also consider how their moral principles might have saved them from the flaws and errors of such characters, and so imagine their own acts of choice writ large on the canvas of history.

Certainly, some women historians communicated powerfully their sense that, had they been in the shoes of a particular historical character, they would have done things quite differently. This sense lies behind Catharine Macaulay's robust, often censorious, character judgements, and her work, in turn, imparted a self-confidently judgemental tone, as well as a radical Whig tendency, to the histories of Lucy Aikin. Aikin's first historical work, the *Memoirs of the Court of Queen Elizabeth* (1818), offered a finessed psychological portrait of Elizabeth as a woman narrowed by her upbringing and hardened by power: 'The disposition of Elizabeth was originally deficient in benevolence and sympathy, and prone to suspicion, pride and anger; and we observe with pain in the progress of her history, how much . . . her high station . . . tended . . . to exacerbate these radical evils of her nature'.[61] Aikin repeatedly censures Elizabeth for failing to rise above the political culture of her time, and treats with sympathy those women, like Lady Catherine Grey for example, who are 'doomed to undergo all the restraints, the persecutions and the sufferings, which in that age formed the melancholy appanage of the younger branches of the royal race, with little participation of the homage or the hopes which some minds would have accepted as an adequate compensation'.[62] Elizabeth lives in a world of intrigue and a world intelligible to the historian only as intrigue: Aikin warns the 'philosophical inquirer' not to look here for evidence of the workings of 'the great moral causes which act upon whole ages and peoples'.[63] Aikin's insight that, as a person and a monarch, Elizabeth was the product of an immature political culture also lends support to her choice of an unfootnoted, flexible and anecdotal mode of historical presentation, rather than a narrative of political events. She carefully defends this choice in the preface: 'it has been the constant endeavour of the writer to preserve to her work the genuine character of Memoirs, by avoiding as much as possible all encroachments on the peculiar province of history'.[64] She offers instead a history that integrates the 'private life' of Elizabeth and other key characters, a 'domestic history of her reign' (including an appendix on domestic architecture) and the 'manners, opinions and literature' of the age.[65] Indeed, the *Memoirs* do represent a genuine and successful attempt (the work reached its sixth edition by 1826) to extend the Enlightenment history of manners into areas of private experience as well as art and literary history, and also to detach it from all but the loosest conjectural scheme of historical development. Aikin's subsequent *Memoirs of the Court of King James the First* (1822) and *Memoirs of the Court of King Charles the First* (1833) were informed by a similar project, if less often reprinted.

The success of Aikin's historical works no doubt encouraged the elderly Mary Hays to return to history after an absence of some years, with her *Memoirs of Queens, Illustrious and Celebrated* (1821). In her *Historical Dialogues for Young Persons* (1806–8) she had made the case for emotional history ('we must feel an interest and a personal sympathy in the books we read, to give them their effect on the heart and mind', argues the main speaker in the dialogues), and she had contributed the third volume to a children's *History of England* (1806), started by Charlotte Smith.[66] Aikin's influence was more productively felt, however, by her friend Elizabeth Benger, and when Benger predeceased her, Aikin wrote a biographical notice celebrating her historical achievement.[67] Benger enjoyed modest fame as a *salonnière*, playing host to literary figures such as Anna Barbauld, Elizabeth Hamilton and Edward Bulwer-Lytton, and as the author of biographical memoirs of Anne Boleyn, Mary, Queen of Scots and Elizabeth of Bohemia.[68] Her historical works are remarkably readable and scholarly examples of the hybrid historical memoir genre. What they have in common is their focus upon flawed but sympathetic and intelligent women at sea in a treacherous world yet somehow managing to retain their self-possession. Benger tries to evoke the ambiguous moral territory inhabited by women in a world utterly different from her own. She always insists upon this absolute historical difference, a difference that becomes vivid to us, for instance, when we look at the paintings of past eras: 'In contemplating this antiquated portraiture of our country, we are admonished, by certain internal feelings, of the immeasurable distance between us.'[69] It is the sensibility of the central female character that mediates the alien, yet nationally formative, history of the early modern period to Benger's readers. Her account of Anne Boleyn recreates, often by inference from the sources, the queen's private feelings and terrors as a way into the story of the Reformation, itself the story *par excellence* of private female feelings impinging on the state. Benger's more accomplished *Memoirs of the Life of Mary Queen of Scots* (1823) uses Mary as the organising sensibility for an account of Scotland in transition from the medieval to the modern age and in the process of Reformation. The Protestant Whig orientation of her story comes from William Robertson's *History of Scotland*; as, for example, when she writes that 'religious controversy' in Scotland was, ironically, not an impediment to the 'progress of civilisation' but 'the harbinger of moral and intellectual improvement'.[70] But what were to Robertson and his generation distinct 'stages' in the progress of society are to Benger 'phases' in an organic progress of cultural growth, expressed in the collective character of their historical inhabitants. She writes in great detail about the sixteenth-century France of Mary's early years as being 'under a phasis never again to be exhibited, where the gigantic image of the old feudal monarchy was still seen lingering in the glorious morning light that suddenly broke on Europe', describing its poets, its art, and its glittering, callous nobility.[71] Benger's greatest interest lies in the kind of mind that such a system of manners might have formed, and she uses documentary sources, including previously unpublished letters, to bring the voice of Mary and other characters to life, as in the case of the French court, where she offers, as she puts it, 'a sketch of the habits and opinions prevailing in that circle in which her mind and manners were formed, and which, at a later period, continued to influence her conduct and character'.[72]

Benger's evocation of Mary certainly involves a great deal of inferential emotional colouring, as for instance when she speculates that Mary's 'chagrins' about her husband's drinking 'were somewhat softened by the hope, which she was now permitted to cherish, of giving an heir to the ancient house of Bruce'.[73] Where evidence is lacking, as most notoriously on the question of Mary's involvement with the murder of her husband, Bender relies upon a trans-historical notion of the frailty and kindness of the female sex.[74] In the main, however, her presentation of Mary is far less sentimental than that of earlier eighteenth-century historians. Benger's Mary has all the limitations of her historical 'phasis' and poor education, and these are her downfall from the moment she arrives in Scotland as 'a woman, possessing all the susceptibility of her sex, who had hitherto been taught to believe that she inspired only sentiments of affection, and who now was, for the first time, regarded with distrust or aversion'.[75] Mary is fallible, morally ambiguous and yet sympathetic in Benger's story in a way that (with the honourable and significant exception of Robertson's account) differs from the more polarised eighteenth-century treatments, including, for example, the gushing defences of her satirised by Jane Austen in her mock *History of England*. In her hilarious, youthful squib ('by a partial, prejudiced, and ignorant Historian'), Austen declares that her 'principal reason' for writing the history is 'to prove the innocence of the Queen of Scotland', and gushes about Mary's sufferings at the hands of wicked Queen Elizabeth: 'Oh! What must this bewitching Princess whose only friend was then the Duke of Norfolk, and whose only ones now are Mr. Whitaker, Mrs Lefroy, Mrs Knight and myself . . . what must not her noble mind have suffered when informed that Elizabeth had given orders for her Death!'[76] Austen's satire of women's history seems implausibly gossipy until one reads Hester Thrale's *Retrospection* (1801), a historical account of the eighteenth century published ten years later, and comprised largely of cosy, drawing-room character judgements of the same kind.[77]

Jane Austen had some sympathy for Catherine Morland, the flawed heroine of *Northanger Abbey* (1817) who is bored by history: '"the quarrels of popes and kings, with wars or pestilences, in every page; the men all so good for nothing, and hardly any women at all – it is very tiresome"'. Her friend Eleanor Tilney is more open to the charms of modern history, and speaks warmly of Hume and Robertson, and her serious-minded brother also leaps to the defence of '"our most distinguished historians"'.[78] Peter Knox-Shaw, in his study *Jane Austen and the Enlightenment*, has argued that, notwithstanding her youthful squib, Austen was at one with the Tilneys on this question, and quite receptive to the influence of Enlightenment history.[79] He makes this case as part of his wider argument that Austen is best understood not as a nostalgic, Tory opponent of Jacobinism and radicalism, but as a legatee of the moderate, sceptical 'Anglo-Scottish' Enlightenment. The argument is persuasive, not least for the connections it draws between the undogmatic, Latitudinarian Anglicanism Austen inherited from her father, her liking for moral qualities of 'benevolence' in her characters and the ethics and epistemology she indirectly imbibed from Scottish Enlightenment philosophers.[80] Like the Enlightenment historians, and like the women historians who were inspired by their work to depict queens and princesses experiencing at first hand different stages of society, Austen was committed to understanding her female characters as inhabitants of very particular states of 'manners'. Where she differs from contemporary female historians, however, is in the virtual absence of any sense, in her works, of a more general progress of society. Knox-Shaw notes the presence of ideas of social progress in the publications of her brother James Austen, but does not otherwise press this case.[81] He detects, rather, an element of Malthusian pessimism on this subject, redolent of the 'food shortages, economic blockade, national debt' that dominated the national landscape of Austen's adult life, and that surfaces in her depiction in *Mansfield Park* of Fanny Price's dirty, overcrowded family home in Portsmouth.[82]

PART II

THE POPULATION QUESTION

Malthus's *An Essay on the Principle of Population* was first published in 1798, and then reissued in a substantially enlarged edition in 1803, with further revised editions appearing until 1826. Austen would have known of the work, at the very least on account of its notorious proposition that population growth will always outstrip food supply, until checked, inevitably, by famine, disease or war. She read approvingly the work of some Evangelicals whose depictions of the social and economic realm as a domain of trial and exemplary suffering incorporated Malthus's picture of human life as a struggle against scarcity.[83] Her novels offer an implicit endorsement, at least, of Malthus's prescription, in the 1803 version of the *Essay*, for late and prudent marriages as the best way to transform unruly natural passion into more equal and enduring affection between men and women.[84] Austen never ventured very far down the road of Malthusian pessimism or, indeed, of the Evangelical conviction of sin. Yet her novels, combining as they do highly particularised and implicitly historicised depictions of states of 'manners' with a historical sensibility engaged, not with progress, but with the struggle to maintain family prosperity and order, might be said to offer a Malthusian version of the Enlightenment. This makes sense only if we first consider to what extent Malthus himself was a part of that Enlightenment. He has more often been regarded as marking the end-point of the Enlightenment idea of the progress of society in that, on the eve of the 1801 population census that revealed that the population of England had reached 8.9 million and that of Scotland 1.6 million, he showed the definitive ecological constraints to that progress. In Malthus's wake economic theorists such as David Ricardo abandoned Smith's notion of a natural harmony of interests, in favour of competition and conflict between stratified social groups, and were, for a time, reluctant to imagine the economy as something that can grow and expand. The rise, from the 1780s, of Evangelical Christianity placed a parallel emphasis upon man's helplessness in this world, and deliberately tried to put an end to the dilute, amiably benevolent Latitudinarian Anglicanism of the eighteenth century. The decline, following the American and especially the French Revolutions, of the Enlightenment, Latitudinarian consensus, that had proved so hospitable to ideas of female social prominence, was hastened by what Boyd Hilton has described as a new 'neo-conservative ("Throne and Altar") ideology'. This ideology set itself against, but never entirely suffocated, 'two competing versions of liberalism' that survived and regrouped in the mid nineteenth century: the first, a radicalism based on civil rights, the second, the residual, progressive socio-economic thinking of the Enlightenment.[85] What had been a dominant mode of Enlightenment thought became for a time an embattled strand of nineteenth-century liberalism or 'philosophic Whiggism'. The legacy of Smith, Robertson and Hume was nurtured at Edinburgh University by Dugald Stewart and at Glasgow by John Millar in what was from the 1790s a climate of considerable political repression. The new generation of Scottish-educated Whigs included politicians such as Henry Brougham and John Russell, and intellectuals such as James Mackintosh and Francis Jeffrey, a founder editor (with Brougham and Francis Horner) of the *Edinburgh Review*, the periodical that did most to promulgate the philosophic Whiggism of the Scottish Enlightenment to the generation that supported the Reform Act of 1832. Stewart, as we will see, was much more sanguine than Malthus about population growth and its benefits to the nation, and more interested than his English contemporary in the relationship between sexual behaviour and 'manners'. It is nevertheless important to see both men as participants in the same late Enlightenment conversation about the possibilities and limits of the progress of society, and its implications for women as well as men.

The connection of Malthus and Stewart to the ongoing Enlightenment, or philosophic Whiggism, of the nineteenth century is now well established. Malthus's most authoritative interpreter, Donald Winch, has argued for the 'centrality of Malthus to the process by which Smith's political economy, as well as other historical and anthropological insights connected with Smith's Scottish contemporaries, became an integral part of Anglican thinking about society during the first third of the nineteenth century'.[86] Malthus's Evangelical interpreters may have taken his doctrine of checks to population as proof that human sexuality is both a trial and a bringer of punishment, but Malthus himself had a philosophic Whiggish faith in the possibility of social melioration within the limits of economic productivity. Malthus certainly felt, like his Scottish forebears, that this melioration ought to include an improvement in the status and treatment of women, and like them, also, he believed that some improvement had already come about as European societies moved through successive stages of development. The population question naturally lends itself to the subject of women, as sexual partners and breeders, and the social progress of women occupied a significant part of the first, 1798 edition of Malthus's *Essay*. Malthus's immediate targets were Condorcet and Godwin with their wildly optimistic visions (in his view) of the possibility of unlimited social and moral improvement. He engages more subtly, however, with Scottish conjectural history, including the particular account it offers of the awakening over time, and delayed gratification of erotic desire, and the opportunities this offers for female social agency. On some points he is in disagreement with his Scottish predecessors. Contrary to what Smith, Millar and others suggested, Malthus takes it as axiomatic that 'the passion between the sexes is necessary and will remain nearly in its present state' throughout history.[87] It follows from this, despite what Robertson had written in his *History of America*, that the passion between the sexes is no less ardent in savage societies than in civilised ones. Malthus does not disagree that conditions for women in primitive societies are unbearably harsh, but attributes this not to a lack of sexual interest on the part of their men, but to poor nutrition, hard work and frequent miscarriages.[88] The reason, he says, for mistaken speculations such as those about native Americans 'is that the histories of mankind that we possess are histories only of the higher classes', and too little is known about the lives of those who live close to the margin of subsistence, their sexual and marriage practices, fertility levels and rates of infant mortality.[89] Malthus does accept that, even further down the social scale, the general trajectory of history is towards better conditions for women, albeit with many setbacks along the way: in pastoral societies, they enjoy 'greater ease' (although here, 'women [were] exposed to casual plunder in the absence of their husbands'), and in sedentary, agricultural societies later marriages bring some respite from numerous pregnancies, although these can lead to the temptations of fornication or adultery.[90] Modern monogamy proves that the natural tendency of the sex instinct is 'to a virtuous attachment', but this can lead to unfeasibly large families among the respectable poor, as well as to hypocritically punitive social attitudes towards women who commit adultery: 'That a woman should at present be almost driven from society for an offence which men commit nearly with impunity, seems to be undoubtedly a breach of natural justice.'[91] Though an Anglican vicar, Malthus was neither prudish nor overly censorious about the sexual passions that provide the deep ecological basis for his own, very cautious account of the progress of society.

Malthus's 1798 *Essay* represented an intervention in the Scottish Enlightenment account of social progress to the extent that it treated population growth more as an effect of biology (especially female biology) than of institutional or economic arrangements. Scottish thinkers had been deeply interested in population questions, but mainly, following Montesquieu, in relation to the influence of political settings (free citizens tend to be more fertile) or to the tendency of commercial societies to foster population increase by paying higher wages (for Smith, especially).[92] They were sanguine about the benefits of population growth, but often also critical of the tendency of commercial prosperity to cause wealthy women to produce few or no children. The link between luxury and infertility, in Scottish writers as in the work of many other commentators such as Richard Price, was always very ill defined, if greatly insisted upon (what did they mean: birth control, venereal disease? Or, more likely, etiolation of the nervous system).[93] In *The Wealth of Nations*,

Smith wrote of the barrenness of fashionable women in his own time: 'Luxury in the fair sex, while it enflames perhaps the passion for enjoyment, seems always to weaken, and frequently to destroy altogether, the powers of generation'; and Kames, in a section of the *Sketches of the History of Man* entitled the 'Progress of Food and Population', complained that 'a woman enervated by indolence and intemperance, is ill qualified for the severe labour of child-bearing', whereas 'a barren woman among the labouring poor, is a wonder'.[94] For Kames, Smith and Millar the limits of civilisation are reached once luxury starts to contaminate female morals and richer women have fewer babies. None of them specifies the link between declining birth rates and economic decline, although, by implication, it would seem that a dip in population among the affluent reduces consumer demand and so discourages production. A more sophisticated version of this argument, before Malthus, came from the Cambridge University theologian William Paley in a remarkable discussion 'Of Population and Provision' in his *Principles of Moral and Political Philosophy* (1785). Paley, a Latitudinarian natural theologian in the tradition of Butler, was enormously influential (though much reviled by Evangelicals) well into the nineteenth century. He understood fertility within marriage as, in part, a quality-of-life issue: wealth and luxury can encourage people to marry and have families, but they also give men material expectations that they may be reluctant to compromise by giving up the single life: 'men will not marry to *sink* their place or condition in society'.[95] The result, as Paley accurately points out and as so many female novelists of the time portrayed it, is that there are large numbers of unmarried women with 'little opportunity . . . of adding to their income', and too many male wastrels guilty of 'licentious celibacy'.[96] Paley offers no easy remedies for this situation, but he does, in a section on the 'relative duties' of parents, argue that fathers have a duty to provide their daughters with a good education, and to set aside for them a much larger slice of the family inheritance than was usually 'agreeable to modern usage'.[97]

MALTHUS'S OLD MAIDS

Paley was an early convert to Malthus's views on the dangers of overpopulation, and Malthus, in turn, was deeply influenced by Paley's ethical and theological views. From the 1803 edition onwards, Malthus's *Essay* included a new chapter 'Of moral restraint, and the foundations of our obligation to practise this virtue' that profoundly modified the meaning of the whole work by advocating a period of celibacy followed by late marriage as the best remedy for the natural tendency of population to outstrip food production (as a devout Anglican, Malthus could have no truck with contraception as an alternative to this). The 'foundations' of young people's 'obligation' to adopt this behaviour he derived from the principle of theological utility, which he goes on to define, quoting Paley directly, as '"the method of coming at the will of God from the light of nature [by inquiring] into the tendency of the action to promote or diminish the general happiness"'.[98] In other words, Paley's highly individualistic and utilitarian version of natural theology ('nothing really exists', wrote Paley, 'or feels but *individuals*') enabled Malthus to formulate a possible remedy for overpopulation in terms that laid obligations on individuals to promote the public happiness in this life rather than reward in the next.[99] Malthus's revised *Essay* thus gave much greater scope for individual, as well as collective and institutional, agency in redressing the tendency of nature periodically to cull the human species. However, Malthus insists, such a shift in individual behaviour cannot take place without a culture change, particularly in relation to attitudes towards women. One such change, he argues in a chapter 'Of the modes of correcting the prevailing opinions on the subject of Population', is that society must stop stigmatising old maids (who have not burdened society with their children) and treating married women as their social superiors (one is put in mind of Lydia Bennett triumphing over her sisters when she is the first of them to get married). Malthus writes:

It is perfectly absurd, as well as unjust, that a giddy girl of sixteen should, because she is married, be considered by the forms of society as the protector of women of thirty, should come first into the room, should be assigned the highest place at the table, and be the prominent figure to whom the attentions of the company are more particularly addressed.[100]

Secondly, Malthus states in a revision of his earlier argument, the virtue of chastity should not be regarded – *pace* Hume – as the 'forced produce of artificial society', but as something that has 'the most real and solid foundation in nature and reason' since, according to utilitarian theological principles, it is the one virtuous means by which men and women can promote the general happiness.[101] Thirdly, men should stop dismissing women past their mid-twenties as on the shelf, and should marry women closer to their own age. This would have the additional, humane benefit of lessening the desperation that 'drives many women into the marriage union with men whom they dislike' – something that Malthus describes as 'little better than legal prostitutions'.[102]

In transforming the 1798 version of the *Essay* into the more optimistic 1803 version, Malthus drew upon the ethical and theological vocabulary provided by Paley to refashion a work that subsequent commentators readily accepted as consistent with Latitudinarian natural theology.[103] His theologically utilitarian prescriptions for 'moral restraint' also realigned the work more closely with the Scottish Enlightenment idea of delayed gratification as the engine of the progress of society. In the second version of the *Essay*, Malthus revisited his earlier observations about savage and civilised societies, and placed much greater emphasis upon the way that the restricted sexual access to women typical of complex societies can be a force for civilisation more generally: 'the passion is stronger, and its general effects in producing gentleness, kindness, and suavity of manners [are] much more powerful, where obstacles are thrown in the way of a very early and universal gratification'.[104] In contrast to 'savage life', the more restrained passion between the sexes in sophisticated societies tends 'to soften and meliorate the human character, and keep it more alive to all the kindlier emotions of benevolence and pity'.[105] Malthus was famously sceptical about the motivational power of benevolence, as opposed to self-love, but does appear to see the more self-regarding passion of love between the sexes as a major factor in the socialising and civilising process. The individual Christian obligation to moral restraint is thus entirely consistent with the collective endeavour to further the 'gradual and progressive improvement of human society' that, Malthus says at the end, is not entirely precluded by the laws of population growth.[106]

Malthus acknowledged the need for an additional factor in the 'progressive improvement of human society', education, needed particularly to enable the poor to understand how they perpetuate their own poverty, and, by implication, to reconcile them to Malthus's recommended phasing out of poor relief.[107] Malthus did not discuss the matter in detail in the *Essay*, and he did not have much to say about the education of either children (whom he viewed mainly as an affliction) or of women. But he clearly regarded political economy as *in itself* an intellectually and spiritually formative exercise of the mind, in seeking human solutions to the physical necessities imposed by God. It was in this spirit that many nineteenth-century women commentators read and recommended political economy as a valuable part of female education. Perhaps in part because of Malthus's strong emphasis upon the need for a reform of social attitudes towards women as a means of regulating population growth, women writers throughout the century promoted Malthus: he and other political economists and population theorists were seen as valuable in enabling their female readers to understand the interaction between their personal lives as wives and mothers and the underlying human ecology of British society. More simply, political economy could and did seem relevant to the daily lives and educational needs of women.[108] One of the first to promote the idea of an education in population and political economy was Malthus's acquaintance Maria Edgeworth, particularly in her *Popular Tales* for children, published in 1804 and reissued throughout the nineteenth century.[109] Edgeworth in turn was connected to the world of the late Scottish Enlightenment through her acquaintances Elizabeth Hamilton (of whom she eventually wrote a memoir) and Dugald Stewart.[110]

Stewart himself addressed the question of population very fully in his lectures on political economy in 1800–1, the series that so electrified Francis Jeffrey, Henry Brougham, James Mill and other young listeners. His notes for these were not published until 1856, after his death, but they show that despite treating political economy as a separate discipline, he took a broad approach to the subject as part of the study of human behaviour, of ethics, of the progress of society and of the laws of nature. On this last subject, and in relation to his opening discussion of population, he disagreed with Malthus: 'He seems to me to lay by far too little stress on the efficacy of those arrangements which nature herself has established for the evils in question.'[111] Stewart went on to enunciate his theory that population growth – as affected by such factors as 'political institutions which regulate the sexual connection' and 'by the state of manners relative to the connection between the sexes' – was largely consistent with economic growth, with social progress and with liberal political institutions. All this he keyed to a stadial model of social evolution, albeit one that placed much greater emphasis than his Scottish forebears on history as the unfolding of the promptings of the moral sense and upon natural human proclivities. These proclivities include 'the delicacy and modesty which seem to be *natural* to the other sex', and these in turn graft a 'moral union on the instinctive passion', and over the long term promote monogamous marriage as a norm.[112] He argues that modern (essentially indissoluble) monogamous marriages are the most favourable to high birth rates, more so than the Roman forms of marriage discussed by Gibbon.[113] In examining the way that manners affect population growth, Stewart looks at unfair property laws and at the unduly high financial expectations that deter young men from marriage and procreation. He underlines the importance of education in making people aware of the relationship of their sexual behaviour to personal and national prosperity by ending the lectures with a section 'Of Education'. This, according to surviving notes, included a section on the 'Importance of the Education of the Female Sex', and mentioned the 'pernicious tendency of some late systems to obliterate the characteristical qualities bestowed on them by Nature, and to counteract her obvious intentions with respect to their peculiar sphere in Civilized Society'.[114] By implication, women who were educated to understand what nature intended their role in the progress of society to be, would be able to further that progress as wives and mothers. This can be connected to Stewart's moral philosophical view, first expressed in his *Outlines of Moral Philosophy* (1793), that women and men have a measure of free will.[115] Their will enables them, with the assistance of education, to interpret and implement the divinely instituted laws of nature in order to bring about the moral and material progress of mankind.

POLITICAL ECONOMY AS FEMALE EDUCATION

The lectures that Stewart built around the published *Outlines* were reported by his students as containing wide-ranging discussions of the (presumably civil, rather than political) rights of women, perhaps along the lines of Hutcheson's *System of Moral Philosophy*.[116] His second wife, Helen D'Arcy Stewart, was a poet and leading Edinburgh hostess, and he apparently encouraged her active interest and input into this part of his work.[117] He may well have felt that the study of the population question, as well as political economy more generally, was a fitting part of female education. By the 1820s, his protégée Maria Edgeworth reported that 'it has now become high fashion with blue ladies to talk political economy'.[118] Anna Barbauld was among those who engaged thoughtfully and critically with political economy and with the work of her acquaintance Malthus.[119] Her example was followed by Jane Marcet in her popular work, *Conversations on Political Economy* (1816). Marcet and her Edinburgh-educated physician husband moved in Whig intellectual circles, and knew Malthus, Brougham, Jeffrey, Edgeworth and Ricardo (the last two were good friends of hers).[120] Her *Conversations* are set out as a dialogue between 'Mrs. B' and her niece Caroline, aimed at making the subject accessible to young people, just, Mrs B. says, as Edgeworth and the Edinburgh university teachers are currently doing, and persuading them that it is 'intimately connected with the daily occurrences of life'.[121] Notwithstanding their intended audience, Marcet pitched the *Conversations* at a very high level, engaging critically with Smith's theory of value and covering topics such as the division of labour, property, foreign trade, and the role of legislation in economic matters, and earning the approbation of Malthus and Ricardo in the process.[122] Marcet's section 'On Wages and Population' takes forward Malthus's idea of population outstripping the means of subsistence, and advances a theory (new at this time) of the determination of wages by the proportion of capital to population stock, and the inevitability that, once the number of people rises and wages fall, population will inevitably 'be checked by distress and disease' and children will die of illnesses and malnutrition.[123] To give some imaginative depth to this point, Marcet paints a picture of a poor mother struggling to look after her large, hungry family ('that mother is frequently obliged to leave them to obtain by hard labour their scanty meal'), and she greatly embellishes Malthus's point that, without education, the poor will never have the prudent foresight to marry late and have fewer babies: 'Education gives rise to prudence, not only by enlarging our understandings, but by softening our feelings, by humanizing the heart, and promoting amiable affections'.[124] To the extent that Marcet's work links political economy with moral philosophical questions, it articulates a theory of human nature as not mainly given over to self-love (as Malthus had done) but as naturally benevolent. Natural benevolence, Mrs B. argues in an echo of Stewart, can often be mistaken in its object (poor relief is a case in point), but it is real, and must be nurtured by knowledge and education.[125]

Marcet's work and friendship had an enormous impact upon Harriet Martineau, the great radical Unitarian populariser of political economy in the ensuing decades. Martineau's *Illustrations of Political Economy* (a series of tales published monthly from 1832 to 1834), published by Brougham's Society for the Diffusion of Useful Knowledge, recommended the benefits of free trade and moral restraint to an envisaged working-class readership. She was attacked as an indelicate woman in the Tory *Quarterly Review* for tackling the subject of population, but this did not prevent the *Illustrations* launching her immensely successful career as a professional writer.[126] Although keen to gain a female as well as male readership for political economy, Martineau's ambivalent attitude towards women's rights and her often doctrinaire belief in the workings of the free market limited her interest in women's access to the economy proper. In this respect, she follows Marcet and indeed most women writers who promoted the subject to female readers. There had been exceptions, notably Priscilla Wakefield, who in her remarkable (if little known) *Reflections on the Present Condition of the Female Sex* (1798, second edition 1817) offered an education in political economy and made a polemical case for improved female access to the labour market. Wakefield, a Quaker educational writer and philanthropist, openly espoused Smith's ideas, particularly on the possibilities for ongoing social progress and the need for productive labour, arguing that women are disbarred, by social prejudice and above all by a lack of education, from employing their 'time and their talents, beneficially to themselves and to the community'.[127] Wakefield then goes on to examine the opportunities and impediments to female participation in the labour market as they apply to different social categories of women. For female servants and tradeswomen, the problem is 'the inequality of the reward of their labour' as well as the fact that 'men monopolize . . . the most advantageous employments'.[128] For labouring poor women, the priority is to wean them off parish charity. Writing before Malthus's ideas had started to dominate public debate on this question, Wakefield unselfconsciously advocates 'inducements to early marriage' as their best way out of dependent poverty, as well as free schooling.[129] The philanthropic, interventionist tone of this section carries over from her discussion of wealthy women who, though 'prohibited from the public service of their country by reason and decorum', ought to promote 'its welfare' as patrons and staff of charitable enterprises.[130] Upper-class women owe it to the country to set the tone of national manners, whereas non-working women of the classes below them should consider engaging in 'the active offices of benevolence', foremost among which is the 'civilization of the poor'.[131]

Although unusual in its insistence on women's entitlement to work, Wakefield's *Reflections* otherwise bear striking similarities to the ideas of Hannah More (whom she praises by name as an exemplary philanthropist), and to More's *Strictures on the Modern System of Female Education*, published the following year.[132] More's much more highly publicised works made a sustained case for women's active engagement in social causes, and an implicit though forceful argument for a consultative role in matters of domestic politics. Lower down the social scale, she tried to inculcate the elementary principles of political economy to men and women alike.[133] Like Wakefield, she regarded the civilisation of the poor as the peculiar prerogative of educated women, and like her, but at far greater length in works such as the *Strictures* and in *Hints towards Forming the Character of a Young Princess* (1805), More advocated a rational education for women to rid them of their usual pleasure-centred silliness, and enable them to gain self-possession and moral autonomy. On this basis, she clearly felt that women would be better equipped to further the progress of civilisation in England: 'The general state of civilized society depends . . . on the prevailing sentiments and habits of women, and on the nature and degree of the estimation in which they are held.'[134] More, once seen as a distasteful and neglected figure, has enjoyed a surge of historical interest in recent years, and has been restored to her rightful prominence as a leading public figure of the late eighteenth to early nineteenth centuries. Yet commentators continue to disagree about how to place her, both in relation to the Enlightenment and to the advancement of women in her own day. A conservative opponent of the French Revolution, her diagnosis of corrupted femininity bears some unlikely yet striking similarities to that of Wollstonecraft.[135] As Anne K. Mellor has argued, More was a fearless and extraordinarily effective advocate of a certain kind of public role for women; this was not, Mellor points out, confined to moral guardianship of national values, but also entailed promoting women's knowledge of household economics as a model for responsible stewardship of the country's domestic affairs.[136]

More, a younger and socially subordinate member of the Bluestocking circle, can, in many ways, be said to have carried the Bluestocking project for a rational education for women and for a female-led reformation of manners. Yet, lest the pendulum swing too far in More's favour, we might also recall the note of caution sounded by historians such as Kathryn Gleadle about the degree to which Evangelical women writers such as More contributed to improvements in women's status in the long run: 'Whilst acknowledging Evangelicalism's importance to the longue durée of growing female confidence and consciousness, its relationship to the specific political demands for women's emancipation . . . is extremely problematic.'[137] At root, there were profound differences of philosophical and theological outlook between More and her Bluestocking acquaintances that shaped not only her emphatically Tory political views but the orientation of her writings about women's status away from notions of social progress and towards those of reformation and recovery. More cannily avoided, in her writings, citations of authors and intellectual reference points that might have narrowed her appeal, and this makes it harder for modern scholars to place her in relation to Enlightenment debate about women. Her prose writings dwell in pious and moralising generalities, yet, from the outset, some of her controversial steeliness glints through. She dedicated her early educational work for girls, *Essays on Various Subjects* (1777), to Elizabeth Montagu, but inserted a passing reference (clearly aimed at Montagu's friend Carter) about the inappropriateness of introducing young girls to Stoic philosophy.[138]

More aired her deepening Evangelical views in her *Estimate of the Religion of the Fashionable World* (1791), making it clear just how far she had travelled from the Latitudinarian and natural theological views held by so many earlier commentators on women's education: 'Under the beautiful mask of an enlightened philosophy', she complained, 'all religious restraints are set at nought.'[139] Here she made one of her longest attacks on the fashionable world, on London society where young girls are allowed out to go to balls and on the thorough-going 'practical irreligion' of the higher ranks that filters down to all below them.[140] Although she professes little concern with doctrine, her High Church views are set out in her generalised attacks on the excessive religious toleration of contemporary society, on rational religion and those principally interested in Christianity as a moral system.[141] She repudiates the idea that hers is an 'age of benevolence', adding that, if there has been an increase in philanthropic activity (implicitly on the part of women, as well as men), this is because there has been an increase in the 'luxury and dissipation which promote . . . distress'.[142] Hers is a religion of the heart, and a morality of the self-denying, Evangelical virtues.

For many contemporary readers, this religion and the controversy it excited, contained, indeed eclipsed, her partiality for rational female education. Even Mary Berry, who noted the unintended resemblance, in the *Strictures on the Modern System of Female Education*, between More's ideas about female education and Wollstonecraft's, was utterly deterred by its religious perspectives, 'a principle radically false, which . . . vitiates every system built upon it and saps the very foundation of morality'.[143] More was hostile not only to tolerant Anglicanism but also to Scottish Enlightenment ideas of common sense and social progress that had so interested Montagu. She accurately placed Malthus in the Scottish camp, dismissing him as 'too thorough a Brougham-ite & Edinburgh Reviewer for me to like'.[144] More's programme – for reformed leadership among the upper classes and a rational education for their middle-class, female foot-soldiers – channelled some of the ideas and energies of the Enlightenment into the assistance and conversion of the poor, as well into as the abolition of the Slave Trade.[145] Yet despite many forays into the public domain, she insistently pictured the home as the control-centre of female activity and a site of insulation from the progress and perils of society.[146]

More operated within and, to an extent capitulated to, a climate of growing scepticism about the benefits of a mixed social sphere. Rousseau had struck a chord in England when he voiced this scepticism to an adoring public of female readers, and offered them, instead of spurious social influence, a fuller sense of what it meant to be a woman, wife and mother. As De Staël wrote in her admiring *Lettres sur . . . Rousseau* (1788), 'Ah! s'il a voulu les [les femmes] priver de quelques droits étrangers à leur sort, comme il leur a rendu tous ceux qui leur appartiennent à jamais!'[147] If the Enlightenment had demonstrated the historical evolution of women's roles within a narrative of ongoing gender differentiation, nineteenth-century British writers limited the possibility of further change by underpinning those roles with ever more solid biological foundations. The language of conjectural history evolved in the nineteenth century – and, with it, the idea that womanhood, whatever its biological content, was, to an important degree, historically contingent and potentially able to share in the progress that society brings. It played a part in the analysis of women's position by Unitarian and Owenite Socialist feminists in the early decades of the nineteenth century.[148] Some writers, notably the radical historian and freethinker Henry Thomas Buckle, argued that the failure of contemporary society to appreciate, in conjectural-historical terms, the contribution of women to progress was in itself an impediment to further improvement. Buckle was the author of the hugely successful *History of Civilization in England* (1857, 1861), a pioneering intellectual history of the secularising and scientific achievements of the Enlightenment. He also gave a public address, published in *Fraser's Magazine* in 1858, on 'The Influence of Women on the Progress of Knowledge' which condensed into a few pages the whole Enlightenment history of women in ancient and modern societies, and urged men, in the interests of science, to be more open to the deductive and imaginative intellectual gifts of women. Women, in Buckle's version of progress, are one half of a historical dialectic of male and female, and he has this aspiration for their future: 'Let us, then, hope that the imaginative and emotional minds of one sex will continue to accelerate the great progress, by acting upon the colder and harder minds of the other sex.'[149] Such dialectics could be serviceable for feminist purposes, as they were for the American feminist Margaret Fuller in her *Woman in the Nineteenth Century* (1845), but, in writers such as Buckle they had the effect of commuting women into a female historical principle, and of confusing the progress of women with progressive feminisation. No such confusion haunted John Stuart Mill and Harriet Taylor, who began their *The Subjection of Women* (1869) with a cold, hard look at the whole question of 'the progress of civilization' (as they were still willing to call it), and how, despite having delivered considerable improvements in the lives of men, it continues to enshrine men's primitive domination over women:

(the general progress of society assisting) the slavery of the male sex has, in all the countries of Christian Europe at least . . . been at length abolished, and that of the female sex has been gradually changed into a milder form of dependence. But this dependence, as it exists at present, is not an original institution, taking a fresh start from considerations of justice and social expediency – it is the primitive state of slavery lasting on, through successive mitigations and modifications occasioned by the same causes which have softened the general manners, and brought all human relations more under the control of justice and the influence of humanity.[150]

Like their Utilitarian forebear Jeremy Bentham, in the early nineteenth century, they were certain that government was not fulfilling its duty to maximise human happiness unless it permitted female as well as male suffrage. But unlike Bentham, with his conviction that men and women are principally motivated by the 'self-regarding affections' and have to be conditioned into sociability, their case for suffrage is linked to a sense that women's moral capacities can best be fulfilled through an active engagement with the world around them ('benevolence', in eighteenth-century language). The delusion of the Enlightenment, for Mill and Taylor, was that the progress of society had, in its 'softening of manners', done anything to realise those capacities in women, still less brought them fully into a community of justice. The achievement of the Enlightenment, however, was that in creating a historical and sociological language through which to understand the progress of men, it made the progress of women towards equal membership of British society both thinkable and desirable.

Notes

INTRODUCTION: THE PROGRESS OF SOCIETY

1. *The Novels and Selected Works of Maria Edgeworth* (12 vols.; London, 1999, 2003), ed. Marilyn Butler *et al.*, volume IX, ed. Susan Manly and Clíona Ó Gallchoir, 214.
2. [Mary Astell], *The Christian Religion, as Profess'd by a Daughter of the Church of England* (London, 1705), 137.
3. See Isabel Rivers, *Reason, Grace and Sentiment: A Study of the Language of Religion and Ethics in England, 1660–1780* (2 vols.; Cambridge, 1991, 2000), II, Introduction.
4. J. G. A. Pocock, *Barbarism and Religion, I. The Enlightenments of Edward Gibbon, 1737–1764* (Cambridge, 1999), *II. Narratives of Civil Government* (Cambridge, 1999), *III. The First Decline and Fall* (Cambridge, 2003), *IV. Barbarians, Savages and Empires* (Cambridge, 2005); Roy Porter, *Enlightenment: Britain and the Creation of the Modern World* (London, 2000); Jonathan I. Israel, *Radical Enlightenment: Philosophy and the Making of Modernity, 1650–1750* (Oxford, 2001) and *Enlightenment Contested: Philosophy, Modernity and the Emancipation of Man, 1670–1752* (Oxford, 2006); John Robertson, *The Case for the Enlightenment: Scotland and Naples, 1680–1760* (Cambridge, 2005).
5. Robertson, *The Case for the Enlightenment*, 33, 28.
6. *Ibid.*, 26–7.
7. J. G. A. Pocock, 'Clergy and Commerce: The Conservative Enlightenment in England' in *L'età dei lumi: Studi storici sul Settecento europeo in onore di Franco Venturi*, ed. Rafaelle Ajello *et al.* (2 vols.; Naples, 1985) and *Barbarism and Religion, I. The Enlightenments of Edward Gibbon*, 5–9.
8. Pocock, *Barbarism and Religion, I. The Enlightenments of Edward Gibbon*, 7.
9. *Ibid.*, 8.
10. B. W. Young, *Religion and Enlightenment in Eighteenth-Century England: Theological Debate from Locke to Burke* (Oxford, 1998). For a useful overview of recent work on the relationship of religion to Enlightenment, see Jonathan Sheehan, 'Enlightenment, Religion, and the Enigma of Secularization: A Review Essay', *American Historical Review*, 108 (2003), 1061–80.

11. On the religious dimensions of the eighteenth-century notion of progress, see David Spadafora, *The Idea of Progress in Eighteenth-Century Britain* (New Haven, 1990).

12. Young, *Religion and Enlightenment,* 2, 8–9, 20.

13. Kathryn Gleadle, *The Early Feminists: Radical Unitarians and the Emergence of the Women's Rights Movement, c.1831–51* (Basingstoke, 1995); Ruth Watts, *Gender, Power and the Unitarians in England, 1760–1860* (London and New York, 1998).

14. John Robertson, 'Women and Enlightenment: A Historiographical Conclusion' in *Women, Gender and Enlightenment,* ed. Barbara Taylor and Sarah Knott (Basingstoke, 2005), 700.

15. *Ibid.,* 701.

16. Young, *Religion and Enlightenment,* ch. 4.

17. Carole Pateman, *The Sexual Contract* (Cambridge, 1988), 3. See also Pateman's revisiting of the arguments in her book in 'Women's Writing, Women's Standing: Theory and Politics in the Early Modern Period' in *Women Writers and the Early Modern British Political Tradition,* ed. Hilda L. Smith (Cambridge, 1998), 378–82. Ruth Perry's study, *Novel Relations: The Transformation of Kinship in English Literature and Culture, 1748–1818* (Cambridge, 2004), traces the growing authority and economic power of brothers over their sisters in the second half of the century. Her evidence is both literary and socio-historical, and it does lend weight to Carole Pateman's idea about the rise of 'fraternal patriarchy' in this period.

18. See most famously, Thomas Laqueur, *Making Sex: Body and Gender from the Greeks to Freud* (Cambridge, Massachusetts, 1990). See also Thomas L. Hankins, *Science and the Enlightenment* (Cambridge, 1985), ch. 5, and Tim Hitchcock, *English Sexualities, 1700–1800* (Basingstoke, 1997).

19. See, especially, E. J. Clery, *The Feminization Debate in Eighteenth-Century England: Literature, Commerce and Luxury* (Basingstoke, 2004).

20. Dror Wahrman, *The Making of the Modern Self: Identity and Culture in Eighteenth-Century England* (New Haven, 2004).

21. Kathryn Gleadle and Sarah Richardson eds., *Women in British Politics, 1760–1860: The Power of the Petticoat* (Basingstoke, 2000) and Elaine Chalus, *Elite Women in English Political Life, c. 1754–1790* (Oxford, 2005).

22. Amy Ericson, 'Property and Widowhood in England, 1660–1840' in *Widowhood in Medieval and Early Modern Europe,* ed. Sandra Cavallo and Lyndan Warner (London and New York, 1999), and *Women and Property in Early Modern England* (London, 1993). Also Susan Staves, *Married Women's Separate Property in England, 1660–1833* (Cambridge, Massachusetts, 1990). On the wider cultural debate, see April London, *Women and Property in the Eighteenth-Century English Novel* (Cambridge, 1999).

23. *The Hardships of the English Laws in Relation to Wives* (London, 1735) is very probably the work of Sarah Chapone, mother-in-law to the Bluestocking educational writer Hester Chapone and close friend of the Bluestocking Mary Delany. The anonymous *The Laws Respecting Women, as they Regard their*

Natural Rights or their Connections and Conduct (London, 1777) was printed by Joseph Johnson, Wollstonecraft's radical publisher. On male contributions to women's rights, see Arianne Chernouk's essay, 'Extending the "Right of Election": Men's Argument's for Women's Political Representation in Late Enlightenment Britain', in Taylor and Knott eds., *Women, Gender and Enlightenment*. This is to form part of a book, *Champions of the Fair Sex: Men and the Creation of Modern British Feminism.*

24. See Mary Thale, 'Women in London Debating Societies in 1780', *Gender and History*, 7 (1995), 5–24; Amanda Vickery, *The Gentleman's Daughter: Women's Lives in Georgian England* (New Haven, 1998); Robert B. Shoemaker, *Gender in English Society, 1650–1850: The Emergence of Separate Spheres?* (London, 1998), chs. 6 and 7; Clare Midgley, *Women Against Slavery: The British Campaigns, 1780–1870* (London, 1992). More generally, Merry E. Wiesner, *Women and Gender in Early Modern Europe* (Cambridge, 1993) and Olwen Hufton, *The Prospect Before Her: A History of Women in Western Europe, Volume I, 1500–1800* (London, 1995).

25. Shoemaker, *Gender in English Society*, 185. Women novelists were prominent, but did not dominate the market in the middle of the century; see James Raven, *British Fiction, 1750–70: A Chronological Checklist of Prose Fiction Printed in Britain and Ireland* (Delaware, 1988), 18. However, they gained a vastly greater market share over the next sixty years to the point where, between 1800 and 1820, they outnumbered men as authors of new novels: Peter Garside, James Raven and Rainer Schöwerling, *The English Novel, 1770–1829: A Bibliographical Survey of Prose Fiction Published in the British Isles* (2 vols.; Oxford, 2000), I, 45–9, II, 73–5.

26. Leonore Davidoff and Catherine Hall, *Family Fortunes: Men and Women of the English Middle Class, 1780–1850* (Chicago, 1987). Amanda Vickery, 'Golden Age to Separate Spheres: A Review of the Categories and Chronology of English Women's History', *Historical Journal*, 36 (1993), 383–414.

27. For example, Boyd Hilton, *A Mad, Bad and Dangerous People? England, 1783–1846* (Oxford, 2006), 363; Anne K. Mellor, *Mothers of the Nation: Women's Political Writing in England, 1780–1830* (Bloomington, Indiana, 2000); Eve Tavor Bannet, *The Domestic Revolution: Enlightenment Feminisms and the Novel* (Baltimore, 2000).

28. Bannet, *The Domestic Revolution*, 8.

29. Harriet Guest, *Small Change: Women, Learning, Patriotism, 1750–1810* (Chicago, 2000), 334. A more pessimistic argument, about the exclusionary effects of the association of the feminine and maternal in discourses of the national, is made by Angela Keane in her fine study, *Women Writers and the English Nation in the 1790s: Romantic Belongings* (Cambridge, 2005).

30. Guest, *Small Change*, 15.

31. *Ibid.*, 14.

32. See Guest's discussion of the domestic in Jane West's *The Mother* (1809) and Felicia Hemans's *The Domestic Affections* (1812), in *Small Change*, 320–4.

33. For example, Charlotte Smith's *The Old Manor House* (1793). See Jackie Labbe's introduction to her edition (Peterborough, Ontario, 2002), 26–8.
34. [Mary Astell], *Some Reflections upon Marriage* in *Political Writings*, ed. Patricia Springborg (Cambridge, 1996), 46.
35. *Ibid.*, 52.
36. Patricia Springborg, *Mary Astell: Theorist of Freedom from Domination* (Cambridge, 2005), 131, 202.
37. *The Ladies Defence* (1701) in *The Poems and Prose of Mary, Lady Chudleigh*, ed. Margaret J. M. Ezell (Oxford, 1993), lines 95–8. On Chudleigh, Egerton, Manley and other women writers of Queen Anne's reign, see Susan Staves, *A Literary History of Women's Writing in Britain, 1600–1789* (Cambridge, 2006), 122–65.
38. *Letters Of the Right Honourable Lady M-y W-y M-e: Written during her Travels in Europe, Asia and Africa* (3 vols.; London, 1763). This was an unauthorised, sometimes inaccurate edition of a copy of her letters, but is quoted here since this is what was available to eighteenth-century readers; I, 19–20, I, 63, II, 35, II, 113.
39. *Ibid.*, II, 33.
40. 'To the Countess of [Mar]', *ibid.*, II, 145–67.
41. Rachel Weil, *Political Passions: Gender, the Family and Political Argument in England, 1680–1714* (Manchester, 1999). Among those who see this language as primarily indicative of a feminist critique of early liberalism are Ruth Perry, 'Mary Astell and the Feminist Critique of Possessive Individualism', *Eighteenth-Century Studies*, 23 (1990), 444–58 and Catherine Gallagher, 'Embracing the Absolute: The Politics of the Female Subject in Seventeenth-Century England', *Genders*, 1 (1988), 24–39.
42. See especially Sarah Prescott, *Women, Authorship and Literary Culture, 1690–1740* (Basingstoke, 2003). Also Alice Wakeley, 'Mary Davys and the Politics of Epistolary Form' in *Cultures of Whiggism: New Essays on English Literature and Culture in the Long Eighteenth Century*, ed. David Womersley, Abigail Williams and Paddy Bullard (Delaware, 2005).
43. [Judith Drake], *An Essay in Defence of the Female Sex . . . In Letter to a Lady . . . Written by a Lady* (London, 1696), 142–3. The best account of Drake and her wider context is Hannah Smith, 'English "Feminist" Writings and Judith Drake's *An Essay in Defence of the Female Sex* (1696)', *The Historical Journal*, 44 (2001), 727–47. See also the seminal article by Lawrence E. Klein, 'Gender, Conversation and the Public Sphere in Early Eighteenth-Century England', in *Textuality and Sexuality: Reading Theories and Practices*, ed. Judith Still and Michael Worton (Manchester, 1993).
44. See Susan J. Owen, 'The Dramatic Language of Sexual Politics' in *Restoration Theatre and Crisis* (Oxford, 1996).
45. Constance Jordan, *Renaissance Feminism: Literary Texts and Political Models* (Ithaca, New York, 1990), 214–20 and the section on 'Depoliticizing Marriage', 286–97.

46. Lawrence Stone, *The Family, Sex and Marriage in England, 1500–1800* (New York and London, 1977). Stone's account has been vigorously contested by social historians: for a summary and useful contribution to this debate, see Naomi Tadmor, *Family and Friends in Eighteenth-Century England: Household, Kinship and Patronage* (Cambridge, 2001), 3–9.
47. See Jordan, *Renaissance Feminism*, ch. 2.
48. For example, Heinrich Cornelius Agrippa von Nettesheim, *De nobilitate et praecellentia foeminei sexus* (1509, translated into English, 1542); William Heale, *An Apologie for Women* (1609), Marie de Gournay, *L'Egalité des hommes et des femmes* (1622).
49. Anne-Thérèse de Marguenat-de-Courcelles, Marquise de Lambert, *Réflexions nouvelles sur les femmes* (Paris, 1727). This was translated into English in 1729. See Jonathan Israel's short section on 'Women, Philosophy and Sexuality' in *Radical Enlightenment*, 82–96.
50. See Hilda L. Smith, *Reason's Disciples: Seventeenth-Century English Feminists* (Urbana, Illinois, 1983) and Erica Harth, *Cartesian Women: Versions and Subversions of Rational Discourse in the Old Regime* (Ithaca, New York, 1992).
51. François Poulain de la Barre, *De L'Egalité des deux sexes, discours physique et moral où l'on voit l'importance de se défaire des préjugez* (1673) (repr. Paris, 1984), 72.
52. *Ibid.*, 54.
53. *Ibid.*, 78.
54. Siep Stuurman, *François Poulain de la Barre and the Invention of Modern Equality* (Cambridge, Massachusetts, 2004), 2.
55. Poulain, *De L'Egalité*, 22–6.
56. *Ibid.*, 30–2.
57. Stuurman, *François Poulain de la Barre*, 281. See, in general, pages 277–83 on editions and the reception of Poulain's work.
58. *Letters to Serena; containing, 1. The origin and force of prejudices . . . By Mr Toland* (London, 1704), xi.
59. *Woman Not Inferior to Man: or A short and modest Vindication of the natural Right of the Fair-Sex to a perfect Equality of Power, Dignity, and Esteem, with the Men. By Sophia, A Person of Quality* (London, 1739), 18. After a second edition in 1740, this work was reprinted in 1743 and again in 1751 as the first part of a volume entitled *Beauty's Triumph: or, The Superiority of the Fair Sex Invincibly Proved* – the editor's stated purpose here was to present Sophia's work alongside the refutation in order to warn his readers of the danger of protesting women. On Sophia's debt to Poulain, see C. A. Moore, 'The First of the Militants in English Literature', *The Nation*, 102 (17 February 1916), 194–6.
60. *Woman Not Inferior to Man*, 2, 27.
61. *Ibid.*, 47. Elizabeth Carter herself seems to have been a little concerned about this, and tried to find out who Sophia was. See Clery, *The Feminization Debate*, 139. Carter's name (as 'Mrs Carte', the translator of Epictetus) is also interpolated into the 1758 translation of *De L'Egalité, Female Rights*

Vindicated; or the Equality of the Sexes Morally and Physcially Proved. By a Lady (London, 1758), 37.

62. Lady Mary Wortley Montagu, *The Nonsense of Common-Sense*, vi (24 January 1738), ed. Robert Halsband (Evanston, Illinois, 1947), 25.

63. Sophia herself gives several apparent clues to her identity, especially in her second work *Woman's Superior Excellence over Man: or, A Reply to the Author of a Late Treatise* (London, 1740): that she is a person 'of Quality', that she enjoys some kind of financial independence ('Thanks to propitious providence the light of life it has placed me in has raised me above the reaches of knaves, and blest me with the liberty of shunning fools', *Woman's Superior Excellence*, 101), and that she used to reside under the wing of her guardian 'Honorio', a good, pious nobleman ('the first of his illustrious family rewarded with a coronet', *ibid.*, 103), politically active ('an excess of loyalty to the prince he loves makes him backward to oppose the measures of a minister he disapproves', *ibid.*, 104) and quite possibly a Catholic (the 'prejudices for the sect he was educated in makes him labour rather to convince himself that the faith he professes is right, than to examine impartially whether it really is so or not', *ibid.*, 104–5).

One possible identification was suggested briefly by 'Medley' in *Notes and Queries*, Series 8, 11 (1 May 1897), 348: that she was Sophia Fermor (1721–45), who made a brilliant marriage to the politician John Carteret, Earl of Granville, and died soon after. She was the daughter of Thomas Fermor (created Earl of Pomfret in 1721) and the remarkable Henrietta Louisa Fermor, Countess of Pomfret, a celebrated letter writer, amateur art historian and friend of Lady Mary Wortley Montagu. The Pomfret family were on the continent from 1738 to 1741, during which time Montagu came to stay with them in Florence: this is recorded in the *Correspondence between Frances, Countess of Hartford . . . and Henrietta Louisa, Countess of Pomfret*, ed. W. M. Bingley (3 vols.; London, 1805).

64. *Woman's Superior Excellence over Man*, 5.

65. *Ibid.*, 21, 59, 28.

66. *Ibid.*, 42.

67. *Ibid.*, 10.

68. John Locke, *Some Thoughts Concerning Education*, ed. John and Jean S. Yolton (Oxford, 1989), 106.

69. *Ibid.*, 210.

70. See the introduction and conduct book extracts in Vivien Jones, ed., *Women in the Eighteenth Century: Constructions of Femininity* (London and New York, 1990), section 1. More generally, Nancy Armstrong and Lennard Tennenhouse, eds., *The Ideology of Conduct: Essays on Literature and the History of Sexuality* (London and New York, 1987).

71. René Pintard, *Le libertinage érudit dans la première moitié du XVIIe siècle* (2 vols.; Paris, 1943).

72. See Michèle Fogel, *Marie de Gournay: itinéraire d'une femme savante* (Paris, 2004).

73. David Wootton, 'Pierre Bayle, Libertine' in *Studies in Eighteenth-Century European Philosophy*, ed. M. A. Stewart (Oxford, 1997).

74. Léo Pierre Courtines, *Bayle's Relations with England and the English* (New York, 1938).

75. On his politics, see M. M. Goldsmith, *Private Vices, Public Benefits: Bernard Mandeville's Social and Political Thought* (Cambridge, 1985), ch. 4.

76. Bernard Mandeville, *The Fable of the Bees: or, Private Vices, Publick Benefits. The Second Edition, Enlarged with many Additions* (London, 1723), 67. The work started life as a poem, *The Grumbling Hive: or, Knaves Turn'd Honest* ([London], 1705), which then appeared with annotations and an essay as *The Fable of the Bees: or, Private Vices, Publick Benefits* (London, 1714). The 1723 text is a greatly expanded version of the 1714 version, and was the first to attract wide public notice. The gender dimension of Mandeville's work is rarely discussed by modern commentators, but see M. M. Goldsmith, '"The Treacherous Arts of Mankind": Bernard Mandeville and Female Virtue', *History of Political Thought*, 3 (1986), 93–114 (mainly on Mandeville's contributions to the *Female Tatler*), and E. G. Hundert, *The Enlightenment's Fable: Bernard Mandeville and the Discovery of Society* (Cambridge, 1994), 205–18.

77. Mandeville, *The Fable of the Bees* (1723), 67–8.

78. [Defoe], *The Fortunes and Misfortunes of the Famous Moll Flanders* (London, 1721 [1722]), 211–13.

79. On Mandeville's debt to Bayle, see Robertson, *The Case for the Enlightenment*, 261–70.

80. Mandeville, *The Grumbling Hive*, 4.

81. [Mandeville], *The Virgin Unmask'd: or, Female Dialogues betwixt an elderly maiden lady, and her niece* (London, 1709), 128.

82. *Ibid.*, 127.

83. Mandeville, *The Fable of the Bees* (1714), 21.

84. *Ibid.*, 65.

85. *Ibid.*, 25.

86. *Ibid.*, 36–7.

87. On women and 'luxury' in eighteenth-century Britain, see Christopher J. Berry, *The Idea of Luxury: A Conceptual and Historical Investigation* (Cambridge, 1994), chs. 5–6 and Maxine Berg and Elizabeth Eger eds., *Luxury in the Eighteenth Century: Debates, Desires and Delectable Goods* (Basingstoke, 2002), part 4: 'A Female Vice?: Women and Luxury'.

88. Mandeville, *The Fable of the Bees* (1723), 55.

89. *Ibid.*, 62.

90. *Ibid.*, 65.

91. *Ibid.*, 151–2.

92. The authoritative account of these writers is Ros Ballaster, *Seductive Forms: Women's Amatory Fiction from 1684–1740* (Oxford, 1992).

93. Delarivier Manley, *The Secret History, or Queen Zarah, and the Zarazians* (Albigion [London], 1705), 33.

94. See Peter Cryle and Lisa O'Connell eds., *Libertine Enlightenment: Sex, Liberty and Licence in the Eighteenth Century* (Basingstoke, 2004).

95. See the discussion of Enlightened libertinage in Barbara Taylor, *Mary Wollstonecraft and the Feminist Imagination* (Cambridge, 2003), 200 ('For elite progressives like Georgiana and Fox, sexuality was not a field of conviction politics' as it would later be for Godwinian radicals and nineteenth-century utopian socialists).

96. Bernard Mandeville, *A Modest Defence of Publick Stews: or, An Essay upon Whoring . . . Written by a Layman* (London, 1724), ed. Richard I. Cook (Los Angeles, 1973), 14, 27. Mandeville's authorship of this work is not absolutely certain, although there are very strong stylistic and philosophical similarities with *The Fable of the Bees*.

97. *Ibid.*, 42.

98. See chapter 2 below, pages 25, 80.

99. On Hume and Mandeville, see Robertson, *The Case for the Enlightenment*, 290–302.

100. Bernard Mandeville, *An Enquiry into the Origin of Honour, and the Usefulness of Christianity in War. By the Author of the Fable of the Bees* (London, 1732), 15. On conjectural history in Mandeville, see Hundert, *The Enlightenment's Fable*, ch. 2.

101. William Law, *Remarks upon a Late Book, Entitled, The Fable of the Bees, or Private Vices, Publick Benefits. In a Letter to the Author. To which is added a Postscript, containing an Observation or two upon Mr. Bayle* (1724) reprinted in J. Martin Stafford ed., *Private Vices, Publick Benefits? The Contemporary Reception of Bernard Mandeville* (Solihull, 1997), 69.

CHAPTER I   ANGLICAN WHIG FEMINISM IN ENGLAND, 1690–1760: SELF-LOVE, REASON AND SOCIAL BENEVOLENCE

1. See, in general, Brian Young, *Religion and Enlightenment in Eighteenth-Century England: Theological Debate from Locke to Burke* (Oxford, 1998) and Isabel Rivers, *Reason, Grace and Sentiment: A Study of the Language of Religion and Ethics in England, 1660–1780* (2 vols.; Cambridge, 1991, 2000).

2. See, in general, Knud Haakonssen ed., *Enlightenment and Religion: Rational Dissent in Eighteenth-Century Britain* (Cambridge, 1996) and Kathryn Gleadle, *The Early Feminists: Radical Unitarians and the Emergence of the Women's Rights Movement, c.1831–51* (Basingstoke, 1995).

3. Ruth Perry, *The Celebrated Mary Astell: An Early English Feminist* (Chicago, 1986), 97.

4. Derek Taylor, 'Clarissa Harlowe, Mary Astell, and Elizabeth Carter: John Norris of Bemerton's Female "Descendants"', *Eighteenth-Century Fiction*, 12 (1999), 19–38.

5. See Dominic Scott, 'Reason, Recollection and the Cambridge Platonists' in *Platonism and the English Imagination*, ed. Anna Baldwin and Sarah Hutton (Cambridge, 1994).

6. Elizabeth Carter, 'Rambler XIV' in *Bluestocking Feminism: Writings of the Bluestocking Circle, 1738–1785*, ed. Gary Kelly *et al.* (6 vols.; London, 1999), vol. II, ed. Judith Hawley, 414.

7. Claudia N. Thomas, *Alexander Pope and his Eighteenth-Century Women Readers* (Carbondale and Edwardsville, Illinois, 1994), 83–101.

8. For example, Catharine Cockburn, *Remarks upon some Writers in the Controversy concerning the Foundation of Moral Virtue and Moral Obligation* (1743) in *The Works of Mrs. Catharine Cockburn* (2 vols.; London, 1751), I, 427–8.

9. *Ibid.*, I, 413.

10. *The Twickenham Edition of the Works of Alexander Pope*, ed. John Butt *et al.* (II vols.; London and New Haven, 1939–69), III-i, *An Essay on Man*, Epistle IV, lines 353–4.

11. John Norris, *Cursory Reflections Upon a Book Call'd, 'An Essay Concerning Human Understanding'* (1690), ed. Gilbert D. McEwen (Los Angeles, 1961), 29.

12. Patricia Springborg, *Mary Astell: Theorist of Freedom from Domination* (Cambridge, 2005), 58–68, and, on the question of authorship and as to whether Masham really was replying to Norris and Astell, 69, 71, 92. Also valuable is William Kolbrener, 'Gendering the Modern: Mary Astell's Feminist Historiography', *The Eighteenth Century: Theory and Interpretation*, 44 (2004), 1–24. See also the introduction to the recent edition: Mary Astell and John Norris, *Letters Concerning the Love of God*, ed. E. Derek Taylor and Melvyn New (Aldershot, 2005).

13. Damaris Cudworth Masham, *A Discourse Concerning the Love of God and Occasional Thoughts in Reference to a Vertuous or Christian Life*, ed. James G. Buickerood (Bristol, 2004), *A Discourse*, 121. See, also, the important article by Sarah Hutton, 'Damaris Cudworth, Lady Masham: Between Platonism and Enlightenment', *The British Journal for the History of Philosophy*, 1 (1993), 29–54. Also Springborg, *Mary Astell*, 67–80 and Ruth Perry, 'Damaris Cudworth Masham, Catharine Trotter Cockburn, and the Feminist Legacy of Locke's Theory of Personal Identity', *Eighteenth-Century Studies*, 35 (2002), 563–76.

14. Masham, *A Discourse Concerning the Love of God*, 68.

15. Mary Astell, *A Serious Proposal to the Ladies, Part II: Wherein a Method is offer'd for the Improvement of their Minds* (London, 1697), 41, 188. On Astell's possible reading of Poulain's *De L'Egalité*, see Springborg, *Mary Astell*, 96.

16. Astell, *A Serious Proposal, Part II*, 266.

17. She engages with *The Reasonableness of Christianity* in detail in *The Christian Religion, As Profess'd by a Daughter of the Church of England* (London, 1705), 65–83. On other contemporary responses to Locke's work, see Victor Nuovo ed., *John Locke and Christianity* (Bristol, 1997).

18. Astell, *The Christian Religion*, 10.

19. *Ibid.*, 96.

20. *Ibid.*, 245.

21. *Ibid.*, 296.
22. *Ibid.*, 278.
23. *Ibid.*, 220. The full discussion occurs at 307–32.
24. *Ibid.*, 322.
25. Masham, *Occasional Thoughts*, 45.
26. *Ibid.*, 227–8.
27. *Ibid.*, 21.
28. *Ibid.*, 84.
29. *Ibid.*, 87, 109.
30. Astell, *The Christian Religion*, 331–2.
31. Masham, *Occasional Thoughts*, 179.
32. In general see Stephen Darwall, *The British Moralists and the Internal 'Ought': 1640–1740* (Cambridge, 1995).
33. John Locke, *Political Essays*, ed. Mark Goldie (Cambridge, 1997), xx and III.
34. John Locke, *An Essay Concerning Human Understanding*, ed. Peter N. Nidditch (Oxford, 1975).
35. *Ibid.*, 357.
36. *Ibid.*, 353.
37. *Ibid.*, 357.
38. John Locke, 'The Epistle to the Reader', *An Essay Concerning Human Understanding ... The Fourth Edition, with large Additions* (London, 1700), sig. C1, recto.
39. Masham, *Occasional Thoughts*, 202.
40. *Ibid.*, 229.
41. Anthony Ashley Cooper, Earl of Shaftesbury, 'An Inquiry Concerning Virtue, or Merit', *Characteristicks of Men, Manners, Opinions, Times ... The Second Edition Corrected* (3 vols.; London, 1714), II, 64.
42. *Ibid.* I am indebted, for this discussion, to Daniel Carey's chapter 'Contesting Diversity: Shaftesbury's Reply to Locke' in his *Locke, Shaftesbury, and Hutcheson: Contesting Diversity in the Enlightenment and Beyond* (Cambridge, 2006). See also Lawrence E. Klein, *Shaftesbury and the Culture of Politeness: Moral Discourse and Cultural Politics in Early Eighteenth-Century England* (Cambridge, 1994).
43. Shaftesbury, 'An Inquiry Concerning Virtue, or Merit', *Characteristicks*, II, 60.
44. Shaftesbury, 'The Moralists, A Philosophical Rhapsody', *Characteristicks*, II, 186. On Shaftesbury and effeminacy, see also G. J. Barker-Benfield, *The Culture of Sensibility: Sex and Society in Eighteenth-Century Britain* (Chicago, 1992), 105–19.
45. See Rivers, *Reason, Grace and Sentiment*, II, ch. 2 and pages 154–5.
46. Shaftesbury, *Characteristicks*, II, 87, 175, 103, 107.
47. *Ibid.*, II, 87.
48. *Ibid.*, II, 171.
49. *Ibid.*, II, 92.
50. *Ibid.*, II, 175.

51. *The Twickenham Edition of the Works of Alexander Pope*, iii-i, Epistle iv, lines 353–6.

52. On Pope and patriarchal, contract and other theories of government, see Howard Erskine-Hill, 'Pope on the Origins of Society' in *The Enduring Legacy: Alexander Pope, Tercentary Essays*, ed. G. S. Rousseau and Pat Rogers (Cambridge, 1988), particularly 85–90. Also Brean S. Hammond, *Pope and Bolingbroke: A Study of Friendship and Influence* (Columbia, Missouri, 1984), 89.

53. On the popularity of this work with women readers, see Thomas, *Alexander Pope*, 83–101.

54. On Cockburn, see the pioneering biography by Anne Kelley, *Catharine Trotter: An Early Modern Writer in the Vanguard of Feminism* (Aldershot, 2002). The best account of her philosophical work is Martha Brandt Bolton, 'Some Aspects of the Philosophy of Catharine Trotter', *Journal for the History of Philosophy*, 31 (1993), 565–88.

55. Cockburn, *Works*, i, 58.

56. *Ibid.*

57. See Kelley, *Catharine Trotter*, 157.

58. *Ibid.*, 166. See Catharine Cockburn, *A Letter to Dr. Holdsworth, occasioned by his sermon preached before the University of Oxford* (London, 1726).

59. Burnet wrote the preface to Cockburn's *A Discourse concerning a Guide in Controversies in Two Letters written to One of the Church of Rome* (London, 1707), the work in which she set out her objections to Roman Catholic doctrine.

60. Astell, *A Serious Proposal, Part II*, 285–6. As Patricia Springborg notes, in arguing in his *Enquiry into the Measures of Submission to the Supream Authority* (1689) that all men are born free, Burnet did not extend that freedom to women. See Mary Astell, *Political Writings*, ed. Springborg (Cambridge, 1996), 4.

61. Gilbert Burnet, *Bishop Burnet's History of His Own Time* (2 vols.; London, 1724, 1734), ii, 653. Burnet was not the only male Anglican to promote educational establishments for women. See Bridget Hill, 'A Refuge from Men: The Idea of a Protestant Nunnery', *Past and Present*, 117 (1987), 107–30.

62. *Ibid.*, ii, 652.

63. T. E. S. Clarke and H. C. Foxcroft, *A Life of Gilbert Burnet, Bishop of Salisbury* (Cambridge, 1907), 439, 548.

64. Elizabeth Burnet, *A Method of Devotion: or, Rules for Holy and Devout Living* (second edn; London, 1709), xxi. The first edition was printed in 1708.

65. *Ibid.*, xv.

66. *Ibid.*, xxvi.

67. *Ibid.*, 25–6.

68. Kelley, *Catharine Trotter*, 15.

69. *Ibid.*, 177–81. Cockburn, *Works*, ii, 386. On the divergent nature and influence of Locke and Clarke, see Young, *Religion and Enlightenment*, ch. 3. For

an account of Clark's place within eighteenth-century moral philosophy and theology, see Rivers, *Reason, Grace and Sentiment*, II, 15–16 and 79–81.

70. Cockburn, *Works*, I, 382.
71. Kelley, *Catharine Trotter*, 187.
72. Cockburn, *Works*, II, 48.
73. Cockburn, 'On Moral Virtue, and its natural tendency to happiness', *Works*, II, 129.
74. Cockburn, *Remarks upon the Principles and Reasonings of Dr. Rutherforth's Essay*, *Works*, II, 33.
75. Cockburn, *Remarks . . . concerning the Foundation of Moral Virtue*, *Works*, I, 427–8.
76. *Ibid.*, I, 413.
77. *Ibid.*
78. See, for example, her letters to her niece about Shaftesbury in *Works*, II, 318 and 329–32.
79. *Ibid.*, I, 412.
80. Letter to her niece (*c.*1734–5), *Works*, II, 280.
81. Kelley, *Catharine Trotter*, 26–2. Catharine Talbot introduced Elizabeth Carter to the works of Cockburn in 1751: see *A Series of Letters between Mrs. Elizabeth Carter and Miss Catharine Talbot, From the Year 1741 to 1770*, ed. Montagu Pennington (2 vols.; London, 1809), II, 49.
82. *The Letters of Mrs. Elizabeth Montagu*, ed. Matthew Montagu (4 vols.; London, 1809–13), III, 222. Also see I, 193, I, 301, II, 112–13.
83. See her comments in her letters to her niece in *Works*, II, 295–6 and 329–32.
84. For example, Norma Clarke, 'Bluestocking Fictions: Devotional Writings, Didactic Literature and the Imperative of Female Improvement' in *Women, Gender and Enlightenment*, ed. Barbara Taylor and Sarah Knott (Basingstoke, 2005), 463; Elizabeth Eger, 'Luxury, Industry and Charity: Bluestocking Culture Displayed' in *Luxury in the Eighteenth Century: Debates, Desires and Delectable Goods*, ed. Maxine Berg and Elizabeth Eger (Basingstoke, 2003); Susan Staves, 'Church of England Clergy and Women Writers' in *Reconsidering the Bluestockings*, ed. Nicole Pohl and Betty A. Schellenberg, *Huntington Library Quarterly*, 65 (2002), 81–103.
85. Montagu Pennington, *Memoirs of the Life of Mrs. Elizabeth Carter* (London, 1807), 86–7.
86. *Ibid.*, 621. On Butler, see especially Rivers, *Reason, Grace and Sentiment*, II, 215–26.
87. Pennington, *Memoirs of . . . Mrs. Elizabeth Carter*, 614.
88. *Ibid.*, 617.
89. *The Letters of Mrs. Elizabeth Montagu*, II, 131, II, 129.
90. *Ibid.*, II, 124.
91. *Letters from Mrs. Elizabeth Carter, to Mrs. Montagu, Between the Years 1755 and 1800*, ed. Montagu Pennington (3 vols.; London, 1817), II, 163.
92. Elizabeth Carter, 'Rambler XIV' in Kelly ed., *Bluestocking Feminism*, II, 411–12.

93. *Ibid.*, II, 414.
94. *Ibid.*, II, 412.
95. Shaftesbury, 'The Moralists: A Philosophical Rhapsody', *Characteristicks*, II, 184.
96. Carter, 'Rambler XIV' in Kelly ed., *Bluestocking Feminism*, II, 414.
97. *An Essay on Man*, epistle ii, ll. 101–02.
98. Elizabeth Carter, *An Examination of Mr. Pope's Essay on Man, Translated from the French of M. Crousaz* (London, 1739). See, for example, page 78.
99. Pennington, *Memoirs of . . . Mrs. Elizabeth Carter*, 119.
100. Kelly ed., *Bluestocking Feminism*, II, 277.
101. *Ibid.*, II, 293.
102. See Rivers, *Reason, Grace and Sentiment*, II, 94.
103. Pennington, *Memoirs of . . . Mrs. Elizabeth Carter*, 132.
104. Kelly ed., *Bluestocking Feminism*, II, 22.
105. *Ibid.*, II, 27.
106. *Ibid.*, II, 28. For a contemporary portrait of a Stoic as a man of both high principles and sensibility, see David Hume's essay 'The Stoic' (1742) in *Essays, Moral and Political and Literary*, ed. Eugene F. Miller (Indianapolis, 1985).
107. Claudia Thomas, '"Th'Instructive Moral, and Important Thought": Elizabeth Carter reads Pope, Johnson and Epictetus', *The Age of Johnson*, 4 (1991), 137–69. The quotation is on page 166.
108. Kelly ed., *Bluestocking Feminism*, II, 21.
109. On the ways in which Carter inhabited and developed the public persona of the learned lady, and on the role played in this by her religious faith, see Harriet Guest, *Small Change: Women, Learning, Patriotism, 1750–1810* (Chicago, 2000), chs. 5 and 6.
110. Pennington, *Memoirs of . . . Mrs. Elizabeth Carter*, 111–37.
111. *The Autobiography of Thomas Secker, Archbishop of Canterbury*, ed. John S. Macauley and R. W. Greeves (Kansas, 1988), 36. The autobiography was not intended for publication, only for consultation by succeeding archbishops. It was, however, written towards the end of Secker's life, and is somewhat caustic and inaccurate in its recollections of events and people.
112. Pennington, *Memoirs of . . . Mrs. Elizabeth Carter*, 118.
113. On Secker's ministry, see Jeremy Gregory, *Restoration, Reformation and Reform, 1660–1828: Archbishops of Canterbury and their Dioceses* (Oxford, 2000).
114. *Remarks on the Athanasian Creed; on a Sermon Preached at the Parish Church of Deal, October 15, 1752* (London, n.d., probably 1753), 22, 48. For the attribution of this work to Carter, see Judith Hawley's introduction to Kelly ed., *Bluestocking Feminism*, II, ix. See also Carter's remark about the unintelligible mystery of the Trinity in 'Objections against the *New Testament*, with Mrs. Carter's Answers to them' printed in Pennington's *Memoirs of . . . Mrs. Elizabeth Carter*, 593.
115. Catharine Talbot, *Essay XXII* in Kelly ed., *Bluestocking Feminism*, III, 103.

116. Talbot, 'Friday', *Reflections* in Kelly ed., *Bluestocking Feminism*, III, 64.
117. 'Self-love' in *The Works of the Late Miss Catharine Talbot*, ed. Montagu Pennington (seventh edn; London, 1809), 144.
118. Clarke, 'Bluestocking Fictions', 463.
119. Talbot to Carter (n.d., *c.*1745) in *A Series of Letters*, I, 118.
120. *The Works of Mary Wollstonecraft*, ed. Janet Todd and Marilyn Butler (7 vols.; London, 1989), I, 29.
121. Mary Hays, *Female Biography; or, Memoirs of Illustrious and Celebrated Women, of all Ages and Countries* (6 vols.; London, 1803).
122. Barbara Taylor, *Mary Wollstonecraft and the Feminist Imagination* (Cambridge, 2003), 106–10.
123. John Robertson, 'Women and Enlightenment: A Historiographical Conclusion' in Taylor and Knott eds., *Women, Gender and Enlightenment*, 700–1.

CHAPTER 2   FROM SAVAGE TO SCOTSWOMAN: THE HISTORY
OF FEMININITY

1. The best overview of the Scottish analysis of women is in Jane Rendall's *The Origins of Modern Feminism: Women in Britain, France and the United States, 1780–1860* (London, 1985), ch. 1.
2. Knud Haakonssen, *Natural Law and Moral Philosophy: From Grotius to the Scottish Enlightenment* (Cambridge, 1996), 7. See also Duncan Forbes, 'Natural Law and the Scottish Enlightenment' in *The Origins and Nature of the Scottish Enlightenment*, ed. R. H. Campbell and Andrew S. Skinner (Edinburgh, 1982).
3. Most famously, David Hume, 'Of the Original Contract' (1748) in *Essays, Moral, Political and Literary*, ed. Eugene F. Miller (Indianapolis, 1985).
4. See Kathryn Gleadle, *The Early Feminists: Radical Unitarians and the Emergence of the Women's Rights Movement, 1831–51* (Basingstoke, 1995), 64–8. On Engels, see Sylvana Tomaselli, 'Civilization, Patriotism and Enlightened Histories of Women' in *Women, Gender and Enlightenment*, ed. Barbara Taylor and Sarah Knott (Basingstoke, 2005), 129–32.
5. Richard B. Sher, *Church and University in the Scottish Enlightenment: The Moderate Literati of Edinburgh* (Edinburgh, 1985) and C. G. Brown, *Religion and Society in Scotland since 1707* (Edinburgh, 1997).
6. See Isabel Rivers, *Reason, Grace and Sentiment: A Study of the Language of Religion and Ethics in England, 1660–1780* (2 vols.; Cambridge, 1991, 2000), II, 157.
7. Francis Hutcheson, *An Inquiry into the Original of our Ideas of Beauty and Virtue; in two Treatises* (London, 1725), 134. Hutcheson is discussed by Daniela Gobetti in *Private and Public: Individuals, Households, and Body Politic in Locke and Hutcheson* (London, 1992) and by Jane Rendall, 'Virtue and Commerce: Women in the Making of Adam Smith's Political Economy'

in *Women in Western Political Philosophy*, ed. Susan Mendus and Ellen Kennedy (Brighton, 1987), 51–6. On Mandeville in Scotland, M. M. Goldsmith, 'Regulating Anew the Moral and Political Sentiments of Mankind: Bernard Mandeville and the Scottish Enlightenment', *Journal of the History of Ideas*, 49 (1988), 587–606.

8. Hutcheson, *An Inquiry*, 202.

9. Francis Hutcheson, *An Essay on the Nature and Conduct of the Passions and Affections* (London, 1728), 169–71.

10. Francis Hutcheson, *A Short Introduction to Moral Philosophy* (Glasgow, 1747), 255, 261.

11. *Ibid.*, 261.

12. *Ibid.*, 257, 256. The origins of society, however, lie in practical necessity rather than in child-rearing. See *A System of Moral Philosophy, in Three Books* (2 vols.; London, 1755), I, 288.

13. *A System*, I, 84; II, 153.

14. *Ibid.*, II, 153, 163.

15. *Ibid.*, II, 164–5.

16. See Rosemarie Zagarri, 'Morals, Manners, and the Republican Mother', *American Quarterly*, 44 (1992), 192–215.

17. See Rivers, *Reason, Grace and Sentiment*, II, 243. The best introduction to Kames is Ian Simpson Ross, *Lord Kames and the Scotland of his Day* (Oxford, 1972).

18. Henry Home Kames, *Sketches of the History of Man* (second edn, 1778), ed. John Valdimir Price (4 vols.; Bristol, 1993), II, 1–2 (first edn, I, 168). Quotations are taken from this revised edition, but a second set of page references are also given to the first edition (2 vols.; Edinburgh, 1774).

19. *Ibid.*, II, 22, 25 (first edn, I, 179, 181).

20. *Ibid.*, II, 41 (first edn, I, 190).

21. Some of the extensive Kames/Montagu correspondence is reprinted in A. F. Tytler, Lord Woodhouselee, *Memoirs of the Life and Writings of the Honourable Henry Home of Kames* (2 vols.; Edinburgh, 1807). The quotations are from *Memoirs*, II, 48, 51. See also Ian Ross, 'A Blue Stocking over the Border: Mrs. Elizabeth Montagu's Aesthetic Adventures in Scotland, 1766', *Huntington Library Quarterly*, 28 (1964–5), 213–33.

22. Mary Catherine Moran, 'Between the Savage and the Civil: Dr John Gregory's Natural History of Femininity' in Taylor and Kuott eds., *Women, Gender and Enlightenment*, 8–29 and my comments on this essay in *ibid.*, 5–6.

23. Quoted by Elizabeth Eger in her 'Luxury, Industry and Charity: Bluestocking Culture Displayed' in *Luxury in the Eighteenth Century: Debates, Desires and Delectable Goods*, ed. Maxine Berg and Elizabeth Eger (Basingstoke, 2003), 202.

24. See Tytler, *Memoirs*, II, 93–6.

25. Montagu to Kames (23 August n.d., probably 1777) in Tytler, *Memoirs*, II, 198.

26. Beattie to Montagu (3 May 1774) in Sir William Forbes, *An Account of the Life and Writings of James Beattie* (second edn, 3 vols.; Edinburgh, 1807), II, 68.
27. Reginald Blunt ed., *Mrs. Montagu: 'Queen of the Blues': Her Letters and Friendships from 1762 to 1800* (2 vols.; London, 1923), I, 268. See also *James Beattie's London Diary, 1773*, ed. Ralph S. Walker, *Aberdeen University Studies*, 122 (1946).
28. Blunt ed., *Mrs Montagu*, I, 233–4.
29. Beattie to Forbes (10 December 1787) in Forbes, *An Account of Beattie*, III, 33–4.
30. James Beattie, *Elements of Moral Science* (2 vols.; Edinburgh, 1790, 1793), II, 137.
31. Thomas Reid, *Essays on the Active Powers of the Human Mind* (London, 1788), 151.
32. See Jane Rendall, '"Women that would plague me with rational conversation": Aspiring Women and Scottish Whigs, c. 1790–1830' in Taylor and Knott eds., *Women, Gender and Enlightenment*, 334–5.
33. David Hume, *A Treatise of Human Nature* (1739–40), ed. Ernest C. Mossner (Harmondsworth, 1984), III, 2, ii.
34. For opposing views of Hume on chastity, see Annette Baier, 'Good Men's Women: Hume on Chastity and Trust', *Hume Studies*, 5 (1979), 1–19 and Christine Battersby, 'An Enquiry Concerning the Humean Woman', *Philosophy*, 56 (1981), 303–12. See also Steven A. Macleod Burns, 'The Humean Female', in *The Sexism of Social and Political Theory*, ed. Lynda Large and Lorenne M. G. Clark (Toronto, 1979), Genevieve Lloyd, *The Man of Reason: 'Male' and 'Female' in Western Philosophy* (Minneapolis, 1984), ch. 3, Baier, 'Hume on a Woman's Complexion' in *The Science of Man in the Scottish Enlightenment*, ed. Peter Jones (Edinburgh, 1989), Nancy Tuana, *Woman and the History of Philosophy* (New York, 1992), 70–82.
35. Hume, *A Treatise of Human Nature*, III, ii, 12, 621.
36. *Ibid.*, 622–3. Smith, in his *Lectures on Jurisprudence*, also argues that the injury of a wife's infidelity is more serious than that of her husband. See Adam Smith, *Lectures on Jurisprudence*, ed. R. L. Meek, D. D. Raphael and P. G. Stein (Oxford, 1978), report of 1762–3, 166.
37. Peter King ed., *The Life of John Locke* (2 vols.; London, 1830), II, 96.
38. David Hume, *Enquiry concerning the Principles of Morals* (1751) in *Enquiries concerning Human Understanding and concerning the Principles of Morals*, ed. L. A. Selby-Bigge, third edn revised by P. H. Nidditch (Oxford, 1975), 191.
39. Hume, 'Of the Rise and Progress of the Arts and Sciences' (1742) in *Essays, Moral, Political and Literary*, 133. See also Hume's essay 'Of Love and Marriage' in *ibid.* (1741, later withdrawn), *Essays*, 556–8.
40. Adam Smith, *The Theory of Moral Sentiments*, ed. D. D. Raphael and A. L. Macfie (Oxford, 1976), 137. The copy text for this edition is the 1790 version.

41. *Ibid.*, 190, 191.
42. See Rendall, 'Virtue and Commerce', 60–2.
43. See F. J. H. Fletcher, '*L'Esprit des lois* before early British Opinion', *Revue de littérature comparée*, 14 (1934), 527–41 and Charles Dédéyan, *Montesquieu ou les lumières d'Albion* (Paris, 1990). Charles de Secondat, baron de Montesquieu, *The Spirit of Laws*, trans. Thomas Nugent (2 vols.; London, 1750). This includes the 'Corrections and Additions communicated by the Author' which were later incorporated into the 1751 French edition. Citations, by book, chapter number and page numbers are drawn from this edition. This translation is also available in an edition by F. Neumann (New York, 1949).
44. See Mona Ozouf, *Les mots des femmes* (Paris, 1995). Montesquieu is not discussed in Lieselotte Steinbrügge's *The Moral Sex: Woman's Nature and the French Enlightenment*, trans. Pamela E. Selwyn (Oxford, 1995) nor in the classic study by Susan Moller Okin, *Women in Western Political Thought* (revised edn, Princeton, 1992). However, Léon Abensour, *La femme et le féminisme avant la Révolution* (Paris, 1923) and Paul Hoffmann, *La Femme dans la pensée des lumières* (Paris, 1977) both discuss Montesquieu. There is a specific study of Montesquieu's allegedly hostile views on women: Jeanette Geffriaud Rosso, *Montesquieu et la féminité* (Pisa, 1977). Pauline Kra, 'Montesquieu and Women' in *French Women and the Age of Enlightenment*, ed. Samia I. Spencer (Bloomington, Indiana, 1984), gives a brief summary of the subject.
45. On the vexed question of Montesquieu and natural law, see Mark H. Waddicor, *Montesquieu and the Philosophy of Natural Law* (The Hague, 1970), and Simone Goyard Fabre, *Montesquieu: la nature, les lois, la liberté* (Paris, 1993).
46. This appeared in England as *Persian Letters*, trans. Mr Ozell (2 vols.; London, 1722), and was reissued in 1730, 1731 and 1760.
47. Montesquieu, *The Spirit*, xiv, ix, 365. However, see also Book xvi, 'How the Laws of domestic Slavery have a Relation to the Nature of the Climate', in which he argues that, in hot climates, women reach puberty at an earlier age and are therefore naturally more likely to find themselves in unequal marriages to older men.
48. The best known study of Montesquieu as a liberal is Thomas L. Pangle, *Montesquieu's Philosophy of Liberalism: A Commentary on the Spirit of the Laws* (Chicago, 1973).
49. Montesquieu, *The Spirit*, xxvi, viii, 198.
50. *Ibid.*, vii, ix, 149. See also vii, iii, and v, vii.
51. *Ibid.*, vii, ix, 148 and vii, iv.
52. *Ibid.*, vii, iv, 143.
53. *Ibid.*, xix, xv, 428.
54. *Ibid.*, xix, xiv.
55. *Ibid.*, xix, xvi, 428.
56. *Ibid.*, xix, xii, 425.

57. On this culture, see Dena Goodman, *The Republic of Letters: A Cultural History of the French Enlightenment* (Ithaca and London, 1994).
58. See Sher, *Church and University*, Nicholas T. Phillipson, 'Culture and Society in the Eighteenth-Century Province: The Case of Edinburgh and the Scottish Enlightenment' in *The University in Society*, ed. Lawrence Stone (2 vols.; Princeton, 1974) and John Dwyer, *Virtuous Discourse: Sensibility and Community in Late Eighteenth-Century Scotland* (Edinburgh, 1987).
59. The term 'conjectural history' was first coined by Dugald Stewart in *Biographical Memoirs of Adam Smith, L.L.D., of William Robertson, D.D. and of Thomas Reid, D.D.* (Edinburgh, 1811), 48–9. The pioneering account is Ronald L. Meek, *Social Science and the Ignoble Savage* (Cambridge, 1976). See also Christopher J. Berry, *Social Theory of the Scottish Enlightenment* (Edinburgh, 1997), including 109–13 on 'Manners and Women'.
60. See Knud Haakonssen, *The Science of a Legislator* (Cambridge, 1981) and his *Natural Law and Moral Philosophy*. Also Istvan Hont and Michael Ignatieff eds., *Wealth and Virtue: The Shaping of Political Economy in the Scottish Enlightenment* (Cambridge, 1983).
61. John Millar, *The Origin of the Distinction of Ranks: or, An Inquiry into the Circumstances which gave rise to Influence and Authority in the Different Members of Society* (1779), ed. John Valdimir Price (Bristol, 1990), 11–12. This text is based on the fourth, corrected edition (Edinburgh, 1806), but I will note page references and differences in the shorter, first edition of this work, *Observations concerning the Distinction of Ranks in Society* (London, 1771, revised 1773). Revisions to the first section of the *Observations* generally elaborate and expand Millar's conjectural history of the passions.
62. J. G. A. Pocock, *Politics, Language and Time* (New York, 1973), 102.
63. William Alexander, *The History of Women, from the Earliest Antiquity to the Present Time* (2 vols.; London, 1779), I, 103.
64. See Margaret Hunt, *The Middling Sort: Commerce, Gender and the Family in England, 1680–1780* (Berkeley, California, 1996).
65. Millar, *The Origin of the Distinction of Ranks*, 100 (first edn, 75).
66. Smith, *Lectures on Jurisprudence*, report of 1762–3, 5. This has been discussed by Rendall, 'Virtue and Commerce', 62–8. See also Chris Nyland, 'Adam Smith, Stage Theory, and the Status of Women', *History of Political Economy*, 25 (1993), 617–40.
67. Smith, *Lectures on Jurisprudence*, 49, 120–1, 60–1.
68. *Ibid.*, 14, 207.
69. *Ibid.*, 207.
70. *Ibid.*, 438 (report dated 1766 of lectures probably delivered 1763–4) and 149. On this subject, see John Dwyer's chapter on 'Smith, Millar and the Natural History of Love' in *The Age of the Passions: An Interpretation of Adam Smith and Scottish Enlightenment Culture* (East Linton, 1998).
71. Smith, *Lectures on Jurisprudence*, 439.
72. *Ibid.*, 439.
73. *Ibid.*, 439.

74. *Ibid.*, 247.
75. Adam Ferguson, *An Essay on the History of Civil Society*, ed. Fania Oz-Salzberger (Cambridge, 1995), 191–3.
76. Montagu to Kames (24 March 1767) in Tytler, *Memoirs*, II, 50–1.
77. On Millar, see William C. Lehmann, *John Millar of Glasgow, 1735–1801: His Life and Thought and Contributions to Sociological Analysis* (Cambridge, 1960), Michael Ignatieff, 'John Millar and Individualism' in Hont and Ignatieff eds., *Wealth and Virtue*, Paul Bowles, 'John Millar, the Four-Stages Theory, and Women's Position in Society', *History of Political Economy*, 16 (1984), 619–38, Bowles, 'Millar and Engels on the History of Women and the Family', *History of European Ideas*, 12 (1990), 595–610, Haakonssen, *Natural Law and Moral Philosophy*, ch. 5.
78. John Craig, 'An Account of the Life and Writings of John Millar', printed as a preface to *The Origin*, lxxvi.
79. Millar, *The Origin*, 108 (not in first edn).
80. *Ibid.*, 34 (first edn, 18). This owes something to Ferguson's account of the subordinate position of women in tribes that have no property or distinction of ranks, *Essay on the History of Civil Society*, 81–3.
81. Millar, *The Origin*, 15–16 (first edn, 3).
82. *Ibid.*, 23 (first edn, 9).
83. *Ibid.*, 32 (first edn, 15).
84. *Ibid.*, 60 (first edn, 'to interrupt the free intercourse of the sexes', 40).
85. *Ibid.*, 58, 62 (first edn, 39; added).
86. *Ibid.*, 76, 79 (first edn, 54; added).
87. *Ibid.*, 85–6 (first edn, 62–3).
88. *Ibid.*, 27–8 (not in first edn).
89. Ignatieff, 'John Millar and Individualism', 338.
90. Millar, *The Origin*, 89–90 (not in first edn).
91. *Ibid.*, 88 (first edn, 63).
92. *Ibid.*, 88–9 (first edn, 64).
93. *Ibid.*, 32, 89 (neither quotation in first edn).
94. *Ibid.*, 100 (first edn, 75).
95. *Ibid.*, 100 (first edn, 75).
96. *Ibid.*, 102 (not in first edn).
97. Jane Rendall, 'Aspiring Women and Scottish Whigs' in Taylor and Knott eds., *Women, Gender and Enlightenment*, 327–8.
98. Millar, *The Origin*, 108 (not in first edn).
99. James Logan, *Elements of the Philosophy of History* (Edinburgh, 1781).
100. William Russell, *An Essay on the Character, Manners, and Genius of Women in Different Ages. Enlarged from the French of M. Thomas* (2 vols.; London, 1773). Antoine Léonard Thomas's popular work, the *Essai sur le caractère des femmes dans les différens siècles* (Paris, 1772), is discussed by Lieselotte Steinbrügge in *The Moral Sex*, 90–9.
101. Russell, *Essay*, II, 17. On Mme Necker's salon, see Goodman, *The Republic of Letters*, 53–89.

102. Russell, *Essay*, I, 98 (Thomas, *Essai*, 61).
103. *Ibid.*, II, 149–55, II, 167.
104. Antoine Léonard Thomas, *An Essay on the Character, the Manners, and the Understanding of Women, in Different Ages. Translated from the French of Mons. Thomas, by Mrs. Kindersley, With Two Original Essays* (London, 1781), iv.
105. Jemima Kindersley, *Letters from the Island of Teneriffe, Brazil, the Cape of Good Hope, and the East Indies* (London, 1777), 138–9, 190–2.
106. Thomas, *An Essay*, trans. Kindersley, iv.
107. See Michèle Duchet, *Anthropologie et histoire au siècle des lumières* (Paris, 1971), and Antonello Gerbi, *The Dispute of the New World*, trans. Jeremy Moyle (Pittsburgh, 1973).
108. *Natural History, General and Particular by the Count de Buffon*, trans. William Smellie (9 vols.; Edinburgh, 1780), II, 403, 411, 419, 423–4.
109. *Ibid.*, II, 467.
110. *Ibid.*, III, 97, 141.
111. See Silvia Sebastiani, '"Race", Women and Progress in the Scottish Enlightenment' in Taylor and Knott eds., *Women, Gender and Enlightenment*, 83–5.
112. On Raynal, see Sankar Muthu, *Enlightenment against Empire* (Princeton, 2003), ch. 3.
113. Jenny Mander, 'No Woman is an Island: The Female Figure in French Enlightenment Anthropology' in Taylor and Knott eds., *Women, Gender and Enlightenment*, 97–116.
114. *Ibid.*, III.
115. Mary Catherine Moran, 'Between the Savage and the Civil', in Taylor and Knott eds., *Women, Gender and Enlightenment*, 8–29.
116. Gregory's early essays were collected as *A Comparative View of the State and Faculties of Man, with those of the Animal World* (London, 1765).
117. William Robertson, *The History of America* (2 vols.; London, 1777). I have discussed the use of conjectural history in this work in *Narratives of Enlightenment: Cosmopolitan History from Voltaire to Gibbon* (Cambridge, 1997), 156–61. The questionnaires can be found in the National Library of Scotland, *Robertson–MacDonald Papers*, MS 3942, ff. 283–6.
118. Robertson, *History of America*, I, 282.
119. *Ibid.*, I, 292, 319.
120. *Ibid.*, I, 321.
121. *Ibid.*, I, 320.
122. *Ibid.*, I, 295.
123. *Ibid.*, I, 290.
124. *Ibid.*, I, 319.
125. Alexander, *The History of Women*, I, 29.
126. *Ibid.*, I, 171.
127. *Ibid.*, I, 260–2.
128. *Ibid.*, I, 218.
129. *Ibid.*, I, 314.

130. *Ibid.*, I, 327.
131. *Ibid.*, II, 313.
132. Vivien Jones, 'Women Writing Revolution: Narratives of History and Sexuality in Wollstonecraft and Williams' in *Beyond Romanticism: New Approaches to Texts and Contexts, 1780–1832*, ed. Stephen Copley and John Whale (London, 1992), 183.
133. Priscilla Wakefield, *Reflections on the Present Condition of the Female Sex; with Suggestions for its Improvement* (London, 1798), 8.
134. Rendall, 'Aspiring Women and Scottish Whigs', 341.
135. Gleadle, *The Early Feminists*, 64–7. Also valuable is Gleadle's *Radical Writing on Women, 1800–1850: An Anthology* (Basingstoke, 2002), 26–41.
136. Kathryn Sutherland, 'Adam Smith's Master Narrative: Women and the *Wealth of Nations*' in *Adam Smith's Wealth of Nations: New Interdisciplinary Essays*, ed. Stephen Copley and Kathryn Sutherland (Manchester, 1995).
137. Haakonssen, *Natural Law and Moral Philosophy*, 180.
138. James Dunbar, *Essays on the History of Mankind in Rude and Cultivated Ages* (London, 1780), 435.
139. *Ibid.*, 143.
140. *Ibid.*, 53–7.
141. *Ibid.*, 407.

CHAPTER 3   ROMAN, GOTHIC AND MEDIEVAL WOMEN: THE HISTORICISATION OF WOMANHOOD, 1750–C.1804

1. See Thomas Preston Peardon, *The Transition in English Historical Writing, 1760–1830* (New York, 1933), chs. 4 and 5.
2. Mark Salber Phillips, *Society and Sentiment: Genres of Historical Writing, 1740–1820* (Princeton, 2000), 295.
3. See Richard Bourke, *Romantic Discourse and Political Modernity: Wordsworth, the Intellectual and Cultural Critique* (London, 1993).
4. J. G. A. Pocock, 'The Political Economy of Burke's Analysis of the French Revolution' in *Virtue, Commerce and History: Essays on Political Thought and History, Chiefly in the Eighteenth Century* (Cambridge, 1985), 199.
5. Dror Wahrman, *The Making of the Modern Self: Identity and Culture in Eighteenth-Century England* (New Haven, 2004), 21 and throughout.
6. See Joseph M. Levine, 'Why Neoclassicism? Politics and Culture in Eighteenth-Century England', *The British Journal for Eighteenth-Century Studies*, 25 (2002), 75–93 and my response in *ibid.*, 99–101.
7. See Philip Ayres, *Classical Culture and the Idea of Rome in Eighteenth-Century England* (Cambridge, 1997) and Caroline Robbins, *The Eighteenth-Century Commonwealthman: Studies in the Transmission, Development and Circumstance of English Liberal Thought* (Cambridge, Massachusetts, 1959).

8. Colin Kidd, *British Identities Before Nationalism: Ethnicity and Nationhood in the Atlantic World, 1600–1800* (Cambridge, 1999). See also Kidd, *The Forging of Races: Race, Scripture and the Protestant Atlantic World, 1600–2000* (Cambridge, 2006), and J. G. A. Pocock, *Barbarism and Religion*, IV, *Barbarians, Savages and Empires* (Cambridge, 2006).

9. Kidd, *British Identities*, 290.

10. Kate Davies, *Catharine Macaulay and Mercy Otis Warren: The Revolutionary Atlantic and the Politics of Gender* (Oxford, 2005), 109–17.

11. Philip Hicks, 'The Roman Matron in Britain: Female Political Influence and Republican Response, ca. 1750–1800', *The Journal of Modern History*, 77 (2005), 35–69. The quotation is on page 39.

12. Laurence Echard, *The Roman History, from the building of the City, to the perfect settlement of the Empire by Augustus Caesar* (London, 1695); Thomas Blackwell, *Memoirs of the Court of Augustus* (3 vols.; Edinburgh and London, 1753–63); Thomas Bever, *The History of the Legal Polity of the Roman State; and of the Rise, Progress, and Extent of the Roman Laws* (London, 1781); Adam Ferguson, *The History of the Progress and Termination of the Roman Republic* (3 vols.; London, 1783).

13. Charles Rollin, *The Roman History, from the Foundation of Rome to the Battle of Actium* (2 vols.; London, 1739–50). This was continued by Jean Baptiste Louis Crevier as *The Roman History* (second edn; 16 vols.; London, 1754). Oliver Goldsmith, *The Roman History, from the Foundation of the City of Rome, To the Destruction of the Western Empire* (2 vols.; London, 1769).

14. Rollin, *Roman History*, II, 279.

15. Blackwell, *Memoirs*, II, 81.

16. Hannah More, *The Inflexible Captive: A Tragedy* (Bristol, 1774), 74.

17. She is compared to Hortensia in *Six Odes, Presented to the Justly-Celebrated Historian, Mrs. Catharine Macaulay* (Bath, 1777), 17–19. [John Adams], *Woman. Sketches of the History, Genius, Disposition, Accomplishments, Employments, Customs and Importance of the Fair Sex, in all Parts of the World. By a friend to the sex* (London, 1790), 28–9. See also Rollin, *Roman History*, XV, 106.

18. See Rollin/Crevier, *Roman History*, XIV, 270–2, 338–9, XV, 171–2.

19. [Sarah Fielding], *The Lives of Cleopatra and Octavia* (London, 1757).

20. See Hicks, 'The Roman Matron', 38, 49. Elizabeth Hamilton, *Memoirs of the Life of Agrippina, the Wife of Germanicus* (3 vols.; Bath, 1804).

21. Goldsmith, *Roman History*, II, 501.

22. Rollin/Crevier, *Roman History*, VII, 39. Blackwell, *Memoirs*, III, 372.

23. For example, Adam Smith, *Lectures on Jurisprudence*, ed. R. L. Meek, D. D. Raphael and P. G. Stein (Oxford, 1978), 143–5.

24. Ferguson, *History of the Progress and Termination*, III, 565.

25. David Hume, 'Of Refinement in the Arts' (originally entitled 'Of Luxury') (1754, 1760) in *Essays, Moral, Political and Literary*, ed. Eugene F. Miller (Indianapolis, 1985), 269. See Christopher J. Berry, *The Idea of Luxury: A Conceptual and Historical Investigation* (Cambridge, 1994) and Maxine

Berg and Elizabeth Eger eds., *Luxury in the Eighteenth Century: Debates, Desires and Delectable Goods* (Basingstoke, 2003).

26. Echard, *Roman History*, 117; Rollin/Crevier, *Roman History* (1754), II, 92; Goldsmith, *Roman History*, I, 150.

27. [Lady Mary Wray, ed.], *An Historical Miscellany* (London, 1771), 94–112 (the extract comes from Hooke's *Roman History*). This *Miscellany* was reprinted three more times during the 1770s. Frances Brooke, *Virginia, A Tragedy, with Odes, Pastorals and Translations* (London, 1756). See also, on the same historical topic, John Dennis, *Appius and Virginia, A Tragedy* (London, 1709) and Samuel Crisp, *Virginia, A Tragedy* (London, 1754). Other works emphasised the sublime but inimitably inhumane devotion of the Roman Republic to the cause of liberty. For instance Hugh Downman's *Lucius Junius Brutus; or, the Expulsion of the Tarquins* (London, 1779), following Nathaniel Lee's superb 1681 play of the same name.

28. John Millar, *The Origin of the Distinction of Ranks*, ed. John Valdimir Price (Bristol, 1990), 125.

29. Edward Gibbon, *The History of the Decline and Fall of the Roman Empire*, ed. David Womersley (3 vols.; Harmondsworth, 1994), II, 779.

30. *Ibid.*, II, 811.

31. *Ibid.*, II, 812.

32. On the legal status of Roman women, see Sarah B. Pomeroy, *Goddesses, Whores, Wives, and Slaves: Women in Classical Antiquity* (1975, repr. London, 1994), ch. 8.

33. Gibbon, *The Decline and Fall*, II, 814; Blackwell, *Memoirs*, III, 372. On Roman marriage and divorce, one scholarly source was John Selden, 'De Nuptiarum apud veteres Romanos' in his *Uxor Ebraica, seu, de Nuptiis et Divortiis ex Iure Civile . . . Veterum Ebraeorum* (London, 1646), 218–23.

34. Gibbon, *The Decline and Fall*, II, 814. See also Smith, *Lectures on Jurisprudence*, 144, which makes a similar point.

35. Gibbon, *The Decline and Fall*, II, 815; Hume, 'Of the Populousness of Ancient Nations' (1752), *Essays*, 400.

36. Blackwell, *Memoirs*, III, 372.

37. Gibbon, *The Decline and Fall*, II, 819.

38. *Ibid.*, II, 823.

39. *Ibid.*, II, 822.

40. *Ibid.*, II, 822.

41. See Amy Louise Erickson, *Women and Property in Early Modern England* (London, 1993), 5.

42. Gibbon, *The Decline and Fall*, I, 481. See, on this subject, Kate Cooper's fascinating study, *The Virgin and the Bride: Idealized Womanhood in Late Antiquity* (Cambridge, MA, 1996).

43. Gibbon, *The Decline and Fall*, I, 481.

44. *Ibid.*, I, 481, note 97.

45. The pioneering treatment of this aspect of Gibbon is Brian Young, 'Gibbon and Sex', *Textual Practice*, II (1997), 517–37.

46. Hamilton, *Memoirs of Agrippina*, III, 263. On Hamilton, see Jane Rendall, 'Writing History for British Women: Elizabeth Hamilton and the *Memoirs of Agrippina*' in *Wollstonecraft's Daughters: Womanhood in England and France, 1780–1920*, ed. Clarissa Campbell Orr (Manchester, 1996).
47. Hamilton, *Memoirs of Agrippina*, III, 263–4.
48. *Ibid.*, III, 35, 252.
49. *Ibid.*, I, 19.
50. *Ibid.*, I, 270 and, in general, ch. x, in which Agrippina gets to know the manners of the Germanic people.
51. Hicks, 'The Roman Matron in Britain', 66–7. Harriet Guest detects a softening and domestication of the British image of Roman motherhood from the late eighteenth century onwards. See *Small Change: Women, Learning, Patriotism, 1750–1810* (Chicago, 2000), 249–51.
52. Edmund Gibson ed., *Camden's Britannia. Britain, or a Chorographicall description of . . . England, Scotland and Ireland* (London, 1695); Edward Lhuyd, *Archaeologica Britannica* (Oxford, 1707). See Joseph M. Levine, *The Battle of the Books: History and Literature in the Augustan Age* (Ithaca, New York, 1991), chapter 11.
53. Kidd, *British Identities*, chs. 4 and 5.
54. *Ibid.*, 185.
55. Julius Caesar, *De Bello Gallico*, v, 14.
56. Millar, *The Origin of the Distinction of Ranks*, 53.
57. *The Works of Tacitus*, trans. Thomas Gordon (2 vols.; London, 1728–31), II, 361. Citations are from this edition. This popular translation was eventually replaced by Arthur Murphy's *The Works of Cornelius Tacitus* (4 vols.; London, 1793).
58. *The Works of Tacitus*, II, 365.
59. *Ibid.*, I, 373–4.
60. Cassius Dio, *Roman History*, LXII, 12, 6.
61. Jodi Mikalachki's *The Legacy of Boadicea: Gender and Nation in Early Modern England* (London, 1998) discusses her as a figure of national identity in the earlier period. I am most grateful to Carolyn D. Williams for allowing me to see her unpublished paper '"The Frantic Woman": Boadicea and English Neo-Classical Embarrassment'.
62. Richard Glover, *A Short History of Boadicea, The British Queen. Being the Story on which the New Tragedy, Now in Rehearsal at the Theatre Royal in Drury Lane, is Founded* (London, 1754).
63. The play was earlier printed from the prompt book as *Boadicea. A Tragedy* (London, 1753).
64. Ambrose Philips, *The Briton. A Tragedy* (London, 1722), 43. The story of Cartimandua, who abandoned her husband for a Roman armour-bearer and incurred the wrath of her people, can be found in Tacitus' *Histories*, 3.45.
65. Kidd, *British Identities*, 188–94.
66. Philippus Cluverius, *Germaniae Antiquae Libri Tres* (Lugduni Batavorum, 1616), I, 179.

67. Simon Pelloutier, *Histoire des Celtes, et particulièrement des Gaulois et des Germains* (2 vols.; The Hague, 1750), I, 509.

68. Kidd, *British Identities*, 187. See Thomas Percy's long preface to his translation of Paul-Henri Mallet, *Northern Antiquities: or A Description of the Manners, Customs, Religion and Laws of the Ancient Danes, And other Northern Nations* (2 vols.; London, 1770). On the rediscovery of Celtic identity and culture, see Joseph Theodoor Leerssen, *Mere Irish and Fior-Ghael: Studies in the Idea of Irish Nationality, its Development and Literary Expression prior to the Nineteenth Century* (second edn, Cork, 1996), 287–93 and the important study by Clare O'Halloran, *Golden Ages and Barbarous Nations: Antiquarian Debate and Cultural Politics in Ireland, 1750–1800* (Cork, 2004).

69. Thomas Carte, *A General History of England* (4 vols.; London, 1747–55), I, 72–3.

70. John Macpherson, *Critical Dissertations on the Origin, Antiquities, Language, Government, Manners, and Religion of the Ancient Caledonians, their Posterity the Picts, and the British and Irish Scots* (London, 1768), dissertation xii. Gibbon relied on this and James Macpherson's findings for his section on ancient Scotland in *The Decline and Fall*, I, 997–9.

71. Macpherson, *Critical Dissertations*, 139.

72. James Macpherson, *The Poems of Ossian and Related Works*, ed. Howard Gaskill with an introduction by Fiona Stafford (Edinburgh, 1996), 17. See also Sylvia Sebastiani, ' "Race", Women and Progress in the Scottish Enlightenment' in *Women, Gender and Enlightenment*, ed., Barbara Taylor and Sarah Knott (Basingstoke, 2005), 86–8 and Lisa Kozlowski, 'Terrible Women and Tender Men: A Study of Gender in Macpherson's *Ossian*' in *From Gaelic to Romantic: Ossianic Translations*, ed. Fiona Stafford and Howard Gaskill (Amsterdam, 1998).

73. Macpherson, *The Poems of Ossian*, 74–5, 100.

74. Hugh Blair, *A Critical Dissertation on the Poems of Ossian, the Son of Fingal* (revised edn of 1765) reprinted in Macpherson, *The Poems of Ossian*, 353.

75. *Ibid.*, 349.

76. *Ibid.*, 350.

77. *Ibid.*, 376.

78. *Ibid.*, 377–8.

79. Elizabeth Montagu to Lord Kames (3 October 1771) in A. J. Tytler ed., *Memoirs of the Life and Writings of the Honourable Henry Home of Kames* (2 vols.; Edinburgh, 1807), II, 95, 96.

80. James Macpherson, *An Introduction to the History of Great Britain and Ireland* (London, 1771), 188. See also Leerssen, *Mere Irish*, 338–40.

81. Kidd, *British Identities*, 200–4.

82. Macpherson, *An Introduction*, 206.

83. *Ibid.*, 206–7.

84. For example, Richard B. Sher, *Church and University in the Scottish Enlightenment* (Edinburgh, 1985), ch. 6.

85. Robert Henry, *The History of Great Britain, From the First Invasion of it by the Romans Under Julius Caesar* (6 vols.; London and Edinburgh, 1771–93), I, 445–7, 456.
86. Mallet, *Northern Antiquities*, I, ii.
87. John Pinkerton, *A Dissertation on the Origin and Progress of the Scythians or Goths* (London, 1787).
88. *Ibid.*, vii.
89. *Ibid.*, 17.
90. *Ibid.*, 69.
91. *Ibid.*, 103.
92. In the early 1790s, Gibbon confirmed that 'the Goths still contrive to be his chosen people; but [he] retains no antipathy to the Celtic savage'. See *The English Essays of Edward Gibbon*, ed. Patricia B. Craddock (Oxford, 1972), 542.
93. Nowadays, the name 'Goths' denotes tribes of the 'ostro-' or 'visi-' variety from Sweden. Following eighteenth-century practice, I will use 'Goths' to mean both Germani and Gotthi. In general, Peter J. Heather, *Goths and Romans, 332–489* (Oxford, 1991).
94. The most important essay on this subject is Jane Rendall, 'Tacitus Engendered: "Gothic Feminism" and British Histories, 1750–1800' in *Imagining Nations*, ed. Geoffrey Cubitt (Manchester, 1998). Still valuable is Samuel Kliger, *The Goths in England: A Study in Seventeenth- and Eighteenth-Century Thought* (New York, 1972). See especially the brief discussion of 'Gothic feminism' on pages 220–3, as well as Kidd, *British Identities*, ch. 9. Caroline Franklin's 'The Colour of a Riband: Patriotism, History and the Role of Women in Helen Maria Williams's *Sketches of the Manners and Opinions in the French Republic* (1801)', *Women's Writing*, 13 (2006), 495–508, offers some valuable reflections on the relationship of women to patriotism in this period.
95. See R. J. Smith, *The Gothic Bequest: Medieval Institutions in British Thought, 1688–1863* (Cambridge, 1987).
96. Hugo Grotius ed., *Historia Gotthorum, Vandalorum et Langobardorum* (Amsterdam, 1655), 65–6.
97. For example, Salvian in *ibid.*, 87.
98. See Howard D. Weinbrot, 'Politics, Taste, and National Identity: Some Uses of Tacitism in Eighteenth-Century Britain' in *Tacitus and the Tacitean Tradition*, ed. T. J. Luce and A. J. Woodman (Princeton, 1993).
99. *The Works of Tacitus*, II, 326, 332.
100. *Ibid.*, II, 331.
101. *Ibid.*, II, 332.
102. *Ibid.*, II, 333.
103. Notably Richard Verstegen, *A Restitution of Decayed Intelligence: In Antiquities* (Antwerp, 1605), 49–50. This work was reissued many times during this century up to 1673. Selden, however, was of the opinion that the Germani

did have a Roman form of divorce: *Uxor Hebraica*, 433, and, in general, chs. 29–30.

104. Millar, *The Origin of the Distinction of Ranks*, 39. See also Millar, *An Historical View of the English Government, from the Settlement of the Saxons in Britain to the Accession of the House of Stuart* (London, 1787), 36–7.

105. Henry Home Kames, *Sketches of the History of Man* (1778), ed. John Valdimir Price (4 vols.; Bristol, 1993), II, 70.

106. William Alexander, *The History of Women, from the Earliest Antiquity to the Present Time* (2 vols.; London, 1779), I, 259, 262.

107. Gibbon, *The Decline and Fall*, I, 243.

108. Karen O'Brien, *Narratives of Enlightenment: Cosmopolitan History from Voltaire to Gibbon* (Cambridge, 1997), 199–201. On Gibbon's use and modification of Tacitus, see David Womersley, *The Transformation of The Decline and Fall of the Roman Empire* (Cambridge, 1988), ch. 6.

109. Gibbon, *The Decline and Fall*, I, 235. See also II, 212–13.

110. *Ibid.*, I, 237. Also I, 241.

111. *Ibid.*, I, 244.

112. Gibbon expresses considerable admiration for the colourful and astute Theodora, a former prostitute, distancing himself from 'Those who believe that the female mind is totally depraved by the loss of chastity' (*ibid.*, II, 567).

113. In the second volume, he tells the story, with great compassion, of the Gothic princess Honoria who, at sixteen, had an affair with a chamberlain: 'Her guilt and shame (such is the absurd language of imperious man) were soon betrayed by the appearances of pregnancy' (*ibid.*, II, 332). She is exiled and eventually driven, by ill usage and intolerance, into the arms of Attila the Hun. Brian Young has found a poem from the 1780s, addressed to Gibbon by the father of a seduced daughter, in which he blames the girl's downfall on her enthusiasm for *The Decline and Fall*, and, in particular, for his rendition of the Honoria story ('Gibbon and Sex', 530, 533–7).

114. Gibbon, *The Decline and Fall*, I, 245, 244.

115. *Ibid.*, I, 84.

116. *Ibid.*, I, 230.

117. Mallet, *Northern Antiquities*, I, 320. Mallet's work takes, as Percy points out in his preface to this work, a misguidedly Scytho-Celtic view of his source material.

118. See William Zachs, *Without Regard to Good Manners: A Biography of Gilbert Stuart, 1743–1786* (Edinburgh, 1992).

119. Gilbert Stuart, *A View of Society in Europe, in its Progress from Rudeness to Refinement* (Edinburgh, 1778). Discussed by Zachs, *Without Regard*, 96–102 and Colin Kidd, *Subverting Scotland's Past: Scottish Whig Historians and the Creation of an Anglo-British Identity, 1689–c.1830* (Cambridge, 1993), ch. 10.

120. Stuart, *A View of Society in Europe*, 16.

121. *Ibid.*, 19.

122. *Ibid.*, 20.

123. *Ibid.*, 14.
124. *Ibid.*, 61.
125. *Ibid.*, 29–36.
126. Erickson, *Women and Property*, 6.
127. Walter Scott, 'Chivalry' (1818) reprinted in *The Miscellaneous Prose Works of Sir Walter Scott, Bart.* (6 vols.; Edinburgh, 1827), VI, 36–7. The most useful general study of chivalry *per se* is Richard Barber, *The Knight and Chivalry* (revised edn, Woodbridge, Suffolk, 1995).
128. See Mark Girouard, *The Return to Camelot: Chivalry and the English Gentleman* (New Haven, 1981). At intervals, the Hanoverian monarchs tried to revive Edward III's chivalric Order of the Garter. See Christine Gerrard, *The Patriot Opposition to Walpole: Politics, Party, and National Myth, 1725–42* (Oxford, 1994), 224–9. See also the section 'Critical Chivalry' in Jacqueline Labbe, *The Romantic Paradox: Love, Violence and the Uses of Romance, 1760–1830* (Basingstoke, 2000), 16–30.
129. [Richard Hurd], *Letters on Chivalry and Romance* (London, 1762), 10. Another early account of chivalry's origins and effects occurred in Joseph Priestley's *Lectures on History and General Policy*, Lecture 45 (delivered in the late 1760s, published Birmingham, 1788).
130. [Hurd], *Letters on Chivalry and Romance*, 38.
131. Richard Hurd, *Moral and Political Dialogues* (third edn, London, 1765), 198.
132. [Hurd], *Letters on Chivalry and Romance*, 18.
133. On the debate about the western/eastern origins of chivalry, see Kliger, *The Goths in England*, 226–35.
134. Jean-Baptiste La Curne de Sainte-Palaye, *Mémoires sur l'ancienne chevalerie, considerée comme un établissement politique et militaire* (2 vols.; Paris, 1759), translated by Mrs S. Dobson as *Memoirs of Ancient Chivalry. To which are added the Anecdotes of the Times* (London, 1784). The review in the *Gentleman's Magazine*, 54 (1784), 43–4 particularly recommends this edition, on account of Dobson's notes, to female readers. The original French edition of the work was familiar to all major eighteenth-century historians, including, for instance, William Russell, who interpolated sections of the *Mémoires* into his translation of Antoine Léonard Thomas's *Essay on the Character of . . . Women* (2 vols.; London, 1773).
135. The tension between the sense of chivalry as an institution and chivalry as a surface is discussed in Lionel Gossman, *Medievalism and the Ideologies of the Enlightenment: The World and Work of La Curne de Sainte-Palaye* (Baltimore, 1968).
136. Sainte-Palaye, *Memoirs of Ancient Chivalry*, 312.
137. *Ibid.*, 12–13, 81–2.
138. *Ibid.*, 106.
139. *Ibid.*, 109, 122.
140. *Ibid.*, 210.
141. *Ibid.*, 82–3.

142. See J. Q. C. Mackrell, *The Attack on Feudalism in Eighteenth-Century France* (London, 1973).
143. Susannah Dobson, Preface, *Memoirs of Ancient Chivalry*, xx.
144. [Susannah Dobson], *Historical Anecdotes of Heraldry and Chivalry. Tending to Shew the Origin of Many English and Foreign Coats of Arms, Circumstances and Customs* (Worcester, 1795), 172–91, 183.
145. George, Baron Lyttelton, *The History of the Life of King Henry the Second. And of the Age in which he lived* (4 vols.; London, 1767–71), II, 38–9.
146. *Ibid.*, II, 234, 246.
147. *Ibid.*, II, 240.
148. See, for example, *The Letters of Mrs. Elizabeth Montagu*, ed. Matthew Montagu (4 vols.; London 1809–13), III, 291 (on Hume's history), IV, 66–7 (on Voltaire's history) and IV, 210 (on the superiority of Lyttelton to modern anecdotal or philosophical history).
149. See, for example, her effusive letter of 1752 on the Black Prince's tomb in *ibid.*, III, 194–5.
150. Montagu to Carter (3 October 1762) in Gary Kelly *et al.* eds., *Bluestocking Feminism: Writings of the Bluestocking Circle 1738–85* (6 vols.; London, 1999), I, 163–4.
151. *Ibid.*, I, 129.
152. George, Baron Lyttelton, *Letters from a Persian to his Friend at Ispahan* (London, 1735), 157. The Persian Selim is speaking here.
153. Kelly ed., *Bluestocking Feminism*, I, 163.
154. Quoted by Kliger in *The Goths in England*, 230.
155. See Harriet Guest, 'The Wanton Muse: Politics and Gender in Gothic Theory after 1760' in *Beyond Romanticism: New Approaches to Texts and Contexts, 1780–1832*, ed. John Whale and Stephen Copley (London, 1992). Clara Reeve in fact mounts an attack on 'gallantry' in *The Progress of Romance, through Times, Countries, and Manners* (1785) in Kelly ed., *Bluestocking Feminism*, VI, 230–1.
156. Thomas Warton, *The History of English Poetry, from the close of the Eleventh to the Commencement of the Eighteenth Century* (4 vols.; London [Oxford], 1774–90). The first three volumes (1774, 1777, 1781) were published during Warton's lifetime; the last (1790) was posthumously published.
157. *Ibid.*, I, sig. i recto.
158. *Ibid.*, I, sig. i verso–recto.
159. *Ibid.*, I, sig. j verso.
160. James Beattie, *Dissertations Moral and Critical* (London, 1783), 525, 546.
161. Henry, *The History of Great Britain*, IV, 577.
162. David Hume, *The History of England* (6 vols.; Edinburgh and London, 1754–62), I, 423. Hume wrote a very early, bemused 'Historical Essay on Chivalry and Modern Honour' that is discussed and reproduced by Ernest Campbell Mossner in *Modern Philology*, 45–6 (1947–9), 54–60.
163. Gibbon, *The Decline and Fall*, III, 579.

164. William Robertson, *The History of the Reign of the Emperor Charles V* (3 vols.; London, 1769), I, 71.
165. *Ibid.*, I, 71, 70.
166. Millar, *The Origin of the Distinction of Ranks*, 75, 76, 72.
167. *Ibid.*, 78.
168. Adam Ferguson, *An Essay on the History of Civil Society*, ed. Fania Oz-Salzberger (Cambridge, 1995), 191, 193 (italics in the original).
169. Edmund Burke, *Reflections on the Revolution in France, and on the Proceedings of Certain Societies in London Relative to that Event* (1790) in *The Writings and Speeches of Edmund Burke*, volume VIII, ed. L. G. Mitchell (Oxford, 1989), 127, 172.
170. *Ibid.*, 127.
171. J. G. A. Pocock, 'The Political Economy of Burke's Analysis of the French Revolution' in *Virtue, Commerce and History: Essays in Political Thought* (Cambridge, 1985), 199. This essay is briefly but illuminating discussed in relation to Burke's chivalry in Donald Winch's *Riches and Poverty: An Intellectual History of Political Economy in Britain, 1750–1834* (Cambridge, 1996), 175–85.
172. Burke, *Reflections*, 130.
173. 'Speech on Divorce Bill, 29 April, 1771' in *The Writings and Speeches of Edmund Burke*, vol. II, ed. Paul Langford (Oxford, 1981), 357.
174. [Thomas Love Peacock], *Melincourt: By the Author of Headlong Hall* (3 vols.; London, 1817), I, 27–8.
175. Henry Hallam, *A View of the State of Europe during the Middle Ages* (2 vols.; London, 1818), II, 561.
176. See J. W. Burrow, *A Liberal Descent: Victorian Historians and the English Past* (Cambridge, 1981), 30–4.
177. Hallam, *A View of the State of Europe*, II, 545–6.
178. *Ibid.*, II, 553.
179. Scott, 'Chivalry', *Miscellaneous Prose Works*, VI, 26.
180. *Ibid.*, VI, 158.
181. Mary Wollstonecraft, *A Vindication of the Rights of Woman* in *The Works of Mary Wollstonecraft*, ed. Janet Todd and Marilyn Butler (7 vols.; London, 1989), V, 127.
182. Clarissa Campbell Orr, 'Agnes Strikland versus Anna Jameson: the Language of Chivalry, Women's Rights and the Langham Place Group' (unpublished paper).
183. Barbara Taylor, 'Feminists versus Gallants: Sexual Manners and Morals in Enlightenment Britain' in Taylor and Knott eds., *Women, Gender and Enlightenment*. See also my observations on this chapter in *ibid.*, 5–7.
184. Catharine Macaulay, *Observations on the Reflections of the Right Hon. Edmund Burke, on the Revolution in France, In a Letter to the Right Hon. the Earl of Stanhope* (London, 1790), 54.
185. *Ibid.*, 54.

186. [Charles Lamb], *Elia: Essays which have Appeared under that Signature in the London Magazine* (London, 1823), 181–2.
187. John Stuart Mill, 'Modern French Historical Works', *Westminster Review* (1826), in *The Collected Works of John Stuart Mill*, ed. John M. Robson (33 vols.; Toronto, 1963–91), *Essays on French History and Historians*, ed. Robson and John C. Cairns, xx, 45.
188. Mill, 'Modern French Historical Works', 45.
189. *Ibid.*, 47.
190. *Ibid.*, 46.
191. *Ibid.*

CHAPTER 4   CATHARINE MACAULAY'S HISTORIES OF ENGLAND: LIBERTY, CIVILISATION AND THE FEMALE HISTORIAN

1. Notably the major biography of Macaulay: Bridget Hill, *The Republican Virago: The Life and Times of Catharine Macaulay, Historian* (Oxford, 1992).
2. See Philip Hicks, 'The Roman Matron in Britain: Female Political Influence and Republican Response, ca. 1750–1800', *Journal of Modern History*, 77 (2005), 35–69; Kate Davies, *Catharine Macaulay and Mercy Otis Warren: The Revolutionary Atlantic and the Politics of Gender* (Oxford, 2005), 70 and ch. 2.
3. Philip Hicks, 'Catharine Macaulay's Civil War: Gender, History, and Republicanism in Georgian Britain', *Journal of British Studies*, 41 (2002), 170–98. The quotation is on pages 197–8.
4. J. G. A. Pocock, 'Catharine Macaulay: Patriot Historian' in *Women Writers and the Early Modern British Political Tradition*, ed. Hilda L. Smith (Cambridge, 1998), 251.
5. Sylvia Harcstark-Myers, *The Bluestocking Circle: Women, Friendship and the Life of Mind in Eighteenth-Century England* (Oxford, 1990), 24, 256. Montagu to Hester Thrale (*c.* January 1779). This MS letter is quoted by Davis, in *Catharine Macaulay and Mercy Otis Warren*, 174.
6. Catharine Macaulay Graham, *Letters on Education. With Observations on Religious and Metaphysical Subjects* (1790), ed. Jonathan Wordsworth (Oxford, 1994), 268.
7. *Ibid.*, 268.
8. *Ibid.*, 210.
9. *Ibid.*, 271, 272–3.
10. Catharine Macaulay, *Loose Remarks on Certain Positions to be Found in Mr. Hobbes's 'Philosophical Rudiments of Government and Society', with a Short Sketch of a Democratical Form of Government, In a Letter to Signor Paoli* (London, 1767). Most of her remarks on Hobbes are directed towards proving that equality is compatible with good, fair government.
11. Pocock, 'Catharine Macaulay: Patriot Historian', 243.

12. Hill, *The Republican Virago*, 16, and Isaac Kramnick, *Republicanism and Bourgeois Radicalism: Political Ideology in Late Eighteenth-Century England and America* (Ithaca, New York, 1990). See also Susan Staves, ' "The Liberty of a She-Subject of England": Rights, Rhetoric and the Female Thucydides', *Cardozo Studies in Law and Literature*, 1 (1989), 161–83.

13. On Macaulay's extensive research for her history, see Hill, *The Republican Virago*, ch. 2, and Bridget and Christopher Hill, 'Catharine Macaulay's *History* and Her Catalogue of Tracts', *The Seventeenth Century*, 8 (1993), 269–85.

14. See Karen O'Brien, *Narratives of Enlightenment: Cosmopolitan History from Voltaire to Gibbon* (Cambridge, 1997), ch. 3.

15. Catharine Macaulay, *The History of England from the Accession of James I to that of the Brunswick Line* (8 vols.; London, 1763–83), v (1771), 383.

16. *Ibid.*, v (1771), 378.

17. *Ibid.*, iv (1768), 159 and 160n.

18. *Ibid.*, i (1763), 274–5.

19. *Ibid.*, v (1771), 382–3.

20. *Ibid.*, i, (1763), 274.

21. *Ibid.*, i (1763), 8.

22. *Ibid.*, v, (1771), 112.

23. *Ibid.*, iii (1767), 332.

24. *Ibid*, vi (1781), xii.

25. Hill, *The Republican Virago*, 41–4.

26. *The European Magazine*, 4 (1783), 331.

27. Caroline Robbins, *The Eighteenth-Century Commonwealthman: Studies in the Transmission, Development and Circumstance of English Liberal Thought from the Restoration of Charles II until the War with the Thirteen Colonies* (Cambridge, MA, 1959); Pocock, 'Catharine Macaulay: Patriot Historian'.

28. Lynne E. Withey, 'Catharine Macaulay and the Uses of History: Ancient Rights, Perfectionism and Propaganda', *The Journal of British Studies*, 16 (1976), 59–83 and Hill, *The Republican Virago*, 31–2.

29. David Hume, 'Of Refinement in the Arts', earlier entitled 'Of Luxury' (1754) in *Essays, Moral, Political and Literary*, ed. Eugene F. Miller (Indianapolis, 1985), 269.

30. Catharine Macaulay, *The History of England from the Revolution to the Present Time in a Series of Letters to a Friend* (Bath, 1778), 314, 308. Davies discusses the highly topical nature of some of the historical parallels suggested in this history: *Catharine Macaulay and Mercy Otis Warren*, 140–6.

31. *The History of England from the Accession of James I*, iv, 125.

32. *Ibid*, iv (1768), 435, 433; viii (1783), 278.

33. *Ibid.*, iv (1768), 430–1.

34. *The History of England from the Revolution to the Present Time*, 72.

35. *Ibid.*, 5.

36. Bridget Hill, 'Reinterpreting the "Glorious Revolution": Catharine Macaulay and Radical Response' in *Culture and Society in the Stuart Restoration*,

ed. Gerald Maclean (Cambridge, 1995), 279. Also valuable in this context is Barbara Brandon Schnorrenberg, 'An Opportunity Missed: Catharine Macaulay on the Revolution of 1688', *Studies in Eighteenth-Century Culture*, 20 (1990), 231–40.

37. Macaulay, *The History of England from the Accession of James I*, VIII (1783), 276.
38. *Ibid.*, VIII (1783), 275.
39. *Ibid.*, VIII (1783), 277.
40. *Ibid.*, VIII (1783), 293.
41. See Isaac Kramnick, *Bolingbroke and his Circle: The Politics of Nostalgia in the Age of Walpole* (Cambridge, MA, 1968).
42. Macaulay, *The History of England from the Accession of James I*, VIII (1783), 293.
43. *Ibid.*, VIII, 334.
44. *Ibid.*, VIII, 330.
45. *Ibid.*, VIII, 329–30.
46. Macaulay, *Loose Remarks*, 37.
47. Withey, 'Catharine Macaulay and the Uses of History', 72.
48. Hill, *The Republican Virago*, ch. 3; John Brewer, *Party Ideology and Popular Politics at the Accession of George III* (Cambridge, 1976), 204, 261.
49. Peter N. Miller, *Defining the Common Good: Empire, Religion and Philosophy in Eighteenth-Century Britain* (Cambridge, 1996), 352.
50. Catharine Macaulay Graham, *A Treatise on the Immutability of Moral Truth* (London, 1783).
51. *Ibid.*, vi, 2.
52. *Ibid.*, 9, 14.
53. *Ibid.*, 21, 25.
54. *Ibid.*, 163, 307. She goes much further than Carter in her brave and unconventional defence of the Stoic practice of suicide, 'a real excellence in their system', *ibid.*, 303.
55. King's work was translated by Edmund Law as *An Essay on the Origin of Evil* in 1731, and went through five editions to 1781.
56. Macaulay, *A Treatise*, 36.
57. *Ibid.*
58. In the introduction to the *Treatise*, Macaulay says that she read Clarke after writing the work, but that 'this very eminent divine preaches exactly the same doctrine' as herself: *A Treatise*, viii. Sarah Hutton, 'Liberty, Equality and God: The Religious Roots of Catharine Macaulay's Feminism' in *Women, Gender and Enlightenment*, ed. Barbara Taylor and Sarah Knott (Basingstoke, 2005), 540–1. This is a valuable article, but is entirely misleading in its placing of Macaulay within an Arminian tradition of liberal theology (page 545).
59. Macaulay, *A Treatise*, 223.
60. *Ibid.*, 258.
61. This section can be found in *ibid.*, 192–268.

62. *Ibid.*, 193, 194.
63. *Ibid.*, 241–3.
64. *Ibid.*, 261.
65. Isabel Rivers, *Reason, Grace and Sentiment: A Study of the Language of Religion and Ethics in England, 1660–1780* (2 vols.; Cambridge, 1991, 2000), II, 212–14.
66. Macaulay, *A Treatise*, xiv.
67. Hill, *The Republican Virago*, 155.
68. Macaulay, *The History of England from the Accession of James I*, III (1767), 450; VII (1781), 493–6; I (1763), xiii.
69. *Ibid.*, IV, 8n.
70. Macaulay, *The History of England from the Revolution to the Present Time*, 367.
71. Macaulay, *The History of England from the Accession of James I*, IV (1768), 431.
72. *Ibid.*, I (1763), x.
73. Susan Wiseman, 'Catharine Macaulay: History, Republicanism and the Public Sphere' in *Women, Writing and the Public Sphere, 1700–1830*, ed. Elizabeth Eger, Charlotte Grant, Cliona o Gallchoir and Penny Warburton (Cambridge, 2001), 192.
74. Macaulay, *The History of England from the Accession of James I*, VIII (1783), 319.
75. *Ibid.*, VIII (1783), 318.
76. Harriet Guest, *Small Change: Women, Learning, Patriotism, 1750–1810* (Chicago, 2000), 205.

CHAPTER 5   GOOD MANNERS AND PARTIAL CIVILISATION IN THE
WRITINGS OF MARY WOLLSTONECRAFT

1. See Barbara Taylor, 'Feminists versus Gallants: Sexual Manners and Morals in Enlightenment Britain' in *Women, Gender and Enlightenment*, ed. Barbara Taylor and Sarah Knott (Basingstoke, 2005), 30–52, and also my introductory remarks on this essay, 5–7.
2. Barbara Taylor, *Mary Wollstonecraft and the Feminist Imagination* (Cambridge, 2003), Gary Kelly, *Revolutionary Feminism: The Mind and Career of Mary Wollstonecraft* (London, 1992), Janet Todd, *Mary Wollstonecraft: A Revolutionary Life* (London, 2000).
3. Most famously, Cora Kaplan, 'Wild Nights: Pleasure/Sexuality/Feminism' in *Sea Changes: Essays on Culture and Feminism* (London, 1986).
4. William Godwin, *Memoirs of the Author of a Vindication of the Rights of Woman* (1798), ed. Pamela Clemit and Gina Luria Walker (Petersboroug, Ontario, 2001), 56. This tendency has been reversed by Taylor, *Mary Wollstonecraft*, ch. 3, 'For the Love of God'.

5. See John Robertson, 'Women and Enlightenment: A Historiographical Conclusion' in Taylor and Knott eds., *Women, Gender and Enlightenment*, 700–2.
6. The review was written for the *Analytical Review* (November 1790) and is reprinted in *The Works of Mary Wollstonecraft*, ed. Janet Todd and Marilyn Butler (7 vols.; London, 1989), VII, 314 (hereafter *Works*).
7. Catharine Macaulay, *Letters on Education. With Observations on Religious and Metaphysical Subjects* (London, 1790). The edition used here is the Woodstock facsimile with an introduction by Jonathan Wordsworth (Oxford, 1994), xii.
8. *Ibid.*, 152.
9. *Ibid.*, 472.
10. *Ibid.*, 212.
11. *Ibid.*
12. Wollstonecraft, *Works*, VII, 314.
13. Wollstonecraft, *A Vindication of the Rights of Woman: with Strictures on Political and Moral Subjects* (London, 1792), *Works*, V, 206–7; hereafter *A Vindication*. For a discussion of Wollstonecraft on chastity as a 'subjective principle' rather than a 'prohibitive code', see Taylor, *Mary Wollstonecraft*, 118.
14. Wollstonecraft, *Works*, VII, 318.
15. Macaulay, *Letters on Education*, i. See also her praise of Hartley in *A Treatise on the Immutability of Moral Truth* (London, 1783), xvi and 113.
16. *Hartley's Theory of the Human Mind, on the Principle of the Association of Ideas*, ed. Joseph Priestley (London, 1775); *Observations on Man, His Frame, His Duty and His Expectations*, with an introduction by David Hartley (Hartley's son) (London, 1791).
17. Hartley, *Observations on Man*, ed. Theodore Huguelet (2 vols.; Gainsville, Florida, 1966), II, 67, 56. This section was included in Priestley's edition.
18. On Wollstonecraft's probable reading of Hartley, see Taylor, *Mary Wollstonecraft*, 110.
19. Macaulay, *Letters*, 484, 163–4.
20. *Ibid.*, 272.
21. *Ibid.*
22. *Ibid.*, 300.
23. *Ibid.*, 205.
24. *Ibid.*, 206.
25. *Ibid.*
26. Penny A. Weiss, *Gendered Community: Rousseau, Sex and Politics* (New York, 1993), 36–53. See also Joel Schwartz, *The Sexual Politics of Jean-Jacques Rousseau* (Chicago, 1984) and Judith Still, *Justice and Difference in the Works of Rousseau* (Cambridge, 1993).
27. Jean-Jacques Rousseau, *Emilius and Sophia: or, A New System of Education* (2 vols.; London, 1762), II, 154. This was the standard eighteenth-century translation.

28. Jean-Jacques Rousseau, *A Discourse upon the Origin and Foundation of the Inequality among Mankind* (London, 1756), 109. Again, the standard translation.

29. Macaulay, *Letters*, 214, 210.

30. Rousseau, *A Discourse upon . . . Inequality*, 81.

31. Macaulay, *Letters*, 215.

32. *Ibid.*, 50. The phrase 'moral complicity of the sexes' is taken from Diana Coole's illuminating discussion of Rousseau and Wollstonecraft in *Women in Political Theory: From Ancient Misogyny to Contemporary Feminism* (Hemel Hempstead, 1993), 90.

33. Bridget Hill, 'The Links between Mary Wollstonecraft and Catharine Macaulay: New Evidence', *Women's History Review*, 4 (1995), 177–92. See also Taylor, *Mary Wollstonecraft*, 48–50.

34. Wollstonecraft, *A Vindication, Works*, v, 175.

35. In 1787, Wollstonecraft wrote 'I am now reading Rousseau's Emile, and love his paradoxes', *The Collected Letters of Mary Wollstonecraft*, ed. Ralph M. Wardle (Ithaca, New York, 1979), 145. On Wollstonecraft and Rousseau, see Taylor, *Mary Wollstonecraft*, 73–93 and Todd, *Mary Wollstonecraft*, 181–4.

36. Macaulay, *Letters*, 224.

37. *Ibid.*, 229.

38. For example, G. J. Barker-Benfield, 'Mary Wollstonecraft: Eighteenth-Century Commonwealthwoman', *The Journal of the History of Ideas*, 50 (1989), 95–115.

39. Taylor, *Mary Wollstonecraft*, 212. An important article on the relationship between late eighteenth-century dissenting radicals and the republican tradition is Mark Philp, 'English Republicanism of the 1790s', *The Journal of Political Philosophy*, 6 (1998), 235–62.

40. Sylvana Tomaselli, *A Vindication of the Rights of Men and A Vindication of the Rights of Woman* (Cambridge, 1995), xvi; Jane Rendall, '"The Grand Causes which Combine to Carry Mankind Forward": Wollstonecraft, History, Revolution', *Women's Writing*, 4 (1997), 155–72.

41. Mary Wollstonecraft, *The Female Reader; or Miscellaneous Pieces in Prose and Verse . . . For the Improvement of Young Women. By Mr. Cresswick, Teacher of Elocution* (London, 1789) in volume IV of *Works*.

42. Review of a work entitled 'Letters on the Manners of the French', *Works*, VII, 341–2 (including a reference to the 'profundity of Montesquieu', VII, 342).

43. See Peter N. Miller, *Defining the Common Good: Empire, Religion and Philosophy in Eighteenth-Century Britain* (Cambridge, 1994), and Isaac Kramnick, *Republicanism and Bourgeois Radicalism: Political Ideology in Late Eighteenth-Century England and America* (Ithaca, New York, 1990).

44. Mary Wollstonecraft, *An Historical and Moral View of the Origin and Progress of the French Revolution; and the Effect It Has produced in Europe* (London, 1794), *Works*, VI, 115.

45. Wollstonecraft, *A Vindication of the Rights of Men*, *Works*, v, 59.
46. *Ibid.*, v, 24.
47. Todd, *Mary Wollstonecraft*, 186.
48. Wollstonecraft, *A Vindication of the Rights of Men*, *Works*, v, 10.
49. *Ibid.*, v, 46.
50. *Ibid.*, v, 25.
51. Taylor, 'Feminists versus Gallants', in Taylor and Knott, eds., *Women, Gender and Enlightenment*, 34.
52. Wollstonecraft, *A Vindication*, *Works*, v, 70. These notes were published by Godwin in 1798 as 'Hints [Chiefly designed to have been incorporated in the Second Part of the Vindication of the Rights of Woman]' and are reproduced in *Works*, v, 271–6.
53. Wollstonecraft, *A Vindication*, *Works*, v, 90.
54. *Ibid.*, v, 73.
55. *Ibid.*
56. *Ibid.*, v, 66, 93.
57. *Ibid.*, v, 264.
58. *Ibid.*, v, 234. On the Shaftesburian strand of influence in Wollstonecraft's work, see Chris Jones, *Radical Sensibility: Literature and Ideas on the 1790s* (London, 1993), 104–7.
59. Wollstonecraft, *A Vindication*, *Works*, v, 219.
60. *Ibid.*, v, 256.
61. Thomas Paine, *Common Sense* (1776) in *Rights of Man, Common Sense and Other Political Writings*, ed. Mark Philp (Oxford, 1995), 5. On Wollstonecraft as a liberal political theorist, see Coole, *Women in Political Theory*, ch. 5. See also Moira Gatens, '"The Oppressed of My Sex": Wollstonecraft on Reason, Feeling and Equality' in *Feminist Interpretations and Political Theory*, ed. Mary Lyndon Shanley and Carole Pateman (Cambridge, 1991), and Shanley, 'Mary Wollstonecraft on Sensibility, Women's Rights, and Patriarchal Power' in *Women Writers and the Early Modern British Political Tradition*, ed. Hilda L. Smith (Cambridge, 1998). A case against a liberal reading of the second *Vindication* is made by Virginia Sapiro in *A Vindication of Political Virtue: The Political Theory of Mary Wollstonecraft* (Chicago, 1992).
62. See her letter to her sister Everina of 22 March 1788 (*Collected Letters*, 173), and her *Analytical* review of her own translation in 1789, *Works*, VII, 60–6.
63. Jacques Necker, *Of the Importance of Religious Opinions. Translated from the French of Mr. Necker* (London, 1788), *Works*, III, 20.
64. Taylor, *Mary Wollstonecraft*, ch. 3.
65. *Ibid.*, 109–10.
66. Isabel Rivers, *Reason, Grace and Sentiment: A Study of the Language of Religion and Ethics in England, 1660–1780* (2 vols.; Cambridge, 1991, 2000), II, 172.
67. *A Vindication*, *Works*, v, 170, 95.

68. Wollstonecraft, *Mary, A Fiction* (1788), *Works*, I, 29. *A Vindication*, *Works*, v, 115.

69. Wollstonecraft, *A Vindication*, *Works*, v, 254.

70. *Ibid.*, v, 255.

71. Richard Price, *A Review of the Principal Questions in Morals*, ed. D. D. Raphael (Oxford, 1948), 109.

72. Wollstonecraft, *A Vindication*, *Works*, v, 254.

73. *Ibid.*, v, 112.

74. *Ibid.*, v, 125.

75. *Ibid.*, v, 127.

76. *Ibid.*, v, 127–8. Rousseau, *Emilius and Sophia*, II, 162.

77. Wollstonecraft, *A Vindication*, *Works*, v, 126.

78. Kaplan, *Sea Changes*, 41.

79. *Ibid.*, 35.

80. The best discussion of this split is Vivien Jones, '"The Tyranny of the Passions": Feminism and Heterosexuality in the Fiction of Wollstonecraft and Hays' in *Political Gender: Texts and Contexts*, ed. Sally Ledger, Josephine McDonagh and Jane Spencer (London, 1994).

81. Wollstonecraft, *A Vindication*, ch. 2. On Fordyce and Gregory, see John Dwyer, *Virtuous Discourse: Sensibility and Community in Late Eighteenth-Century Scotland* (Edinburgh, 1987), ch. 5, and Mary Catherine Moran, 'Between the Savage and the Civil: Dr John Gregory's Natural History of Femininity' in Taylor and Knott, eds., *Women, Gender and Enlightenment*, 8–29.

82. Wollstonecraft, *A Vindication*, *Works*, v, 129.

83. The opposite case – that Wollstonecraft particularly associates corrupt femininity with economic consumption – is advanced by Harriet Guest in her article 'The Dream of a Common Language: Hannah More and Mary Wollstonecraft', *Textual Practice*, 9 (1995), 303–23.

84. Wollstonecraft, *A Vindication*, *Works*, v, 145.

85. *Ibid.*, v, 40.

86. It is clear, from the 'Hints' towards the second part of the *Vindication*, that Wollstonecraft was becoming increasingly interested in the relationship between sexuality and the social mechanisms of restraint. 'In Otaheite [Tahiti]', she remarks, 'love cannot be known, where the obstacles to irritate an undiscriminate appetite, and sublimate the simple sensations of desire till they mount to passion, are never known' (*Works*, v, 271). These remarks are similar to Scottish Enlightenment ideas about primitive sexuality, but also stem from her thoughts about questions of love and desire. See Jane Moore, 'Wollstonecraft's Secrets', *Women's Writing*, 4 (1997), 247–60.

87. This reading is indebted to Claudia L. Johnson's argument that, for Wollstonecraft, 'the problem undermining society in her view is feminized men': *Equivocal Beings: Politics, Gender, and Sentimentality in the 1790s* (Chicago, 1995), 23.

88. Wollstonecraft, *Analytical Review* (1790), *Works*, VII, 240.

89. Wollstonecraft, *Collected Letters*, 231.
90. Jane Rendall, in the most authoritative account of this work, '"The Grand Causes"', lists contemporary reviews, including an extract from the *Historical View* in the *Scots Magazine* entitled 'On the Degeneracy of Morals Incident to Polished Manners, particularly in France'. This title, as Rendall argues, precisely captures Wollstonecraft's philosophical ambitions.
91. Wollstonecraft, *An Historical View*, *Works*, VI, 121, 230. In the context of a different kind of analysis, Tom Furniss writes that 'Wollstonecraft's central strategy is to identify the feminine with the *ancien régime* and the masculine with bourgeois radicalism'. *Edmund Burke's Aesthetic Ideology* (Cambridge, 1993), 191. On Wollstonecraft, gender and revolution, see Todd, *Mary Wollstonecraft*, 211–20.
92. Wollstonecraft, *Collected Letters*, 218.
93. Wollstonecraft, *Works*, VI, 444.
94. Kelly, *Revolutionary Feminism*, 147.
95. Wollstonecraft, *Works*, VI, 444.
96. *Ibid.*, VI, 445.
97. Wollstonecraft, *Collected Letters*, 257.
98. See Hedva Ben-Israel, *English Historians on the French Revolution* (Cambridge, 1968), 17. Steven Blakemore argues that Wollstonecraft only comes close to 'criticizing the revolutionary idea' when she 'mocks the vainglorious French for trying to implement a radical idea too quickly': *Crisis in Representation: Thomas Paine, Mary Wollstonecraft, Helen Maria Williams, and the Rewriting of the French Revolution* (Madison, Wisconsin, 1997), 141. By contrast, Harriet D. Jump observes that 'it becomes difficult to see why twentieth-century commentators have described Wollstonecraft's attitude [to the Revolution] as optimistic', in her article '"The Cool Eye of Observation": Mary Wollstonecraft and the French Revolution' in *Revolution in Writing: British Literary Responses to the French Revolution*, ed. Kelvin Everest (Milton Keynes, 1991), 114. Jane Rendall concurs that the *Historical View* is essentially a history of failure ('"The Grand Causes"', 165). Gary Kelly suggests that 'her argument posits . . . a "good" if misguided Revolution of 1789 to 1792, a "bad" Revolution of 1793 to the time of her writing, and a restoration of the "good" Revolution in the future' (*Revolutionary Feminism*, 154).
99. The review appeared in *The British Critic*, 6 (1794), 29–36. *The New Annual Register* account was printed separately as *An Impartial History of the Late Revolution in France* (2 vols.; London, 1794), and remained one of the fullest and most popular contemporary histories of the Revolution.
100. James Mackintosh, *An Historical Sketch of the French Revolution from its Commencement to the Year 1792* (London, 1792), 244–5. The work was reviewed by Wollstonecraft for the *Analytical*; see *Works*, VII, 425–30. J. P. Rabaut Sainte-Etienne, *Précis historique de la Révolution française* (Paris, 1792). Among the British historians of the early 1790s, Wollstonecraft and John Gifford (J. R. Green) are among the few to blame the duke for inciting

the march on Versailles: See Gifford, *The Reign of Louis XIV; and Complete History of the French Revolution* (London, 1794), 402. Some of Wollstonecraft's primary sources are discussed by Janet Todd in the introduction to her facsimile edition of the *Historical View* (New York, 1975).

101. Thomas Christie, *Letters on the Revolution of France, and on the New Constitution Established by the National Assembly* (London, 1791), 64.

102. F. M. de Kerverseau, G. Clavelin *et al.*, *Histoire de la Revolution de 1789, et de l'établissement d'une constitution en France* (7 vols.; Paris, 1790). She may also have read John Talbot Dillon, *Historical and Critical Memoirs of the General Revolution in France In the Year 1789* (London, 1790) (a liberal, constitutional account), and Henry Frederic Groenvelt, *Letters containing an account of the Late Revolution in France* (London, 1792) (contains an eye-witness account of the storming of the Bastille).

103. Wollstonecraft, *An Historical View, Works*, VI, 111.

104. *Ibid.*, VI, 111.

105. *Ibid.*, VI, 70.

106. *Ibid.*, VI, 123.

107. *Ibid.*, VI, 121.

108. On the relationship of the *Historical View* to this tradition, see Taylor, *Mary Wollstonecraft*, 211–12.

109. Wollstonecraft, *Works*, VI, 227, 44, 226.

110. Vivien Jones gives a persuasive literary reading of the *Historical View* in terms of novelistic paradigms and the violent sublime in 'Women Writing Revolution: Narratives of History and Sexuality in Wollstonecraft and Williams' in *Beyond Romanticism: New Approaches to Texts and Contexts, 1780–1832*, ed. Stephen Copley and John Whale (London, 1992). See also Jones, 'Femininity, Nationalism and Romanticism: The Politics of Gender in the Revolution Controversy', *History of European Ideas*, 16 (1993), 299–305.

111. Wollstonecraft, *An Historical View, Works*, VI, 221, 166.

112. *Ibid.*, VI, 143.

113. *Ibid.*, VI, 209. See Blakemore, *Crisis in Representation*, 133–8, and Jones's analysis in 'Women Writing Revolution', of the way in which Enlightenment history, Gothic narrative and the 'sexual plot' of the Duc d'Orléans converge at this point.

114. Wollstonecraft, review dated 1791, *Works*, VII, 375.

115. *Ibid.*, VII, 376. Wollstonecraft also reviewed the first history of the American Revolution by Thomas Gordon (as she states on p. 376 of this review). The review is omitted from Todd and Butler's edition. For a detailed discussion of Ramsay's history, see my *Narratives of Enlightenment: Cosmopolitan History from Voltaire to Gibbon* (Cambridge, 1997), ch. 7.

116. Gilbert Imlay, *A Topographical Description of the Western Territory of North America* (London, 1792), 1.

117. *Ibid.*, 40.

118. Wollstonecraft, review of 1791, *Works*, VII, 391.

119. Wollstonecraft, *An Historical View, Works*, VI, 20.
120. *Ibid.*, VI, 20.
121. Reprinted by Penelope J. Corfield in 'The Case of *The Cabinet*: Did Mary Wollstonecraft join the Norwich Radicals?', *The Times Literary Supplement* (21 March 1997), 11–12.
122. Mary Wollstonecraft, *Letters Written During a Short Residence in Sweden, Norway, and Denmark* (1796), *Works*, VI, 346.
123. *Ibid.*, VI, 248.
124. *Ibid.*, VI, 250–1.
125. *Ibid.*, VI, 309.
126. See Olympe de Gouges, *Déclaration des droits de la femme et de la citoyenne* (1791) in *The French Revolution and Human Rights: A Brief Documentary History*, ed. Lynn Hunt (New York, 1996), 124–9. Also Joan Wallach Scott, *Only Paradoxes to Offer: French Feminists and the Rights of Man* (Cambridge, Massachusetts, 1996).
127. See Todd, *Mary Wollstonecraft*, 210. Condorcet, 'Sur l'admission des femmes au droit du cité' in Hunt, ed., *The French Revolution and Human Rights*, 119–21.
128. Marie-Jean-Antoine-Nicolas Caritat de Condorcet, *Outlines of an Historical View of the Progress of the Human Mind* (London, 1795), 178.
129. *Ibid.*, 24, 45, 176.

CHAPTER 6   THE HISTORY WOMEN AND THE POPULATION MEN, 1760–1830

1. Lucy Aikin, *Epistles on Women, Exemplifying their Character and Condition in Various Ages and Nations* (London, 1810), vii, v. According to the new *Dictionary of National Biography*, Aikin also projected a work on the social history of women in the eighteenth century, but this was never completed. The case for Aikin's *Epistles* as a kind of Enlightenment history is made more fully by Kathryn Ready, who also supplies details of Aikin's personal ties to Edinburgh intellectual circles, in 'The Enlightenment Feminist Project of Lucy Aikin's Epistles on Women', *History of European Ideas*, 31 (2005), 435–50.
2. Aikin, *Epistles*, 4, lines 91–2.
3. *Ibid.*, 4, lines 179–80, lines 452–3.
4. Thomas Babington Macaulay, review of Henry Neele, *The Romance of History* (1828) in *Miscellaneous Writings and Speeches* (London, 1882), 157.
5. Mark Salber Phillips, *Society and Sentiment: Genres of Historical Writing in Britain, 1740–1820* (Princeton, 2000), especially 344–7.
6. See the illuminating study by Miriam Elizabeth Burstein, *Narrating Women's History in Britain, 1770–1902* (Aldershot, 2004), 54. On women historians of this period, see also Joan Thirsk's pioneering, 'The History Women' in *Chattel, Servant or Citizen: Women's Status in Church, State and Society*, ed. M. O'Dowd and S. Wichert (Belfast, 1995) and Natalie Zemon

Davis, 'Gender and Genre: Women as Historical Writers' in *Beyond their Sex: Learned Women of the European Past*, ed. Patricia H. Labalme (New York, 1980). Also Bonnie Smith, *The Gender of History: Men, Women and Historical Practice* (Cambridge, Massachusetts, 1998), Devoney Looser, *British Women Writers and the Writing of History, 1670–1820* (Baltimore, 2000), Mary Spongberg, *Writing Women's History Since the Renaissance* (Basingstoke, 2002) and Greg Kucich, 'Women's Historiography and the (dis)Embodiment of Law: Ann Yearsley, Mary Hays, Elizabeth Benger', *Wordsworth Circle*, 33 (2002), 3–6. For a good account of Victorian women historians that makes connections between them and some of their predecessors discussed in this chapter, see Rohan Amanda Maitzen, *Gender, Genre, and Victorian Historical Writing* (New York and London, 1998). Also valuable is Rosemary Mitchell, '"The Busy Daughters of Clio": Women Writers of History from 1820 to 1880', *Women's History Review*, 7 (1998), 107–34 and a version of this article in *Picturing the Past: English History in Text and Image 1830–70* (Oxford, 2000). For comparison, the best discussion of French women historians in this period is Carla Hesse, *The Other Enlightenment: How French Women Became Modern* (Princeton, 2001).

7. See Jane Rendall, '"Women that would plague me with rational conversation": Aspiring Women and Scottish Whigs, *c.* 1790–1830' in *Women, Gender and Enlightenment*, ed. Barbara Taylor and Sarah Knott (Basingstoke, 2005), 334.

8. See Jane Rendall, 'Adaptations: Gender, History, and Political Economy in the Works of Dugald Stewart and Elizabeth Hamilton' in *The Science of Man in the Scottish Enlightenment*, ed. Thomas Ahnert (Cambridge, 2007); *Practical Education: by Maria Edgeworth … and by Richard Lovell Edgeworth* (2 vols.; London, 1798), I, 345. On Edgeworth and Stewart, see Clíona Ò Gallchoir, *Maria Edgeworth: Women, Enlightenment and Nation* (Dublin, 2005), 32.

9. Anna Laetitia Barbauld, *A Legacy for Young Ladies, consisting of Miscellaneous Pieces in Prose and Verse by the late Mrs Barbauld* (London, 1826), 125.

10. *Ibid.*, 130.

11. See Daniel E. White, '"With Mrs Barbauld it is different": Dissenting Heritage and the Devotional Taste' in Taylor and Knott, eds., *Women, Gender and Enlightenment*, 482.

12. *Ibid.*, 483–5.

13. See Harriet Guest, *Small Change: Women, Learning, Patriotism, 1750–1810* (Chicago, 2000), 234–5.

14. Hester Chapone, *Letters on the Improvement of the Mind* in *Bluestocking Feminism: Writings of the Bluestocking Circle, 1738–1785*, ed. Gary Kelly *et al.* (6 vols.; London, 1999), III, 348, 351.

15. *Ibid.*, 186. On women as readers of history, see D. W. Woolf, 'A Feminine Past? Gender, Genre, and Historical Knowledge in England, 1500–1800', *American Historical Review*, 102 (1997), 645–79.

16. Charlotte Cowley, *The Ladies History of England; from the Descent of Julius Caesar, to the Summer of 1780. Calculated for the Use of the Ladies of Great-Britain and Ireland* (London, 1780), i, 508. This is a handsome folio volume, published by subscription. Many of the subscribers were women, including a number of school mistresses.

17. Mary Hays, *Female Biography; or, Memoirs of Illustrious and Celebrated Women, of all Ages and Countries* (6 vols.; London, 1803), v, 292.

18. The best discussion of Scott's histories so far is Betty A. Schellenberg, *The Professionalization of Women Writers in Eighteenth-Century Britain* (Cambridge, 2005), ch. 3. Alessa Johns in *Women's Utopias of the Eighteenth Century* (Urbana and Chicago, 2003), 96–101, usefully links these works to Scott's fiction.

19. Schellenberg, *Women Writers*, 81, 90.

20. Henry Augustus Raymond [Sarah Scott], *The History of Gustavus Ericson, King of Sweden, with An Introductory History of Sweden from the Middle of the Twelfth Century* (London, 1761), viii–ix.

21. *Ibid.*, 210–11, 216.

22. See Voltaire, *Histoire de L'Empire de Russie sous Pierre le Grand* (Geneva, 1759–63). On Gustav's realistic approach to reform, see Scott, *The History of Gustavus Ericson*, 247, 267.

23. See Clarissa Campbell Orr, *Queenship in Britain, 1660–1837* (Manchester, 2002), 236.

24. For example, *The History of Mecklenburgh, from the First Settlement of the Vandals in that Country to the Present Time* (London, 1762), 358.

25. [Sarah Scott], *The Life of Theodore-Agrippa D'Aubigné, containing a succinct account of the most remarkable occurrences during the Civil Wars of France in the reigns of Charles IX. Henry III. Henry IV. And in the Minority of Lewis XIII* (London, 1772), viii. The subject may have been suggested by the sixteenth dialogue of Lyttelton's *Dialogues of the Dead* (1760) in which the widow of the sixteenth-century Huguenot hero Admiral de Coligni talks about the glory of her life lived for the Protestant cause.

26. Jean Dumont ed., *Mémoires de la vie de Théodore-Agrippa D'Aubigné* (Amsterdam, 1731).

27. Letter of 23 October 1757, *The Letters of Mrs. Elizabeth Montagu*, ed. Matthew Montagu (4 vols.; London, 1809–13), IV, 66–7.

28. Sarah Fielding, *The Lives of Cleopatra and Octavia*, ed. R. Brimley Johnson (London, 1928), xliii. The original edition was stated to be 'By the Author of David Simple'.

29. E. Cornelia Knight, *Marcus Flaminius: Or, A View of the Military, Political, and Social Life of the Romans: in A Series of Letters from a Patrician to his Friend* (2 vols.; London, 1792), i, 34–5. This work was dedicated to Horace Walpole.

30. *Ibid.*, i, 147.

31. *Ibid.*, i, 28.

32. Karen O'Brien, 'History and the Novel in Eighteenth-Century Britain', *Huntington Library Quarterly*, 68 (2005), 397–414.

33. Mary Hays, *Historical Dialogues for Young Persons* (3 vols.; London, 1806–8) quoted and discussed in Gary Kelly, *Women, Writing and Revolution, 1790–1827* (Oxford, 1993), 250.

34. Phillips, *Society and Sentiment*, 146.

35. See *The Gentleman's Magazine*, 49 (1779), 258–9 and 360–1.

36. Susannah Dobson, Preface to Sainte-Palaye, *The Literary History of the Troubadours. Containing their Lives, Extracts from their Work, And Many particulars relating to the . . . Twelfth and Thirteenth Centuries* (London, 1779), xii.

37. *Ibid.*, xxiv.

38. *Ibid.*, viii.

39. W. J. Bate and A. B. Strauss eds., *The Rambler* (3 vols.; New Haven, 1969), I, 319.

40. See Phillips, *Society and Sentiment*, ch. 4 ('History, the Novel and the Sentimental Reader').

41. Elizabeth Benger, *Memoirs of the late Mrs. Elizabeth Hamilton. With a Selection from her Correspondence, and other Unpublished Writings* (2 vols.; London, 1818), I, 1–2.

42. Julius Hutchinson ed., *Memoirs of the Life of Colonel Hutchinson . . . Written by His Widow Lucy. Published from the MS by Rev. Julius Hutchinson to which is prefixed The Life of Mrs. Hutchinson, Written by Herself* (London, 1806), i.

43. *Ibid.*, iv–v.

44. *Ibid.*, xi.

45. *Ibid.*, xiii, xii.

46. Francis Jeffrey, review of 'Memoirs of the Life of Colonel Hutchinson', *Edinburgh Review*, 13.25 (October 1808), 4. Aikin, *Epistles on Women*, 4, line 403.

47. Mary Berry, *A Comparative View of the Social Life of England and France, from the Restoration of Charles the Second to the French Revolution* (London, 1828), 41.

48. Mrs John [Elizabeth] Sandford, *Lives of the English Female Worthies* (London, 1833), xiv. This work, containing biographical sketches of Hutchinson and Grey, was the first and only volume of four originally projected.

49. On Macaulay and Russell, see Claire Brock, *The Feminization of Fame, 1750–1830* (Basingstoke, 2006), 61. Aikin, *Epistles on Women*, 4, line 413 and, in general, 4, lines 412–27.

50. [Mary Berry], *Some Account of The Life of Rachael Wriothesley, Lady Russell . . . followed by . . . letters from Lady Russell to her husband, William Lord Russell from 1672–1682* (London, 1819), c. An earlier edition of the *Letters of Lady Rachel Russell* (London, 1773) to other correspondents was designed mainly to vindicate her husband's reputation against the charge of taking bribes from Louis XIV.

51. Berry, *Some Account of . . . Lady Russell*, xx.
52. J. W. Burrow, *A Liberal Descent: Victorian Historians and the English Past* (Cambridge, 1981), 12–13.
53. Berry, *A Comparative View*, i.
54. *Ibid.*, 105–6.
55. *Ibid.*, 99.
56. [Mary Berry], *Social Life in England and France, from the French Revolution in 1789 to that of July 1830* (London, 1831), 9.
57. Berry, *A Comparative View*, 404, 402.
58. Hannah Lawrance, *The History of Women in England* (London, 1843), vi, 365. This goes up to 1200 and is styled 'volume 1' although only one volume ever appeared.
59. Mitchell, *Picturing the Past*, 169.
60. Stella Tillyard, *Aristocrats: Caroline, Emily, Louisa and Sarah Lennox, 1740–1832* (London, 1994) and *A Royal Affair: George III and his Troublesome Siblings* (London, 2006). Tillyard, 'All Our Pasts: The Rise of Popular History', *The Times Literary Supplement*, 5402 (13 October 2006), 8, 7.
61. Lucy Aikin, *Memoirs of the Court of Queen Elizabeth* (2 vols.; London, 1818), II, 104.
62. *Ibid.*, I, 350.
63. *Ibid.*, I, 451.
64. *Ibid.*, I, vii–viii.
65. *Ibid.*, I, iv.
66. Quoted by Kelly in *Women, Writing and Revolution*, 250. Charlotte Smith and Mary Hays, *The History of England, from the Earliest Records to the Peace of Amiens. In a Series of Letters to a Young Lady at School* (3 vols.; London, 1806).
67. Aikin's 'Memoir of Mrs Benger' is prefixed to the third (1827) edition of Elizabeth Benger's *Memoirs of the Life of Anne Boleyn, Queen of Henry VIII* (2 vols.; London, 1821).
68. See Cynthia Lawford, 'Turbans, Tea and Talk of Books: The Literary Parties of Elizabeth Spence and Elizabeth Benger', *Corvey Women Writers Journal* (2004) [www2.shu.ac.uk/corvey/cw3journal].
69. Benger, *Memoirs of the Life of Anne Boleyn*, I, 1.
70. Elizabeth Benger, *Memoirs of the Life of Mary Queen of Scots, with Anecdotes of the Court of Henry II* (2 vols.; second edn, London, 1823), I, 39.
71. *Ibid.*, I, 56.
72. *Ibid.*, I, v.
73. *Ibid.*, II, 126–7.
74. *Ibid.*, II, 204–5.
75. *Ibid.*, II, 49.
76. Jane Austen, 'The History of England from the reign of Henry the 4th to the death of Charles the 1st' (1791) in *The Works of Jane Austen*, ed. R. W. Chapman (6 vols.; third edn, Oxford, 1954), VI, 149, 145. On Victorian

treatments of Mary and Elizabeth, see Maitzen, *Gender, Genre and Victorian Historical Writing*, ch. 6.

77. Hester Lynch Piozzi, *Retrospection, or A Review of the Most Striking and Important Events, Characters, Situations, and Their Consequences, Which the Last Eighteen Hundred years have Presented to the View of Mankind* (2 vols.; London, 1801).

78. Jane Austen, *Northanger Abbey*, 110 in *The Cambridge Edition of the Works of Jane Austen*, ed. Janet Todd *et al.* (9 vols.; Cambridge, 2006).

79. Peter Knox-Shaw, *Jane Austen and the Enlightenment* (Cambridge, 2004), 115–24.

80. *Ibid.*, 222, 8. This must be qualified by Austen's apparent admiration for Thomas Gisborne, a highly effective Evangelical opponent of the most influential late eighteenth-century Latitudinarian, William Paley: Jane Austen, *Letters*, ed. Deirdre Le Faye (Oxford, 1995), 112. Knox-Shaw acknowledges this, while overstating, in my view, the compatibility of Evangelicalism and the Enlightenment: *Jane Austen and The Enlightenment*, 160–6.

81. Knox-Shaw, *Jane Austen and the Enlightenment*, 19–21.

82. *Ibid.*, 160.

83. On Malthus-inspired 'Evangelical economics', see Boyd Hilton, *The Age of Atonement: The Influence of Evangelicalism on Social and Economic Thought, 1795–1865* (Oxford, 1988), 69–70. On the vexed question of Austen and Evangelicalism, see especially Vivien Jones, 'Reading for England: Austen, Taste, and Female Patriotism', *European Romantic Review*, 16 (2005), 221–30.

84. T. R. Malthus, *An Essay on the Principle of Population*, ed. Donald Winch (Cambridge, 1992), 212.

85. Boyd Hilton, *A Mad, Bad, and Dangerous People? England 1783–1846* (Oxford, 2006), 30.

86. Donald Winch, *Riches and Poverty: An Intellectual History of Political Economy in Britain, 1750–1834* (Cambridge, 1996), 237–8.

87. T. R. Malthus, *An Essay on the Principle of Population* (1798), ed. Philip Appleman (New York, second edn, 2004), 19.

88. *Ibid.*, 27.

89. *Ibid.*, 24.

90. *Ibid.*, 28, 30.

91. *Ibid.*, 23, 71.

92. See Sylvana Tomaselli, 'Moral Philosophy and Population Questions in Eighteenth-Century Europe', *Population and Development Review*, 14, supplement: *Population and Resources in Western Intellectual Traditions* (1988), 7–29 and Charles Emil Stangeland, *Pre-Malthusian Doctrines of Population: A Study in the History of Economic Theory* (New York, 1904).

93. Richard Price, *An Essay on the Population of England, From the Revolution to the Present Time* (London, second edn corrected, 1780), 28.

94. Adam Smith, *An Inquiry into the Nature and Causes of the Wealth of Nations*, ed. R. H. Campbell and A. S. Skinner (2 vols.; Oxford, 1976), I, 97. Henry Home Kames, *Sketches of the History of Man* (4 vols.; Edinburgh, 1788), I, 113.
95. William Paley, *Principles of Moral and Political Philosophy: The Second Edition Corrected* (London, 1786), 596.
96. *Ibid.*, 292–3.
97. *Ibid.*, 293.
98. Malthus, *Essay*, ed. Winch, 223.
99. Paley, *Principles*, 587.
100. Malthus, *Essay*, ed. Winch, 273.
101. *Ibid.*, 218.
102. *Ibid.*, 242.
103. See Winch, *Riches and Poverty*, 243–4.
104. Malthus, *Essay*, ed. Winch, 212.
105. *Ibid.*, 212.
106. *Ibid.*, 331.
107. See Winch, *Riches and Poverty*, 278.
108. For an illuminating discussion of this, see Josephine McDonagh, *Child Murder and British Culture, 1720–1900* (Cambridge, 2003). On population theories and later women writers, see the excellent study by Angelique Richardson, *Love and Eugenics in the Late Nineteenth Century: Rational Reproduction and the New Woman* (Oxford, 2003).
109. In *The Novels and Selected Works of Maria Edgeworth*, ed. Marilyn Butler *et al.* (12 vols.; London, 1999, 2003), vol. XII, ed. Elizabeth Eger, Marilyn Butler and Clíona Ò Gallchoir. The editors cite Smith's *Wealth of Nations* as 'the single most important written source' for the *Tales* (viii). Edgeworth also knew David Ricardo the economist, and his sister Sarah Ricardo Porter, herself a notable educational theorist and novelist.
110. Maria Edgeworth, 'Memoir of Mrs. Elizabeth Hamilton', *Monthly Magazine*, 42, part ii (1816).
111. *Lectures on Political Economy* in *The Collected Works of Dugald Stewart*, ed. Sir William Hamilton (11 vols.; 1854–60, reprinted Bristol, 1994), VIII, 207.
112. *Ibid.*, VIII, 74–6.
113. *Ibid.*, VIII, 81.
114. *Ibid.*, VIII, xx. On Stewart and women's education, see Jane Rendall, 'Bluestockings and Reviewers: Gender, Power, and Culture in Britain, *c.* 1800–1830', *Nineteenth-Century Contexts*, 26 (2004), 1–20.
115. Dugald Stewart, 'Of Man's Free Agency' in *Outlines of Moral Philosophy. For the Use of Students at Edinburgh University* (Edinburgh, 1793), 148–51.
116. According to the New Oxford *DNB* entry.
117. John Veitch, 'Memoir of Dugald Stewart' in *Collected Works*, ed. Hamilton, x, pp. i–lxxxix.
118. Letter of 9 March 1822 quoted in Bette Polkinghorn and Dorothy Lampen Thomson, *Adam Smith's Daughters: Eight Prominent Women Economists*

from the Eighteenth Century to the Present (Cheltenham, revised edn, 1998), 11. In 1803, Edgeworth wrote from Scotland to her aunt, 'I have not heard him [Stewart] lecture; no woman can go to the public lectures here, and I don't choose to go in men's or boy's clothes.' Quoted in G. Macintyre, *Dugald Stewart: The Pride and Ornament of Scotland* (Sussex Academic Press, 2003), 117.

119. See Josephine McDonagh, 'Barbauld's Domestic Economy', *Essays and Studies*, 51 (1998), 62–77, especially 68. Malthus had studied at the Warrington Academy, where Barbauld's father taught, and, though not a Unitarian, he remained close to the family.

120. On Marcet's life and her career as a highly successful populariser of science and educationalist, see Bette Polkinghorn, *Jane Marcet: An Uncommon Woman* (Aldermaston, 1993).

121. [Jane Marcet], *Conversations on Political Economy; in which the elements of that science are familiarly explained* (London, 1816), 12, 14, 10. The work reached its seventh, enlarged edition by 1839.

122. Polkinghorn and Thomson, *Adam Smith's Daughters*, 11.

123. Marcet, *Conversations*, 140–1. On Marcet and 'Wages Fund' theory, see J. R. Shackleton, 'Jane Marcet and Harriet Martineau: Pioneers of Economics Education', *History of Education*, 19 (1990), 283–97.

124. Marcet, *Conversations*, 142, 158.

125. *Ibid.*, 163.

126. See Shelagh Hunter, *Harriet Martineau: The Poetics of Moralism* (Aldershot, 1995), 44–6.

127. Priscilla Wakefield, *Reflections on the Present Condition of the Female Sex; with Suggestions for its Improvement* (London, 1798), 8. The work was printed by Wollstonecraft's publisher, Joseph Johnson.

128. *Ibid.*, 150–1.

129. *Ibid.*, 182.

130. *Ibid.*, 95.

131. *Ibid.*, 113.

132. *Ibid.* For a useful introduction to early nineteenth-century debate about women and employment, see Kathryn Gleadle, *Radical Writing on Women, 1800–1850: An Anthology* (Basingstoke, 2002), 77–95.

133. On More generally see Anne Stott, *Hannah More: The First Victorian* (Oxford, 2003).

134. Hannah More, *Strictures on the Modern System of Female Education* (2 vols.; London, 1799), I, 2.

135. See Guest, *Small Change*, 271–89.

136. Anne K. Mellor, 'Hannah More, Revolutionary Reformer' in *Mothers of the Nation: Women's Political Writing in England, 1780–1830* (Bloomington, Indiana, 2002), 13–38. Also very useful in this context is Kathryn Sutherland, 'Hannah More's Counter-Revolutionary Feminism', in *Revolution in Writing: British Literary Responses to the French Revolution*, ed. Kelvin Everest (Milton Keynes, 1991).

137. Gleadle, *Radical Writing on Women*, 13.
138. Hannah More, *Essays on Various Subjects, Principally designed for Young Ladies* (London, 1777), 167. The work went into five editions by 1791. Anne Stott sees this as a work in which More started to distance herself from Bluestocking ideas: *Hannah More*, 36–7.
139. [More], *An Estimate of the Religion of the Fashionable world. By one of the laity* (London, 1791), 31.
140. *Ibid.*, 208, 211, 19.
141. *Ibid.*, ch. 7.
142. *Ibid.*, 42, 45.
143. *Extracts from the Journals and Correspondence of Miss Berry from the Years 1783–1852*, ed. Lady Theresa Lewis (3 vols.; London, 1865), II, 92–3, quoted by Anne Stott, *Hannah More*, 227.
144. Stott, *Hannah More*, 305.
145. As the current Archbishop of Canterbury reminded his audience during his Wilberforce Lecture Trust address (24 April 2007) on the 200th anniversary of the abolition of the slave trade, it was the Christian Evangelical belief in the equality of souls, and not the Enlightenment belief in progress, that motivated the campaign: 'Freedom and Slavery', www.archbishopofcanter bury.org/sermons-speeches.
146. For this reading of More, see Angela Keane, *Women Writers and the English Nation in the 1790s* (Cambridge, 2005), ch. 6.
147. De Staël, *Lettres sur les écrits et le caractère de J. J. Rousseau* (Paris, 1820), 19.
148. See the section 'Analysing Woman's Position' in Gleadle, *Radical Writing on Women*, 26–41.
149. Henry Thomas Buckle, 'The Influence of Women on the Progress of Knowledge', *Fraser's Magazine*, 57.340 (April 1758), 407.
150. *The Subjection of Women* in *The Collected Works of John Stuart Mill*, ed. J. M. Robson (33 vols.; Toronto, 1963–91), XXI, 10–11.

Bibliography

PRIMARY SOURCES

Aikin, Lucy, *Epistles on Women, Exemplifying their Character and Condition in Various Ages and Nations* (London, 1810)
Memoirs of the Court of Queen Elizabeth (2 vols.; London, 1818)
Alexander, William, *The History of Women, from the Earliest Antiquity to the Present Time* (2 vols.; London, 1779)
Astell, Mary, *A Serious Proposal to the Ladies, Part II: Wherein a Method is offer'd for the Improvement of their Minds* (London, 1697)
The Christian Religion, As Profess'd by a Daughter of the Church of England (London, 1705)
Political Writings, ed. Patricia Springborg (Cambridge, 1996)
Astell, Mary and John Norris, *Letters Concerning the Love of God*, ed. E. Derek Taylor and Melvyn New (Aldershot, 2005)
Austen, Jane, *The Cambridge Edition of the Works of Jane Austen*, ed. Janet Todd *et al.* (9 vols.; Cambridge, 2006)
Barbauld, Anna Laetitia, *A Legacy for Young Ladies, consisting of Miscellaneous Pieces in Prose and Verse by the late Mrs Barbauld* (London, 1826)
Beattie, James, *Dissertations Moral and Critical* (London, 1783)
Elements of Moral Science (2 vols.; Edinburgh, 1790, 1793)
Benger, Elizabeth, *Memoirs of the late Mrs. Elizabeth Hamilton. With a Selection from her Correspondence, and other Unpublished Writings* (2 vols.; London, 1818)
Memoirs of the Life of Anne Boleyn, Queen of Henry VIII (2 vols.; London, 1821)
Memoirs of the Life of Mary Queen of Scots, with Anecdotes of the Court of Henry II (2 vols.; second edn, London, 1823)
Berry, Mary, *Some Account of The Life of Rachael Wriothesley, Lady Russell . . . followed by . . . letters from Lady Russell to her husband, William Lord Russell from 1672–1682* (London, 1819)
A Comparative View of the Social Life of England and France, from the Restoration of Charles the Second to the French Revolution (London, 1828)
Social Life in England and France, from the French Revolution in 1789 to that of July 1830 (London, 1831)

Extracts from the Journals and Correspondence of Miss Berry from the Years 1783–1852, ed. Lady Theresa Lewis (3 vols.; London, 1865)

Bever, Thomas, *The History of the Legal Polity of the Roman State; and of the Rise, Progress, and Extent of the Roman Laws* (London, 1781)

Blackwell, Thomas, *Memoirs of the Court of Augustus* (3 vols.; Edinburgh and London, 1753–63)

Brooke, Frances, *Virginia, A Tragedy, with Odes, Pastorals and Translations* (London, 1756)

Buffon, Georges Louis Le Clerc comte de, *Natural History, General and Particular by the Count de Buffon*, trans. William Smellie (9 vols.; Edinburgh, 1780)

Burke, Edmund, *Reflections on the Revolution in France, and on the Proceedings of Certain Societies in London Relative to that Event* (1790) in *The Writings and Speeches of Edmund Burke*, volume VIII, ed. L. G. Mitchell (Oxford, 1989)

Burnet, Elizabeth, *A Method of Devotion: or, Rules for Holy and Devout Living* (second edn; London, 1709)

Burnet, Gilbert, *Bishop Burnet's History of His Own Time* (2 vols.; London, 1724, 1734)

Butler, Joseph, *Fifteen Sermons Preached at the Rolls Chapel* (London, 1726)
  Analogy of Religion, Natural and Revealed, to the Constitution and Course of Nature (London, 1736)

Carte, Thomas, *A General History of England* (4 vols.; London, 1747–55)

Carter, Elizabeth, *Remarks on the Athanasian Creed; on a Sermon Preached at the Parish Church of Deal, October 15, 1752* (London, n.d., probably 1753) (Carter is the probable author of this)
  A Series of Letters between Mrs. Elizabeth Carter and Miss Catharine Talbot, From the Year 1741 to 1770, ed. Montagu Pennington (2 vols.; London, 1809)
  Letters from Mrs. Elizabeth Carter, to Mrs. Montagu, Between the Years 1755 and 1800, ed. Montagu Pennington (3 vols.; London, 1817)

Christie, Thomas, *Letters on the Revolution of France, and on the New Constitution Established by the National Assembly* (London, 1791)

Chudleigh, Mary Lady, *The Poems and Prose of Mary, Lady Chudleigh*, ed. Margaret J. M. Ezell (Oxford, 1993)

Clarke, Samuel, *A Demonstration of the Being and Attributes of God* (London, 1705)
  A Discourse concerning the Unchangeable Obligations of Natural Religion (London, 1706)
  The Scripture–Doctrine of the Trinity (London, 1712)

Cluverius, Philippus, *Germaniae Antiquae Libri Tres* (Lugduni Batavorum, 1616)

Cockburn, Catharine, *A Discourse concerning a Guide in Controversies in Two Letters written to One of the Church of Rome* (London, 1707)
  A Letter to Dr. Holdsworth, occasioned by his sermon preached before the University of Oxford (London, 1726)
  The Works of Mrs. Catharine Cockburn (2 vols.; London, 1751)

Condorcet, Marie-Jean-Antoine-Nicolas Caritat de, *Outlines of an Historical View of the Progress of the Human Mind* (London, 1795)

Cowley, Charlotte, *The Ladies History of England; from the Descent of Julius Caesar, to the Summer of 1780. Calculated for the Use of the Ladies of Great-Britain and Ireland* (London, 1780)

Crisp, Samuel, *Virginia, A Tragedy* (London, 1754)

Dennis, John, *Appius and Virginia, A Tragedy* (London, 1709)

Dobson, Susannah, *Historical Anecdotes of Heraldry and Chivalry. Tending to Shew the Origin of Many English and Foreign Coats of Arms, Circumstances and Customs* (Worcester, 1795)

Drake, Judith, *An Essay in Defence of the Female Sex . . . In Letter to a Lady . . . Written by a Lady* (London, 1696)

Dunbar, James, *Essays on the History of Mankind in Rude and Cultivated Ages* (London, 1780)

Echard, Laurence, *The Roman History, from the building of the City, to the perfect settlement of the Empire by Augustus Caesar* (London, 1695)

Edgeworth, Maria and Richard Lovell Edgeworth, *Practical Education* (2 vols.; London, 1798)

    The Novels and Selected Works of Maria Edgeworth, eds. Marilyn Butler *et al.* (12 vols.; London, 1999, 2003)

Ferguson, Adam, *The History of the Progress and Termination of the Roman Republic* (3 vols.; London, 1783)

    An Essay on the History of Civil Society, ed. Fania Oz-Salzberger (Cambridge, 1995)

Fielding, Sarah, *The Lives of Cleopatra and Octavia*, ed. R. Brimley Johnson (London, 1928)

Forbes, Sir William, *An Account of the Life and Writings of James Beattie* (second edn, 3 vols.; Edinburgh, 1807)

Gibbon, Edward, *The English Essays of Edward Gibbon*, ed. Patricia B. Craddock (Oxford, 1972)

    The History of the Decline and Fall of the Roman Empire, ed. David Womersley (3 vols.; Harmondsworth, 1994)

Gibson, Edmund ed., *Camden's Britannia. Britain, or a Chorographicall description of . . . England, Scotland and Ireland* (London, 1695)

Godwin, William, *Memoirs of the Author of a Vindication of the Rights of Woman*, ed. Pamela Clemit and Gina Luria Walker (Petersboroug, Ontario, 2001)

Goldsmith, Oliver, *The Roman History, from the Foundation of the City of Rome, To the Destruction of the Western Empire* (2 vols.; London, 1769)

Gordon, Thomas trans., *The Works of Tacitus* (2 vols.; London, 1728–31)

Grotius, Hugo ed., *Historia Gotthorum, Vandalorum et Langobardorum* (Amsterdam, 1655)

Hamilton, Elizabeth, *Memoirs of the Life of Agrippina, the Wife of Germanicus* (3 vols.; Bath, 1804)

Hartley, David, *Hartley's Theory of the Human Mind, on the Principle of the Association of Ideas*, ed. Joseph Priestley (London, 1775)

Observations on Man, His Frame, His Duty and His Expectations, with an introduction by David Hartley (London, 1791)

Observations on Man, ed. Theodore Huguelet (2 vols.; Gainsville, Florida, 1966)

Hays, Mary, *Female Biography; or, Memoirs of Illustrious and Celebrated Women, of all Ages and Countries* (6 vols.; London, 1803)

Historical Dialogues for Young Persons (3 vols.; London, 1806–8)

Henry, Robert, *The History of Great Britain, From the First Invasion of it by the Romans under Julius Caesar* (6 vols.; London and Edinburgh, 1771–93)

Hume, David, *The History of England* (6 vols.; Edinburgh and London, 1754–62)

Enquiries concerning Human Understanding and concerning the Principles of Morals, ed. L. A. Selby-Bigge, third edn revised by P. H. Nidditch (Oxford, 1975)

A Treatise of Human Nature (1739–40), ed. Ernest C. Mossner (Harmondsworth, 1984)

Essays, Moral and Political and Literary, ed. Eugene F. Miller (Indianapolis, 1985)

Hurd, Richard, *Letters on Chivalry and Romance* (London, 1762)

Moral and Political Dialogues (third edn, London, 1765)

Hutcheson, Francis, *An Inquiry into the Original of our Ideas of Beauty and Virtue; in two Treatises* (London, 1725)

An Essay on the Nature and Conduct of the Passions and Affections (London, 1728)

A System of Moral Philosophy, in Three Books (2 vols.; London, 1755)

Hutchinson, Julius ed., *Memoirs of the Life of Colonel Hutchinson . . . Written by His Widow Lucy. Published from the MS by Rev. Julius Hutchinson to which is prefixed The Life of Mrs. Hutchinson, Written by Herself* (London, 1806)

Imlay, Gilbert, *A Topographical Description of the Western Territory of North America* (London, 1792)

Johnson, Samuel, *The Rambler*, ed. W. J. Bate and A. B. Strauss (3 vols.; New Haven, 1969)

Kames, Henry Home, Lord, *Sketches of the History of Man* (2 vols.; Edinburgh, 1774)

Sketches of the History of Man (second edn, 1778), ed. John Valdimir Price (4 vols.; Bristol, 1993)

Kelly, Gary *et al.* eds., *Bluestocking Feminism: Writings of the Bluestocking Circle, 1738–1785* (6 vols.; London, 1999)

Kindersley, Jemima, *Letters from the Island of Teneriffe, Brazil, the Cape of Good Hope, and the East Indies* (London, 1777)

King, Peter ed., *The Life of John Locke* (2 vols.; London, 1830)

Knight, Ellis Cornelia, *Marcus Flaminius: Or, A View of the Military, Political, and Social Life of the Romans: in A Series of Letters from a Patrician to his Friend* (2 vols.; London, 1792)

Lawrance, Hannah, *The History of Women in England* (London, 1843)

Lhuyd, Edward, *Archaeologica Britannica* (Oxford, 1707)

Locke, John, *An Essay Concerning Human Understanding . . . The Fourth Edition, with large Additions* (London, 1700)

An Essay concerning Human Understanding, ed. Peter N. Nidditch (Oxford, 1975)

Some Thoughts Concerning Education, ed. John and Jean S. Yolton (Oxford, 1989)

Political Essays, ed. Mark Goldie (Cambridge, 1997)

Logan, James, *Elements of the Philosophy of History* (Edinburgh, 1781)

Lyttelton, George Baron, *Letters from a Persian to his Friend at Ispahan* (London, 1735)

The History of the Reign of King Henry II. And of the Age in which he lived (4 vols.; London, 1767–71)

Macaulay, Catharine, *The History of England from the Accession of James I to that of the Brunswick Line* (8 vols.; London, 1763–83)

Loose Remarks on Certain Positions to be Found in Mr. Hobbes's 'Philosophical Rudiments of Government and Society', with a Short Sketch of a Democratical Form of Government, In a Letter to Signor Paoli (London, 1767)

The History of England from the Revolution to the Present Time in a Series of Letters to a Friend (Bath, 1778)

A Treatise on the Immutability of Moral Truth (London, 1783)

Observations on the Reflections of the Right Hon. Edmund Burke, on the Revolution in France, In a Letter to the Right Hon. the Earl of Stanhope (London, 1790)

Letters on Education. With Observations on Religious and Metaphysical Subjects, ed. Jonathan Wordsworth (Oxford, 1994)

Mackintosh, James, *An Historical Sketch of the French Revolution from its Commencement to the Year 1792* (London, 1792)

Macpherson, James, *The Poems of Ossian and Related Works*, ed. Howard Gaskill with an introduction by Fiona Stafford (Edinburgh, 1996)

An Introduction to the History of Great Britain and Ireland (London, 1771)

Macpherson, John, *Critical Dissertations on the Origin, Antiquities, Language, Government, Manners, and Religion of the Ancient Caledonians, their Posterity the Picts, and the British and Irish Scots* (London, 1768)

Mallet, Paul-Henri, *Northern Antiquities: or A Description of the Manners, Customs, Religion and Laws of the Ancient Danes, And other Northern Nations*, trans. Thomas Percy (2 vols.; London, 1770)

Malthus, Thomas Robert, *An Essay on the Principle of Population*, ed. Donald Winch (Cambridge, 1992)

An Essay on the Principle of Population (1798), ed. Philip Appleman (New York, second edn, 2004)

Mandeville, Bernard, *The Grumbling Hive: or, Knaves Turn'd Honest* ([London], 1705)

The Virgin Unmask'd: or, Female Dialogues betwixt an elderly maiden lady, and her neice (London, 1709)

The Fable of Bees: or, Private Vices, Publick Benefits (London, 1714)

The Fable of the Bees: or, Private Vices, Publick Benefits. The Second Edition, Enlarged with many Additions (London, 1723)

A Modest Defence of Publick Stews (London, 1724), ed. Richard I. Cook (Augustan Reprint Society, Los Angeles, 1973)

An Enquiry into the Origin of Honour, and the Usefulness of Christianity in War. By the Author of the Fable of the Bees (London, 1732)

Manley, Delarivier, *The Secret History, or Queen Zarah, and the Zarazians* (Albigion [London], 1705)

Marcet, Jane, *Conversations on Political Economy; in which the elements of that science are familiarly explained* (London, 1816)

Masham, Damaris Cudworth, *A Discourse Concerning the Love of God and Occasional Thoughts in Reference to a Vertuous or Christian Life*, ed. James G. Buickerood (Bristol, 2004)

Mill, John Stuart, *The Collected Works of John Stuart Mill*, ed. J. M. Robson (33 vols.; Toronto, 1963–91)

Millar, John, *Observations concerning the Distinction of Ranks in Society* (London, revised edn, 1773)

The Origin of the Distinction of Ranks: or, An Inquiry into the Circumstances which gave rise to Influence and Authority in the Different Members of Society (1779), ed. John Valdimir Price (Bristol, 1990)

An Historical View of the English Government, from the Settlement of the Saxons in Britain to the Accession of the House of Stuart (London, 1787)

Montagu, Elizabeth, *The Letters of Mrs. Elizabeth Montagu*, ed. Matthew Montagu (4 vols.; London, 1809–13)

Mrs. Montagu: 'Queen of the Blues': Her Letters and Friendships from 1762 to 1800, ed. Reginald Blunt (2 vols.; London, 1923)

Montagu, Lady Mary Wortley, *Letters Of the Right Honourable Lady M-y W-y M-e. Written during her Travels in Europe, Asia and Africa* (3 vols.; London, 1763)

Montesquieu, Charles de Secondat Baron de, *Persian Letters*, trans. Mr Ozell (2 vols.; London, 1722)

The Spirit of Laws, trans. Thomas Nugent (2 vols.; London, 1750)

More, Hannah, *The Inflexible Captive: A Tragedy* (Bristol, 1774)

Essays on Various Subjects, Principally designed for Young Ladies (London, 1777)

An Estimate of the Religion of the Fashionable world. By one of the laity (London, 1791)

Strictures on the Modern System of Female Education (2 vols.; London, 1799)

Norris, John, *Cursory Reflections Upon a Book Call'd, 'An Essay Concerning Human Understanding'* (1690), ed. Gilbert D. McEwen (Los Angeles, 1961)

Paine, Thomas, *Rights of Man, Common Sense and Other Political Writings*, ed. Mark Philp (Oxford, 1995)

Paley, William, *Principles of Moral and Political Philosophy: The Second Edition Corrected* (London, 1786)

Peacock, Thomas Love, *Melincourt: By the Author of Headlong Hall* (3 vols.; London, 1817)

Pelloutier, Simon, *Histoire des Celtes, et particulièrement des Gaulois et des Germains* (2 vols.; The Hague, 1750)

Pennington, Montagu, *Memoirs of the Life of Mrs. Elizabeth Carter* (London, 1807)

Pinkerton, John, *A Dissertation on the Origin and Progress of the Scythians or Goths* (London, 1787)

Pope, Alexander, *The Twickenham Edition of the Works of Alexander Pope*, ed. John Butt *et al.* (11 vols.; London and New Haven, 1939–69)

Poulain de la Barre, François, *De L'Egalité des deux sexes, discours physique et moral où l'on voit l'importance de se défaire des préjugez* (1673) (repr. Paris, 1984)

Price, Richard, *An Essay on the Population of England, From the Revolution to the Present Time* (London, second edn corrected, 1780)

A Review of the Principal Questions in Morals, ed. D. D. Raphael (Oxford, 1948)

Reid, Thomas, *Essays on the Active Powers of the Human Mind* (London, 1788)

Robertson, William, *The History of the Reign of the Emperor Charles V* (3 vols.; London, 1769)

The History of America (2 vols.; London, 1777)

Rollin, Charles, *The Roman History, from the Foundation of Rome to the Battle of Actium* (2 vols.; London, 1739–50)

Rousseau, Jean-Jacques, *A Discourse upon the Origin and Foundation of the Inequality among Mankind* (London, 1756)

Emilius and Sophia: or, A New System of Education (2 vols.; London, 1762)

Russell, William, *An Essay on the Character, Manners, and Genius of Women in Different Ages. Enlarged from the French of M. Thomas* (2 vols.; London, 1773)

Sainte-Palaye, Jean-Baptiste de la Curne de, *Mémoires sur l'ancienne chevalerie, considerée comme un établissement politique et militaire* (2 vols.; Paris, 1759)

The Literary History of the Troubadours. Containing their Lives, Extracts from their Work, And Many particulars relating to the . . . Twelfth and Thirteenth Centuries, trans. Susannah Dobson (London, 1779)

Memoirs of Ancient Chivalry. To which are added the Anecdotes of the Times, trans. Susannah Dobson (London, 1784)

Sandford, Elizabeth, *Lives of the English Female Worthies* (London, 1833)

Scott, Sarah, *The History of Gustavus Ericson, King of Sweden, with An Introductory History of Sweden from the Middle of the Twelfth Century* (London, 1762)

The History of Mecklenburgh, from the First Settlement of the Vandals in that Country to the Present Time (London, 1762)

The Life of Theodore-Agrippa D'Aubigné, containing a succinct account of the most remarkable occurrences during the Civil Wars of France in the reigns of Charles IX. Henry III. Henry IV. And in the Minority of Lewis XIII (London, 1772)

Scott, Sir Walter, *The Miscellaneous Prose Works of Sir Walter Scott, Bart.* (6 vols.; Edinburgh, 1827)

Secker, Thomas, *The Autobiography of Thomas Secker, Archbishop of Canterbury*, ed. John S. Macauley and R. W. Greeves (Kansas, 1988)

Selden, John, *Uxor Ebraica, seu, de Nuptiis et Divortiis ex Iure Civile . . . Veterum Ebraeorum* (London, 1646)

Shaftesbury, Anthony Ashley Cooper, third Earl of, *Characteristicks of Men, Manners, Opinions, Times . . . The Second Edition Corrected* (3 vols.; London, 1714)

Smith, Adam, *The Theory of Moral Sentiments*, ed. D. D. Raphael and A. L. Macfie (Oxford, 1976)

An Inquiry into the Nature and Causes of the Wealth of Nations, ed. R. H. Campbell and A. S. Skinner (2 vols.; Oxford, 1976)

The Glasgow Edition of the Works and Correspondence of Adam Smith (7 vols.; Oxford, 1976)

Lectures on Jurisprudence, ed. R. L. Meek, D. D. Raphael and P. G. Stein (Oxford, 1978)

'Sophia', *Woman Not Inferior to Man: or A short and modest Vindication of the natural Right of the Fair-Sex to a perfect Equality of Power, Dignity, and Esteem, with the Men. By Sophia, A Person of Quality* (London, 1739)

Woman's Superior Excellence over Man: or, A Reply to the Author of a Late Treatise (London, 1740)

Staël-Holstein, Anne Louise Germaine baronne de, *Lettres sur les écrits et le caractère de J. J. Rousseau* (Paris, 1820)

Stewart, Dugald, *Outlines of Moral Philosophy. For the Use of Students at Edinburgh University* (Edinburgh, 1793)

Biographical Memoirs of Adam Smith, L.L.D., of William Robertson, D.D. and of Thomas Reid, D.D. (Edinburgh, 1811)

The Collected Works of Dugald Stewart, ed. Sir William Hamilton (11 vols.; 1854–60, reprinted Bristol, 1994)

Stuart, Gilbert, *A View of Society in Europe, in its Progress from Rudeness to Refinement* (Edinburgh, 1778)

Talbot, Catharine, *The Works of the Late Miss Catharine Talbot*, ed. Montagu Pennington (seventh edn; London, 1809)

A Series of Letters between Mrs. Elizabeth Carter and Miss Catharine Talbot, From the Year 1741 to 1770, ed. Montagu Pennington (London, 1809)

Thomas, Antoine Léonard, *Essai sur le caractère des femmes dans les différens siècles* (Paris, 1772)

An Essay on the Character of . . . Women, trans. William Russell (2 vols.; London, 1773)

An Essay on the Character, the Manners, and the Understanding of Women, in Different Ages. Translated from the French of Mons. Thomas, by Mrs. Kindersley, With Two Original Essays (London, 1781)

Toland, John, *Letters to Serena; containing, 1. The origin and force of prejudice* (London, 1704)

Thrale [Piozzi], Hester, *Retrospection, or A Review of the Most Striking and Important Events, Characters, Situations, and Their Consequences, Which the Last Eighteen Hundred years have Presented to the View of Mankind* (2 vols.; London, 1801)

Tytler, A. F., Lord Woodhouselee ed., *Memoirs of the Life and Writings of the Honourable Henry Home of Kames* (2 vols.; Edinburgh, 1807)

Verstegen, Richard, *A Restitution of Decayed Intelligence: In Antiquities* (Antwerp, 1605)

Wakefield, Priscilla, *Reflections on the Present Condition of the Female Sex; with Suggestions for its Improvement* (London, 1798)

Walker, Ralph S. ed., *James Beattie's London Diary, 1773*, Aberdeen University Studies, 122 (1946)

Warton, Thomas, *The History of English Poetry, from the close of the Eleventh to the Commencement of the Eighteenth Century* (4 vols.; London [Oxford], 1774–90)

Wollstonecraft, Mary, *The Collected Letters of Mary Wollstonecraft*, ed. Ralph M. Wardle (Ithaca, New York, 1979)

The Works of Mary Wollstonecraft, ed. Janet Todd and Marilyn Butler, with the assistance of Emma Rees-Mogg (7 vols.; London, 1989)

A Vindication of the Rights of Men and A Vindication of the Rights of Woman, ed. Sylvana Tomaselli (Cambridge, 1995)

Wray, Lady Mary ed., *An Historical Miscellany* (London, 1771)

SECONDARY SOURCES

Abensour, Léon, *La femme et le féminisme avant la Révolution* (Paris, 1923)

Armstrong, Nancy and Lennard Tennenhouse, *The Ideology of Conduct: Essays on Literature and the History of Sexuality* (London and New York, 1987)

Ayres, Philip, *Classical Culture and the Idea of Rome in Eighteenth-Century England* (Cambridge, 1997)

Baier, Annette, 'Good Men's Women: Hume on Chastity and Trust', *Hume Studies*, 5 (1979), 1–19

Baldwin, Anna and Sarah Hutton eds., *Platonism and the English Imagination* (Cambridge, 1994)

Ballaster, Ros, *Seductive Forms: Women's Amatory Fiction from 1684–1740* (Oxford, 1992)

Bannet, Eve Tavor, *The Domestic Revolution: Enlightenment Feminisms and the Novel* (Baltimore, 2000)

Barber, Richard, *The Knight and Chivalry* (revised edn, Woodbridge, Suffolk, 1995)

Barker-Benfield, G. J., 'Mary Wollstonecraft: Eighteenth-Century Commonwealthwoman', *The Journal of the History of Ideas*, 50 (1989), 95–115

The Culture of Sensibility: Sex and Society in Eighteenth-Century Britain (Chicago, 1992)

Battersby, Christine, 'An Enquiry Concerning the Humean Woman', *Philosophy*, 56 (1981), 303–12

Ben-Israel, Hedva, *English Historians on the French Revolution* (Cambridge, 1968)

Berg, Maxine and Elizabeth Eger eds., *Luxury in the Eighteenth Century: Debates, Desires and Delectable Goods* (Basingstoke, 2003)

Berry, Christopher J., *The Idea of Luxury: A Conceptual and Historical Investigation* (Cambridge, 1994)

Social Theory of the Scottish Enlightenment (Edinburgh, 1997)

Blakemore, Steven, *Crisis in Representation: Thomas Paine, Mary Wollstonecraft, Helen Maria Williams, and the Rewriting of the French Revolution* (Madison, Wisconsin, 1997)

Bolton, Martha Brandt, 'Some Aspects of the Philosophy of Catharine Trotter', *Journal for the History of Philosophy*, 31 (1993), 565–88

Bourke, Richard, *Romantic Discourse and Political Modernity: Wordsworth, the Intellectual and Cultural Critique* (London, 1993)

Bowles, Paul, 'Millar and Engels on the History of Women and the Family', *History of European Ideas*, 12 (1990), 595–610

Brewer, John, *Party Ideology and Popular Politics at the Accession of George III* (Cambridge, 1976)

Brock, Claire, *The Feminization of Fame, 1750–1830* (Basingstoke, 2006)

Burrow, J. W., *A Liberal Descent: Victorian Historians and the English Past* (Cambridge, 1981)

Burstein, Miriam Elizabeth, *Narrating Women's History in Britain, 1770–1902* (Aldershot, 2004)

Campbell, R. H. and Andrew S. Skinner eds., *The Origins and Nature of the Scottish Enlightenment* (Edinburgh, 1982)

Carey, Daniel, *Locke, Shaftesbury, and Hutcheson: Contesting Diversity in the Enlightenment and Beyond* (Cambridge, 2006)

Chalus, Elaine, *Elite Women in English Political Life, c. 1756–1790* (Oxford, 2005).

Clarke, T. E. S. and H. C. Foxcroft, *A Life of Gilbert Burnet, Bishop of Salisbury* (Cambridge, 1907)

Clery, E. J., *The Feminization Debate in Eighteenth-Century England: Literature, Commerce and Luxury* (Basingstoke, 2004)

Coole, Diana, *Women in Political Theory: From Ancient Misogyny to Contemporary Feminism* (Hemel Hempstead, 1993)

Cooper, Kate, *The Virgin and the Bride: Idealized Womanhood in Late Antiquity* (Cambridge, MA, 1996)

Corfield, Penelope J., 'The Case of *The Cabinet*: Did Mary Wollstonecraft join the Norwich Radicals?', *The Times Literary Supplement* (21 March 1997), 11–12

Coutines, Léo Pierre, *Bayle's Relations with England and the English* (New York, 1938)

Cryle, Peter and Lisa O'Connell eds., *Libertine Enlightenment: Sex, Liberty and Licence in the Eighteenth Century* (Basingstoke, 2004)

Darwall, Stephen, *The British Moralists and the Internal 'Ought': 1640–1740* (Cambridge, 1995)

Davidoff, Leonore and Catherine Hall, *Family Fortunes: Men and Women of the English Middle Class, 1780–1850* (Chicago, 1987)

Davies, Kate, *Catharine Macaulay and Mercy Otis Warren: The Revolutionary Atlantic and the Politics of Gender* (Oxford, 2005)

Davis, Natalie Zemon, 'Gender and Genre: Women as Historical Writers' in *Beyond their Sex: Learned Women of the European Past*, ed. Patricia H. Labalme (New York, 1980)

Duchet, Michèle, *Anthropologie et histoire au siècle des lumières* (Paris, 1971)

Dwyer, John, *Virtuous Discourse: Sensibility and Community in Late Eighteenth-Century Scotland* (Edinburgh, 1987)

The Age of the Passions: An Interpretation of Adam Smith and Scottish Enlightenment Culture (East Linton, 1998)

Eger, Elizabeth, 'Luxury, Industry and Charity: Bluestocking Culture Displayed' in Maxine Berg and Elizabeth Eger eds., *Luxury in the Eighteenth Century: Debates, Desires and Delectable Goods* (Basingstoke, 2003)

Erickson, Amy Louise, *Women and Property in Early Modern England* (London, 1993)

Fogel, Michèle, *Marie de Gournay* (Paris, 2004)

Franklin, Caroline, 'The Colour of a Riband: Patriotism, History and the Role of Women in Helen Maria Williams's Sketches of the Manners and Opinions in the French Republic', *Women's Writing*, 13 (2006), 495–508

Garside, Peter, James Raven and Rainer Schöwerling, *The English Novel, 1770–1829: A Bibliographical Survey of Prose Fiction Published in the British Isles* (2 vols.; Oxford, 2000)

Gerbi, Antonello, *The Dispute of the New World*, trans. Jeremy Moyle (Pittsburgh, 1973)

Gerrard, Christine, *The Patriot Opposition to Walpole: Politics, Party, and National Myth, 1725–42* (Oxford, 1994)

Girouard, Mark, *The Return to Camelot: Chivalry and the English Gentleman* (New Haven, 1981)

Gleadle, Kathryn, *The Early Feminists: Radical Unitarians and the Emergence of the Women's Rights Movement, c.1831–51* (Basingstoke, 1995)

Radical Writing on Women, 1800–1850: An Anthology (Basingstoke, 2002)

Gleadle, Kathryn and Sarah Richardson eds., *Women in British Politics, 1760–1860: The Power of the Petticoat* (Basingstoke, 2000)

Gobetti, Daniela, *Private and Public: Individuals, Households, and Body Politic in Locke and Hutcheson* (London, 1992)

Goldsmith, M. M., *Private Vices, Public Benefits: Bernard Mandeville's Social and Political Thought* (Cambridge, 1985)

'"The Treacherous Arts of Mankind": Bernard Mandeville and Female Virtue', *History of Political Thought*, 7 (1986), 93–114

'Regulating Anew the Moral and Political Sentiments of Mankind: Bernard Mandeville and the Scottish Enlightenment', *Journal of the History of Ideas*, 49 (1988), 587–606

Goodman, Dena, *The Republic of Letters: A Cultural History of the French Enlightenment* (Ithaca and London, 1994)

Gossman, Lionel, *Medievalism and the Ideologies of the Enlightenment: The World and Work of La Curne de Sainte-Palaye* (Baltimore, 1968)

Gregory, Jeremy, *Restoration, Reformation and Reform, 1660–1828: Archbishops of Canterbury and their Dioceses* (Oxford, 2000)

Guest, Harriet, 'The Wanton Muse: Politics and Gender in Gothic Theory after 1760' in *Beyond Romanticism: New Approaches to Texts and Contexts, 1780–1832*, ed. John Whale and Stephen Copley (London, 1992)

'The Dream of a Common Language: Hannah More and Mary Wollstonecraft', *Textual Practice*, 9 (1995), 303–23

Small Change: Women, Learning, Patriotism, 1750–1810 (Chicago, 2000)

Haakonssen, Knud, *Natural Law and Moral Philosophy: From Grotius to the Scottish Enlightenment* (Cambridge, 1996)

Haakonssen, Knud ed., *The Science of a Legislator* (Cambridge, 1981)
  Enlightenment and Religion: Rational Dissent in Eighteenth-Century Britain (Cambridge, 1996)
Hallam, Henry, *A View of the State of Europe during the Middle Ages* (2 vols.; London, 1818)
Hankins, Thomas L., *Science and the Enlightenment* (Cambridge, 1985)
Harcstark-Myers, Sylvia, *The Bluestocking Circle: Women, Friendship and the Life of Mind in Eighteenth-Century England* (Oxford, 1990)
Harth, Erica, *Cartesian Women: Versions and Subversions of Rational Discourse in the Old Regime* (Ithaca, New York, 1992).
Heather, Peter J., *Goths and Romans, 332–489* (Oxford, 1991)
Hesse, Carla, *The Other Enlightenment: How French Women Became Modern* (Princeton, 2001)
Hicks, Philip, 'Catharine Macaulay's Civil War: Gender, History, and Republicanism in Georgian Britain', *Journal of British Studies*, 41 (2002), 170–98
  'The Roman Matron in Britain: Female Political Influence and Republican Response, ca. 1750–1800', *The Journal of Modern History*, 77 (2005), 35–69
Hill, Bridget, 'A Refuge from Men: The Idea of a Protestant Nunnery', *Past and Present*, 117 (1987), 107–30
  The Republican Virago: The Life and Times of Catharine Macaulay, Historian (Oxford, 1992)
  'Reinterpreting the "Glorious Revolution": Catharine Macaulay and Radical Response' in *Culture and Society in the Stuart Restoration*, ed. Gerald Maclean (Cambridge, 1995)
  'The Links between Mary Wollstonecraft and Catharine Macaulay: New Evidence', *Women's History Review*, 4 (1995), 177–92
Hill, Bridget and Christopher Hill, 'Catharine Macaulay's *History* and Her Catalogue of Tracts', *The Seventeenth Century*, 8 (1993), 269–85
Hilton, Boyd, *The Age of Atonement: The Influence of Evangelicalism on Social and Economic Thought, 1795–1865* (Oxford, 1988)
  A Mad, Bad, and Dangerous People? England 1783–1846 (Oxford, 2006)
Hitchcock, Tim, *English Sexualities* (Basingstoke, 1997)
Hoffmann, Paul, *La Femme dans la pensée des lumières* (Paris, 1977)
Hont, Istvan and Michael Ignatieff eds., *Wealth and Virtue: The Shaping of Political Economy in the Scottish Enlightenment* (Cambridge, 1983)
Hufton, Olwen, *The Prospect Before Her: A History of Women in Western Europe, Volume I, 1500–1800* (London, 1995)
Hundert, E. G., *The Enlightenment's Fable: Bernard Mandeville and the Discovery of Society* (Cambridge, 1994)
Hunt, Margaret, *The Middling Sort: Commerce, Gender and the Family in England, 1680–1780* (Berkeley, California, 1996)
Hunter, Shelagh, *Harriet Martineau: The Poetics of Moralism* (Aldershot, 1995)
Hutton, Sarah, 'Damaris Cudworth, Lady Masham: Between Platonism and Enlightenment', *The British Journal for the History of Philosophy*, 1 (1993), 29–54

Israel, Jonathan I., *Radical Enlightenment: Philosophy and the Making of Modernity, 1650–1750* (Oxford, 2001)
   Enlightenment Contested: Philosophy, Modernity and the Emancipation of Man, 1670–1752 (Oxford, 2006)
Johns, Alessa, *Women's Utopias of the Eighteenth Century* (Urbana and Chicago, 2003)
Johnson, Claudia L., *Equivocal Beings: Politics, Gender, and Sentimentality in the 1790s* (Chicago, 1995)
Jones, Chris, *Radical Sensibility: Literature and Ideas on the 1790s* (London, 1993)
Jones, Peter ed, *The Science of Man in the Scottish Enlightenment* (Edinburgh, 1989)
Jones, Vivien, *Women in the Eighteenth Century: Constructions of Femininity* (London and New York, 1990)
   'Women Writing Revolution: Narratives of History and Sexuality in Wollstonecraft and Williams' in *Beyond Romanticism: New Approaches to Texts and Contexts, 1780–1832*, ed. Stephen Copley and John Whale (London, 1992)
   'Femininity, Nationalism and Romanticism: The Politics of Gender in the Revolution Controversy', *History of European Ideas*, 16 (1993), 299–305
   '"The Tyranny of the Passions": Feminism and Heterosexuality in the Fiction of Wollstonecraft and Hays' in *Political Gender: Texts and Contexts*, ed. Sally Ledger, Josephine McDonagh and Jane Spencer (London, 1994)
   'Reading for England: Austen, Taste, and Female Patriotism', *European Romantic Review*, 16 (2005), 221–30
Jordan, Constance, *Renaissance Feminism: Literary Texts and Political Models* (Ithaca, New York, 1990)
Kaplan, Cora, *Sea Changes: Essays on Culture and Feminism* (London, 1986)
Keane, Angela, *Women Writers and the English Nation in the 1790s: Romantic Belongings* (Cambridge, 2005)
Kelley, Anne, *Catharine Trotter: An Early Modern Writer in the Vanguard of Feminism* (Aldershot, 2002)
Kelly, Gary, *Revolutionary Feminism: The Mind and Career of Mary Wollstonecraft* (London, 1992)
   Women, Writing and Revolution, 1790–1827 (Oxford, 1993)
Kidd, Colin, *Subverting Scotland's Past: Scottish Whig Historians and the Creation of an Anglo-British Identity, 1689–c.1830* (Cambridge, 1993)
   British Identities Before Nationalism: Ethnicity and Nationhood in the Atlantic World, 1600–1800 (Cambridge, 1999)
Klein, Lawrence E., 'Gender, Conversation and the Public Sphere in Early Eighteenth-Century England', in *Textuality and Sexuality: Reading Theories and Practices*, ed. Judith Still and Michael Worton (Manchester, 1993)
   Shaftesbury and the Culture of Politeness: Moral Discourse and Cultural Politics in Early Eighteenth-Century England (Cambridge, 1994)
Kliger, Samuel, *The Goths in England: A Study in Seventeenth- and Eighteenth-Century Thought* (New York, 1972)

Knox-Shaw, Peter, *Jane Austen and the Enlightenment* (Cambridge, 2004)

Kolbrener, William, 'Gendering the Modern: Mary Astell's Feminist Historiography', *The Eighteenth Century: Theory and Interpretation*, 44 (2004), 1–24

Kramnick, Isaac, *Bolingbroke and his Circle: The Politics of Nostalgia in the Age of Walpole* (Cambridge, MA, 1968)

Republicanism and Bourgeois Radicalism: Political Ideology in Late Eighteenth-Century England and America (Ithaca, New York, 1990)

Labbe, Jacqueline, *The Romantic Paradox: Love, Violence and the Uses of Romance, 1760–1830* (Basingstoke, 2000)

Laqueur, Thomas, *Making Sex: Body and Gender from the Greeks to Freud* (Cambridge, Massachusetts, 1990)

Leerssen, Joseph Theodoor, *Mere Irish and Fíor-Ghael: Studies in the Idea of Irish Nationality, its Development and Literary Expression prior to the Nineteenth Century* (second edn, Cork, 1996)

Lehmann, William C., *John Millar of Glasgow, 1735–1801: His Life and Thought and Contributions to Sociological Analysis* (Cambridge, 1960)

Levine, Joseph M., *The Battle of the Books: History and Literature in the Augustan Age* (Ithaca, New York, 1991)

Lloyd, Genevieve, *The Man of Reason: 'Male' and 'Female' in Western Philosophy* (Minneapolis, 1984)

London, April, *Women and Property in the Eighteenth-Century English Novel* (Cambridge, 1999)

Looser, Devoney, *British Women Writers and the Writing of History, 1670–1820* (Baltimore, 2000)

Mackrell, J. Q. C., *The Attack on Feudalism in Eighteenth-Century France* (London, 1973)

Macleod Burns, Steven A., 'The Humean Female' in *The Sexism of Social and Political Theory*, ed. Lynda Large and Lorenne M. G. Clark (Toronto, 1979)

Maitzen, Rohan Amanda, *Gender, Genre, and Victorian Historical Writing* (New York and London, 1998)

McDonagh, Josephine, 'Barbauld's Domestic Economy', *Essays and Studies*, 51 (1998), 62–77

Child Murder and British Culture, 1720–1900 (Cambridge, 2003)

Meek, Ronald L., *Social Science and the Ignoble Savage* (Cambridge, 1976)

Mellor, Anne K., *Mothers of the Nation: Women's Political Writing in England, 1780–1830* (Bloomington, Indiana, 2002)

Midgley, Clare, *Women Against Slavery: The British Campaigns, 1780–1870* (London, 1992)

Mikalachki, Jodi, *The Legacy of Boadicea: Gender and Nation in Early Modern England* (London, 1998)

Miller, Peter N., *Defining the Common Good: Empire, Religion and Philosophy in Eighteenth-Century Britain* (Cambridge, 1996)

Mitchell, Rosemary, *Picturing the Past: English History in Text and Image 1830–70* (Oxford, 2000).

Moore, Jane, 'Wollstonecraft's Secrets', *Women's Writing*, 4 (1997), 247–60

Nuovo, Victor ed., *John Locke and Christianity* (Bristol, 1997)

Nyland, Chris, 'Adam Smith, Stage Theory, and the Status of Women', *History of Political Economy*, 25 (1993), 617–40

O'Brien, Karen, *Narratives of Enlightenment: Cosmopolitan History from Voltaire to Gibbon* (Cambridge, 1997)

  'History and the Novel in Eighteenth-Century Britain', *Huntington Library Quarterly*, 68 (2005), 397–414

Ó Gallchoir, Clíona, *Maria Edgeworth: Women, Enlightenment and Nation* (Dublin, 2005)

O'Halloran, Clare, *Golden Ages and Barbarous Nations: Antiquarian Debate and Cultural Politics in Ireland, 1750–1800* (Cork, 2004)

Okin, Susan Moller, *Women in Western Political Thought* (revised edn, Princeton, 1992)

Orr, Clarissa Campbell, *Queenship in Britain, 1660–1837* (Manchester, 2002)

Owen, Susan J., *Restoration Theatre and Crisis* (Oxford, 1996)

Ozouf, Mona, *Les mots des femmes* (Paris, 1995)

Pangle, Thomas L., *Montesquieu's Philosophy of Liberalism: A Commentary on the Spirit of the Laws* (Chicago, 1973)

Pateman, Carole, *The Sexual Contract* (Cambridge, 1988)

Peardon, Thomas Preston, *The Transition in English Historical Writing, 1760–1830* (New York, 1933)

Perry, Ruth, *The Celebrated Mary Astell: An Early English Feminist* (Chicago, 1986)

  'Mary Astell and the Feminist Critique of Possessive Individualism', *Eighteenth-Century Studies*, 23 (1990), 444–58

  'Damaris Cudworth Masham, Catharine Trotter Cockburn, and the Feminist Legacy of Locke's Theory of Personal Identity', *Eighteenth-Century Studies*, 35 (2002), 563–76

  Novel Relations: The Transformation of Kinship in English Literature and Culture, 1748–1818 (Cambridge, 2004)

Phillips, Mark Salber, *Society and Sentiment: Genres of Historical Writing in Britain, 1740–1820* (Princeton, 2000)

Phillipson, Nicholas T., 'Culture and Society in the Eighteenth-Century Province: The Case of Edinburgh and the Scottish Enlightenment' in *The University in Society*, ed. Lawrence Stone (2 vols.; Princeton, 1974)

Philp, Mark, 'English Republicanism of the 1790s', *The Journal of Political Philosophy*, 6 (1998), 235–62

Pintard, René, *Le libertinage érudit dans la première moitié du XVIIe siècle* (2 vols.; Paris, 1943)

Pocock, J. G. A., *Politics, Language and Time* (New York, 1973)

  Virtue, Commerce and History: Essays on Political Thought and History, Chiefly in the Eighteenth Century (Cambridge, 1985)

  'Clergy and Commerce: The Conservative Enlightenment in England' in *L'età dei lumi: Studi storici sul Settecento europeo in onore di Franco Venturi*, ed. Rafaelle Ajello *et al.* (2 vols.; Naples, 1985)

Barbarism and Religion, I. The Enlightenments of Edward Gibbon, 1737–1764 (Cambridge, 1999), *II. Narratives of Civil Government* (Cambridge, 1999), *III. The First Decline and Fall* (Cambridge, 2003), *IV. Barbarians, Savages and Empires* (Cambridge, 2005)

Pohl, Nicole and Betty A. Schellenberg eds., 'Reconsidering the Bluestockings', *Huntington Library Quarterly*, 65 (2002)

Polkinghorn, Bette, *Jane Marcet: An Uncommon Woman* (Aldermaston, 1993).

Polkinghorn, Bette and Dorothy Lampen Thomson, *Adam Smith's Daughters: Eight Prominent Women Economists from the Eighteenth Century to the Present* (Cheltenham, revised edn, 1998)

Pomeroy, Sarah B., *Goddesses, Whores, Wives, and Slaves: Women in Classical Antiquity* (1975, repr. London, 1994)

Porter, Roy, *Enlightenment: Britain and the Creation of the Modern World* (London, 2000)

Prescott, Sarah, *Women, Authorship and Literary Culture, 1690–1740* (Basingstoke, 2003).

Raven, James, *British Fiction, 1750–70: A Chronological Checklist of Prose Fiction Printed in Britain and Ireland* (Delaware, 1988)

Ready, Kathryn, 'The Enlightenment Feminist Project of Lucy Aikin's Epistles on Women', *History of European Ideas*, 31 (2005), 435–50

Rendall, Jane, *The Origins of Modern Feminism: Women in Britain, France and the United States, 1780–1860* (London, 1985)

'Virtue and Commerce: Women in the Making of Adam Smith's Political Economy' in *Women in Western Political Philosophy*, ed. Susan Mendus and Ellen Kennedy (Brighton, 1987)

'Writing History for British Women: Elizabeth Hamilton and the *Memoirs of Agrippina*' in *Wollstonecraft's Daughters: Womanhood in England and France, 1780–1920*, ed. Clarissa Campbell Orr (Manchester, 1996)

'"The Grand Causes which Combine to Carry Mankind Forward": Wollstonecraft, History, Revolution', *Women's Writing*, 4 (1997), 155–72

'Tacitus Engendered: "Gothic Feminism" and British Histories, 1750–1800' in *Imagining Nations*, ed. Geoffrey Cubitt (Manchester, 1998)

'Adaptations: Gender, History, and Political Economy in the Works of Dugald Stewart and Elizabeth Hamilton' in *The Science of Man in the Scottish Enlightenment*, ed. Thomas Ahnert (Cambridge, 2007)

Enlightenment, ed. Thomas Ahnert (Cambridge, 2008)

Richardson, Angelique, *Love and Eugenics in the Late Nineteenth Century: Rational Reproduction and the New Woman* (Oxford, 2003).

Rivers, Isabel, *Reason, Grace and Sentiment: A Study of the Language of Religion and Ethics in England, 1660–1780* (2 vols.; Cambridge, 1991, 2000)

Robbins, Caroline, *The Eighteenth-Century Commonwealthman: Studies in the Transmission, Development and Circumstance of English Liberal Thought from the Restoration of Charles II until the War with the Thirteen Colonies* (Cambridge, Massachusetts, 1959)

Robertson, John, *The Case for the Enlightenment: Scotland and Naples, 1680–1760* (Cambridge, 2005)

Ross, Ian, 'A Blue Stocking over the Border: Mrs. Elizabeth Montagu's Aesthetic Adventures in Scotland, 1766', *Huntington Library Quarterly*, 28 (1964–5), 213–33

Ross, Ian Simpson, *Lord Kames and the Scotland of his Day* (Oxford, 1972)

Sapiro, Virginia, *A Vindication of Political Virtue: The Political Theory of Mary Wollstonecraft* (Chicago, 1992)

Schellenberg, Betty A., *The Professionalization of Women Writers in Eighteenth-Century Britain* (Cambridge, 2005)

Schnorrenberg, Barbara Brandon, 'An Opportunity Missed: Catharine Macaulay on the Revolution of 1688', *Studies in Eighteenth-Century Culture*, 20 (1990), 231–40.

Schwartz, Joel, *The Sexual Politics of Jean-Jacques Rousseau* (Chicago, 1984)

Scott, Joan Wallach, *Only Paradoxes to Offer: French Feminists and the Rights of Man* (Cambridge, Massachusetts, 1996)

Shackleton, J. R., 'Jane Marcet and Harriet Martineau: Pioneers of Economics Education', *History of Education*, 19 (1990), 283–97

Sheehan, Jonathan, 'Enlightenment, Religion, and the Enigma of Secularization: A Review Essay', *American Historical Review*, 108.4 (2003), 1061–80

Sher, Richard B., *Church and University in the Scottish Enlightenment: The Moderate Literati of Edinburgh* (Edinburgh, 1985)

Shoemaker, Robert B., *Gender in English Society, 1650–1850: The Emergence of Separate Spheres?* (London, 1998)

Smith, Bonnie, *The Gender of History: Men, Women and Historical Practice* (Cambridge, Massachusetts, 1998)

Smith, Hannah, 'English "Feminist" Writings and Judith Drake's *An Essay in Defence of the Female Sex* (1696)', *The Historical Journal*, 44 (2001), 727–47

Smith, Hilda L., *Reason's Disciples: Seventeenth-Century English Feminists* (Urbana, Illinois, 1983)

Smith, Hilda L. ed., *Women Writers and the Early Modern British Political Tradition* (Cambridge, 1998)

Smith, R. J., *The Gothic Bequest: Medieval Institutions in British Thought, 1688–1863* (Cambridge, 1987)

Spadafora, David, *The Idea of Progress in Eighteenth-Century Britain* (New Haven, 1990)

Spencer, Samia, ed., *French Women and the Age of Enlightenment* (Bloomington, Indiana, 1984)

Spongberg, Mary, *Writing Women's History Since the Renaissance* (Basingstoke, 2002)

Springborg, Patricia, *Mary Astell: Theorist of Freedom from Domination* (Cambridge, 2005)

Stafford Fiona and Howard Gaskill eds., *From Gaelic to Romantic: Ossianic Translations* (Amsterdam, 1998)

Stafford, J. Martin ed., *Private Vices, Publick Benefits? The Contemporary Reception of Bernard Mandeville* (Solihull, 1998)

Stangeland, Charles Emil, *Pre-Malthusian Doctrines of Population: A Study in the History of Economic Theory* (New York, 1904)

' "The Liberty of a She-Subject of England": Rights, Rhetoric and the Female Thucydides', *Cardozo Studies in Law and Literature*, 1 (1989), 161–83

Married Women's Separate Property in England, 1660–1833 (Cambridge, Massachusetts, 1990)

Staves, Susan, *A Literary History of Women's Writing in Britain, 1600–1789* (Cambridge, 2006)

Steinbrügge, Lieselotte, *The Moral Sex: Woman's Nature and the French Enlightenment*, trans. Pamela E. Selwyn (Oxford, 1995)

Still, Judith, *Justice and Difference in the Works of Rousseau* (Cambridge, 1993)

Stone, Lawrence, *The Family, Sex and Marriage in England, 1500–1800* (Harmondsworth, 1977)

Stott, Anne, *Hannah More: The First Victorian* (Oxford, 2003).

Stuurman, Siep, *François Poulain de la Barre and the Invention of Modern Equality* (Cambridge, Massachusetts, 2004)

Sutherland, Kathryn, 'Hannah More's Counter-Revolutionary Feminism', in *Revolution in Writing: British Literary Responses to the French Revolution*, ed. Kelvin Everest (Milton Keynes, 1991)

'Adam Smith's Master Narrative: Women and the *Wealth of Nations*' in *Adam Smith's Wealth of Nations: New Interdisciplinary Essays*, ed. Stephen Copley and Kathryn Sutherland (Manchester, 1995)

Tadmor, Naomi, *Family and Friends in Eighteenth-Century England: Household, Kinship and Patronage* (Cambridge, 2001)

Taylor, Barbara, *Eve and the New Jerusalem: Socialism and Feminism in the Nineteenth Century* (London, 1983)

Mary Wollstonecraft and the Feminist Imagination (Cambridge, 2003)

Taylor, Barbara and Sarah Knott eds., *Women, Gender and Enlightenment* (Basingstoke, 2005)

Taylor, Derek, 'Clarissa Harlowe, Mary Astell, and Elizabeth Carter: John Norris of Bemerton's Female "Descendants"', *Eighteenth-Century Fiction*, 12 (1999), 19–38

Thale, Mary, 'Women in London Debating Societies in 1780', *Gender and History*, 7 (1995), 5–24

Thirsk, Joan, 'The History Women' in *Chattel, Servant or Citizen: Women's Status in Church, State and Society*, ed. M. O'Dowd and S. Wichert (Belfast, 1995)

Thomas, Claudia N. '"Th'Instructive Moral, and Important Thought": Elizabeth Carter reads Pope, Johnson and Epictetus', *The Age of Johnson*, 4 (1991), 137–69

Alexander Pope and his Eighteenth-Century Women Readers (Carbondale and Edwardsville, Illinois, 1994)

Tillyard, Stella, *Aristocrats: Caroline, Emily, Louisa and Sarah Lennox, 1740–1832* (London, 1994)

'All Our Pasts: The Rise of Popular History', *The Times Literary Supplement*, 5402 (13 October 2006)

Todd, Janet, *Mary Wollstonecraft: A Revolutionary Life* (London, 2000).

Tomaselli, Sylvana, 'Moral Philosophy and Population Questions in Eighteenth-Century Europe', *Population and Development Review*, 14, supplement: *Population and Resources in Western Intellectual Traditions* (1988), 7–29

Tuana, Nancy, *Woman and the History of Philosophy* (New York, 1992)

Vickery, Amanda, *The Gentleman's Daughter: Women's Lives in Georgian England* (New Haven, 1998)

Waddicor, Mark H., *Montesquieu and the Philosophy of Natural Law* (The Hague, 1970)

Wahrman, Dror, *The Making of the Modern Self: Identity and Culture in Eighteenth-Century England* (New Haven, 2004)

Watts, Ruth, *Gender, Power and the Unitarians in England, 1760–1860* (London and New York, 1998)

Weil, Rachel, *Political Passions: Gender, the Family and Political Argument in England, 1680–1714* (Manchester, 1999)

Weinbrot, Howard D., 'Politics, Taste, and National Identity: Some Uses of Tacitism in Eighteenth-Century Britain' in *Tacitus and the Tacitean Tradition*, ed. T. J. Luce and A. J. Woodman (Princeton, 1993)

Weisner, Merry E., *Women and Gender in Early Modern Europe* (Cambridge, 1993)

Weiss, Penny A., *Gendered Community: Rousseau, Sex and Politics* (New York, 1993)

Winch, Donald, *Riches and Poverty: An Intellectual History of Political Economy in Britain, 1750–1834* (Cambridge, 1996)

Wiseman, Susan, 'Catharine Macaulay: History, Republicanism and the Public Sphere' in *Women, Writing and the Public Sphere, 1700–1830*, ed. Elizabeth Eger, Charlotte Grant, Clíona ÓGallchoir and Penny Warburton (Cambridge, 2001)

Withey, Lynne E., 'Catharine Macaulay and the Uses of History: Ancient Rights, Perfectionism and Propaganda', *The Journal of British Studies*, 16 (1976), 59–83

Womersley, David, *The Transformation of The Decline and Fall of the Roman Empire* (Cambridge, 1988)

Woolf, D. W., 'A Feminine Past? Gender, Genre, and Historical Knowledge in England, 1500–1800', *American Historical Review*, 102 (1997), 645–79

Wootton, David, 'Pierre Bayle, Libertine' in *Studies in Eighteenth-Century European Philosophy*, ed. M. A. Stewart (Oxford, 1997)

Young, Brian, 'Gibbon and Sex', *Textual Practice*, 11 (1997), 517–37

Young, Brian, *Religion and Enlightenment in Eighteenth-Century England: Theological Debate from Locke to Burke* (Oxford, 1998)

Zachs, William, *Without Regard to Good Manners: A Biography of Gilbert Stuart, 1743–1786* (Edinburgh, 1992)

Zagarri, Rosemarie, 'Morals, Manners, and the Republican Mother', *American Quarterly*, 44 (1992), 192–215

Index

Printed in Great Britain
by Amazon.co.uk, Ltd.,
Marston Gate.